Freud in Oz

Freud

in

At the Intersections of Psychoanalysis and Children's Literature

Kenneth B. Kidd

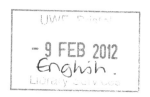

University of Minnesota Press

Minneapolis

London

Earlier versions of the Introduction and chapter 2 were previously published as "Children's Literature and Psychoanalysis: The Case for Complementarity," *Lion and the Unicorn* 29, no. 1 (January 2004): 109–30. An earlier version of chapter 4 was published as "Wild Things and Wolf Dreams: Maurice Sendak, Picture-Book Psychologist," in *The Oxford Handbook of Children's Literature,* ed. Julia Mickenberg and Lynne Vallone (New York: Oxford University Press, 2011). An earlier version of chapter 6 was previously published as "'A' Is for Auschwitz: Psychoanalysis, Trauma Theory, and the Children's Literature of Atrocity," *Children's Literature* 33 (2005): 120–49.

Published by the University of Minnesota Press
111 Third Avenue South, Suite 290
Minneapolis, MN 55401-2520
http://www.upress.umn.edu

Library of Congress Cataloging-in-Publication Data

Kidd, Kenneth B.
    Freud in Oz : at the intersections of psychoanalysis and children's literature / Kenneth B. Kidd.
        p.   cm.
    Includes bibliographical references and index.
    ISBN 978-0-8166-7582-1 (hc : alk. paper)
    ISBN 978-0-8166-7583-8 (pbk. : alk. paper)
    1. Children's stories, English—History and criticism.   2. Children's stories, American—History and criticism.   3. Psychoanalysis and literature.   4. Children in literature.   5. Child psychology in literature.   6. Psychology in literature.   7. Young adult fiction, English—History and criticism.   8. Young adult fiction, American—History and criticism.   I. Title.
    PR830.P74K53 2011
    809'.89282—dc23

JWE, BRISTOL LIBRARY SERVICE   2011017141

Printed in the United States of America on acid-free paper

The University of Minnesota is an equal-opportunity educator and employer.

18 17 16 15 14 13 12 11   10 9 8 7 6 5 4 3 2 1

Contents

Introduction: Reopening the Case of Peter Pan

"THE SERIOUS STUDY OF CHILDREN'S LIT-
erature," writes Michael Egan in a 1982 essay
on *Peter Pan,* "may be said to have begun with
Freud" (37). Freud was interested in a genre now
firmly associated with childhood, the fairy tale,
and thanks to his encouragement, "almost every single major psychoanalyst wrote at least one paper applying psychoanalytic theory to
folklore" (Dundes 1987, 21). But though the serious study of children's
literature began with Freud, we may also say that psychoanalysis
developed in part through its engagement with children's literature.
Psychoanalysis used children's literature to articulate and dramatize
its themes and methods, turning first to folklore and the fairy tale and
then to materials developed during child analysis and to children's literary texts, especially classic fantasies such as *Alice's Adventures in
Wonderland, Through the Looking-Glass, and What Alice Found There,*
and *Peter Pan.*[1] While Freud and the first analysts did not think of
themselves as engaging with "children's literature," their work helped
advance as well as reshape that literature.

Children's literature has in turn appropriated and even influenced
psychoanalysis. As psychoanalysis underwent dissemination and adaptation, two newer genres of children's literature—the picturebook[2]

and the adolescent (now young adult, or YA) novel—were fashioned as psychological (perhaps also psychoanalytic) in form and function. Put another way, the picturebook and the adolescent novel were two narrative forms in and around which psychoanalysis underwent dissemination and adaptation. Children's literature more broadly is now often understood as creative psychological work undertaken on behalf of the young subject. This is particularly true for these two genres. Authors and illustrators of these genres have accrued and asserted a kind of lay psychological expertise. Meanwhile, we can see in both classical and revisionist psychoanalysis the imprint of children's literature and its professional study.

Freud in Oz is about the historical and contemporary relationship between children's literature and psychoanalysis. That relationship has been sometimes collaborative and sometimes antagonistic, at times favoring one project or discourse over the other. Even so, it is best understood as two-way, or mutually constitutive. While my title might call up dreams (or nightmares) of Sigmund Freud in Oz—with Freud, say, as the not-so-innocent abroad or as the Wizard himself—I use "Freud" and "Oz" as markers for psychoanalysis and children's literature and for their intersections. *Freud in Oz* might also be titled *Oz in Freud*, in that children's literature is shown to be as much a shaping presence within psychoanalysis as psychoanalysis is within children's literature.[3]

Freud in Oz thus revises existing "case writing" on children's literature and psychoanalysis, in particular Jacqueline Rose's influential *The Case of Peter Pan; or, The Impossibility of Children's Fiction.* Appropriating the psychoanalytic genre of the case history (more on this in chapter 3), *The Case of Peter Pan* ushered into children's literature studies a timely and useful hermeneutics of suspicion. It did so, however, by pitting psychoanalysis against children's literature, which Rose sees as equivalent to the classic Romantic view of childhood as a time of innocence and simplicity. According to Rose, children's fiction claims an "impossible" relation of adult to child (1984, 1), one presuming the transparency of language alongside the retrievability of childhood.[4] The fantasy of the child as emblematic of a "lost truth and/or moment in history" (43) is one we never leave behind but rather repeat endlessly, from John Locke to Jean-Jacques Rousseau, all the way to Bruno Bettelheim and Maurice Sendak, in her view. For Rose, it is Freud (and Jacques Lacan) who tells more truthfully the story of childhood, exposing it as a myth that gives coherence to otherwise alarming experiences of self and otherness. If we learn to read the real Freud, she says, and not the revisionist Freud of ego psychology, we will realize that Freud sought to dismantle the ideologies allegedly underwriting children's literature, among them the idea that "childhood is part of a strict developmental sequence at the end of which stands the cohered and rational consciousness of the adult mind" (13).[5]

In her introduction to *The Trial(s) of Psychoanalysis,* Françoise Meltzer emphasizes the asymmetry of psychoanalysis and literature, looking back to Shoshana Felman's essay "To Open the Question." In that essay, Felman proposes a "real *dialogue*" between psychoanalysis and literature, one that would necessarily prevent "a unilateral monologue of psychoanalysis about literature" (1977, 6; emphasis in the original). Meltzer points to the difficult nature of such a dialogue, given "the totalizing teleology of psychoanalysis" (1987, 3). "Finding a place for psychoanalysis," she remarks, "is in part so difficult because it often shifts the rules of the game and, like a child, pretends that the other had agreed upon them from the outset" (5). This figuration of psychoanalysis as the willful, domineering child is itself suggestive, given the child's centrality to both psychoanalysis and children's literature. In any case, as Rose's work suggests, the teleology of psychoanalysis seems especially totalizing in the case of children's literature. Scholars working on so-called adult literature have come to emphasize the influences of literature on psychoanalysis, but no such emphasis has yet marked children's literature studies. This is unfortunate, for there is a history of children's literature *within* psychoanalysis, beginning with Freud's interest in fairy tales or with his inclusion of Rudyard Kipling's *The Jungle Books* in a 1906 top-ten list of "good books" (Gay 1990, 98).[6]

Rose's polemic has not gone unchallenged by scholars of children's literature; Marah Gubar, Perry Nodelman, Kimberly Reynolds, and David Rudd, among others, have offered substantive critiques.[7] What interests me most, however, is Rose's particular choice of *Peter Pan* as an illustrative or exemplary text. As Nodelman notes in an early and largely critical review of Rose, *Peter Pan* is made "to stand for children's literature" but is also set as an exception to that literature (1985, 98–99)—and, I would add, as a creative version or analogue of psychoanalysis. *Peter Pan* is bound up with the fiction of childhood yet also serves as the closest thing we have to psychoanalysis in the imaginative register. Rose's use of *Peter Pan* as nearly a version of psychoanalysis suggests not so much the exceptionality of that text (since it is also allegedly representative) as the potential of children's literature to be close to psychoanalysis in various ways. In opposing children's literature and psychoanalysis through *Peter Pan,* she also draws them together, suggesting an alternative line of theorizing.

In his engaging *The Hidden Adult,* Nodelman refines his earlier critique of Rose into a new theory of children's literature that affirms its adult dimensions as precisely what makes children's literature coherent and meaningful. Adults, he suggests, simultaneously believe both that childhood is different from adulthood and also that children must grow into adulthood and thereby lose their distinctiveness. This belief in difference alongside future sameness, he thinks, affects how adults write children's books—and how children read those books:

> Children's books encourage readers to consider what it means
> to see or think in ways usually considered to be childlike—
> ways defined by their relative lack of knowledge or complexity. They open a discourse about what children are, about
> how they are different from adults, and about the relative
> merits of the different qualities. And in doing so, they invite
> their readers, not just adults but also children, to think about
> what it means to be a child and what it means, therefore,
> to know less than older people do. In a sense they replicate
> the foundational situation of their writing—an adult knowing more writing for children because children know less
> and need to understand the implications of knowing less.
> (2008, 22)

Like Rose, Nodelman detects the adult in children's literature, but that adult is not necessarily a villain. If we accept children's literature as adult in composition and texture, then we can begin thinking through what it means to claim adult or child status, or to shuttle between those identities. "As Rose's own provocative discussion reveals," he writes, "children's literature criticism becomes valuable exactly at the point at which the constructedness of the child readers implied by children's literature becomes a focus of attention" (161).[8]

In saying that the hidden adult verifies rather than undermines children's literature, Nodelman inverts Rose's argument but maintains its psychoanalytic scaffolding, especially its child–adult dialectic. Nodelman calls the psychoanalytic understanding of childhood "central and particularly instructive" (170). A key claim is that children's books have adult "shadow texts" that comprise what the author (or narrator) cannot or will not say to the child directly but that can be read between the lines. Nodelman's "shadow text," like the "hidden adult," is psychoanalytically derived but also revisionist.[9] "What texts of children's literature might be understood to sublimate or keep present but leave unsaid," he clarifies, "is a variety of forms of knowledge— sexual, cultural, historical—theoretically only available to and only understandable by adults" (206). The presence of the hidden adult and the shadow text is what makes children's literature intelligible as a "genre," he asserts. Nodelman's understanding of shadow text suggests the diffusion or expansion of psychoanalytic terminology; his might seem a rather secular kind of psychoanalytic theorizing. His book, like my own, participates in the ongoing life of psychoanalytic engagement with children's literature (or vice versa). And while he uses terms like "sublimation," "the uncanny," and "the unconscious," Nodelman gives this genre a history, dating it to the expansion of capitalism and the emergence of childhood as a concept and commodity, based in and around books, toys, and other children's forms. Nodelman's emphasis on the economic and materialist origins of children's literature, alongside his very instructive use of Pierre Bourdieu in talking about the field of children's literature, grounds and keeps in check the psychoanalytic energies of his work.

I dwell on *The Hidden Adult* because it is the only text since Rose's to offer a theory of children's literature derived in part from psychoanalysis, even as it also represents the antidote to Rose: written from inside the field of children's literature studies by a respected scholar, exhaustive in its command of the literature, incorporative of just about every theoretical tradition, and ambivalent about its own commitments to synthesis and definition. *Freud in Oz* is less ambitious, neither a theory of children's literature nor an account of the field. *Freud in Oz* does not rework Rose or Nodelman but rather takes instructions from both (especially the latter) while pursuing another kind of case history, one suggested by Egan's comments about Freud, *Peter Pan,* and the

wooing an eligible heiress from the post-modernist elite in the
Duchy of Durkheim. The princess's followers were outraged.
They pointed out how divided the prince's own partisans
had always been. Sweet Princess Childlit would at last have
brought some respectability to a prince unable to control the
factions in his own camp, all of whom professed fealty to him
as the descendant of Empress Psyche, yet none of whom could
agree on how to present him best, or, for that matter, how to
present themselves. The wedding did not take place. Soon the
Board of Canonizers issued an edict pronouncing both groups
to be out of the system. Hereafter, their passports would be
stamped with the word "MARGINAL" in red Gothic print.
(1990, 131–32)

In his subsequent commentary, Knoepflmacher expresses hope for a
marriage after all, and a good one at that, one based on mutual respect rather than convenience. Psychological criticism, he says, must
acknowledge the nuance and sophistication of children's literature. He
is particularly opposed to single-theorist interpretation, arguing for
multiple perspectives to illustrate the "fluidity" and "multiformity" of
children's texts (132). "Above all," he insists, "theories should be put
into the service of texts and not the other way around" (133). Putting
aside the gendering and heteronormativity of this fantasy—why not
Prince Childlit and Princess Psychian, or Prince and Prince, Princess
and Princess?—we can say that by 1990 our couple was carrying on a
torrid affair, even if not a great marriage.

The critical scene continues to diversify, with articles appearing in
all the major journals and with two special issues of the *Children's Literature Association Quarterly* devoted to the topic, the second exploring Freud's concept of *unheimlich* (the uncanny).[13] In addition to single-
theorist readings, other kinds of psychoanalytic work include analyses
of genre alongside psychodynamic themes, such as the work of Karen
Coats (1999) and Martha Westwater (2000) on adolescence and abjection, and Lucy Rollin (1992) on nursery rhymes and baby–mother interaction, and also overview chapters on psychoanalytic criticism such as
those by Bosmajian in Peter Hunt's *Understanding Children's Literature* (1999) and by Roderick McGillis in *The Nimble Reader* (1996).[14]
Evident in such work is the diversification of psychoanalytic theory

beyond the triumvirate of Freud, Carl Gustav Jung, and Bettelheim. While more should be done along those lines, as Mary Galbraith (2001a) and David Rudd (2001) suggest in their respective reviews of Rollin and West's *Psychoanalytic Responses to Children's Literature,* the field has certainly expanded beyond its original scenes.

In addition to the grander theorizing of Rose and Nodelman, I see four kinds of critical projects involving psychoanalysis and children's literature: (1) using psychoanalysis to explain and interpret children's literature and its function, (2) using children's literature to explain or clarify psychoanalysis, (3) explaining how children's literature helps children psychologically, and (4) historicizing the relationship(s) between children's literature and psychoanalysis. A quick review of these projects will help clarify what *Freud in Oz* does and does not attempt.

Most scholarship belongs to the first category, regardless of whether the critical orientation is single- or poly-theorist or whether the literary subject is a single text or genre or some mixture thereof. A strong example is Eric L. Tribunella's *Melancholia and Maturation: The Trauma of Loss in American Children's Literature* (2010). Drawing on psychoanalytic and queer theoretical work on mourning, melancholia, and attachment, Tribunella proposes that many American children's books require their protagonists to sacrifice loved objects as part of their ostensible maturation. Child characters must give up beloved dogs, same-sex best friends, faith in democracy, and so forth, undergoing a melancholic makeover in subject formation. To be adult for Tribunella is always to have loved and lost. Tribunella proposes further that fictional children are subjected to traumatic situations precisely because real children are supposed to be shielded from such situations. Through shrewd analysis of children's texts as well as of teacher rationales and other materials, he makes a persuasive case for an American master plot of melancholic maturation. The book compares favorably to other works of criticism that mobilize psychoanalytic conceits to illuminate the dynamics of American national and popular culture, such as Priscilla Wald's *Constituting Americans* (1995) and Elizabeth Bronfen's *Home in Hollywood* (2004).

Some exercises in the interpretation of children's literature also function as introductions to psychoanalytic theory, not unlike graphic novel primers such as Richard Appignanesi and Oscar Zarate's *Freud for*

Beginners (1979). A good example is Rollin and West's *Psychoanalytic Responses to Children's Literature*. Another, more theoretically sophisticated such primer is Karen Coats's *Looking Glasses and Neverlands* (2004). Coats finds in children's literature confirmation of Lacan's theories of subject formation through language. Whereas Rose practices oppositional case writing, Coats offers a persuasive complementary approach to Lacan and children's literature, suggesting that the latter confirms the former. There is some irony here, in that Lacan was particularly resistant to the practice of child analysis, seeing it as a danger to adult (mature) psychoanalysis.[15] The child is generally acknowledged as a legitimate subject of psychological discourse *except* in the most "rigorous" (adult) variants, especially that of Lacan. Moreover, Rose reports that her "controversial subtitle," "The Impossibility of Children's Fiction," was "born of a 1975 encounter with Jacques Lacan, who responded when I told him I was preparing a PhD on children's writing, '*Est-ce qu'il peut exister une littérature pour enfants?*'—a question which profoundly resonated with the disturbing subtext I was in the process of uncovering" (Rose, quoted in Rudd and Pavlik 2010, 227–28).[16] And yet, it is evident that Lacan's theory of subject formation is organized around the question of the child and the child's access to the symbolic. There are even scattered references in Lacan to *Alice*.[17] Though children's literature hides the adult, as Nodelman holds, psychoanalysis sometimes also hides the child, as Lacan hopes. Lacan is the master theorist for Coats, not a historical subject, and so there is no discussion of this problem.[18] Nonetheless, Coats's pairing of Lacan and children's literature amounts to a challenge of Lacan's adultism.

The third kind of project, explaining how children's literature works psychologically for its young readers, is of great interest to many and spills over into reader-response criticism and memoir. Trying on various psychosocial theories of development (Bettelheim, Piaget, Arthur N. Applebee), Francis Spufford puzzles out his adult identity in his memoir *The Child That Books Built* (2002) by revisiting the books and genres that most preoccupied his childhood self. Faith in the psychological efficacy of children's literature is a particular hallmark of developmental and cognitive psychology, from Piaget to Applebee, author of the influential *The Child's Concept of Story* (1978). Educational psychologist Nicholas Tucker combines Piagetian with Freudian analysis in his *The*

Child and the Book in order to illuminate the emotional and also cognitive appeal of certain books for children; "psychological" for Tucker spans both dimensions of mental life. Tucker keys certain ages or developmental periods to certain genres. He places "fairy stories, myths and legends," for instance, after "first books (ages 0–3)" and "story and picture-books (ages 3–7)," reversing a trend toward seeing fairy tales as the first genre of children's literature (a trend discussed in my chapter 1). Tucker concludes that as children mature, they become more accepting of literary and psychological complexity. His discussion approaches literary criticism, for, as he points out:

> the discussion of the psychological appeal of any particular
> book often brings one very close to making literary judgments,
> too, since literary sensitivity when writing for the young can
> also be described in terms of the skills with which an author
> responds to various psychological and imaginative needs
> within his or her audience. (1981, 1–2)

Examining the role of reading in subject formation well beyond childhood are studies by J. A. Appleyard and Michael Steig.[19]

Lucy Rollin's *Cradle and All* belongs to this third category, as well as to the first. Working with object relations theory and ego psychology as well as Freudian analysis, Rollin holds that nursery rhymes serve and encode the psychological needs of young children. "To me," she writes, "nursery rhymes suggest the containment of strong urges and the use of defensive and adaptive maneuvers in the service of maturation" (1992, xv). Children do not read nursery rhymes but rather hear them and experience them bodily; nursery rhymes are chanted or sung by adults holding, tickling, or playing with children. Nursery rhymes, she suggests, are adventures in trust, risk, and transitional relation, in which bodily contact with the parent can be critical. They both terrify and soothe, moving the child toward symbol formation and language mastery.[20] Rollin positions her research as an extension of the psychoanalytic literature on fairy tales. We might also include in this category Jack Zipes's *Why Fairy Tales Stick* (2006), which attributes the survival of certain fairy tales to their psycho-evolutionary use-value. Zipes and Rollin use psychoanalytic theory to explain the appeal and persistence of children's genres.

Freud in Oz makes no psychological claims about the staying power of texts or genres, nor does it offer psychoanalytic readings per se. In a sense, it tries to see psychoanalysis through children's literature, but it does not use the latter to explain or justify the former. *Freud in Oz* aspires to the fourth kind of project, those that attempt to historicize the relationship(s) between children's literature and psychoanalysis. In an essay on Freud's Wolf Man case, for example, Michelle A. Massé proposes that children's literature and psychoanalysis both "seek to represent the child as a 'rounded' individual with a complete, if not yet fully shaped identity" (2003, 151). A more developed inquiry along these lines is Juliet Dusinberre's *Alice to the Lighthouse: Children's Books and Radical Experiments in Art*. Dusinberre points to the imbrication of children's literature and psychological child study from the late nineteenth century forward. "When the late nineteenth century found that its researches into origin and development focused attention on the child," writes Dusinberre, "it simultaneously produced for those children a literature which revealed as clearly as possible adult hopes for the new generation" (1987, 32). Dusinberre chronicles that simultaneous process, noting the influence not only of Freud but also of Charles Darwin, Friedrich Froebel, and others. This period also marks the start of professional commentary on children's literature. As her title suggests, Dusinberre argues further for the influence of Victorian children's authors on modernist writing.

In "Apertures in the House of Fiction," Holly Blackford likewise draws provocative comparisons between the child study movement that began in the late nineteenth century and the "novel methods" of imaginative writers otherwise as diverse as Lewis Carroll, Henry James, and L. M. Montgomery. Child study pioneers such as Darwin, James Sully, and Bernard Perez, she notes, insisted both on the mysteriousness of the child's mental life and on the importance of studying it. They lobbied for the close observation of children, especially children at play, as a means of access to the otherwise enigmatic (when not inaccessible) child mind. Imaginative writers likewise embraced what Blackford calls "the paradox of the child subject": "While human consciousness should be studied in the child, the precise nature of a child's insight will forever elude, and yet require the interpretations of, adults" (2007, 370, 372). In his essay "Child's Play," for instance, Robert

Louis Stevenson, while forging ahead with creative investigations such as *Treasure Island* and *A Child's Garden of Verses,* laments how the "coloured windows" of adult consciousness block insight into childhood (1877, n.p.). The child's unknowability, I would add, was so enthusiastically affirmed that it functioned more as an incitement to discourse than as an obstacle to inquiry. The challenge of knowing the child made possible literary and theoretical interpretation, just as much later the "impossibility" of children's literature made possible (and was itself part of) a theoretical program.

Blackford asserts that with *Through the Looking-Glass,* Carroll affirms but also ironizes child study. Proponents of child study, she writes, sought to uncover "the very structure of consciousness by deducing it from the content of play and children's animate theories. In *Looking-Glass* this is a hopeless game because play is such a stream that it continually shifts and undoes its prior meaning" (2007, 379). *Through the Looking-Glass* thus performs the fantasy of knowing the child alongside and through the child's inscrutability. Of course, Carroll's book appeared before the major documents of child study and might be said to anticipate as much as ironize them. Blackford does understand Carroll's narrative as foundational, saying that he "sets up the major questions of the field" (374). Certainly he raises the question of just how knowable a child might be through play, a question that still drives child psychology. Blackford in fact holds that child study became developmental psychology.[21]

In "Good Friends, or Just Acquaintances?" Nicholas Tucker wonders whether psychological discourse might influence how children's authors design their work.[22] The "number of nods within [children's literature] aimed in the direction of any specific school of psychology have always been sparse," he admits. Instead, children's authors

> become their own psychologists when reconstructing their own childhoods and that of the imaginary characters they invent. Any child psychologists writing with similar authority about childhood matters can in this sense seem rivals to children's authors rather than colleagues. (1992, 156)

This was the rivalry of Sendak and Bettelheim in reverse; as I note in chapter 4, Bettelheim recognized Sendak as a child expert and sought to discredit his most influential picturebook. Even so, Tucker believes that children's authors are likely to make use of the psychological programs of the day, whether deliberately or not. This simultaneous acceptance of and resistance to psychological discourse makes for "something of a psychological mishmash" (157). In Tucker's estimation, the only early psychologist whose theories have been followed "to the letter" by creative writers is Rousseau (158). He credits the ideas of Locke, Froebel, Freud, and Piaget with some influence on imaginative literature. More contemporary trends within psychology have yet to have much impact on the writing of children's books, he holds. He concludes by noting, "What possible effects [imaginative] literature may in turn have had upon psychological thinking over the years remains an even more mysterious and still relatively unexplored topic" (173). Like Dusinberre and Blackford, Tucker points the way to the kind of analysis I am attempting.[23] Tucker is the only one to speculate that children's authors assert and are endowed with a kind of expertise on childhood, an idea I pursue with respect to the picturebook and the adolescent novel.

Plotting for the Read

When I began this project, I wanted to theorize the intersection between psychoanalysis and children's literature as a third space or transitional zone in the tradition of D. W. Winnicott. Winnicott seems to be the theorist of choice these days in revisionist psychoanalysis as well as in some ventures in queer theory that resist gloomy rehashings of melancholic subject formation and the death drive.[24] It is easy enough to think of scholarship as belonging to Winnicott's ever-expansive category of "cultural experience" as discussed in his *Playing and Reality* (1989), forged in the necessarily paradoxical space of play and interactive exchange. More to the point, my subject is really neither children's literature nor psychoanalysis but rather their interactions and odd offspring—what J. M. Barrie, in describing Peter Pan (half bird, half boy) in *The Little White Bird,* calls the "Betwixt-n-Between." *Freud in Oz* is about that Betwixt-n-Between. Besides, there is no discrete or stable object called "psychoanalysis" or "children's literature" to begin with; these terms signify ever-shifting constellations of ideas, forms, and practices.[25] Both children's literature and psychoanalysis depend upon paradox, and all the more so their encounters with one another. But because my project is more historical than theoretical, and because Winnicott is part of the story I am telling, *Freud in Oz* is a traditional kind of cultural history, one recognizing its objects of inquiry as dynamic, fuzzy, and enmeshed.

Terminology is tricky in a project such as this. The distinction between "psychoanalysis" and "psychology," for example, is itself part of the history under scrutiny. In and around children's literature we can see a shift from psychoanalysis more properly to broader discourses of the psychological, precisely because children's literature has functioned as a site of psychoanalytic adaptation and refashioning. While psychoanalysis continues to signify in relation to children's literature, psychoanalysis has also been transformed into other discourses of the psychological, some new, some recyclings of earlier such discourses. Writers who claim or are granted insight into the psychic lives of children do not generally think of themselves as psychoanalytic (or even psychological) in outlook or affiliation. The problem of terminology is the problem of cultural translation and remaking. Any attempt to discuss the history and ongoing life of psychoanalysis is fraught with peril, so vast and complex is the subject and so intense are personal and professional relations to it.

That said, psychology predates, persists alongside, and survives Freud; modern psychology tends toward the empirical and experimental and generally does not maintain the key terms or concepts of Freud or even of revisionist psychoanalysis. "Psychology" remains an umbrella term, an overarching discourse of mind and mental life that encompasses psychoanalysis but also behaviorism, third-force psychology, empirical psychology, and so forth. But psychology can also be opposed to psychoanalysis, invoked against Freud's unsettling ideas about sexuality, the unconscious, and the death drive. Some historians of psychology see it as offering up a more palatable version of Freud. In *Freud in Oz,* I use "psychology" both ways, to mean a larger category including psychoanalysis and as a marker for more oppositional projects. Sometimes I mean something more specific, such as developmental psychology or humanistic psychology. Where possible, I follow general uses within the scholarship, using terms like "object relations theory," "ego psychology," and the "relational tradition."

By "psychoanalysis" I mean Freudian theory and the so-called clas-

INTRODUCTION   xxi

sical tradition. Fidelity to Freud is one marker of psychoanalysis; hence
the inclusion of Lacan in that category, despite the significant revisions
of Lacan's return to Freud. For Lacan and for others, psychoanalysis
means a commitment to Freud's principles and attitudes. Freud, they
feel, is the proper name for psychoanalysis. This is the party line adopted by Rose; Rose names Freud while really operating in the tradition of Lacan (indeed, putting herself in Lacan's place as the master
theorist who returns to Freud). I would place Melanie Klein and Anna
Freud in Freud's camp, despite the more radical innovations of the former and despite concern that ego psychology hijacked Freud's project.

Freud in Oz begins with classical psychoanalysis but gravitates
toward American culture and American popular psychology because
that is where the encounter of psychoanalysis and children's literature
has most vividly played out, especially since the mid-twentieth century.
While some of the key texts I consider are British in origin, they have
entered a distinctly American orbit, used to justify (sometimes also to
exorcise) psychoanalysis in the popular domain. *Freud in Oz* thus gives
priority to the Americanization of psychoanalysis. Once upon a time,
the story goes, Freud came to America, bringing by his own account
the "plague" of psychoanalysis. But Freud also worried that America
would contaminate psychoanalysis, suppressing its more troubling insights and transforming it into a practical program of uplift. His fears
were perhaps justified. As Joel Pfister points out, Americans tended
to glamorize the psychological, gravitating to early self-help titles
such as William J. Fielding's 1922 *Caveman within Us* (Pfister 1997,
183). Americans merged psychoanalysis with pragmatism and home-
grown ego psychology, preferring the perfectible ego to the intractable
unconscious.[26] Revisionist Freudianism surged during the 1940s, and
by the 1960s, humanist or third-force psychology had effected a shift
away from the treatment of neurosis to the search for happiness and
self-actualization.

In place just after midcentury was a white middle-class therapeutic culture with little use for the hard lessons of Freud, according to a
host of observers on the American scene. The most famous assessment
along these lines comes from sociologist Philip Rieff, who saw in 1966
a "triumph of the therapeutic" at the expense of Freud's analytic.[27] By
"therapeutic" Rieff means not a particular practice but rather a cultural

disposition. In his view, people "specialize at last, wittingly, in techniques that are to be called, in the present volume, 'therapeutic,' with
nothing at stake beyond a manipulatable sense of well-being. This is
the unreligion of the age, and its master science" (1966, 13). Freud and
the classical tradition, he proposes, "has been ruined by the popular
(and commercial) pressure upon it to help produce a symbolic for the
reorganization of personality" (21). While the therapeutic is not re-
stricted to America, it found there a "most congenial climate" (54).[28]
Versions of this critique came in the next decade from Christopher
Lasch and Richard D. Rosen, Lasch denouncing an American "culture
of narcissism" (1979) and Rosen the proliferation of "psychobabble."
"Everything must now be spoken," writes Rosen. "The sexual revolution, this therapeutic age, has culminated in one profuse, steady stream
of self-revelation, confessed profligacy, and publicized domestic and intra-
psychic trauma" (1975, 17).[29] "Whereas Freud saw a mortgage that could
never be entirely paid off," Rosen continues, "the human potential movement hints at a final freedom and a life lived in the black" (21–22). French
sociologist Pierre Bourdieu takes the more cynical view, attributing
"the rise of the therapeutic morality" to "the constitution of a corps of
professionals" who preside over the "art of living" (1998, 369–70) and
thereby shore up their own authority at the expense of everyone else;
Bourdieu, incidentally, mentions the "Peter Pan complex" as one among
the "'liberationist' commonplaces" of the therapeutic ethic's "psychobabble" (368) (see chapter 4). I try for neutrality in this debate about the
improvement or exploitation of psychoanalysis, even as I make some
judgments about the consequences of popularization.

Across the scene of Freudian loyalty, revision, and rejection, children's literature has remained an important part of the cultural conversation about the psychosocial lives of children. Each historical moment
is marked by certain conceptions and uses of children's literature, even
as children's literature has exerted its own influences upon psychological discourse. The first two chapters of *Freud in Oz* examine the
place and status of children's literature within early or more classical psychoanalysis. Children's literature obviously existed before psychoanalysis, but it gained new urgency in its wake, at once benefiting from psychoanalytic attention and encouraging such attention in
the first place. Chapter 1 focuses on the psychoanalytic engagement

with the fairy tale, from the foundational ideas of Freud and Jung to current fairy-tale studies. As Tucker notes, psychoanalysts have long ignored children's books and "concentrated on those traditional fairy stories and myths that most clearly lend themselves to Freudian interpretation" (1992, 163). Tales from the Brothers Grimm were especially popular. And because those stories were understood to be traditional, observes Tucker—as well as "of the people"—analysts could take up fairly dramatic topics (cannibalism, torture, incest, bestiality, murder) with less fear of protest or censorship. Such interpretive practice, I would add, keeps psychoanalysis at the center of fairy-tale discourse and claims for psychoanalysis the popularity of its subject material.

Analytical attention to the fairy tale bestowed upon it a new kind of value. The psychoanalytic literature on the fairy tale gradually began to intersect with the widespread belief that the fairy tale is "for" children, so that by midcentury, the fairy tale was broadly received both as a psychological genre and as a cornerstone for children's literature. Bettelheim, writing in 1976, goes out of his way to discredit modern children's literature in order to champion the fairy tale as the most appropriate and authentic of childhood's literary forms. Such sanctification of the fairy tale, however, exacts a price, including the suppression of the rich diversity of children's literature with respect to genre, mood, tone, audience, and conditions of production and reception.

Chapter 2 first proposes that the subdiscipline of child psychoanalysis, or child analysis, brought psychoanalytic attention to other narrative forms associated with or produced by children, even as it was also *like* children's literature, involving as it did child–adult play and collaborative storytelling. In its attention to children's play especially, child analysis helped shift attention to symbol formation and creative work, thereby affirming the idea of children's literature. Child analysis, that is, helped textualize childhood, such that children's play-work— their stories and drawings—became just as legitimate an object of inquiry as children themselves. At the same time, the practice of child analysis mirrored the practice of writing children's books, most notably in the case of A. A. Milne's Pooh stories. This chapter, too, begins with Freud, specifically Freud's case history of Little Hans, but more significant is the work of Klein and then Winnicott, whose poetics of play helped set the agenda for children's literature and its translation with the fairy tale, from the foundational ideas of Freud and Jung to current fairy-tale studies. As Tucker notes, psychoanalysts have long ignored children's books and "concentrated on those traditional fairy stories and myths that most clearly lend themselves to Freudian interpretation" (1992, 163). Tales from the Brothers Grimm were especially popular. And because those stories were understood to be traditional, observes Tucker—as well as "of the people"—analysts could take up fairly dramatic topics (cannibalism, torture, incest, bestiality, murder) with less fear of protest or censorship. Such interpretive practice, I would add, keeps psychoanalysis at the center of fairy-tale discourse and claims for psychoanalysis the popularity of its subject material.

Analytical attention to the fairy tale bestowed upon it a new kind of value. The psychoanalytic literature on the fairy tale gradually began to intersect with the widespread belief that the fairy tale is "for" children, so that by midcentury, the fairy tale was broadly received both as a psychological genre and as a cornerstone for children's literature. Bettelheim, writing in 1976, goes out of his way to discredit modern children's literature in order to champion the fairy tale as the most appropriate and authentic of childhood's literary forms. Such sanctification of the fairy tale, however, exacts a price, including the suppression of the rich diversity of children's literature with respect to genre, mood, tone, audience, and conditions of production and reception.

Chapter 2 first proposes that the subdiscipline of child psychoanalysis, or child analysis, brought psychoanalytic attention to other narrative forms associated with or produced by children, even as it was also *like* children's literature, involving as it did child–adult play and collaborative storytelling. In its attention to children's play especially, child analysis helped shift attention to symbol formation and creative work, thereby affirming the idea of children's literature. Child analysis, that is, helped textualize childhood, such that children's play-work—their stories and drawings—became just as legitimate an object of inquiry as children themselves. At the same time, the practice of child analysis mirrored the practice of writing children's books, most notably in the case of A. A. Milne's Pooh stories. This chapter, too, begins with Freud, specifically Freud's case history of Little Hans, but more significant is the work of Klein and then Winnicott, whose poetics of play helped set the agenda for children's literature and its translation into an adult concern. That translation or remaking is the focus of the chapter's second part. By way of the discourse of "Poohology," or usually pop-psychological or pop-philosophical writing centered around Milne's *Winnie-the-Pooh* and *The House at Pooh Corner,* I show how the ongoing interiorization of the child as within the adult—the legacy of Freud himself—has transformed the Pooh books from children's books to books that belong to the inner child in all of us. Child analysis, play, and these children's literary classics meet up in child-themed but adult-oriented Poohology.

Chapter 2 begins to shift focus away from the presence of children's materials or proto–children's literature within classical psychoanalytic discourse and toward the circulation of officially recognized children's "classics" within popular and applied psychoanalysis. Tucker notes that the "ignorance of modern children's literature among most psychologists is typical, although some psychoanalytic critics did eventually get round to discussing classics from the more immediate past" (1992, 163). This restriction of children's material to fairy tales and early classics is strategic on the part of analysts, but it is also a consequence of the proliferation of children's books. Analysts and therapists appeal to the classics because they are well-known, although Tucker asserts that "common knowledge today about any modern classic for children can no longer be taken for granted" (164). Certainly we cannot expect accurate or faithful uses of these texts; they are useful because everyone claims them but usually without having read them.

Chapter 3 attends to psychoanalytic interpretation of and popular case writing around the Golden Age classics *Alice, Peter Pan,* and *The Wonderful Wizard of Oz.* Psychoanalytic and literary case writing on these classics both reflects their cultural standing and contributes to it. While we can argue for connections between psychoanalysis and the original texts of these classics, I concentrate, as with the second part of chapter 2, more on their aftertexts, in the form of case rewritings. Case work on Lewis Carroll and J. M. Barrie especially rehearses what I call the immaturity critique of American culture, even though neither was American. While psychoanalytic criticism of children's literature did not appear until later, psychoanalytic and pop-psychoanalytic assessments of famous authors who wrote about childhood were being published as early as 1920 and have continued to influence popular attitudes.[30] *Alice* and *Peter Pan* are ostensibly about the immaturity of their authors, their fans, or both, and *The Wonderful Wizard of Oz* is similarly assumed to hide the adult, even if not so much the adult's psychopathology.

The next two chapters shift attention from the positioning of children's literature within psychoanalysis to the psychoanalytic and psychological texture of the picturebook (chapter 4) and the adolescent novel (chapter 5). Whereas the fairy tale and the Golden Age classic have been incorporated into psychoanalysis, the picturebook and the adolescent novel were fashioned from the start as psychological, thus authorizing their best practitioners as partners in child-rearing. Other genres of children's literature may also have psychological coordinates, but not so explicitly or consistently.

In various ways the picturebook represents and textualizes child play, sometimes including the adult, sometimes not. This is one characteristic or marker of what I am calling picturebook psychology, the subject of chapter 4. There I focus on author-illustrator Maurice Sendak, whose long and very successful career touches on most, perhaps all the major moments of picturebook psychology. Picturebook psychology began with child study, child analysis, and progressive educational work and has since been revised by humanistic ego psychology and more recently bibliotherapy. Sendak underwent Freudian analysis and was trained by author-illustrators with ties to child analysts and educational reform. He developed his picturebooks out of his own experiences, his own recollections of childhood, and his informal observation and sketching of children at play. Moreover, with *Where the Wild Things Are* (1963), Sendak updates Freud's famous dream of the Wolf Man, giving picturebook psychology a neo-Freudian makeover and establishing psychological wildness as the very stuff of child life. In "Good Friends, or Just Acquaintances?," Tucker remarks that "neither Freud nor his followers, almost all of whom led conventional middle-class existences, would ever have countenanced a modern children's literature giving direct expression to the unsocialized, aggressive and acquisitive forces existing within every individual" (1992, 163). Sendak makes possible just such a modern children's literature, perhaps especially for those who lead conventional middle-class existences, through his carefully framed story of "wild" Max's rebellion and return. While picturebook psychology as I am imagining it is a many-splendored thing, Sendak makes an ideal figurehead and spokesman and has in fact embraced the role of lay child expert. The chapter concludes with some discussion of the 2009 film version by Spike Jonze, as well as Dave Eggers's novelization, published the same year.

"Stated broadly," writes Anne Scott MacLeod, "the path of American adolescent novels has been from outward to inward, from concern with the young adult's relationship to the larger community to a nearly exclusive emphasis on the adolescent's inner feelings" (1997, 125). Chapter 5 follows that path. I mark three stages in the psychologization of the genre, beginning with the articulation of adolescence as a psychological as well as a literary category, followed by the construction of a problem interior along familiar lines of gender and sexuality, and ending with the conversion of that problem interior into "young adulthood," a state marked by confidence (proximity to adulthood) and by vulnerability (proximity to childhood). While I suggest the importance of authorial expertise in this chapter also, I do not focus on it at length, in part because no single author seems as representative as Sendak is for picturebook psychology. Instead I emphasize the positioning of young adult authors as themselves young adults, in and around what Julia Kristeva calls the "adolescent economy of writing." The young adult author must maintain proximity to youth but must also be sufficiently grown up to model problem solving. Because there is less distance between young adult and adult than between child and adult, there is potentially more indeterminacy in the identity of the young adult author, whereas the picturebook psychologist is not easily mistaken for a child. The chapter also argues against the conflation of adolescence with abjection, a tendency in some recent scholarship.

Operative in these genres, and especially in the picturebook and the young adult novel, is a trend toward what Elizabeth Baer calls a "'literature of atrocity' for children" (2000, 381), Holocaust centered and influenced by the themes and conceits of psychoanalysis. Serving also as a conclusion to the book, chapter 6 treats contemporary trauma writing for children and young adults as the latest and most problematic iteration of the triumph of the therapeutic, or of the merging of psychological discourse and children's literature. I turn first to some young adult texts addressing the Holocaust and genocidal trauma, then to first-wave picturebook work about the September 11, 2001, terrorist attacks. Despite the broader energies of picturebook psychology, these books tend toward cultural and political conservatism, affirming what Lauren Berlant calls "infantile citizenship" (1997, 21). It is notable that while Holocaust titles for young readers took some time to materialize, 9/11 picturebooks appeared as early as 2002. These books register few of the political or psychosocial complexities of terrorism; instead, they reassert American innocence around the figure of the vulnerable child subject. While not necessarily representative of trauma writing more generally, such texts underscore the dangers of a pop-psychological children's literature that gives up or dumbs down the child–adult dialectic and the conceit of the unconscious.

Now that the book is finished, I see (shadow?) texts that failed or refused to materialize. I might have taken a longer historical view, starting perhaps with the relays between child-rearing/pedagogical discourse and eighteenth-century children's literature. Given that modern psychology follows literature historically and also borrows generously from it, it seems plausible that early Anglo-American children's literature may have established some of the ground rules for child-centered psychological discourse especially. As one of my readers suggested, I might also have considered how contemporary children's literature pushes back against psychoanalysis by putting it on the couch, as it were, subjecting it to literary investigation and treatment. Certainly there are plenty of portraits of analysts and therapists in children's books, not all so flattering. Robert Cormier's young adult novel *I Am the Cheese* (1977), which I mention in chapter 5, interrogates not only the analyst figure but the whole enterprise of therapy and memory work. There are surely other examples, especially in our moment of postmodernism and metafiction. Doing these things—pushing the project both backward and forward in time and considering an even broader range of materials—might have resulted in a stronger case for the influence of children's literature upon psychoanalysis. A more suspicious project might have positioned children's literature and psychoanalysis alike as both manipulative of and, equally, indebted to the vulnerable state called childhood. Even so, I have settled for a more modest and cheerful story of entanglement and exchange. If I haven't managed to put children's literature on the couch, I hope that I've at least called sufficient attention to psychoanalysis's debts to the materials and forms of childhood.

1. Kids, Fairy Tales, and the Uses of Enchantment

T HE IDEA THAT THE FAIRY TALE IS AN APPRO-
priate narrative genre for children predates psychoanalysis, but psychoanalysis nurtured that idea,
building upon existing associations of childhood and
primitive/folk culture. Psychoanalytic advocacy for
the fairy tale began long before Bruno Bettelheim made the case in *The
Uses of Enchantment* (1976). Bettelheim mobilizes familiar psychoanalytic arguments about the fairy tale, while addressing the issue of
children's literature directly. Bettelheim disparages modern children's
books and insists that the fairy tale is the *real* children's literature, exactly because it is so psychologically useful. Fairy tales, he thought,
encourage children to work through various unconscious dilemmas.
But Bettelheim could teach us how to read fairy tales psychoanalytically because Sigmund Freud had already learned from fairy tales and
incorporated them into psychoanalytic discourse.

By the time Bettelheim published his book, the fairy tale was understood not simply as *a* genre of children's literature but indeed as
its foundational and thus *most important* genre. Thus Leslie Fiedler
declares that fairy tales "are the first form of 'children's literature'"
(1973, xi). William Kerrigan and Jack Zipes agree, calling the fairy tale
"the primal form of children's literature" (Kerrigan 1985, x) and "the

classical genre for children" (Zipes 1983; this is part of the subtitle to his *Fairy Tales and the Art of Subversion*). This chapter proposes that psychoanalytic attention to the fairy tale helped enshrine it as a cornerstone of children's literature and child development. The fairy tale is perhaps *not* so representative of children's literature; not all fairy-tale scholars see it as a children's genre. Psychoanalysis helped consolidate its status as such.

At the same time, psychoanalysis took a cue from the fairy tale and from discourse about the fairy tale's function and importance. We can see in the themes and forms of psychoanalysis the influence of fairy-tale discourse as well as the other way around. We do have to look more closely to see the former, because psychoanalysis did not profess interest in children's literature until well into the twentieth century. Earlier, psychoanalysis expressed interest in the fairy tale as a children's form, one showing up in patient histories and overlapping with common dream material. Rather than conceptualize the fairy tale as children's literature, however, Freud and subsequent analysts approached it in the context of folk culture, with its alleged correspondences to the primitive mind. For Freud, the fairy tale belonged not to children's literature but rather to the individual child, even when the same tale surfaced in multiple case histories. Even so, some understanding of fairy tales as the narrative stuff of childhood was operative in psychoanalysis. As much as Bettelheim, Freud knew that fairy tales were useful to analysts as well as to children and their caregivers.

This chapter examines the interrelation of psychoanalysis and the fairy tale, in and around the question of children's literature. I show how Freud and others capitalized upon but were also instructed by fairy-tale discourse, so that psychoanalysis has certain fairy-tale correlates. The chapter also explores the consequences of this interrelation for psychoanalysis, for children's literature, and for the study of children's narrative. The psychoanalytic study of the fairy tale heightened the genre's status as children's literature—as canon, in a sense—even as it gave fairy-tale and children's literature studies a critical method and a strong psychoanalytic inflection. Psychoanalysis, in turn, has been kept relevant and useful by its association with fairy tales. The relationship between psychoanalysis and the fairy tale might be described as symbiotic, mutually dependent and beneficial.

Freud and Fairy-Tale Discourse

Fairy-tale scholars largely agree that the fairy tale came to be thought of as primarily for children in the eighteenth century, as adult literate and literary culture moved in other directions and as the fairy tale migrated in association from the folk to the child-folk, to unlettered and ostensibly simple people. Whereas the folktale is still associated with folkish adults, the fairy tale is widely presumed to be a form of children's literature.[1] There are various scholarly accounts of this transformation and its consequences. As Maria Tatar notes, the "process by which adult entertainment was translated into children's literature was a slow one with a long transitional period when the line between the two was by no means clear" (1987, 21). The sorting of children's and adult literature along the orality/literacy line was ongoing in the nineteenth century. Tatar points especially to the case of the Grimms' 1812 *Kinder- und Hausmärchen (Nursery and Household Tales)*, which began as a scholarly tome with preface and explanatory notes, only to be refashioned by the second edition as a collection of stories appropriate for children because of its ostensible proximity to the oral tradition. This refashioning, at the hands of Wilhelm Grimm in particular, was part of a broader rewriting of the fairy tale as being for children. As early as the 1830s, the English extravaganza producer and French fairy-tale translator J. R. Planché felt obliged to remake fairy tales into appropriate fare for adults, so thoroughly had they already been claimed for children. Planché blamed Charles Perrault and Madame d'Aulnoy for this ostensible infantilization. The association of fairy tales with children's literature was firmly in place by the time of Freud.

Freud and his scientific predecessors were less interested in the fairy tale's literary status or in questions about its major audience than in what the fairy tale could reveal about "primitive" man. The allegedly natural association of children with fairy tales, as Jacqueline Rose points out, emerges from a "preoccupation with cultural infancy and national heritage," a metanarrative in which children and the "folk" are made equivalent (1984, 56). That metanarrative influenced and in turn was supported by popular adaptations of evolutionary theory in the nineteenth century. The evolutionary notion of recapitulation, first articulated by Ernst Haeckel (and popularly summed up as "ontogeny recapitulates phylogeny"), found widespread application and adaptation from the nineteenth century forward, underwriting and overlapping with a broader theory of evolutionary social progress. Caucasian child and non-Caucasian primitive or savage (and sometimes the criminal) were said to be at the same developmental stage or level, and the theory was sometimes even extended to nations, with, say, the "cultural infancy" of Western nations being ostensibly equivalent to the maturity of primitive cultures. Freud and other analysts later made extensive use of recapitulation and these ostensible correspondences.

Even so, it is no accident that Freud and his colleagues kept encountering folklore and fairy tales (which they tended to conflate). Fairy tales were already known and loved across Europe and were especially cherished in Germany, where they represented a proto-nationalistic collective. In the nineteenth century, in and around nationalistic movements, scholars and collectors considered folktales expressions of the folk soul or psyche—as belonging to and thus reflecting the psyches of the people. Mythic and anthropological conceptions of the fairy tale echoed the evolutionary doctrines of the day, linking folk and fairy tales to ostensibly primitive levels of individual and group development. Freud and his colleagues took a cue from philologists as well as from anthropologists and folklorists, recognizing in dreams, fairy tales and even parapraxes the power (even magic) of words. They generally maintained the principle of recapitulation, seeing parallels among primitive people, children, and young nations, likening folklore to children's "researches" and to national legends.[2]

Freud made frequent appeals to fairy tales, examining particular variants alongside the genre more broadly. His 1913 paper "The Occurrence in Dreams of Material from Fairy Tales" (1963c), for instance, tells the story of a patient who dreamed of Rumpelstiltskin, and both "Little Red Riding Hood" and "The Wolf and the Seven Little Goats" are pivotal to the famous Wolf Man case of 1918 (1963e). Freud approached the fairy tale much as he approached dreams: as symptomatic expressions of wish fulfillment. Fairy tales, in other words, play out the usual dynamics of sexual repression and its consequences. Because fairy tales openly suspend reality and openly indulge in "wish-fulfillments, secret powers, [and] omnipotence of thoughts," notes Freud in his 1919 essay "The Uncanny," they do not achieve the kind of uncanny effects typical of more literary productions, such as E. T. A. Hoffmann's *The Sandman*. "Who would be so bold as to call it uncanny," writes Freud, "when Snow-White opens her eyes once more?" (1955, 246). The fairy tale, for Freud, was not a complex form, though it afforded insight into complex minds.

Fairy-tale analysis was not simply a by-product of psychoanalysis but rather a key genre through which psychoanalysis was practiced and disseminated. "Actually," notes Alan Dundes, "almost every single major psychoanalyst wrote at least one paper applying psychoanalytic theory to folklore" (1987, 21). The list includes Karl Abraham, Ernest Jones, Otto Rank, Carl Gustav Jung, Herbert Silberer, and Franz Ricklin—the last of whom published a book-length study of fairy tales as wish-fulfillment in 1908, sixty-plus years before Bettelheim took up the subject (Ricklin 1915).[3] Moreover, some of this literature (much of it German) focused on the child and adolescent, notably Charlotte Bühler's *Das Märchen und die Phantasie des Kindes* (The fairy tale and the child's imagination; 1918) and Bruno Jöckel's *Der Weg zum Märchen* (The pathway to understanding the fairy tale; 1939). Freud and his colleagues appealed to the fairy tales because they were turning up in analysis and because they could be used to spread the gospel of psychoanalysis. Fairy tales provided a common cultural reference point. As Dundes shows, Freud did not just encourage the analysis of folktales; he actively sought out folklorists who could demonstrate the power of psychoanalysis through analysis of folklore.[4] He encouraged his students to develop their knowledge of folklore and fairy tales and accepted an invitation from the Austrian folklorist Friedrich S. Krauss to write a preface to the German translation of John G. Bourke's 1913 study *Scatalogic Rites of All Nations* (Dundes 1987, 7).

Freud's invocation of fairy tales often accompanies the invocation of allegedly more adult literature, as if Freud hoped to cover all bases, appealing to and speaking the language of common folk as well as more learned men and thereby achieving the broadest possible audience. Freud used his education in classical literature not only to dramatize psychoanalysis (hence the borrowing of Oedipus from Sophocles) but to give it a classical—even classically tragic—feel and appeal.[5] Psychoanalysis was situated within the male homosocial curriculum of European education, Sarah Winter (1999), emphasizes, ensuring both widespread recognition and cultural legitimacy. Freud sought to reach other men of his class and intellectual interests, and folding Sophocles into his discourse was one strategy for outreach.[6] Psychoanalysis functions still as intellectual capital for the educated classes, both in its own right and as part of that broader thing called theory.

But the story of Oedipus, of course, was a folktale before it became a play, and if Freud sought to legitimize his work through the classics, he also sought to popularize it through stories of the folk. In Freud's work, classical material coexists peacefully with fairy tales and less tragic, more populist or folkish material. In *The Interpretation of Dreams*, Oedipus is but one of the many figures dramatizing psychic life. In the second of four sections devoted to "typical dreams" in chapter 5, "The Material and Sources of Dreams," Oedipus is introduced almost casually, as literary evidence of the universal childhood wish that loved ones should die. In the first of those four sections, Freud discusses the typical dream of being naked, which he reads as fulfillment of the desire to exhibit oneself, and there he turns to Hans Christian Andersen's original fairy tale "The Emperor's New Clothes." After devoting several pages to this narrative and the dream-wish of exhibition, Freud notes that the connections between typical dreams and classic fairy tales "are neither few nor accidental" (1965, 279). "The Emperor's New Clothes," of course, did not come to occupy so central a place in the Freudian universe as has the story of Oedipus, but Freud did make strategic if local use of Andersen's tale. Whereas Oedipus demands a "tragic" recognition of the truths of psychoanalysis, "The Emperor's New Clothes" offers comic engagement with the psychopathology of everyday life.

The Interpretation of Dreams, moreover, could be read as a collection of folktale-like dreams in common, analogous to the tale collections of the Grimms or Perrault. We might make the same case for *The Psychopathology of Everyday Life,* a collection of representative parapraxes and errors. It is not a stretch to see Freud as a collector-scholar-theorist of folk material. Perhaps Freud intuited this method from tale collectors and scholars. Early folklore studies was structuralist in orientation, offering taxonomies of tale-type lineage and derivation; Freud likewise offers taxonomies of representative, overlapping dreams and mistakes, suggesting the structuralist energies of his own broader project. Whether deliberately fashioned after folklore studies or not, Freud's engagement with fairy tales goes beyond his thematization of fairy tale as symptom.

In *Making American Boys* (2004), I propose along similar lines that Freud's case histories of the Rat Man (of 1909) and the Wolf Man be understood as psychoanalytic variants on the feral tale, the story of a human animal living among other animals or otherwise not fully socialized into human culture. Freud adapted the feral tale to psychoanalytic ends, I suggest, but in the process psychoanalysis was also shaped by the feral tale, especially in the form of popular psychology about men and their inner wildness. Freud positioned himself as a teller of fabulous tales by turning his male patients especially into heroic if also pitiable characters, most famously the Rat Man and the Wolf Man. Talking animals abound in folklore and fairy tales, as in anthropology, and psychoanalysis seems to have been formulated with such creatures in mind. Freud's insistent and often colorful presentation of humans as, in fact, human *animals* maintains fidelity to Darwinian critique of human exceptionalism.

While Freud's texts do not particularly look like fairy tales—just the opposite, at first glance—fairy-tale discourse more broadly provided a kind of exemplary history and method for Freud. The talking cure requires that the analysand talk freely and openly while the analyst textualizes his or her story—writing it down, rearranging it, finding subtext, making it public or pedagogical, and so forth. Psychoanalysis, in short, performs as much as it thematizes the transformation of oral narrative—the patients' stories—into written text. Simon Grolnick makes this argument as well:

> In other words, psychoanalysis itself stands within the
> folkloristic tradition. The patient and the analyst tell and
> retell, interpret and reinterpret the story of the patient. Oral
> tradition prevails until, in the fashion of Perrault or Grimm,
> the decision is made to write up and publish a case report.
> (1986, 212)

Psychoanalysis remains a system of oral delivery as much as a system of writing (indeed, the two are in perpetual tension, as not a few commentators have underscored). But while it fetishizes orality and the child-folk subject, it actually favors literacy and textuality, thus affirming and speeding up the orality-to-literacy metanarrative of folklore and folklore and fairy-tale studies. Psychoanalysis has made the fairy tale even more textual and more literary, often to the point of dismissing oral tradition.

Beautiful Material

Psychoanalytic attention to the fairy tale helped shift the fairy-tale conversation from the question of morality to the question of psycho-social instrumentality. From that orientation, a powerful case can be made for appropriateness, arguing that the fairy tale is ideal for kids not merely because it enchants but also because it disturbs, unsettles, even terrifies. Psychoanalytic discussion of the fairy tale did not so much abandon the issues of morality and aesthetics as reframe them in the idiom of analysis.

Franz Ricklin's *Wünscherfüllung und Symbolik im Märchen* appeared in 1908, and in 1915 it was translated as *Wishfulfillment and Symbolism in Fairy Tales,* monograph 21 in the (American-published) Nervous and Mental Disease Monograph Series. Ricklin, a clinical psychiatrist, was determined not merely to analyze "such *beautiful, inviting material* as fairy tales" but "to bear a weapon" in the "struggle for and against the Freudian theories" in psychiatry especially (1915, 1; emphasis mine). While the interpretive scheme is strictly Freudian, the book is thoughtful and nuanced, with Ricklin worrying over questions of "historical pedigree" (2), tale variation, and the politics of translation and language. ("Is not every word a symbol!" he declares [26].) Ricklin draws upon a wide range of fairy-tale material, including Icelandic, Italian, and Russian tale collections as well as German sources other than the Grimms. He blends tale analysis with patient case histories, focusing like Freud on dreams with fairy-tale material. "The human psyche," he writes early on, "is always still a fairy poetess" (3).

Whereas Ricklin emphasized the invitational beauty of fairy tales, Hermine Hug-Hellmuth, generally recognized as the first child analyst, positions such beauty as the child's heritage, anticipating later declarations by children's literature critics. In her 1924 work "New Ways to the Understanding of Youth" she writes, "Fairy tales and sagas, songs and sounds should become a precious heritage for the child's soul. They speak simply but powerfully about the old days with simple experiences and primitive feelings at a time when the child is still susceptible and inclined" (1991c, 191). Precisely because they are so exciting, fairy tales should be carefully screened, she thinks. "We know that the child's waiting desires, imaginations, feelings, and impulses will jump like wild animals onto the corresponding literature," she continues, "and that's why we don't recommend reading frightening stories at bedtime and why we recommend to parents to keep their bookcase locked from their children" (191). Hug-Hellmuth, in short, does not see fairy tales as useful in the way Bettelheim does, instead hewing to the classical view of fairy tale as symptom while also stressing their aesthetic appeal. Her conception of the fairy tale as a "precious heritage" is echoed by later advocates within children's literature.

As in so many areas, Melanie Klein is a transitional figure in her orientation to fairy tales. Klein's ideas about infantile aggression have not been popular in the United States, as they make difficult the kind of upbeat theorizing about ego development typical of Americanized psychoanalysis. In her 1921 "The Development of the Child," Klein reviews the interest of a young boy named Fritz (in fact, Klein's son Erich) in fairy-tale material. Like Freud's Wolf Man, Fritz is both afraid of and obsessed with wolves in fairy tales and picturebooks, and also like the Wolf Man, he dreams about wolves. The Grimms' tales, she notes, nearly always elicit anxiety manifestations (1988a, 52), thus serving as a kind of litmus test for mental health. Klein proposes that psychoanalysis will give us the insight and maturity with which to experience these tales in all their heady, violent glory, including their encouragement of normal sadistic fantasy in children. Klein here moves into Bettelheim territory, her interest in enchantment more focused on aggression than on sexuality.

Whereas for Freud the fairy tale offered something like a side path to the individual unconscious, for Freud's disciple-turned-rival Jung the fairy tale led to the collective unconscious and its repertoire of ostensibly universal symbols and forms, or archetypes. Although Jung was more interested in myth than in the fairy tale, he did discuss the fairy tale as an archetypal form, notably in "The Phenomenology of the Spirit in Fairytales" ("Zur Phanomenologie des Geistes im Märchen," 1948) but also in "On the Psychology of the Trickster-Figure" ("Zur Psychologie der Schelmenfigure," 1954).[7] Jung's approach to myth and the fairy tale has been enormously influential.

In "The Phenomenology of the Spirit of Fairytales," Jung holds that fairy tales in all or most cultures incorporate the archetype of "spirit," or the presence of the collective unconscious within the psyche of a person. This "spirit" can be manifested with the proper guidance and attitude. Evidence of its existence can be gleaned from our ability to solve problems beyond our usual cognitive and rational resources. Fairy tales, he thinks, are "spontaneous, naïve, and uncontrived products[s] of the psyche" that cannot express "anything else except what the psyche actually is" (Jung 1959, 239). Jung elaborates this theory of the fairy tale against the sexual-symptomatic analysis of Freud. For Jung, "spirit" unifies the good and evil encountered in fairy tales, and indeed unifies all aspects of the form. Within fairy tales, spirit may be personified by characters like a "wise old man," a "dwarf," even "animal forms" (213). Archetypes, he proposes, sometimes approach consciousness and can be partly perceived through forms ostensibly made of psychic energy itself, including the fairy tale.

Jung's thoughts on childhood are explored at length in "The Psychology of the Child-Archetype" ("Zur Psychologie des Kind-Archetypus," 1941), which mentions fairy tales although the primary focus is myth. For Jung, childhood is the primitive stage of life prior to the development of individual ego—*and* a stage or state to which we should aspire. Jung's system is cyclical as well as linear; the child, or rather the Child archetype, represents wisdom that may be reclaimed.[8] Jung emphasizes the futurity of this archetype: "The child is potential future" (1949, 115). But he also insists that the child is "thus both beginning and end, an initial and a terminal creature. The initial creature existed before man was, and the terminal creature will be when man is not. . . . the 'child' symbolizes the pre-conscious and the post-conscious nature of man" (134). Jung also gave attention to children's dreams, in a series of seminars not published until after his death.[9] While there are significant differences between Freud and Jung, both saw the child as an analogue to primitive man, in keeping with the principle of recapitulation.

"Freud may still be the genius of choice for the learned elite of the late twentieth century," writes Richard Noll, "but it is clear that, in sheer numbers alone, it is Jung who has won the cultural war and whose works are more widely read and discussed" (1994, 6).[10] Although Jung was no more attuned to "children's literature" than was Freud, analytical psychology has further ratified the fairy tale as a cultural form and as one in proximity to childhood. Moreover, for Jung and his followers, the fairy tale is not tied to psychopathology; rather, its association with the unconscious is positive, the stuff of "spirit" rather than destructive affect or even simple neurosis. Jung's spiritual and esoteric tendencies have encouraged fairy-tale interpreters to see the genre as a source of wisdom and higher consciousness.[11] Whereas for Freudians fairy tales point to infantile dramas, for Jungians fairy tales reveal spiritual truths. Jung even seems to position analytical psychology as being on a par with fairy tales. His friend and disciple Marie-Louise von Franz similarly calls fairy-tale language "the international language of all mankind" (1996, 27–28).[12] Analytical psychology is not privileged over the fairy tale but rather acts as its coconspirator and translator.

Jacqueline Rose claims that Jung "has in fact been much better received than Freud in relation to children's literature" (1984, 18), thanks largely to Freud's emphasis on sexuality. While I am not sure that Jung still overshadows Freud in children's literature studies, Rose is right to note that Jungian readings of children's literature have long proliferated, readings that apply Jungian ideas about archetypes—chief among them the Shadow, the Anima, and the Animus, as well as the Child—as well as the concept of individuation. As with Freudian readings, not a few Jungian analyses of the fairy tale and other genres are vulgar or reductive, missing out on the complexities of Jung's actual discourse.[13] In any case, Jungian criticism of children's literature originates more with the work of von Franz and other Jungian commentators than with Jung himself. Because the Child archetype can and should be sought after by the adult, Jung's system does not itself support the idea of a separate "children's literature"; rather, Jung emphasized the intertwining of child and adult forms (or Forms). Fairy tales, myths, and dreams do make up for Jung a literature of the Child archetype. Jung appeals to this archetype to emphasize the integrative psychological work we should all undertake. Even so, the literature of the Child archetype, in Jung and especially in pop-Jungian discourse, supports a modern and largely affirmative conception of children's literature.

Not all the texts in which children take an interest, or which adults devise for them, would qualify for Jung as literature of the Child archetype. In Jungian terms, children's literature might be literature that returns us to the Child archetype and to knowledge of the collective unconscious. "The child-motif," writes Jung, "represents the preconscious, childhood aspect of the collective psyche" (1949, 111). Jung's understanding of the child in literature has perhaps been more influential than that of Freud, who did not stress the unity of genres in which the child was called up or called forth. Together, Freud and Jung make a compelling case for the intimacy of childhood and the fairy tale.

Fairy Tales, Fantasy, and Useful Children's Books: The American Scene

In the United States, psychoanalytic interest in the fairy tale merged with and supported a fairy-tale friendly popular culture, generally speaking. Perrault's 1697 *Histoires ou contes du temps passé* was translated into English as early as 1729, the Grimms' *Kinder- und Hausmärchen* in 1823. By the end of the nineteenth century, these and other collections of fairy tales had reached a wide American audience, inspiring the likes of Nathaniel Hawthorne and Lydia Maria Child to experiment with the genre. In the September 1881 issue of the *Atlantic Monthly,* John Fiske takes note of the popularity of fairy tales and remarks that every new translation has increased readerly demand. The fairy tale apparently resonated with residually Puritan American literature and with various newer genres of sensational literature.[14]

American attitudes towards fairy tales have long been mixed, but for the most part, fairy tales were accepted in the nineteenth century as proto-therapeutic. So, too, with sensational literature, despite widespread fears about the excitable young imagination. In "Books for Our Children," which appeared in 1865 in the *Atlantic Monthly,* the Reverend Samuel Osgood argued that children's books need to stimulate the imagination and stressed the importance of play, the subject of my next chapter. Children's books, held Osgood, must facilitate imaginative engagement with the so-called real world *and* keep alive the fantasy worlds of childhood. More optimistic still is Thomas Wentworth Higginson's spirited 1879 defense of "sensational" boy books by Oliver Optic (William Taylor Adams) and Horatio Alger Jr., which he presented at the meeting of the American Library Association (see Darling 1968). His defense anticipates the twentieth-century argument for fairy tales, from the first wave of psychoanalysis forward. Fairy tales, we now think, enable psychosocial development, giving outlet to yearnings and nurturing creativity. Assuming assessments like those of Osgood and Higginson to be representative, it would seem that belief in child-centered as well as sensational narrative was already allied with faith in the child's imaginative powers before psychoanalysis took up the cause. Perhaps that faith emanated from the literature itself, to some degree.

The 1920s saw the eruption of the so-called fairy-tale wars between progressive educators led by Lucy Sprague Mitchell, founder of the Bureau of Educational Experiments (informally known as the Bank Street School from its address), and more traditionally minded book advocates led by librarian and critic Anne Carroll Moore. Moore was especially vocal in defending fairy tales, myths, and legends against the encroachments of the modern realist (usually urban) tale for children, which Mitchell was encouraging at Bank Street. This discussion took the form of a debate about the merits of "fantasy," meaning both fantastical narratives and psychological fantasy (also *ph*antasy) as theorized by Freud, Klein, and others. As Jacalyn Eddy reports, child experts at first inveighed against fantasy, but gradually the tables turned, with the experts often championing fantasy along psychological lines (2006, 110–17).

By midcentury, both child psychology and commentary on fairy tales emphasized the importance of fantasy and imaginative narrative, dismissing residual concerns about escapism. Arguments in favor of fantasy tended to be psychoanalytic in formulation, if not always explicitly, since fantasy was seen as emanating from unconscious processes, instinctual drives, or both. "Books for children have," notes Kate Friedlaender, "even in the early days of Psychoanalysis, aroused its interest. Up till now it has chiefly concerned itself with the Fairy-Tale, literature for older children only rarely playing a part in analytical research" (1942, 129). Friedlaender, a psychiatrist, makes the case that books appealing to children in the latency stage do so because they help children meet psychological challenges. Decades before Bettelheim, she identifies a number of features common to favorite latency-period books, features also more explicitly present in fairy tales, she notes. These include orphanhood or dramatic changes in circumstance for the main character, which she likens to the family romance, as well as the regular "taming" of bad adults alongside an impossible goodness in child character, symptomatic of "certain functions of the Ego's defence-mechanisms" (138). In short, she proposes that children read for emotional satisfaction rather than for information, which brings them into conflict with adults. They love fantasy, she notes, and prefer substandard literature that speaks to them emotionally to more literary material that does not. The adult classics they like best, she notes, are likewise those with the same themes and emphases as appear in favored latency-period books and fairy tales, books such as *Jane Eyre* and *David Copperfield*. Friedlaender urges adults to give greater consideration to the psychodynamic dimensions of reading and to "avoid prohibitions of every kind" when it comes to children's reading (150). Tacitly she acknowledges that the insights of psychoanalysis have been anticipated by imaginative literature.

In 1946 Martha Wolfenstein, staff psychiatrist for the Walden School in New York City and future collaborator of Margaret Mead, made a similar assessment.[15] Wolfenstein reports on an interesting experiment in applied psychology, designed to see how a children's story about the birth of a sibling and with a strong fantasy element might affect a young child and his or her mother. Commissioned by Wolfenstein and her team, established children's author Leo Rosten wrote a story (without pictures) called *Sally and the Baby and the Rampatan,* in which young Sally, faced with the arrival of a sibling but ignorant of the facts of life, fantasizes that the baby will be a "rampatan," an animal part duck, part bunny, and part pussycat. Sally asserts control over the situation, refusing to tell her mother what a "rampatan" might be. The rampatan fantasy, remarks Wolfenstein, "expresses with the ingenuous condensation of a dream image the wishes of the child in the given situation: the wish to create something as the parents have . . . the wish to determine what the baby will be, the wish to outdo the Mother, to destroy the Mother's baby and at the same time to make restitution" (1946, 3–4).

Ten four-year-old subjects and their mothers were presented with this story in various settings, and the results were analyzed through interviews and individual play sessions (complete with doll sets and art materials). Wolfenstein discovers that the children most likely to dislike the rampatan fantasy belonged to the mothers most inclined to repress discussions of sexuality and to deny the emotional complexity of childhood, whereas the children most likely to enjoy the fantasy belonged to the mothers more willing to see their children as sexual and sometimes hostile little creatures. The fantasy element of the rampatan ensures the proper unconscious processing of standard psychological anxieties, she concludes, and sublimation is infinitely preferable to repression. Like Friedlaender, Wolfenstein argues that aesthetic merit should always be secondary to affective power. Wolfenstein goes one step further than Friedlaender by showing what happens when mothers resist the importance of fantasy, thereby positioning mothers as potential hindrances and shoring up her own authority as a child expert. The adult more generally, she declares, "seems to have little ability for cathecting fantasy" (28).[16]

Whereas Friedlaender and Wolfenstein spoke on behalf of the experts, Josette Frank—educator, anthology editor, and executive director of the Child Study Association of America—served as an intermediary of sorts between the experts and parents seeking advice about children and their books. As Lynn S. Cockett (1996) details, Frank is one of a number of women in the first half of the twentieth century who wrote about children's reading for parents in mass-market publications such as *Good Housekeeping* and *Parents Magazine.* Cockett documents through this literature a shift away from moralistic understandings of children's literature and toward more contemporary concerns with both the child's developmental needs and the needs of parents who want to be involved with their children's reading. In an essay in the winter 1948–49 issue of *Child Study,* the Child Study Association's official journal (aimed primarily at parents), Frank concurs with the contemporary emphasis on the importance of fantasy and children's emotions, associating them with "mental hygiene" rather than with psychoanalysis.[17] She acknowledges and approves of the newer emphasis on children's pleasure in reading but notes that didactic stories persist. "Practically every kind of child behavior has been exploited recently in stories for the young," she notes, and most of those stories "are cheerful and positive" (1948–49, 6). Frank is more cautious than Friedlaender and Wolfenstein in her assessment of this shift toward pleasure and fantasy, however, noting, "There are things which reading can and cannot do for children. Books cannot substitute for experiences. . . . Neither can reading motivate emotions, overcome defects, or revise personality patterns" (26). Contra Wolfenstein and more-alarmist expert opinion,

Frank sees parents as uniquely qualified to preside over the emotional lives of their children and to find material best suited for them.

A decade or so earlier, Frank had published a book called *What Books for Children? Guideposts for Parents,* which argues for a new kind of valuation of children's books, one based more on emotional and developmental relevance. "We will save ourselves many heartaches," she writes, "if we think of our children's reading not in terms of 'culture'—of good books or bad, or of more books or fewer—but rather as an avenue of expression and inner satisfaction for each according to his needs" (1937, 23). Appealing briefly to the wisdom of psychoanalytic psychiatry concerning the appeal of fairy tales, she emphasizes that parents and children do not necessarily want the same thing from literature, and that the child's needs always come first.[18] "The important thing is not that a child shall read all the good books which are available or which his parents read before him," she writes, "but that what he does read shall have meaning and value *for him* and that he shall know how to find the books which have" that value and meaning (80). She is not worried about less-than-literary narrative and in fact even acknowledges its appeal. She likens series reading to the measles— harmless enough and perhaps even beneficial.

By midcentury, fantasy narrative, with the fairy tale center stage, was widely deemed essential to the psychological health of children. This was probably the combined effect of psychoanalytic advocacy and the imaginative literature itself. Parents generally came to accept their children as vexed and pleasure-seeking creatures who could be coaxed into responsible selfhood. Jack Zipes may be right that fantasy "was really on the defensive while appearing to be on the offensive," that if anything it was "used to compensate for the growing rationalization of culture, work, and family life in western society" (1983, 171). Whether liberatory, normative, or both, the clinical and popular literature on fairy tale and fantasy prepared the way for Bettelheim.

The Uses of Enchantment

At the time of his death in 1990, Bettelheim was one of the most respected psychologists in the world, praised for his work at the Sonia Shankman Orthogenic School in Chicago, a residential treatment center for children, and for his writings on the Holocaust, autism, kibbutz life, and childhood. From 1968 to 1973, he ran an advice column in *Ladies' Home Journal* for mothers, titled "Dialogue with Mothers" after his 1962 *Dialogues with Mothers* (itself based on a series of talks for mothers given at the University of Chicago); other books dealing with childhood and parenting include *Love Is Not Enough: The Treatment of Emotionally Disturbed Children* (1950), *Truants from Life: The Rehabilitation of Emotionally Disturbed Children* (1955), *The Children of the Dream* (1969), and *A Good Enough Parent: A Book on Child-Rearing* (1987). Already well-known, he became famous thanks to *The Uses of Enchantment,* his fairy-tale study that also functioned as a child-rearing book of sorts. The book was the recipient of both the National Book Award and the National Book Critics Circle Award and was praised by the likes of Harold Bloom, Leslie Fiedler, and John Updike. In 1995 it was named by the New York Public Library as one of the most influential volumes of the century (Pollak 1988, 351). *The Uses of Enchantment* enjoyed such success because it effectively synthesized and repackaged decades of psychoanalytic research on childhood and fairy tales.

Anyone versed in the scholarship on fairy tales knows the criticisms that have rightly been made of Bettelheim's study, chiefly that it is indifferent to tale variation and historical context and that it has an overriding commitment to Freudian hermeneutics.[19] In *Off with Their Heads!,* Maria Tatar takes Bettelheim's role as a public intellectual seriously when she also accuses him of siding with parents against children. In fact, she finds that attitude to be common among scholars. "With few notable exceptions," she writes, "nearly every study of children's fairy tales published in this century has taken the part of the parent. . . . For a book that champions the interests of children, *The Uses of Enchantment* is oddly accusatory toward children" (1992, xvii–xxii). In Tatar's view, Bettelheim's refusal to acknowledge the sociohistorical realities of child abuse or any sort of adult hostility toward children—a position in line with Freud's emphasis on the child's polymorphous perversity—has the effect of making children into villains. The "transhistorical assumption of a disturbed child and a healthy adult" (xxiv) has been nurtured by psychoanalysis, she holds, and Bettelheim's book is "deeply symptomatic of our own culture's thinking about children" (xxv).

I find this critique persuasive, but I would stress the complexity of Bettelheim's vision, not only in *The Uses of Enchantment* but also in his larger body of work. Even in the fairy-tale study, Bettelheim does not, in fact, position himself so unequivocally against children, nor does he remain entirely faithful to Freudian theory. *The Uses of Enchantment* pointedly situates the child as existential hero engaged in the "struggle for meaning" (the title of his introduction) by way of the fairy tale. Bettelheim's ideas about the psychological value of fairy tales are usefully understood in light of his lifelong interest in the feral tale.[20] Long before he wrote about fairy tales, he wrote about feral children, beginning with a famous case of wolf-girls in Midnapore, India. In so doing, he fashioned after Freud his own psychoanalytic variants of the feral tale, in which parents—and specifically mothers—are villains. Bettelheim did not believe that trauma only comes from within; as early as 1943, he focused his attention on the devastating effects of concentration camp imprisonment and other environmental realities, including beastly parenting. In this respect, he was a pioneer in trauma studies, as David James Fisher hints (2008, 38–39). Adults are not blameless in his work. Bettelheim has in fact been charged with a special hostility toward mothers, particularly in his autism study, *The Empty Fortress: Infantile Autism and the Birth of the Self,* first published in 1967.

Operating from the standard psychoanalytic assumption that children are repeating the developmental history of the species, *The Uses of Enchantment* is divided into two sections, the first dealing with the "need for inner integration" and the second with "oedipal problems" (1976, 90). While he does not shrink from invoking Freud, Bettelheim appeals strategically to contemporary faith in "integration" before he returns to the thornier issue of oedipality. In part 2 he ingeniously rediscovers the story of Oedipus in the form of a fairy tale, offering a comparison of the Oedipus story with the fairy tale "Snow White and the Seven Dwarves." In this way, he positions himself as Freud's successor.[21] At the same time, he takes a more radical position by implying that the fairy tale is an *improvement* on the tale of Oedipus, in that "Snow White" offers the child hope, unlike the Greek legend. In fairy tales, he remarks, "the hero's story shows how these potentially destructive infantile relations can be, and are, integrated into developmental processes," whereas in myth, including the myth of Oedipus, "there is only insurmountable difficulty and defeat" (198). In the final section of the book, Bettelheim turns to the "life cycle" model of neo-Freudian Erik Erikson, reading the fairy tale "Cinderella" as a lesson in autonomy and integration. Bettelheim urges that children be raised on fairy tales so they can mature. As Dundes points out, Bettelheim's conviction on this point is more obvious from the title of the German translation of the book: *Kinder brauchen Märchen,* or "Children need fairy tales" (Dundes 1991, 73). Further, to allow children the freest engagements, holds Bettelheim, adults should *tell* the stories, again and again, rather than let children read them. And never should they reveal to the child the fairy tale's psychological attraction; that would spoil the enchantment.

Bettelheim emigrated to the United States in 1939 and was in many ways an Americanized analyst, pragmatic and open to revisionist thought. *The Uses of Enchantment* is often described as resolutely Freudian, but the book indicates Bettelheim's simultaneous commitments to classical and revisionist psychoanalysis and to competing views of childhood.[22] Consider, for example, this representative passage from the introduction:

> This is exactly the message that fairy tales get across to the child in manifold form: that a struggle against severe difficulties in life is unavoidable, is an intrinsic part of human existence—but that if one does not shy away, but steadfastly meets unexpected and often unjust hardships, one masters all obstacles and at the end emerges victorious. (1976, 8)

Here, as throughout the book, a traditionally Freudian outlook meets the more utopian perspective of ego psychology, which overlaps considerably with the American-dream narrative of success through adversity. *The Uses of Enchantment* is not only a book of interpretation but also a child-rearing primer, its readings designed for practical use. Bettelheim speaks of the importance of "personality integration" and "healthy human development" (12), in keeping with both Jungian tradition and humanistic or third-force psychology. He also acknowledges the importance of play, affirming the contributions of Klein and Jean Piaget on play and symbolization. In fact, he positions the encounter with fairy tales after play as the next "solution" to unconscious challenges:

> Some unconscious pressures in children can be worked out through play. But many do not lend themselves to it because they are too complex and contradictory, or too dangerous and socially disapproved. . . . Knowing fairy tales is a great help to the child, as illustrated by the fact that many fairy stories are acted out by children, but only after children have become familiar with the story, which they never could have invented on their own. (55)

Bettelheim's psychoanalytic formulations are certainly problematic from a contemporary perspective, especially with respect to gender and sexuality. For instance, he approves of doll play among boys, but only if it can be sublimated by maturity. He recommends that homosexual desires be kept unconscious. Even so, he refuses to pathologize either children or fairy tales, emphasizing the resourcefulness of the former and remarking (contra Freud) that the latter "are not neurotic symptoms" (19). He takes parents to task for their "fear of fantasy" (122). Most critically, he express faith in the complementarity of children's forms and psychoanalysis, remarking that "the fairy-tale answer [to the question of human identity] is the same one which psychoanalysis offers: To avoid being tossed about and, in extreme cases, torn apart by our ambivalences requires that we integrate them" (89–90). Whereas Freud understood psychoanalysis as offering insight but not necessarily dramatic change, Bettelheim grants the fairy tale great transformative power as well as foreknowledge of the wisdom of psychoanalysis, claiming that "the form and structure of fairy tales suggest images to the child by which he can structure his daydreams and with them give better direction to his life" (7). Fairy tales got there first, he seems to say.

The Uses of Enchantment is about fairy tales, not children's literature, as Bettelheim is quick to emphasize. He finds children's literature—"modern stories"—insufficiently deep and useful. "The pre-primers and primers from which [the child] is taught to read in school," writes Bettelheim, "are designed to teach the necessary skills, irrespective of meaning. The overwhelming bulk of the rest of so-called 'children's literature' attempts to entertain or to inform, or both. But most of these books are so shallow in substance that little of significance can be gained from them" (4). "The deep inner conflicts originating in our primitive drives and our violent emotions are all denied in much of modern children's literature" (10). Only fairy tales offer the right balance of conflict and hope, in his view.

Bettelheim knows very little about children's literature and seems unaware of the ascendance of fantasy in American literature and culture, which made possible such a favorable reception for his own book. Friedlaender, Wolfenstein, and Frank had already granted the psychological benefits of the fairy tale to other forms of children's narrative, in effect setting up the fairy tale as a template for good children's literature. While Bettelheim's psychology was far from rigid, his faith in form was strikingly so: in his mind, only the fairy tale can enable "personality integration." Bettelheim was old-fashioned in many respects, and his fidelity to the fairy tale may reflect nostalgia for the Old World. For whatever reasons, Bettelheim refused to recognize other fantasy forms, famously objecting to Maurice Sendak's *Where the Wild Things Are* as insufficiently attuned to the child's inner life. As I discuss in chapter 4, Bettelheim wrote against Sendak's book—now viewed as *the* picturebook fantasy—in one of his "Dialogue with Mothers" columns, at some level recognizing Sendak as a rival authority on childhood (Bettelheim 1969).

While Bettelheim endorses the fairy tale as authentic children's literature, he does not examine the difficulties attendant on such a claim. Is the fairy tale real children's literature because it appeals to real children, we might ask, or because it reflects the folk-childish-unconscious mind, or some combination thereof? These possibilities are somewhat in conflict, in that individual meaning making in and around fairy tales requires some level of mature awareness of their import and value; might not such awareness run counter to unconscious needs and desires? Freud "used" fairy tales with his patients, helping them see how fairy tales screen infantile fears and fantasies; according to Bettelheim, children ostensibly use fairy tales themselves, with parents functioning as analyst surrogates.

In more ways than one, *The Uses of Enchantment* is not original work. As I have suggested, Bettelheim builds on the groundswell of support for fantasy. But there is more to the story. There is good evidence that *The Uses of Enchantment* was plagiarized from Julius E. Heuscher's *A Psychiatric Study of Fairy Tales: Their Origin, Meaning, and Usefulness* (1963). Joan Blos was the first to make this discovery in 1978, with Alan Dundes and especially Bettelheim's biographer Richard Pollak following up on the story. Heuscher's study "was rich with psychological gingerbread," writes Pollak, "and like the hungry Hansel, Bettelheim helped himself" (1988, 343). Pollak's side-by-side comparisons of passages from the two books make obvious the derivative nature of Bettelheim's book. "Bettelheim had been in this forest before," continues Pollak, "scrambling for nuts and berries that would give him something to say about concentration camps or parenting or autism or kibbutzism or the youth culture, but seldom digesting his pickings before announcing their meaning to a waiting world" (347). Dundes is more measured, finding Bettelheim's study "infinitely superior" to Heuscher's, whose work he calls "a confusing mix of Freudian, Jungian, and anthroposophical theories" (1991, 80), but faulting Bettelheim for this "sin of commission" as well as for neglecting other relevant work (76–77).[23]

Heuscher's book is indeed a mishmash of ideas, but Heuscher himself thinks we have surpassed the strictly "natural-scientific" orientation of Freud (1963, 43) and argues for a composite approach. For Heuscher, the fairy tale helps us "regain the spiritual or moral impulses which can liberate our imprisoned 'everyday Ego.' This Ego," he continues, "is captured in a narrow materialistic world just like Rapunzel who is jailed by the witch in a stone tower" (vi). Heuscher's vision of the fairy tale is very much one of collective spirituality and empowerment, one motivated by the alleged dangers of materialism. Heuscher sees reflected in the fairy tale three "epochs" of both individual and historical life: a prematerialistic period, a materialistic one, and a (future) postmaterialistic phase. Even more than most psychologically oriented commentators, he idealizes the child as especially receptive to the fairy tale's visual and narrative magic. In the last chapter of *A Psychiatric Study of Fairy Tales*, "The Child and the Fairy Tale," he asserts, like Bettelheim, that "fairy tales have an educational and therapeutic value" (186). Heuscher's utopian faith in the genre may well have tempered the Freudian tendencies of Bettelheim, causing the latter also to emphasize the fairy tale's transformative potential.[24] When Heuscher learned of the plagiarism, he quite generously responded, "We all plagiarize. I plagiarize. Many times, I am not sure whether it came out of my own brain or if it came from somewhere else. . . . I am only happy that I would have influenced Bruno Bettelheim" (cited in Pollak 1988, 351).

Is the alleged plagiarism less scandalous if we understand Bettelheim as the most successful in a long line of psychoanalytic commentators on fairy tales? With this subject at least, he is more popularizer than original thinker, and his book has in turn spawned a cottage industry of bibliotherapeutic writing on fairy tales. There is Sheldon Cashdan's *The Witch Must Die: The Hidden Meaning of Fairy Tales* (1999), for instance, as well as Catherine Orenstein's *Little Red Riding Hood Uncloaked: Sex, Morality, and the Evolution of a Fairy Tale* (2002). Orenstein pays homage to Bettelheim, who, she says, "almost single-handedly catapulted the modern genre into vogue" (11–12). These are but two of the many sequels to *The Uses of Enchantment* that trend away from the scholarly monograph and toward popular, applied psychology.

Do You Believe in Magic?

As children's literature criticism developed, librarians and literary scholars turned to fairy tales for insights into childhood and as a template for children's narrative more generally. Psychoanalysis borrows from the fairy tale, but literary criticism also borrows from psychoanalysis, especially when it comes to children's narrative. One example is Canadian librarian Lillian Smith's 1953 textbook *The Unreluctant Years: A Critical Approach to Children's Literature.*[25] In her first chapter, titled "The Case for Children's Literature," Smith insists upon the differences between children and adults and upon the need to respect those differences in writing for children. She notes that "the adult's conception of what constitutes a children's book [does not] coincide always with that of the child. . . . Children are a race whose experience of life is different from that of adults" (Smith 1991, 5). Smith's book is organized by genre, beginning with a chapter on fairy tales, in which she emphasizes their staying power and transformative potential. Smith holds that the fairy tale helps children manage their fears. "Against the limitless terrors of a child's own imaginations," she remarks, "are set the limits opposed by the conventions of the fairy tale" (50). She quotes Walter de La Mare's claim in his 1940 work *Animal Stories* that fairy tales "may feed the imagination, enlighten the mind, strengthen the heart, show us *ourselves*" (quoted in Smith 1991, 51; emphasis La Mare's). "In turning from one kind of fairy tale to another," she remarks, "a child finds, in their variety, a deepening and broadening of emotional sympathy" (51). She remarks that children "are aware, consciously or unconsciously, that in hero stories they find experience. Beyond their glamour and magic and romance there is something tough and real" (84).

Most histories of Anglo-European children's literature, as well as textbooks on children's literature, consider fairy tales and the oral tradition the foundation of children's literature. Even when fairy-tale literature is not presented as a precursor to ostensibly more adult or more literary genres, it is nearly always positioned as coming first in the child's experience of stories and thus as setting certain patterns of expectation. It is not that fairy tales have been grandfathered into children's literature, but rather that the modern understanding of children's literature was argued for on the basis of the fairy tale's value and the broader uses of enchantment. The general story of Anglo-American children's literature is that entertainment began to displace didacticism in the nineteenth century, as fairy tales and fantasy became more popular. I would call this the progressive hypothesis of children's literature, the idea that children's literature gets freer in form and content with time and ostensibly gives free reign to the child's imagination. Such freedom probably constitutes yet another chapter in the rationalization of child-centered discourse or in the instrumentalization of children's forms (per Michel Foucault, this might be the disciplinary hypothesis). After centuries of contestation, fairy tales were made authoritative in our own time through a rhetoric of children's psychological, emotional, imaginative needs: children *need* to fantasize, to dream, to sail to where the wild things are. Amusement, play, and fantasy are core terms in the newer language of child development, not displacing didacticism or rationality but giving them a makeover. Fantasy is the new realism. The ongoing debate about the psychological appropriateness of fairy tales for children is part of the fairy tale's long history of adult–child negotiation and helps maintain rather than undermine the fairy tale's centrality to children's literature.

Not only are fairy tales seen as foundational, but also cultural preference has shifted away from narratives that teach rationality and character development and toward narratives that distill as well as model psychological challenges. Introducing a new forum of ideas in a special issue of *Children's Literature in Education* in 1978, children's author Joan Blos turns immediately to the subject of children's literature and child psychology, emphasizing their "reciprocal content and corresponding statements" (1978, 101) and pairing remarks by psychologists about childhood with passages from classic children's books. Writers and psychologists seem to know the same truths, she observes. More to the point, she connects good children's books to fairy-tale wisdom:

> We begin by recalling that in the old tales repetition, over time, has tended to refine their material to what folklorist Tristam P. Coffin has aptly termed "the emotional core" of the narrative. We note that in more cases than not that core locates in childhood the great and most *universal aspect* of human experience. Equipped with our insight we speculate that the regression that underlies creativity—whether practiced by a contemporary author with an electric typewriter or a story teller by the hearth or kitchen fire—put that emotionally relevant material into the stories in the first place, and that it is this presence in the stories that makes them appeal to children. The tale, in other words, achieves by evolution what the children's book of excellence has by virtue of its author's skill, as well as that person's tolerance for the particular kind of regressive experience demanded by valid art. (104)

This universalizing attitude is one serious consequence of the conflation of fairy tales with children's literature at large. Not only are differences among fairy tales and tale types thereby collapsed, but fairy tales as a group define "good" children's books, as measured by an "emotional core" produced through "the particular kind of regressive experience demanded by valid art." By this standard, books that are deliberately crafted rather than forged from the primal depths do not qualify as good children's books. Without regression, suggests Blos, there can be no emotional core and therefore no art.

The sanctification of the fairy tale as the real, original, or good children's literature exacts a price, including the suppression of the actual diversity of children's literature with respect to genre, mood, tone, audience, conditions of production and reception, and so forth. Bettelheim, for instance, finds Johann David Wyss's 1812 book *The Swiss Family Robinson* lacking because, quite simply, it is not a fairy tale, and thus "did not hold out any promise that [an unnamed adolescent reader's] life would take a turn for the better—a hope which would have made life much more bearable for her" (1976, 131).

Another consequence of such fairy-tale sanctification is the dominance of developmental theories about childhood reading, which co-exist uneasily with the universal-transcendent model of children's literature represented by Blos above. Even though fairy tales represent the child's first and most powerful contact with children's literature, the child is also expected to leave them behind. "I was given [fairy tale] collections to read—two or three of the Andrew Lang coloured *Fairy Books,* French anthologies, Hans Christian Andersen," reports Marina Warner, "but I was expected to grow out of them, I could tell" (1994, xiv). Warner has made a career out of resisting that expectation. Nicholas Tucker, in his age-graded guide to children's literature, ranks fairy tales as best suited for children around age seven; he puts fairy tales, myths, and legends after nursery rhymes and "story and picture-books" (1981) but before early fiction, comics, and literature for older children. Tucker has in mind the child's reading ability and puts picture-based texts before fairy tales for this reason, but others have argued that fairy tales should be experienced before or alongside picturebooks, as they encourage the move from orality to literacy. "It is precisely through fairy tales and fantasy," affirms Tatar in *Enchanted Hunters,* "that children learn to move beyond magical thinking" (2009, 140), coming to prefer the magic of words.

This logic harkens back not so much to Freud as to ego psychology and other traditions of developmental psychoanalytic theory. In *The Magic Years: Understanding and Handling the Problems of Early Childhood,* Selma H. Fraiberg, a popular childhood expert and professor of child psychoanalysis at the California School of Medicine, writes that the first five years of a child's life are "'magic' years because the child in his early years is a magician—in the psychological sense. His earliest conception of the world is a magical one; he believes that his actions and his thoughts can bring about events" (1959, ix). Fraiberg endorses the developmental model without giving up Freud and Klein, asserting that if we did not provide monsters to children, they would invent their own (she makes this point in a chapter called "Witches, Ogres, Tigers, and Mental Health"). Fraiberg's vision is Freudian, even as she acknowledges the influences of ego psychology and anticipates humanist psychologist Carl Rogers with section titles like "On Becoming a Person" (Roger's book with the same title was published in 1961). Fraiberg's book, which sold well and was widely reviewed, typifies the period's faith in practical, distilled psychoanalytic wisdom.

Children's literature is still regularly framed as progressing from simple to complex textual encounters and from simple to complex psychological tasks. Eschewing the traditional language of developmental stages, J. A. Appleyard argues for a sequence of reading roles beginning in childhood and running through adulthood: the reader as player, as hero/heroine, as thinker, as interpreter, and as pragmatist (1990, 14–15). Early childhood features the reader as player, and Appleyard talks first about young children who play with (you guessed it) fairy tales and their characters, Snow White specifically. He then stresses the affective power of fantasy and magical thinking, citing Bettelheim in support (36–37). If children are to grow into critical thinkers, the logic runs, they must get past magical thinking and the fairy-tale fetish. The positioning of the fairy tale as the first form of children's literature, then, supports two variations on the fairy-tale-as-magic theme. Childhood is at once envisioned as a magical place to which adults (especially creative writers) can return via the fairy tale and analogous forms (Blos's universal-transcendent model) and a stage of life that should be left behind in search of "higher" magic (the developmental model).

In summary, the psychoanalytic presentation of the fairy tale as the exemplary form of children's literature enabled an expansion of genres—from fairy tales to other imaginative genres—and of keywords, such as "magic," "enchantment," and "play." Across the twentieth century, psychoanalytic writing on the fairy tale helped authorize a broader discourse on the forms and uses of enchantment. The broadening of terms accompanied and facilitated a broadening of the canon, so that certain children's classics are now invoked alongside the fairy tale in illustration of theoretical or interpretive claims.[26] At the same time, that broadening has its limits or conditions, and texts or genres that fail to meet fairy-tale standards can be pushed to the sidelines.

Under the Influence: Fairy-Tale Studies

The fairy tale's partial takeover of children's literature—and the psychoanalytic coordinates of that takeover—also has consequences for academic criticism. The field of children's literature studies within English and related humanities fields began to take shape around the same time that Bettelheim's fairy-tale book appeared, with the founding of the Children's Literature Association and of specialized journals, book series, and graduate programs. Scholars of children's literature have advocated a broad and diverse understanding of that literature even as they continue to study the fairy tale. Even so, it is no accident that fairy-tale scholarship enjoys great visibility and circulation within and especially outside children's literature studies. A recent example is Ruth B. Bottigheimer's *Fairy Tales: A New History* (2009), featured prominently in a 2009 article in the *Chronicle of Higher Education*. Jack Zipes and Maria Tatar, first-rate scholars to be sure, have likewise benefited from ongoing fascination with the fairy tale within the public sphere.[27]

Psychoanalytic engagement with the fairy tale has left its mark on fairy-tale scholarship. "We tend to believe," notes Elizabeth Wanning Harries, "that the fairy tales we know and love come from ancient oral sources, that their appearance in print is a late and somewhat disturbing development. And we tend to believe that they are an expression of the deep wisdom and knowledge of the 'folk'" (2001, 12). Classical psychoanalysis affirms these beliefs, endorsing the orality-to-literacy metanarrative despite evidence of a more complicated process of fairy-tale emergence. Harries has challenged such faith, which persists in some scholarship. So has Bottigheimer, who has argued in several monographs that fairy tales are literary in origin as well as in destination. In *Fairy Tales: A New History,* she pulls no punches: "Folk invention and transmission of fairy tales has no basis in verifiable fact. Literary analysis undermines it, literary history rejects it, social history repudiates it, and publishing history (whether of manuscripts or of books) contradicts it" (2009, 1).[28] Focusing especially on "rise tales"—tales in which a lowly protagonist climbs the social ladder—Bottigheimer provides instead a book-based history that traces the canon of Perrault and Grimm back to the sixteenth- and seventeenth-century Italian authors Giambattista Basile and Giovan Francesco Straparola. This point has been made before, but as Bottigheimer emphasizes, the "oralist-privileging" history of fairy tales still reigns even in specialist scholarship.[29] The matter is far from settled, most fairy-tale scholars now taking the view that fairy tales are a provocative and confusing mixture of oral and literary tradition (and perhaps also, of wonder and realism).

Even Max Lüthi's formalist-narratological approach to the fairy tale emphasizes its "abstract style" but thereby suggests a psychological function for the fairy tale. While the fairy tale itself has little psychological content for Lüthi, he speculates that its "abstract style" encourages psychological engagement:

> The individual characters of a folktale are thus seen as components of a human personality, and in essence the folktale represents a psychological process. The abstract stylization of the tale, together with the figurative quality of its human beings and animals, is called on to witness that tales do not deal with fully individualized persons or the portrayal of an external world; rather, they represent an internal reality. Even if this conclusion cannot be proven absolutely, one still must grant that precisely because the folktale never directly expresses the psychological, its characters and events can easily be taken as symbolic images of inner potentialities and processes. (1982, 117–18)[30]

Furthermore, fairy-tale scholars have had to contend with the towering influence of Bettelheim. Zipes and Tatar especially have developed their analytical projects against as well as through Bettelheim.[31] Zipes is the fairy godfather not only of fairy-tale studies but also of theoretical children's literature studies, having cofounded the journal *The Lion and the Unicorn,* established the first monograph series on children's literature, and generally functioned as a galvanizing presence for the field. Published seven years after Bettelheim's blockbuster, Zipes's *Fairy Tales and the Art of Subversion: The Classical Genre for Children and the Process of Civilization* approaches the fairy tale not as a psychological symptom or cure but as a "symbolic act" to be understood historically and culturally. The fairy tale, he writes, is "intended to transform a specific oral folk tale (and sometimes a well-known literary tale) . . . [to] address the concerns of the educated and ruling classes of late feudal and early capitalistic societies" (1983, 6). "We must remember that the fairy tale for children originated in a period of absolutism when French culture was setting standards of *civilité* for the rest of Europe," he notes. "Exquisite care was thus taken to cultivate a discourse on the civilization process through the fairy tale for the benefit of well-raised children" (9).

Zipes finds Bettelheim's approach "unhistorical and too glib" (32), a familiar criticism. Zipes emphasizes instead "the development of the individual and family in different societies in relation to the civilizing process," calling his approach "an historical psychological point of view" (32–33). "Beauty and the Beast" tales are important not because they enable children to work through their fears and fantasies, Zipes insists, but rather because these tales "set standards for sexual and social conduct which complied with inhibiting forms of socialization and were to be internalized by the readers and auditors of the tale" (33). His inspiration is Norbert Elias's *The Civilizing Process,* a Freudian study of the relays between the "psychogenetic" development of the species and the "sociogenetic" evolution of society. This emphasis, of course, on the parallelism of social body and the individual subject owes something to recapitulation theory. While Freud often leaned automatically on recapitulation theory, he was also critically engaged with the question or problem of ontogenetic–phylogenetic correspondence. In some ways, even as he offers a sociohistoricist or Marxist–materialist response to Bettelheim, Zipes shares this engagement, drawing on Elias who draws on Freud.

Zipes has since published a remarkable number of fairy-tale studies. His 2006 *Why Fairy Tales Stick: The Evolution and Relevance of a Genre* reconsiders the argument of *Fairy Tales and the Art of Subversion,* using recent evolutionary studies of human cognition to theorize about the psychocultural reasons for narrative canonicity.[32] That is, he returns psychology to the scene of explanation. After twenty-five years of reflection, he concludes that classical fairy tales "did not become stable and establish their value . . . simply because they reinforced the ideological norms of patriarchal societies. They spoke to the conflicts and predicaments that arose out of the attempts by social orders to curb and 'civilize' our instinctual drives." Fairy tales, in short, "enabled listeners and readers to envision possible solutions to their problems so that they could survive and adapt to their environment" (2006, xii). Drawing on linguistics, epidemiology, evolutionary psychology, and genetics, Zipes theorizes that we prefer certain stories because they help us adapt to often-harsh realities. At the same time, Zipes still follows Freud's general model of instincts and the workings of civilization. Zipes rejects Bettelheim but continues to engage with Freudian theory.

Tatar variously criticizes, affirms, and imitates Bettelheim's fairytale work. Her first book, *The Hard Facts of the Grimms' Fairy Tales,* is both historicist and psychological in orientation. She likens fairy tales to dreams but says that "rather than giving us personalized wishes and fears, they offer collective truths, realities that transcend individual experience and that have stood the test of time." "This is not to say that folktales and folklore function as repositories of a sort of Jungian collective unconscious," she is quick to clarify. "Rather, they capture psychic realities so persistent and widespread that they have held the attention of a community over a long time" (1987, xvi). "For all its excesses, psychoanalytic criticism has scored numerous successes in its encounters with fairy tales" (55). While she emphasizes the historical and cultural aspects of tale variation and transmission, she insists that the fairy tale "lends itself more readily to literary and psychological analysis than to historical inquiry" (57).

Tatar is openly critical of Bettelheim in *Off with Their Heads!,* accusing him of siding with parents and suppressing tales "that run counter to the Freudian orthodoxy" (1992, xxii) and aligning him with Sendak as champion of a masculinist empowerment fantasy. "Bettelheim endows children with a power over the text that they do not in reality possess," she declares. "The fact that fairy tales guide feelings and control responses gives the lie to the notion that children work their way from dependence to autonomy through literature" (77). The ideal of the innocent, naive child "has haunted the children's literature industry since its inception," she writes. "For this reason, fairy tales, which seem to

represent both the childhood of fiction and the fiction of childhood, occupy a special position in the hierarchy of children's literature" (79).
Tatar also registers the triumph of the therapeutic: "Our own culture
has moved into yet another mode of telling children's stories, one that
might be best described as empathetic/cathartic, resting as it does on a
therapeutic model" (90).

This critique disappears in her 2009 book *Enchanted Hunters,*
which was aimed at a broader audience and marketed, in fact, as "in
the tradition of Bruno Bettelheim's landmark *Uses of Enchantment*"
(dust jacket). (Her title, by the way, derives from Vladimir Nabokov's
Lolita.) Sendak and Bettelheim return as pioneers: "Sendak, like the
renowned child psychologist Bruno Bettelheim, endorses a therapeutic
model that embraces fantasy as a way of working through the complex
primal emotions of childhood" (119). Whereas *Hard Facts* and *Off with
Their Heads!* are concerned with the history and transmission of fairy
tales, *Enchanted Hunters* focuses on the aesthetic and emotional engagement of readers of children's literature more generally. Tatar presents her work as a contact zone between her own desire to "break the
spell" with the readerly belief in literary magic (6), as evidenced in her
interviews and autoethnographies of reading. The result is a decidedly
pro-magic book, in which Tatar presents herself and is presented by her
publisher as an improved Bettelheim, an expert on enchantment and
the enchanted hunters called children.

Perhaps the psychoanalytic texture of fairy-tale scholarship has
been mostly a good thing. And perhaps I am overstating the case; fairy-
tale scholarship is certainly a rich undertaking, with many intellectual
and cultural aspects and influences. Still, I would stress that a psychoanalytic understanding of the fairy tale is very pervasive in academic
as well as in popular culture, so much so that we do not always see it
clearly.

Whatever its effects on children's literature studies, the association
of the fairy tale and psychoanalysis has certainly benefited the latter. The
fairy tale has furnished much grist for the psychoanalytic mill, extending its relevance and giving it a popular (even populist) tone. We might
protest that, say, Cashdan's *The Witch Must Die* is not properly psychoanalytic, but I see this and other texts of pop-psychology as continuous

with Freud's fairy-tale commentary and his commitment to the applied analysis of folklore. Freud believed in lay analysis and wanted psychoanalysis to have wide purchase; the fairy tale has achieved this goal better than all the psychoanalytic institutes combined. Moreover, the fairy tale has helped maintain childhood at the center of psychoanalysis.

More recently, the fairy tale has been remodeled as a key genre in what has been called the "children's literature of atrocity." The fairy tale has been a preferred genre for negotiating not only the existential challenges of everyday life but more extraordinary experiences of trauma. This emphasis also extends back to Freud and Bettelheim, and it has been picked up by a number of trauma theorists who see in the fairy tale an imaginative reckoning with otherwise unspeakable loss and shock. The final chapter of *Freud in Oz* takes up trauma writing for the young, starting with fairy-tale forms. First, however, comes a consideration of magic's companion term, another word for the uses of enchantment and one central to child analysis: "play."

2. Child Analysis, Play, and the Golden Age of *Pooh*

> You probably won't see me again at the MLA, but
> remember: somewhere a Bear and his Best Critic
> will always be playing.
>
> > —Frederick Crews, as "N. Mack Hobbs,"
> > *Postmodern Pooh*

IN A PROVOCATIVE ESSAY ABOUT THEORY AND psychoanalysis, Michael Payne likens scenes of child sexual curiosity in Freud's 1908 *The Sexual Theories of Children* (1963d) to chapter 7 of A. A. Milne's 1926 *Winnie-the-Pooh,* about the alarming arrival of Kanga and Baby Roo in the 100 Aker Wood. "The subsequent, charming conversation among Pooh, Piglet, and Rabbit," writes Payne,

> is a wonderfully zany exercise in theory construction arising
> out of such concerns as these: Who are these strange animals
> with their odd ways who have just intruded into our forest,
> especially having as they do a pocket in the mother's body for
> the baby? If rabbits had pockets for babies, how many would
> they have to have? (Rabbit's Answer: 18, including the one
> for a pocket handkerchief.) What are we going to do about
> this sudden intrusion of an unexpected baby, a mother with
> an unusual body, and other strange and disturbing uncertain-
> ties? (2005, 2–3)

Payne sees in Milne and Freud both a double-consciousness, "in which the reader is invited to identify simultaneously with the youthful perspective of a more or less innocent fictional character and with the more critically reflexive persona of the narrator" (1). We theorize with the child, but also with the adult attending to the child.

Payne underscores the commitment within psychoanalysis to the play of language and ideas in and around childhood, beginning with Freud and extending to the work of Adam Phillips, a writer and contemporary psychoanalyst (in fact, a child analyst). In so doing, however, Payne also underscores the resemblances of children's literature to psychoanalysis and theory. Whereas Jacqueline Rose mobilizes psychoanalysis against children's literature, Payne sees them as analogous, even parallel enterprises. Payne's essay was one of the inspirations for my book, suggesting as it does that we might make a case very different from the one Rose makes, and also by way of a classic text. Payne's use of *Pooh,* however, is no more accidental than is mine in this chapter, or than Rose's use of *Peter Pan.* Just as Rose writes in the wake of broader case writing about *Peter Pan,* Payne and I write in the wake of Poohology, or Pooh-centric discourse.

Poohology emerged from Milne's books and from the material culture of Pooh, which had been expanding dramatically since the 1920s, spanning games, toys, tea sets, clothes, and all kinds of pop-culture items.[1] The first Pooh songbook was published in 1926 and was dedicated to the recently born Princess Elizabeth of Great Britain (Sibley 2001, 96). Poohology proper began later, probably with Alexander Lenard's Latin translation of Milne's book, *Winnie ille Pu* (1958), produced as a teaching aid and the first foreign-language title on the *New York Times* bestseller list. Next up was Frederick Crews's hilarious if vicious satire *The Pooh Perplex* (1963), ostensibly a "freshman casebook" on literary criticism. Poohology mobilizes *Pooh* toward various ends, which might be generally called pedagogical. Much more so than the case writing I take up in the next chapter, Poohology imitates while extending *Pooh* stylistically or thematically. That is, while case writing about *Peter Pan* or *Alice* or *The Wonderful Wizard of Oz* shows some fidelity to those source texts, Poohology often looks a great deal like *Pooh,* quoting extensively from Milne as well as adopting his playful, minimalist style. Poohology is the playful repetition and interpretation of source text.

While Payne's essay is not primarily about *Pooh,* it uses *Pooh* to draw suggestive comparisons among children's literature, psychoanalysis, and critical theory and thus works somewhat like Poohology. My chapter, too, makes use of *Pooh* and might be called historicist Poohology. I show how this classic has long been bound up with psychoanalytic and pop-psychological discourse. *Pooh* began to accrue psychological interest in the 1920s, when child analysis was being developed. The books were then a subject not of psychoanalytic investigation but rather of an analogous investigation into play and the child–adult relationship. The child analysts did not use *Pooh;* nor were they generally attuned to "children's literature" beyond the fairy tale. But as Payne suggests of Freud, they were pursuing some of the same themes that preoccupied Milne and were coming up with some of the same treatments. The ongoing overlap of child analysis and children's literature helped transform *Pooh* into Poohology.

This chapter first revisits early child analysis with this larger trajectory in mind. Before turning to the *Pooh* books, I suggest that child analysts made accommodation for children's materials and thus for children's literature. The chapter then explores Poohology vis-à-vis the transformation of child analysis, which involved both object relations theory and ego psychology. While child analysis persists under other rubrics, it has also been folded back into the broader discourse of psychoanalysis, in large measure because the child, while still an observable creature, is increasingly a metaphor for adult interiority—for Freud, the excavated or reconstructed child; for pop-psychologists, the inner child or child within. *Pooh* became popular in part because it resonated with child analysis; Poohology thrives because it has been easy to shape as an adult, if still child-themed, domain. Even more than child analysis, Poohology made the playing or childish adult central to its imaginary.

Psychologists, philosophers, and literary critics, among others, have claimed Pooh as poster bear. Exercises in Poohology sometimes work at the expense of *Pooh* or children's literature, and sometimes in support of them. Readers are expected to identify variously and sometimes simultaneously with Pooh (child) and with Milne (adult). Poohology is a form of popular psychology and child analysis and literary criticism and theory. Across these variations, though, Poohology refashions the children's classic into a plaything for adults, supporting the interiorization of childhood and of childhood's forms. If *Pooh* belongs to the inner child in all of us, then *Pooh* is something like a collective inner text. Poohology, along with its concomitant *Pooh*-interiorization, positions its practitioners as playful wise guys in the tradition of Milne himself.

Child Study, Child Analysis, and Children's Literature

"Children," writes Sigmund Freud in his introduction to August Aichhorn's 1925 book *Wayward Youth* (Freud 1983), "have become the main subject of psycho-analytic research and have thus replaced in importance the neurotics on which its studies began." Freud acknowledges here both the influence of child analysis, which he encouraged, and also the broader psychoanalytic reorientation from adult to the adult's remembered or inner child. Child analysis itself was indebted to and significantly reworked the transatlantic project of child study, which grew out of evolutionary science as well as empiricist (observational) psychology. While child study can be traced to the late-eighteenth-century work of Dietrich Tiedemann in Germany, it did not get fully underway until the late nineteenth century. In 1877 Hippolyte Taine published an essay on childhood language acquisition in the English journal *Mind;* it was followed the same year by Charles Darwin's "A Biographical Sketch of an Infant," the first of the so-called baby biographies. Child study organizations were established first in America, then in Britain, Germany, France, and Belgium.[2] Pivotal figures in these developments include American psychologist G. Stanley Hall, who founded several journals and launched the National Association for the Study of Childhood, and British psychologist James Sully, author in 1895 of the influential *Studies of Childhood.* As Sully explains in the introduction to that work, "Our modern science is before all things historical and genetic, going back to beginnings so as to understand the later and more complex phases of things as the outcomes of these beginnings" (2000, 4).

A key concern of child study and of child analysis after it was children's play. Portraits of the playing child were of course already central to various literary traditions. In 1762 in *Emile,* Jean-Jacques Rousseau argues for playfully exploratory rather than passive learning, and not long after, Richard and Maria Edgeworth affirm in their theoretical and imaginative works the significance of child play. In this respect, "didactic" literature such as that of the Edgeworths is not so far removed from the ostensibly more playful fantasy literature of Lewis Carroll and company. The Victorians were quite preoccupied with the topic of play. In "Child's Play" (1878), Robert Louis Stevenson conceptualizes play not only as the stuff of childhood but also as a strategy for coping with reality, anticipating psychoanalytic work on the uses of enchantment. Scientific discourse on play, in and around child study, was proliferating by century's end, building on literary discussions of play as well as early educational theory on the topic. Across this literature, play was a unifying motif more than an easily definable activity or a term of consensus. "We talk . . . glibly about [children's] play, their make-believe, their illusions," notes Sully in his first chapter, "The Age of Imagination," "but how much do we really know of their state of mind when they act out a little scene of domestic life, or of the battlefield?" (2000, 27). Play was and remains an overdetermined and elusive concept or set of concepts, which is probably the secret of its staying power.

While child study advocates like Sully and Hall assigned great significance to play as a research topic, the child analysts went further, adopting play as a clinical and discursive method as well. We can see in Sully the kind of playful inquiry characteristic of child analysis, but Sully never quite argues for play as a mode of analytical discourse. While there is much overlap between child study and child analysis, the conceptualization of analysis *as* play was a distinguishing feature of the latter, carried forward into object relations theory and ego psychology. The lay discourse of Poohology likewise claims play as method as much as theme.

While he encouraged child analysis, Freud did not generally practice it himself, preferring to work with the inner children of adult analysands. As Carolyn Steedman and Holly Blackford (among others) have noted, Freud's child is more theoretical construct than real-world inhabitant. For critics of Freud, this theorization or interiorization of childhood represents an abandonment of children, a preference for abstraction over reality, or both. Steedman's view is more neutral; she argues in *Strange Dislocations* (1995) that in the wake of psychoanalysis especially, the child came to stand for the idea of human interiority, assigned both a place (the unconscious) and a time (the past). But child analysis did begin with Freud, and Freud did engage in one exemplary case of child analysis. True to form, Freud conducted the case indirectly, meeting with the child only once and relying primarily on the reports of the child's father, Max Graf, a musicologist and a member of Freud's social circle.[3] The case became that of Little Hans, more formally "Analysis of a Phobia in a Five Year Old Boy," published in 1909. "I have for many years been urging my pupils and my friends to collect observations on the sexual life of children," he explains, thus encountering "the reports which I received at regular intervals about little Hans," which "soon began to take a prominent place" (1963a, 48) in his thinking.

Freud was probably attracted to the Hans reports because of their similarities to the Rat Man case history, on which he was then also working. Little Hans suffers from a horse phobia, brought about, according to Freud, by sibling rivalry and oedipal conflict, the usual stuff of child psychosocial drama. Like the Rat Man, Little Hans plays out Freud's theories about infantile sexuality and oedipal drama as articulated in 1900 in *The Interpretation of Dreams*. There is much in the case study reminiscent of classic child study; for Freud as for Sully and Hall before him, children are little primitives, naturally perverse but innocent of culture, destined through the principles of recapitulation to reenact the developmental history of the human race.[4] As I argue in *Making American Boys* (2004), Freud wrote his own psychoanalytic variants of the feral tale, notably the Rat Man and Wolf Man case histories but also that of Little Hans. Unlike the Wolf Man, Hans successfully resolves his animal phobia, thereby attesting to the therapeutic as well as theoretical value of psychoanalysis.

While Freud does not interact with Hans directly, he communicates and in a sense plays with Hans through his father, even as he plays with the ideas and anxieties that Hans is working through. Hans is for Freud an exemplary child subject, a "little Oedipus" (1963a, 135, 148) and a "positive paragon of all the vices" (57) while still destined for a happy outcome. He is at once wily and innocent, a gently delinquent noble savage who struggles against "sivilization" and thereby embodies the spirit of psychoanalysis. He is at once id and ego, little Oedipus and little Freud, neurotic enough to fear horses yet normal enough to represent the healthy, curious child. Peter Rudnytsky demonstrates that Freud in fact knew the Graf family better than he let on, suggesting that Freud downplays that closeness to disguise his countertransference, his need for Hans as a psychoanalytic child hero. Freud's declaration that the case was a total success indicates his strong desire that Hans be a representative subject. I would add that Freud alternately aligns himself with Hans and with Hans's father, identifying with both child and adult positions and thus fashioning psychoanalysis as theoretical play in the manner described by Payne. Just as Mark Twain poses Tom Sawyer against the model boy of the village, so too Freud poses Little Hans against the model child of conventional child-rearing. In that respect, Freud aligns himself with Little Hans as much as with the adult authority. Freud is particularly attentive to and defensive of Little Hans's lies, which he reads as revenge for the lies of his parents regarding the origin of babies (the classic story that storks deliver babies).[5] Freud playfully conspires with Hans against his father and enjoins the reader to do likewise. Hans struggles heroically toward knowledge against the misleading of adults.[6] Freud praises "our young investigator," who has "come somewhat early upon the discovery that all knowledge is patchwork, and that each step forward leaves an unsolved residue behind" (138).

In "Family Romances," published the previous year, Freud remarks that imaginative activity "is one of the essential characteristics of neurotics and also of all comparatively highly gifted people," and one that emerges "first in children's play" (1963b, 42). In the case of Little Hans, Freud nearly seems to recast psychoanalysis as child play, emphasizing the inquisitive spirit and intuitive wisdom that marks both. While Freud remained skeptical about the play methods of Melanie Klein, he directs attention to the play-work of Little Hans, to his stories and his sketches. What make Hans a representative (child) subject are not only his polymorphous perversity and oedipal desire but also the rich play of his symbolic activity, his dreams and daydreams and lies and storytelling. Hans does not only play; he fantasizes about play and even carries on a playful dialogue with Freud by way of his father (who takes messages from Hans to Freud). As such, he helps Freud see the possibilities in child analysis, the connections between child research and adult theory construction. The child's speech, the stories he tells, the pictures he draws, and his interactions with adults: these are the key elements of child analysis as Freud modeled it. Payne is right to see in Freud's work the foundation for playful, child-centered discourse.

In *Beyond the Pleasure Principle,* published in 1920, Freud makes reference to the early analytical literature on child play and contributes his own anecdote, about a simple game invented by his one-and-a-half-year-old grandson. This very young and mostly preverbal child, Freud reports, had a habit of throwing small objects under the bed, into a corner, or otherwise out of sight, then going after and retrieving the object. He also threw a wooden reel with a piece of string attached to it over the edge of his curtained cot and then pulled the reel back into sight. While doing these things he would utter the word *fort* (German for "gone") followed by a joyful *da* ("back"). Freud realized that this was a game of disappearance and return designed to manage the boy's anxiety about the coming and going of his mother. The boy's "great cultural achievement," says Freud, was not protesting when his mother left (1961, 14). The *fort/da* game—what Lucy Rollin and Mark West call "the most famous children's game in psychoanalysis" (1999, 5)— was for Freud evidence of the child's growing ability to symbolize. The processes of play-symbolization were increasingly the focus of child analysis.

By the 1920s, child analysis had become a major transatlantic undertaking. Across Europe, child guidance clinics were set up as part of an ambitious, politically progressive agenda to establish free psychoanalytic treatment centers and thereby help transform civil society (Danto 2005). In and around this movement, Freud and his Hungarian colleague Sándor Ferenczi stressed that the analysis of children would make significant intellectual contributions to the discipline, and they encouraged women in particular to pursue work along these lines. Freud inspired his daughter Anna to expand upon her work as a teacher by becoming a child analyst, and to that end, Anna, with Dorothy Burlingham and Eva Rosenfeld, opened the Heitzing School in Vienna, a psychoanalytically oriented program in early childhood education.[7] Meanwhile, Ferenczi was helping his analysand Melanie Klein pursue her own research into the psychic life of young children, first in Berlin and later in London. Hermine Hug-Hellmuth had paved the way, and Klein and Anna Freud were quick to follow. Child analysis was assumed to be the natural calling of women, and especially of mothers.[8]

By 1911, Freud knew Hug-Hellmuth's pioneering work on child analysis and recommended it for publication (MacLean and Rappen 1991, 8). Hug-Hellmuth joined the Vienna Psychoanalytic Society in 1913, apparently the first gentile member and only the third woman to be admitted. Hug-Hellmuth held a doctorate in physics but had turned her attention toward the fields of education and psychoanalysis, first developing a system of child observation and then actually psychoanalyzing children. Her published work on the subject dates to 1912.[9] In 1920, she attended the Sixth Congress of the International Psychoanalytic Association, where she presented "On the Technique of Child-Analysis." There she describes her efforts to prepare the child for analysis, specifying that she does not analyze children younger than seven years old. She takes up the question of transference and acknowledges the precariousness of the relationship between the child's analyst and the parents. At issue also is the relationship between education and psychoanalysis. "The curative and educative work of analysis," she avers, "does not consist only in freeing the young creature from his sufferings, it must also furnish him with moral and aesthetic values" (1991e, 138). "Her views," writes Danto, "found their way into education, parenting, and child welfare facilities and her practice of treating children in their own homes was picked up by the emerging social work profession" (2005, 57). Hug-Hellmuth was the first to focus on analytic technique in child analysis.

Like Klein, Hug-Hellmuth used toys in child analysis,[10] but she did not liken the play of children to the dreamwork, a foundational comparison for Klein. A central challenge for child analysis was to find a method for accessing the child's unconscious, since children could not often verbalize well. Whereas Hug-Hellmuth and Anna Freud felt that analysis was appropriate only for older children and that the talking cure remained the appropriate method, Klein had a very different vision of the child's inner life and eagerly embraced the idea that play functioned like the dreamwork, illuminating that life. Her interest in play began with her observations of her son Erich (alias "Fritz"), but it was with another patient, Rita, that Klein discovered the usefulness of toys. Later she would identify the play technique as the defining element of her practice. While Anna used toy play to gain the trust of child patients, she was skeptical of its analytical value. The "Controversial Discussions" between Anna Freud and Klein in the 1940s revolved around Klein's assertion that the child's unconscious could be accessed through play, including toy play.[11] Whereas Sully, in 1895, calls play "the working out into visible shape of an inner fancy" (2000, 35), he and Anna Freud are content to observe play. Klein, by contrast, initiates and actively engages in it.

Klein furnished her child patients with "deep" and rather adult interpretation even as she played intently with them. Her play involved explanation and other discourses of talk. For Klein, to play with the child was to play with the unconscious itself. "For some psychoanalysts," writes child analyst Adam Phillips, "describing the child replaced describing the unconscious, or the dreamwork. Or rather, describing the child *was* to describe the unconscious. The child was, as it were, the unconscious *live;* you could see it in action. It had been found; in fact, you could virtually talk to it" (2001, 42; emphasis in the original). This formulation of unconscious-as-child persists in the wake of a newer formulation, the ego-as-child (and the child-as-ego).

Klein's work has often been devalued, especially in the United States, but her influence on subsequent theorists is undisputed. To borrow from D. W. Winnicott, she was the good enough theoretical mother who authorized psychoanalysts to play—with their clients, with other therapists, and with psychoanalytic theory. Her first paper on child observation, "The Development of a Child," from 1921, bears a strong affinity to Freud's case history of Little Hans. For example, Hans and Klein's analysand Fritz are both fascinated with transport (Hans with coaches and carts, Fritz with electric cars; both use boxes in play). Both boys watch transport activities from the window because they fear the street. Both are intensely curious, not just about sexuality but about human existence more broadly, and are actively engaged with the stories of adults; both are told the stork story. Both play with their widdlers or *wiwimachers* and are preoccupied with excrement. Freud recommends the sexual enlightenment of children; Klein eloquently warns of the dangers of repression and "injury to the instinct for knowledge" (1988a, 20). These and other resemblances suggest the staying power of Freud. Klein moves the analysis in some different directions, but only after respectfully situating her study of Fritz vis-à-vis that of Little Hans.

In this 1921 piece, Klein begins to identify the phantasies of young children, moving toward her later view that all children have schizophrenic tendencies and suffer from an immense amount of anxiety and aggression that is at once sadistic and masochistic. Even when parents do their best to encourage a child's curiosity, some repression of sexual curiosity and interest will occur, she explains in this essay, so that the child may temporarily shut down, refusing to ask questions or tell stories or play. She describes exactly this phase in the life of Fritz. The solution, she suggests, is for the parent to round out the child's knowledge about reproduction and birth, to supply whatever information is missing, even if the child seems resistant. Once Klein furnishes Fritz with said information, things turn around. He begins to play and tell stories, learns to read, and expresses interest in "everything in the world" (33). If the mother-analyst can cooperate with and even intensify the child's curiosity, stories and symbolic play and developmental progress will follow. Klein emphasizes the extreme nature of Fritz's subsequent phantasies: "He related more and more numerous and extensive phantasies, very frequently about the devil but also about the captain, Indians, robbers and wild animals as well" (39). These phantasies, moreover, are rarely subject to secondary elaboration; they afford direct and undistorted access to the unconscious. And what they show is not pretty. The unconscious world of the young child, according to Klein, is populated by terrifying figures that represent the child's parents, in keeping with the paranoid-schizophrenic position. Whereas Bruno Bettelheim later focused on the child's attraction to fairy tales, Klein emphasizes that the tales come *from* as much as *to* the child. The child produces those phantasies on his or her own.

To demonstrate the power of these internal objects and fantasies, Klein began to study children's use of external objects, including toys. Nearly any object could be a toy and could affirm the reality of objects within. In 1923, in one of her early essays, "The Role of the School in the Libidinal Development of the Child," Klein shows how the pedestrian objects of the classroom—desk, slate, penholder, chalk—bespeak internal objects and imagoes. Klein in fact links children's mastery of the alphabet with their libidinal and symbolic maturation. Young Fritz/Erich re-creates the erotics of the schoolroom within the confines of Klein's consulting room, playing with the cushions on her divan, drawing various characters, even doing math homework. "It can be repeatedly demonstrated," Klein writes in that essay, "that behind drawing, painting and photography there lies a much deeper unconscious activity: it is the procreation and production in the unconscious of the object represented" (1988c, 72). I return to the subject of children's drawing in chapter 4; here I want to note that by describing even the letters of the alphabet as objects and by likening child's play to the free association of adults, Klein alters our understanding of language and narrative. Hence the importance of objects such as toys and books to the study of childhood; studying children's forms is not so far removed from the direct observation of children, the logic runs.

In her 1930 work "The Importance of Symbol Formation in the Development of the Ego," otherwise known as the case of Little Dick, Klein emphasizes how destructive desires, in tandem with the dread to which they give rise, enable the child's ability to symbolize. For Klein, symbolization offers relief from the intense anxieties and hostilities of early childhood. In this essay, she acknowledges the influence of Ferenczi and Ernest Jones, both of whom also speculated on the origin of symbolization (and by way of folklore). Revising an earlier formulation of the problem, Klein writes:

> Since the child desires to destroy the organs (penis, vagina, breasts) which stand for the objects [the adults to whom those organs belong], he conceives a dread of the latter. This anxiety contributes to make him equate the organs in question with other things; owing to this equation these in their turn become objects of anxiety, and so he is impelled constantly to make other and new equations, which form the basis of his interest in the new objects and of symbolism. (1988b, 220)

For Klein, symbolization is motivated by aggression and anxiety, not by the child's curiosity. "Thus," she continues, "not only does symbolism come to be the foundation of all phantasy and sublimation but, more than that, it is the basis of the subject's relation to the outside world and to reality in general" (221). Little Dick suffers from an arrest of symbolization. Because his ego's defenses against sadistic wishes are "excessive and premature" (232), he is no longer able to bring into phantasy the sadism he feels toward his mother. Play is a bid for survival. "Play for Klein," notes Mary Jacobus, "was not necessarily fun, or creative, or even particularly playful. It was a serious form of meaning-making—often compulsive, repetitive, and anxious, with its own syntax, rules, and narrative conventions" (2005, 91).

Klein's apperception of play was not limited to the child's physical manipulation of objects but eventually included the play of words, linguistic and semantic play, alongside the more nonverbal forms of interaction and fantasy. "By relying on the interplay of the child's diverse semiotic codes, the creativity of psychodrama, and the interplay among the signifiers of free association," holds Julia Kristeva, "Melanie unwittingly foresaw the path that analytic treatment would take in the wake of Freud" (2001, 56). Klein's attention to language, which anticipates Jacques Lacan's "return" to Freud, also anticipates the semiotic interest in literature. Whereas Freud recognized man as a symbol user, suggests Kristeva, Klein described the child as a symbol maker.

Klein did not comment on children's literature per se, but she was interested in fairy tales. The good–bad splitting of characters in fairy tales, thought Klein, confirmed her theories of the child's splitting of the mother into the good and bad breast. We might also propose that Klein's positioning as a mother-analyst brings her closer to the realm of children's literature—especially since she analyzed her own children, reading to them, listening to their stories, and telling stories back to them. This is nearly Kristeva's take on Klein: "And what did the mother-analyst do? She made up stories, she played, and she told tales" (41). Klein's work with children was conducted in England, Kristeva stresses, a country quite hospitable to literatures of the child. "The child appears to be the object of desire par excellence of the English imaginary," writes Kristeva. "Does this mean that it was real necessity, and not happenstance, that fated Klein to realize her talent in England rather than someplace else?" (37). Kristeva also frames Klein as an interpreter of children's literature, not just for adults but also for children, as she interpreted their play directly to them.

Of course, child analysts focused on texts produced by children, not texts by adults written for children. Their work thus might seem easily distinguishable from children's literature, if we hold to a narrow definition of such. But by collaborating with children—by playing and drawing with them, by transforming their stories into written narrative—child analysts might also be considered authors for children, in a sense.

The interactive nature of child analysis in conjunction with its emphasis on symbolic and creative activity aligns it with the project of writing
for children. By contemporary standards, in fact, child analysis is more
like children's literature than is the fairy tale. At the least, we can say
that child analysis engendered interest in children's forms, by which
I mean the physical and emotional selves of children but also various
kinds of texts produced by or for them, from dreamwork and play-work
to more concrete drawings, stories, and other productions. The attention of child analysts to play further affirmed children's literature as a
project and practice. In turn, a writer like Milne might be considered
a lay child analyst. Milne's child-centered stories, moreover, have always drawn an adult audience, further aligning them with the adult
discourse of analysis. While I would not claim *Pooh* as a case history,
or analytical writing as children's literature exactly, the now-standard
observation that children's literature is always already adult in composition and concern gives the lie to any easy distinctions among such
materials.

Winnicott-the-Pooh

Reflecting on autobiographical accounts of doll play by Charles Baude-
laire and Rainer Maria Rilke, Marina Warner notes that

> [the] question of the real haunts the psychology of play and
> through play, the theory of fantasy: is the state of animation
> that the power of thought can conjure sufficient to make real-
> ity present? . . . Many writers for children, following in the
> wake of many fundamental myths, have attempted to answer
> this question with a resounding "Yes!" and invented fictions
> that do bring toys to life in a parallel world where playing for
> real can indeed really work. (2009, 5)

Warner points to Carlo Collodi's 1883 work *The Adventures of Pinocchio* and Margery Williams's 1922 book *The Velveteen Rabbit,* but
Pooh also qualifies. Moreover, Milne, like the child analysts, interacts
directly with the child both inside and outside the text under construction. Whereas Collodi's character Geppetto is the maker of Pinocchio,
Milne represents himself as the coauthor of *Pooh.* For Milne as for the

child analysts, and especially Klein, it is the exchange between adult and child that animates or realizes an imagined world.

The articulation of child analysis was taking place at the same time that Milne introduced Pooh. The year 1926 saw the appearance not only of *Winnie-the-Pooh* but also of Anna Freud's *Introduction to the Technique of the Analysis of Children.* There she explains how she seeks the child's cooperation in analysis, taking steps to bond with the child not only by engaging in supportive conversation but by becoming "useful" and "interesting" to the child, even interacting with his or her playthings. "In the case of a little girl who was undergoing her preparation," she reports, "I zealously crocheted and knitted during her appointments, and gradually clothed all her dolls and teddy bears" (1946, 10). *Pooh,* of course, had inspiration in the stories that Milne devised with his young son Christopher Robin about Christopher's beloved teddy bear and other toy characters. Pooh debuts simply as "Teddy Bear" in 1924 in *When We Were Very Young,* then morphs first into Edward Bear and finally into Winnie-the-Pooh.[12] While Milne was its author-narrator and Christopher its reader-protagonist, *Pooh* seems to have emerged from a collaborative play experience. Milne not only observed Christopher's toy/bear play but participated in it; he then transformed that narrated play into a book, one in which Milne is also a character of sorts, talking with Pooh as well as with Christopher Robin.[13]

Milne sought to engage his son, not to analyze him. But there are correspondences between Milne's compositional methods and the techniques of child analysis. Milne and the child analysts fashioned analogous, even parallel discourses of child–adult play. I would position Milne somewhere between the more laissez-faire style of child analysis practiced by Anna Freud and the more participatory mode of Klein. In terms of child–adult interactivity, *Pooh* is closer to Klein, but tonally *Pooh* has more in common with the genteel and more detached Anna, as well as with Hug-Hellmuth.

Whatever the parallels between *Pooh* and the play-centered practices of child analysis, *Pooh* does not explicitly surface in psychoanalytic discourse until D. W. Winnicott's now-classic 1971 text *Playing and Reality.* While Erik Erikson also did much to promote and expand the significance of play, it was the British Winnicott who made brief if suggestive use of *Pooh.* The object relations tradition, to which

Winnicott was closer, was more preoccupied than ego psychology with what I have been calling children's materials. A respected pediatrician, Winnicott worked under Klein initially and also analyzed one of her children. He was the central figure of the so-called middle group of British child analysts who avoided formal alignment with either Anna Freud (ego psychology) or Klein (object relations theory). Winnicott played a pivotal role in the reconceptualization of the infant away from the self-enclosed, largely passive infant of Freud to the more outward-bound, interactive infant of object and attachment theory.[14] While on good terms with Klein, Winnicott rejected her portrait of the child as war-torn and tyrannical. He also emphasized the mother's role as a real-life presence in the child's development. Winnicott and other members of the middle group, notably Marion Milner, urged the protection of the child's illusion of omnipotence—akin to what Freud called "magical thinking." It was Milner who added the term "illusion" to the psycho-analytic repertoire (Jacobus 2005, 102).

Winnicott's major innovation was the idea of "transitional" objects and phenomena, first articulated in the early 1950s and refined across his later work. Transitional objects and phenomena are those that occupy and designate "the intermediate area of experience, between the thumb and the teddy bear, between the oral erotism and the true object-relationship, between primary creative activity and projection of what has already been introjected, between primary unawareness of indebtedness and the acknowledgement of indebtedness" (1989, 2). In *Playing and Reality* Winnicott enlarges this notion, suggesting that we never fully relinquish this "intermediate area of experience" and that transitional phenomena form the core of everyday adult living, which he sees as always already "creative." For Winnicott, everything can be play, even psychoanalysis, which he calls "a highly specialized form of playing in the service of communication with oneself and others" (41). Ideally, thinks Winnicott, the transitional object survives its use/abuse at the hands of the child and fades away in importance, replaced by transitional "phenomena" or more abstract kinds of inner–outer play.

Winnicott's work remains seductive because it promises a more cheerful perspective on the child's psychosocial development as well as on the adult's creativity. Jacobus finds that Winnicott's theory of transitional phenomena "verges on being a theory of magical cultural diffusion" (2005, 112). The "poetics of play in British Object Relations preserves the most magical aspects of psychological thinking," she writes, "if only in viewing the child as both origin and prototype of creativity" (95). Looking at Winnicott, Milner, and Susan Isaacs, Jacobus suggests that magical thinking is performed as much as analyzed in object relations theory.

A fuller analysis might trace the ways in which national cultures of play were predisposed to embrace Winnicott's upbeat account of transitional space, playing, and creativity. Lisa Jacobson, for instance, argues that by 1940, American family and child experts had successfully "promoted a new vision of children's play that promised to restore the primacy of family ties and combat the allure of mass recreation" (2004, 161). Jacobson points to the rise of home playgrounds and playrooms; moreover, she suggests, parenting became less authoritarian and more playful, paving the way for Winnicott's reformulation of adult life as play.[15] Moreover, American child study, notes Nicholas Sammond (2005), has long tended toward the production of the "normal" child rather than the treatment of the neurotic child, even before the advent of ego psychology with its mainstreaming energies; such an emphasis might have enabled a Winnicottian outlook on child and adult players both.

Winnicott twice invokes Pooh as the exemplary transitional object in *Playing and Reality*. First, from the inaugural page: "My own approach derives from my study of babies and children, and in considering the place of these phenomena in the life of the child one must recognize the central position of Winnie the Pooh" (xi). And second, from the chapter "Playing: A Theoretical Statement": "A. A. Milne, of course, immortalized Winnie the Pooh. Schulz and Arthur Miller, among other authors, have drawn on these [transitional] objects that I have specifically referred to and named" (40). Winnicott is referring here to Linus's blanket in Charles M. Schulz's *Peanuts* comic strip and to that in Miller's 1963 children's book *Jane's Blanket*. Lois Kuznets notes that the 100 Aker Wood functions as "a transitional country" (1994, 47), reading Milne's work by way of Winnicott and also Jean Piaget. The lesson here is not only that Winnicott and Piaget have useful things to say about play and child development, but also that authors like Milne and Miller do too, and have often gotten there first. Winnicott seems to have recognized as much, acknowledging children's culture as an intermediate area of experience in which inner and outer realities are negotiated.

Winnicott was the first clinician-theorist to understand *Pooh* as dramatizing the psychodynamic work of childhood. Though not a Poohologist, Winnicott also operates somewhat like Pooh Bear and somewhat like Milne within psychoanalytic and cultural discourse, modeling wisdom-in-simplicity, embracing paradox, and authorizing others to claim his stories. Winnicott's theoretical statement on playing is also a playful statement on theory. While his work probably did not directly influence Poohology, it shares with that discourse a style of bold but gentle theorizing reminiscent of Milne himself. As child analysis developed over the century from Anna Freud and Klein to Winnicott and beyond, it was effectively (re)masculinized. The ostensible "independence" of Winnicott and his middle group, however progressive in other respects, points to a familiar masculinist claim to autonomy and originality. Winnicott's distinctive style, moreover, bespeaks something like mastery; in fact, he seems most authoritative when the most playful rhetorically. In claiming play as the province of adults, too, Winnicott helps authorize a tradition of male-authored, inner-child-themed Poohology.[16]

Sing Ho! for the Life of a Bear! (Some Versions of Poohology)

Observing that by 1975, *Winnie-the-Pooh* had sold over one million copies, Carol A. Stanger remarks, "These numbers can be partially explained by the fact that while *Pooh* was published as a children's book, it was often taken over for adult reading" (1987, 34). She points to Alison Lurie's "Back to Pooh Corner," in which Lurie notes that "all through high school and college [she and her friends] went on speaking [Milne's] language, seeing people and events in his terms" (1973, 11). Stanger concludes that despite the book's "almost totally male cast of characters" (1987, 35), Milne's text makes space for women readers through its emphasis on emotion, nurturing, self-acceptance, and promise of "a kinder, more humanistic time" (47). Milne, she holds, chose to "assimilate the maternal role" by positioning himself as the narrator of bedtime stories about Pooh Bear (47), which positions Milne (like

Winnicott) as a good-enough mother determined to provide a safe but playful holding environment for his child readers.

Whatever *Pooh*'s appeal to women or Milne's maternal tendencies, the adult takeover of *Pooh* has been both distinctly American and lop-sidedly male.[17] Only one of the texts I treat below is female-authored. Moreover, male Poohologists stay close to Milne's texts because Milne's language and episodic structure make adaptation quite easy. Unlike what the case writing indicates for *Alice, Peter Pan,* and *The Wonderful Wizard of Oz,* Poohology seems not to have a dark side. *Pooh* itself seems not to have a dark side; even Eeyore's melancholy is comic. Perhaps that is why Americans especially have been drawn to Milne's stories; they seem to resonate with the American self-help and pop-meditational narrative.

Winnie-the-Pooh and *The House at Pooh Corner* are generally understood as end texts of the Golden Age fantasy tradition inaugurated by *Alice* in 1865. *Pooh,* holds Jackie Wullschläger, "sprang from [Milne's] own happiness just as Carroll's or Barrie's fantasies grew out of their disappointments" (1995, 177). Unlike the authors of earlier Golden Age texts, who were "mavericks, lonely, eccentric, emotionally unbalanced or odd in appearance, Milne was handsome and clever, well-off and well-liked" (177). (Only later did Milne suffer bitter disappointments, among them estrangement from his son.) Though Wullschläger's outlook is reductive, she is perhaps right to call Milne's work "the fantasy tamed," emphasizing Milne's move away from the zany mindscapes of Carroll and J. M. Barrie and into the reassuringly familiar and domestic space of the 100 Aker Wood, populated by children's toys rather than wild animals or mythical creatures (197). She finds in Milne's work a "self-mockery" that was "the death-knell of children's fantasy" (179). Humphrey Carpenter offers a similar assessment, subtitling his chapter on Milne "farewell to enchanted places" (1987, 197).

But even if *Pooh* brought an end to the Golden Age tradition, in part by being more authentically for children,[18] the stories live on not only through the Walt Disney Company—whose adoption of the books was probably the first phase of their Americanization—but also through various lifestyle primers or humor books pitched to adults. The ostensible simplicity of the books, along with their snug domesticity and sense of security, makes them attractive as well as elastic. *Pooh* seems to lend itself to "lite" thought, to the sort of subject primers that now proliferate in the form of comic books or graphic novels (for example, Richard Appignanesi and Oscar Zarate's 1979 *Freud for Beginners*). *Pooh* makes the ideal delivery system for popular, everyday philosophy and psychology—and also for the disparagement of academic or otherwise "serious" intellectual work. The populism of Poohology tends at times toward anti-intellectualism, or at least toward some mockery of scholasticism, in keeping with the teasing tendencies of Milne's texts.

In *The Child and the Book*, Nicholas Tucker points out that Milne's *Pooh* books "show children—through the character of Pooh—how easy it is for an immature mind to misconstrue things. The mistakes of Pooh and Piglet especially recall the muddled, egocentric world of small children's thinking" (1981, 98). *Pooh* shows adults the same thing, according to one of the more sincere exercises in Poohology, Dorothy G. Singer and Tracey A. Revenson's *A Piaget Primer: How a Child Thinks:* "The charm of A. A. Milne's work and his intuitive understanding of child psychology," the authors explain, "inspired us to interpret Jean Piaget's developmental theory through the use of literary examples" (1977, xi). Intended primarily for parents and teachers, the book found first life as an article by Singer published in *Psychology Today. A Piaget Primer* "aims for maximum simplicity without diluting Piaget's work" (3). Singer and Revenson use excerpts not only from *Pooh* but also from *Alice*, Norton Juster and Jules Feiffer's *The Phantom Tollbooth*, Crockett Johnson's *Harold and the Purple Crayon*, and the *Peanuts* comic strip to illustrate Piagetian concepts such as accommodation, conservation, and object permanency. Like Piaget, they suggest, good children's authors find instructive material in the "mistakes" of children; the mistakes, while funny, underscore how children think, why, and to what effects.[19]

In *Philosophy and the Young Child*, Gareth Matthews reads *Pooh* as illustrating the curiosity rather than the immaturity of child minds. Writers for children, he notes, "have been almost the only important adults to recognize that many children are naturally intrigued by philosophical questions" (1980, 56). As evidence he points to Milne's *Pooh* books as well as to L. Frank Baum's *Oz* books, James Thurber's *Many Moons*, Carroll's *Alice* books, and Arnold Lobel's *Frog and Toad*

Together. Matthews does not argue that children's stories are philo-sophical treatises; rather, he contends that such stories are written in a style he calls "philosophical whimsy," "raising, wryly, a host of basic epistemological and metaphysical questions familiar to students of phi-losophy" (59). Philosophy, he thinks, should remain attuned to the ques-tions and conundrums of childhood, even as children should be encour-aged to maintain their philosophical interests.

The American literary critic Frederick Crews outright reverses the child–adult hierarchy in his satire of literary criticism, *The Pooh Per-plex,* the first major work of Poohology. For Crews, it is adults rather than children who misconstrue things and suffer from muddled ego-centrism. Attempting to make *Pooh* illustrate their various theories of literature, literary critics end up underscoring their own limitations, suggests Crews. In Milne, notes Wullschläger, "the mocking tone is everywhere" (1995, 190), and the same is true in Crews. A mock stu-dent casebook, *The Pooh Perplex* spoofs schools of literary criticism in vogue in the early 1960s. Tellingly, Crews's parody emerges from his love-turned-hate affair with psychoanalysis. In 1966, three years *after* the publication of *The Pooh Perplex,* Crews published *The Sins of the Fathers,* a Freudian interpretation of Nathaniel Hawthorne and still a respected monograph. Later, however, Crews was to repudiate psychoanalysis in books such as *Out of My System* (1975) and *Skeptical Engagements* (1986), but as early as *The Pooh Perplex* we can see the beginnings of that long and ongoing repudiation. Spoofing psychoanal-ysis was the first step in disavowing it.

Marxist, archetypal, Leavisite, philological, neo-Aristotelian, and "cultural" criticism all get served by Crews. There are two riffs on psy-choanalytic criticism. The first, "Poisoned Paradise: The Underside of *Pooh,*" is a pop-psychoanalytic reading in the spirit of Leslie Fiedler, who saw in classic American literature a pattern of boyish, homoerotic escape from the plots of adult (heterosexual) society. In "Poisoned Para-dise," "Myron Masterson" acknowledges the "polymorphous perversity" of all children's books but reminds us that fortunately, perversity is part of our repressed collective unconscious and "the average child never knows, as it were, what is hitting him. And thus we can go back to the nursery with a clear conscience and an armload of restored clas-sics" (Crews 1963, 43). Masterson then tenders an oedipal analysis of the 100 Aker Wood crew, including Christopher Robin. In fact, he says, "The real subject of the book is Christopher Robin's loss of his mother, which is alternately symbolized, accepted, protested against, denied, and homoerotically compensated for in the various 'nursery' stories of the plot" (45). Masterson offers the Fiedlerian formula of "the inevitable homoerotic alternative to compulsory innocence" (49)—citing a passage from Milne in which Piglet is "agog at the thought of seeing Christopher Robin's blue braces again"—and concluding, "Christopher Robin is flattered and attracted by this fetishistic response to his little striptease, but he is naturally reluctant to enter into serious relations with a pig" (50).

The second spoof of psychoanalysis harkens back to old-school and faithful Freudian case history: "A. A. Milne's Honey-Balloon-Pit-Gun-Tail-Bathtub complex," by "Karl Anschauung, M.D.," "one of the last survivors of Freud's original circle of Viennese followers" (125). Dr. Anschauung likens Milne's bear-phobia to the horse-phobia of Freud's Little Hans and detects in Milne a fascination with anal birth and the phallic mother. The focus here is Milne's honey-balloon complex. Milne, says the good doctor, should present himself for treatment, as his case "is a relatively simple one of advanced animal-phobia and obsessional defense, somewhat complicated it is true by anal-sadistic and oral-helpful fantasies" (136).

The Pooh Perplex concludes with "Prolegomena to Any Future Study of *Winnie-the-Pooh*," by "Professor Smedley Force": "I want you to help me enforce a twenty-year moratorium on further emetic 'critical studies' of *Pooh*. . . . I also trust that you will return to your universities with a sense that, bibliographically and scientifically speaking, we are on the threshold of the GOLDEN AGE OF *POOH*! [Applause.]" (149; emphasis in the original). More than one critic has emphasized how powerfully Force/Crews succeeded in this moratorium; Crews's book "silenced almost all work on Milne for decades," notes Wullschläger, "and it is still difficult to write a line about Pooh without hearing Crews's satiric laughter over one's shoulder" (1995, 198). In 2001, Crews published a sequel, *Postmodern Pooh*, purportedly a transcript of a Modern Language Association (MLA) special session (from which I take my chapter epigraph).[20]

Crews uses humor to work through his growing ambivalence about psychoanalysis. In *Skeptical Engagements,* published more than twenty years after *The Pooh Perplex,* Crews presents Freudianism as essentially a cult, "an ingenious witches' brew of speculative neurophysiology, mythic conceptualizing about subterranean psychic agents, literary charm, debaters' tricks, mendacious therapeutic claims, and spicy and grotesque sexual tales" through which "Freud eventually captured the fancy of a civilization" (1986, xv). Responding to Freud's thoughts on the resistance to psychoanalysis, Crews counters "that for many intellectuals psychoanalysis has been, not a blow to human pride in general, but a means of elevating pride among a corps of privileged knowers who, by subscribing to the Freudian movement, rescue themselves from doubt and insignificance" (34). This passion for psychoanalysis among intellectuals, according to Crews, and the passion for theoretical systems more generally, are symptomatic of intellectual weakness, even if not also laziness.

"What Crews is trying to suggest in both of his Pooh books," suggests Jan Susina in a review of the second, "is that the best way to show the limitations or flaws of a critical approach is to apply it to a children's text" (2002, 276). Presumably Susina means that for Crews, the ostensibly simple, innocent children's text best exposes the absurdities of professional discourse. For Crews, perhaps, the children's text is simple and thus profound. Or perhaps children's classics, and this one in particular, are such. The ease with which Crews develops his mock readings suggests the openness of *Pooh,* which might even be thought great literature because the stories lend themselves to so many meanings. Presumably it would be difficult to perform such a range of readings on just any children's text. I do not think Crews means to champion *Pooh* per se. He could be banking on the opposite assumption, that the silliness of criticism is particularly obvious when it takes seriously a less-than-literary text. The critique works either way. *The Pooh Perplex* may have discouraged scholarship on Milne, but it also licensed subsequent ventures in Poohology. We might even claim the book as a kind of negative form of children's literature criticism.

Carpenter calls Crews's choice of *Pooh* shrewd, as the stories "are almost completely without layers of secondary meaning" (1987, 202). But as Nodelman avers in *The Hidden Adult* (2008), every children's text has an implied "shadow" text of nuance and complexity. Crews's choice of material is shrewd because Milne's stories have a surface appearance that suggests depth. Adult, or at least double, meaning hovers at every turn, so that the books seemed proto-post-modern, destined not only for Disneyfication but also for the mining and recycling we now see everywhere in popular culture. My guess is that Crews is a fan of Milne—and that Milne would most probably have applauded Crews. Milne's books may be addressed to the child and may capture the workings of the child's mind, but they do so very much for the entertainment of adults (not so much, as Singer and Revenson have it, for their instruction). So too with *The Pooh Perplex*.[21]

Whereas Payne invokes *Pooh* to authorize the play of ideas in and around psychoanalysis, Crews uses the books to make fun of just such play. Whereas Payne sees in them a generative mode of child–adult theorizing, Crews positions Pooh as the bear who exposes the "follies of the wise."[22] Like Pooh, suggests Crews, literary critics are misdirected and clueless, if sometimes sweet and endearing. At the same time, Pooh plays the role of the wise fool, exposing greater foolishness through his own modest and perhaps deceptive brand of naïveté. The wisdom of Pooh as it plays out in the narrative depends upon Pooh's not quite getting things right, easily converted into getting things right after all. Crews gets to have it both ways, aligning himself with Pooh but also with Milne. As in Milne's work, content and style are linked; Crews satirizes style to get at content, the ponderousness of Karl Anschauung, M.D., underscoring the heavy-handed pedantry of first-generation psychoanalysis.

Crews uses *Pooh* to signal that he is growing up as a critic, leaving behind the theorized academy and, especially, psychoanalysis. And yet nobody knows better than Crews just how difficult such renunciation is. Crews opts out of psychoanalytic interpretive method, but not out of psychoanalysis; in fact, he continues to be preoccupied with psychoanalysis as a force shaping popular and academic culture. Crews is not unlike other sons of Freud whose rebellion keeps them close, playing out the family romance of psychoanalysis after ostensibly leaving home. Crews's ostensible rejection of psychoanalysis became a template for all his critical work, which, though engaging and persuasive at points, has a repetitive lesson: the emperor has no clothes. Obviously *The Pooh Perplex* did nothing to silence literary criticism on other books, suggesting not so much the irrelevance of critique but the capacity of analysis for humor and even parody. Much psychoanalytic work from Freud forward addresses itself to humor and is itself funny. The success of Crews's joke book probably owes something to the playful and humorous side of psychoanalysis, which engages *Pooh* both in spite of and in the wake of Crews.

Continuing the populist pedagogy of Poohology, and occupying a middle zone (transitional space?) between Singer and Revenson's earnest mobilizations of *Pooh* and Crews's satire, are Benjamin Hoff's bestsellers *The Tao of Pooh* and *The Te of Piglet*. Like Crews, Hoff is disdainful of scholasticism, celebrating instead the wisdom of simple folk; unlike Crews, he uses *Pooh* to deliver an earnest message about the validity and proper Western practice of Taoism. The books are designed as a series of conversations between the author and Milne's characters, imitating the structure of Milne's texts, in which we experience occasional intrusions by the narrator. Hoff talks to Pooh, and Pooh talks back. Pooh, explains Hoff in the first volume, embodies "P'u," which Hoff translates as the "Uncarved Block." Whereas other Milne characters define themselves through action or activity, Pooh just *is*— hence the wisdom of Pooh. Admitting that there are many forms as well as interpretations of Taoism, Hoff holds that "the basic Taoism that we are concerned with here is simply a particular way of appreciating, learning from, and working with whatever happens in everyday life" (1983, 5). For Hoff, Pooh the Uncarved Block enables that basic understanding, modeling a psychoblissology of everyday life. Owl, for Hoff, is the anti-Pooh, the Scholar, "the Brain, the Academician, the dry-as-dust Absentminded Professor" who—like Confucius—"divides all kinds of things into little categories and compartments" (25). Owl is an "Academic Mortician, whose bleached-out Scholarly Dissertations contain no more of the character of Taoist wisdom than does the typical wax museum" (26). The scholar, thinks Hoff, hoards knowledge, "writing pompous and pretentious papers that no one else can understand, rather than working for the enlightenment of others" (26). Thought itself seems to be dangerous: "The surest way to become Tense, Awkward, and Confused is to develop a mind that tries too hard—one that thinks too much" (77).

Hoff is no less critical of more rugged models of American manhood, "from the Miserable Puritan" to the "Restless Pioneer" and the "Lonely

Cowboy" and on forward to the "Bisy Backson" of Milne's text (103). Westerners and especially Americans are rootless and restless, opines Hoff, always yearning for something bigger and better when the secret to happiness is within. "What is that magic, mysterious something? Nothing. To the Taoist, Nothing is *something* and Something—at least the sort of thing that many consider to be important—is really nothing at all" (143). Against the Scholar-adult Hoff poses the Pooh-child. "The adult is not the highest stage of development. The end of the cycle is that of the independent, clear-minded, all seeing Child. That is the level known as wisdom. When the *Tao Te Ching* and other wise books say things like, 'Return to the beginning; become a child again,' that's what they're referring to" (151). The voice of Pooh "calls to us with the voice of a child's mind" (155).

The *Te of Piglet* offers more of the same and is nearly twice as long; this time around Hoff takes the opportunity to weigh in on various issues of the day, such as the Gulf War. The campaign against scholasticism continues:

> Then one day, while quoting to someone from A. A. Milne's *Winnie-the-Pooh,* I got an Idea. I could write a book explaining Taoism through the characters in *Winnie-the-Pooh* and *The House at Pooh Corner.* That would, it seemed to me, release Taoist wisdom from the grip of the Overacademics and restore to it the childlike awareness and sense of humor that they had taken away. (1993, 3)

Piglet rather than Pooh is the protagonist; if Pooh is the Uncarved Block, or Nothing at all, then Piglet embodies *Te,* which Hoff glosses as "Virtue of the Small." While amusing, the *Te of Piglet* is more pontification than play.

In "The Taoism of the Western Imagination and the Taoism of China," scholar and "overacademic" Russell Kirkland calls the *Tao of Pooh* "popular fluff" (2009, 2). In Kirkland's view, a project such as Hoff's is little more than another exercise in cultural theft and "spiritual colonialism" (14). "To many," he writes, "'Taoism' has come to be imagined—and I emphasize the word 'imagined'—as a living spiritual ideal into which anyone today—particularly the individual American—can easily step" (2). With the help of Hoff, thinks Kirkland, Americans have turned Taoism from a complex and culturally attuned religious and cultural tradition into an easy, portable, individualistic spirituality. Westerners have been free to "indulge their own egos and to make money in the commercial book market" (10). Kirkland sees Hoff as infantilizing Taoism by way of a children's classic:

> Do the Taoists of traditional or modern China follow a truth
> that they would be willing to explain in terms of Western
> children's stories, or in terms of the various other elements
> of modern American life encountered in comparable books—
> books published not to present the beliefs of Chinese Taoists
> to modern readers, but rather to generate profit for the author
> and the publisher by selling a sanitized, imaginary "Tao" to
> the middle-class American consumer? (14)

"Don't Pooh-pooh Taoism," he urges in a related essay (1998, 113).[23]

Pooh is thus made to represent both the true message of Taoism and shameless American appropriation. The struggle over the right to represent and interpret Taoism in an American context is not unlike the struggle to represent and interpret psychoanalysis, even if Taoism is viewed positively by both Hoff and Kirkland. Further, the American popularization of Taoism is akin to the American popularization of psychoanalysis, in that both discourses have been dehistoricized and transformed into a generic rhetoric of personal spiritualism.

Pooh's drift into the self-help toolbox is obvious in two Poohology trilogies. Roger E. Allen's *Winnie-the-Pooh on Management* (1994), which applies "lessons" in human psychology from Milne to the business world, was followed by *Winnie-the-Pooh on Problem Solving* and *Winnie-the-Pooh on Success* (Allen and Allen 1995, 1997). While playful, these books are in earnest. On the other hand, John Tyerman Williams's trilogy offers a more tongue-in-cheek look at philosophy, "the ancient mysteries," and psychology, in (respectively) *Pooh and the Philosophers* (1996), *Pooh and the Millennium* (1999), and *Pooh and the Psychologists* (2000). Perhaps it is easier or less dangerous to mock philosophy than the practical vocations? In the last volume, subtitled *In Which It Is Proven That Pooh Bear Is a Brilliant Psychotherapist*, Williams presents Pooh as a clinician whose seeming ineptitude actually proves his genius (Pooh-as-Uncarved Block). Pooh helps Piglet to mature, Rabbit to confront his xenophobia, Owl to communicate with the masses, and Eeyore to beat depression. Like all good therapists, hints Williams, Pooh is eclectic, borrowing from Freud, Jung, Winnicott, Piaget, and even Lacan. We get surprisingly good overviews of these theorists. Though more irreverent, Williams is no less informative than Allen. Humor is not an antagonist of self-help and indeed is often one of its more effective modes or guises. Perhaps even *The Pooh Perplex* works as comic self-help for overacademics. Poohology moves in mysterious ways.

While Milne initially welcomed the success of his Pooh stories, he came to resent their overshadowing of his work for adults. As Christopher Robin, Milne tried to bid farewell to Pooh as early as the final chapter of *The House at Pooh Corner*:

> "Pooh," said Christopher Robin earnestly, "if I—if I'm not quite—" he stopped and tried again—"Pooh, *whatever* happens, you *will* understand, won't you?"
>
> "Understand what?"
>
> "Oh, nothing." He laughed and jumped to his feet. "Come on!"
>
> "Where?" said Pooh.
>
> "Anywhere," said Christopher Robin. (1957, 313; emphasis in the original).

Pooh was not so easily left behind. Not only did the public, to Milne's frustration, care more about his Pooh stories than about his other publications, but Milne himself couldn't stop writing about Pooh. "As a discerning critic points out," writes Milne in his autobiography (first titled *It's Too Late Now*), "The hero of my latest play, God help it, was 'just Christopher Robin grown up.' So that even when I stop writing about children, I still insist on writing about people who were children once. What an obsession with me children are become!" (1944, 287).

Everything Is Play, Play Is Everything

The poetics of play, to borrow Jacobus's suggestive phrase, has helped elevate the writing and criticism of literature for children both before and in the wake of psychoanalysis. As historians of children's literature routinely note, beginning in the late eighteenth century, didactic and rationalistic children's literature was challenged by a literature of play and amusement, one that began in England and eventually made its way to the United States; this advance ostensibly represents the dawn of a new sensibility. The ascendance of play marks less a dramatic shift in sensibility than a modernization of terms; play is the new rationality, a new term for symbolic work and the making of meaning. Karín Lesnik-Oberstein thus finds that "'amusement' starts its career as a form of claimed love and commitment to learning" and remains "the cry of educators up to the present day" (1994, 68). Margaret and Michael Rustin hold that children's literature is always already child's play, even when play is not thematized. The authors they examine create emotional depth through "symbolic equivalents or containers for states of feeling," which amounts to "a kind of poetic communication, analogous to the symbolizations of children's imaginative play" (1987, 3).

Play found new urgency and expression with the advent of child study and child analysis. I have ventured in this chapter that children's materials are at the heart of child analysis and that across its history of expansion and modification, child analysis has affirmed the cause of children's literature. The career of *Pooh* is one index to this relationship. These are not only children's books but also something like a lay form of child analysis. In our Golden Age of *Pooh,* even the most adult discourses have become playful and child-affiliated. *Pooh,* while ostensibly a "children's classic," is increasingly the stuff of adult popular discourse. *Pooh* can be both things because the child reader is merged with the inner child. The possibility that everything is play and play is everything hinges not only on the interiorization of the playful/playing child within the adult, but also on the adult's assimilation of the children's book. Poohologists don't just read *Pooh;* they become *Pooh,* absorbing and mimicking its lessons and rhythms. With a little help, so can you.

3. Three Case Histories

Alice, Peter Pan, and *The Wizard of Oz*

> I want to tell you about a syndrome in our society
> that is causing a lot of problems. We all know
> it's there, but until now nobody has labeled or
> explained it.
>
> —Dan Kiley, *The Peter Pan Syndrome:*
> *Men Who Have Never Grown Up*

ACQUELINE ROSE'S *THE CASE OF PETER PAN* (1984) is not only the best-known theoretical statement on children's literature; it is also the best-known example of what we might call literary-critical case writing: the building of an argument or analysis around a single text, usually literary, and in this instance a text for children. Rose was not the first to practice such case writing. We recall Crews's *The Pooh Perplex,* addressed in chapter 2, which satirizes not only schools of literary analysis but also the freshman pedagogical casebook on a literary text. To very different ends, Crews and Rose capitalize on and in turn extend the "hypercanonicity" (to use Jonathan Arac's term for Twain's *Huck Finn*) of a children's classic. Because *Pooh* and *Peter Pan* are already so diffuse or overdetermined, Crews and Rose can range far afield of the text proper to address larger literary and cultural issues.

A less well known but equally fascinating exercise in case writing is Jennifer Stone's essay on "Pinocchiology." Noting that virtually every major writer and cultural critic in Italy has written about Carlo Collodi's 1881 book *The Adventures of Pinocchio: Story of a Puppet,* Jennifer Stone criticizes Pinocchiology for its obsession with native

Italian culture and its evasion of Sigmund Freud's insights into the psyche, an evasion she dubs the "Pinocchio Complex." Pinocchiologists, she thinks, ignore or downplay Freud's ideas about infantile sexuality, the unconscious, and the Oedipus complex. "The resistance to Freud in Italy," she writes, "is such that even an acknowledged 'phallic' nose is subsumed by the innocence of childhood and by the immaculacy of the Virgin Madonna-Fairy-Godmother" (1994, 329). Stone promises us the *true* story of *Pinocchio*.[1]

Stone and Rose both assert that "we" fly away from the hard lessons of Freud into the Neverland of childhood and "children's fiction." Like Stone, Rose recognizes the complexities of her literary source text, using them alongside Freudian and Lacanian theory to emphasize the politics of misreading and denial. Unlike Crews, who is not particularly invested in the status of the *Pooh* books, Rose and Stone juxtapose the maturity of the source text with the screen dream of simple stories for simple folks (children). The problem is not *Pinocchio* or *Peter Pan* but "children's fiction," whether it takes the form of actual fiction or the governing fiction of childhood's innocence.

Such literary-critical case writing on the children's classic is always already psychoanalytic in form as well as content. *The Pooh Perplex* may be a parody, but it is nonetheless still a casebook, one through which Crews rehearses his reservations about psychoanalysis and in which psychoanalytic discourse nonetheless enjoys favor. Unlike Crews, Rose and Stone enthusiastically embrace the discourse of psychoanalysis, adapting one of its principal genres, the case study or case history. Rose and Stone do not just want to set the literary record straight; they want to teach us the real lessons of psychoanalysis, continuing Freud's project by using one of Freud's preferred forms. Like Freud, they imagine a reader resistant to their lessons, a reader clinging to ignorance or innocence despite indications of trouble or complexity. "We have been reading the wrong Freud to children" (1984, 12), Rose intones, suggesting our resistance to or deliberate misunderstanding of Freud.

Case writing on children's literature undertakes not only the education of the reader but also a broader critique of innocence, ignorance, or immaturity. Built into the case history form is the assumption that people usually prefer simplicity to complexity, even if not also ignorance to knowledge. The critique of American male immaturity has special resonance and staying power. It dates back at least to Van Wyck

Brooks's 1920 book *The Ordeal of Mark Twain,* a Freudian critique of the ostensible immaturity of Twain and his reading public of ostensibly boyish men, and extends to Dwight Macdonald's 1953 analysis of mass culture as producing "adultized children and infantile adults" (1957, 66). Americans in Macdonald's view cling to "our cult of youth" and "the sentimental worship of Mother as if we couldn't bear to grow up and be on our own. Peter Pan might be a better symbol of America than Uncle Sam" (66). These and other assessments were wrapped up with anxieties about "Momism" and the feminization and infantilization of American men. As early as 1948, literary critic Leslie Fiedler argues that American literature is really an escapist, homoerotic literature for boys, suggesting that American culture has yet to mature. In *Love and Death in the American Novel,* Fiedler elaborates on this theme and singles out "the ritual praise of good-badness as the true Americanism" (1960, 284–85), stopping just short of coining a complex. Fiedler's scheme of development—boyhood to manhood, homoeroticism to heterosexuality—is loosely Freudian, even if Fiedler does not attribute immaturity to an American resistance to Freud.[2] The immaturity critique has been picked up by self-help writing in the last few decades, which likewise finds literature symptomatic of cultural problems. Ignoring the ironies of J. M. Barrie's text(s), psychologist Dan Kiley takes Peter Pan as a realistic figure and bad role model, diagnosing American men as immature and boyish, as suffering from the "Peter Pan Syndrome" (PPS).

Kiley wants American men to grow up and get married, and Fiedler wants straight male maturity in the canon as well as in the culture. Rose and Stone, in contrast, want "us" (Italians and all) to stop hiding behind "children's fiction." Stone and Rose use *Pinocchio* and *Peter Pan* respectively to suggest and model a better (more mature) kind of analysis. Unlike Kiley and Stone, Rose does not apply her observations to a particular national culture; her "we" seems to mean Anglo-American culture. But even Rose resorts to the trope of the flighty boy to indict immaturity: we must man up to Freud, she suggests. Rose and Stone both imply that there is something immature about evading Freud (and for Rose, Jacques Lacan).

While Stone and Rose are obliged as scholars to respect the specifics of their source texts—or at least, are more inclined to do so— Kiley plays fast and loose with *Peter Pan,* conflating the rich, often bizarre texts of Barrie with Disney's and other adaptations or variants. Kiley's is a collective, generalized *Peter Pan*. While Kiley's immaturity thesis seems, well, immature, I want to emphasize that Kiley shares with Rose and Stone a concern about immaturity. Moreover, Kiley, like Rose, challenges (while also benefiting from) the popular mythology of Peter Pan; he refuses happy-go-lucky, fairy-dust sprinkling Peter as a role model. Kiley's *The Peter Pan Syndrome* (1983) was published one year before Rose's *The Case of Peter Pan*. Kiley and Rose are contemporaries and have in common an investment in psychological discourse, as well as the practice of mobilizing a children's classic on behalf of an interpretive program.

This chapter focuses on the evolution and consequences of case writing on three children's classics: *Alice, Peter Pan,* and the world of *Oz,* both L. Frank Baum's books and the movies based on them. Scholarly case writing on these classics derives in part from psychoanalytic case studies of these books or their authors and from the relays between those case studies and popular case writing. Rose's analysis draws not only on the Freudian case study but also on the ongoing notion that there is something hidden or duplicitous about *Peter Pan* and something incomplete about our reckonings with it. For Perry Nodelman, the "hidden adult" is more benign, but the formulation is the same: *Peter Pan,* and children's literature generally, has depths and shadows, adult tendencies or investments that have yet to be fully acknowledged. With both *Alice* and *Peter Pan,* critical case writing takes a cue from psychoanalytic case writing and from broader anxiety about man–child sexuality in and around these classics, discernible in popular retellings and adaptations, which I am treating as popular case writing. *The Wizard of Oz* has likewise been framed as having a repressed adult history; recent adaptations or sequels such as Geoff Ryman's novel *Was* or Gregory Maguire's novel *Wicked* imagine the not-so-hidden adult and even predatory aspects of Oz. The immaturity thesis is thus also the thesis of hidden, repressed, or unrealized maturity. This thesis, so central to psychoanalytic case writing, circulates widely in popular case writing as well, in and around these three classics especially.

I also suggest that case writing helped make these texts into classics, not in spite of their adult tendencies but because of them. Literature, especially the novel, already shares certain commitments with the psychoanalytic case study, including a focus on the origin, development, and consequences of "character" and interiority. Beyond those mutualities, psychoanalytic, literary-critical, and popular case writing further enhanced the status of these three classics even as it positioned them as having suppressed adult features. *Alice, Peter Pan,* and *The Wizard of Oz* are invoked in and mobilized by both classical and more popular strains of psychoanalysis, used to support complex theoretical arguments as well as crude rhetorics of self-help and cultural assessment.[3] These and other Golden Age texts, more clearly than the picturebook or the fairy tale, are addressed to adult as well as child subjects. Adult retellings of such texts continue their questioning of the adult–child relation, often maintaining more fidelity to the source texts than do retellings for children.[4] In this respect, they are closer to the narrative forms of psychoanalysis, which also have both child and adult coordinates (case histories being about childhood but not intended for child readers).

Alice predates the invention of psychoanalysis, while *The Wonderful Wizard of Oz* and *Peter Pan* first appeared during Freud's lifetime. These texts coexist with psychoanalysis as much as they find themselves subject to it. They share with psychoanalysis key themes and concerns and might be said to be literary analogues of it. All three are fantasies, and their fantastic characters and plots probably made them attractive to psychoanalysts already invested in fairy tales and in the uses of enchantment. All three feature dreams, with *Alice* and the cinematic *The Wizard of Oz* explicitly framed as dream tales. All ironize the idea of innocence to some degree. Retellings of these three classics—what have been called aftertexts—are heavily influenced by these first associations and by subsequent case writing. *Alice, Peter Pan,* and *The Wizard of Oz* were already popular, but their entanglements with psychoanalysis and with case writing, in and around their dissemination in print and film media, made them all the more so.

What follows are case histories of case histories. I use "case writing" loosely, referring not only to the kind of work performed by analysts and literary critics but also to pop-psychological variations on that work as well as to the broader narrative framing of literature and film. The larger cultural presentation of Lewis Carroll (the pen name of Charles Ludwig Dodgson) as a case of arrested development, for example, and of *Alice* as a story of man–girl love, constitutes for me case writing, alongside the more specialized discourse of Freud, Rose, or Kiley.[5]

Golden Age Case Writing

Before taking up particular narratives, a few words about so-called Golden Age scholarship. Much of what I am calling case writing depends upon the conceit of a "Golden Age" as well as upon the so-called cult of the child, theorized by George Boas. We might think of these as positive and negative versions of the same idea. A term of affirmation, "golden age" tends toward unreflective nostalgia and narrow canonicity. "In modern histories of children's literature and fantasy," notes Carolyn Sigler, "the 'Golden Age' of Victorian fantasy has been reified as the work of [a] small group of male writers, including [John] Ruskin, Charles Kingsley, George MacDonald, J. M. Barrie, and, of course, Lewis Carroll" (1998, 352–53). Roger Lancelyn Green seems to have brought the phrase into children's literature scholarship with his 1962 essay "The Golden Age of Children's Books." Green's is actually one of the more diversified accounts; he includes not only male-authored texts that have remained hypercanonical but also Catherine Sinclair's 1839 *Holiday House,* William Makepeace Thackeray's 1855 *The Rose and the Ring,* and the domestic novels of Mrs. Molesworth. Green takes the Golden Age conceit in part from Kenneth Grahame's autobiographical 1895 book *The Golden Age,* not written for children but very much about childhood. Green notes that Grahame's book "presented childhood as a thing in itself: a good thing, a joyous thing—a new world to be explored, a new species to be observed and described. Suddenly children were not being written down to any more—they were being written up" (1980, 12). Like *Alice* before it, *The Golden Age* "had a marked effect even on writers already well in their stride" (13). The conceit of the Golden Age performs as much as describes an attitude. It is code for an idealized past alongside an ongoing view of childhood as everyone's golden age. Critics have lately used the term with skepticism, even as affirmation of the literature itself continues.

Golden Age case writing in the genre of literary criticism tends toward psychonationalistic conceptions of the subject and toward a gentler, almost affirmative immaturity thesis. In *Secret Gardens: The Golden Age of Children's Literature,* Humphrey Carpenter points to a distinctly British literary refusal of traditional religion and the attendant "search for a mysterious, elusive Good Place" (1987, 13), beginning with *Alice* and continuing through A. A. Milne's 1926 *The House at Pooh Corner.* Loss of religious faith, he proposes, alongside anxieties about the future of the British Empire, led children's authors to escape "down the rabbit hole," into Wonderland and other enchanted places. Carpenter is not overly critical of this tendency—he certainly does not use the term "cult"—but he does imply that Golden Age writers turn away from the real world perhaps too much. In *Audacious Kids: Coming of Age in America's Classic Children's Books,* Jerry Griswold points to the "metaphoric reciprocity" (1992, 14) between America and the child in and around books published between 1865 and 1914. Griswold suggests that books of the American Golden Age tend toward realism rather than fantasy, and their stories usually take the form of an orphan story with strong oedipal dynamics. An orphaned child makes a journey, finds friends and foes, and comes of age; Griswold calls this overarching plot "The Three Lives of Childhood." He attributes the peculiarly American persistence of this plot to a variety of factors and echoes Carpenter in acknowledging that American classics have escapist and pastoral tendencies, albeit more outward-bound ones.

While there is a touch of the immaturity thesis to their work, Carpenter and Griswold propose that Golden Age books became classics because they resonated with and gave expression to collective hopes and fears. They suggest a national psyche or zeitgeist whose features can be deduced from the production and reception of individual texts. Perhaps because his book depends more explicitly on archetypal reading, Griswold registers without resolving the tension between "psychological explanations" and "national considerations," between "American Motifs" and "Historical Considerations" (these are his section headings). The "metaphoric reciprocity" between child-self and nation allows an uneasy but productive truce between archetypal-psychological and sociohistorical analysis. Carpenter offers psychological insights but resists seeing his work as psychological, framing it instead as genre criticism. In his preface, he notes that while he did write early papers on the "personal psychology" of Golden Age authors, those papers never amounted to much. Most of the Golden Age authors "were in some respect psychological curiosities, people whose personal difficulties in the real world had driven them inwards and helped to develop the childlike side of their imagination" (1987, ix). However, the "links between these authors proved to be not in their lives, but on the deeper levels of the books themselves" (x).

These two studies have been influential precisely to the degree that they bring pop-psychoanalytic perspectives to Golden Age texts, not unlike novelistic and filmic engagements. Carpenter and Griswold capitalize on and extend the psychological popularity of the Golden Age canon. In his review of *Audacious Kids*, Bruce A. Ronda describes the book as a "lively survey" and a "collection of lecture notes" rather than a deep critical study (1995, 192). "Griswold's psychological readings," writes Ronda, "seem largely reliant on a kind of popular Freudianism" (192). While I share Ronda's belief that children's literature deserves serious analysis, the "popular Freudianism" of Griswold's study should not necessarily give us pause. Put another way, the popular Freudianism of *Audacious Kids* cannot simply be attributed to limitations or idiosyncrasies on Griswold's part; rather, it is built into the narrative-explanatory apparatus of the Golden Age idea as well as particular traditions of case writing. Griswold's work represents a different but still insightful kind of academic work on Golden Age literature from, say, Rose's *The Case of Peter Pan*. But both are influenced by and in turn influence the play of psychoanalytic ideas in and around children's literature. Historically, Golden Age case writing has functioned as a macro version of case writing on individual texts, reflecting popular rather than academic psychoanalysis and favoring stories of national or cultural immaturity.

Other scholarship on the period, notably that of U. C. Knoepflmacher (1998) and Marah Gubar, resists the Golden Age conceit and the homogenization–case writing–immaturity thesis it seems to engender, emphasizing the diversity of literature from the period and complicating the child–adult relation. In *Artful Dodgers* (2009), Gubar offers a timely and powerful corrective to the dominant critical understanding of Golden Age children's literature, emphasizing that writers from the period did *not* uniformly portray childhood as a time of pastoral innocence; rather, they typically saw children as coproducers and collaborators in both literature and life. Gubar makes her case against not only the idealized, utopian tradition of Golden Age analysis but also the more suspicious perspective on childhood associated with Rose and others. Rose's account, after all, inverts the usual cheerful story about Golden Age literature, turning innocence into a problem but likewise insisting on its omnipresence. Rose backdates the problem of the innocence to Jean-Jacques Rousseau, claiming that children's literature has ever since merely repeated the same story about childhood's innocence, simplicity, and transparency. Gubar, on the other hand, identifies what is distinctive about Golden Age children's literature, looking at a range of texts and genres and resisting the homogenizing force of negative and positive case writing alike.

While Gubar makes a good case for rethinking Golden Age literature in its cultural and historical context, I am less concerned here with the original literature than with what has been done with and to it. I understand that source texts do not always authorize their aftertexts and that Golden Age authors enjoyed richer, more complex personalities than we might know from ventures in case writing.

Good Carroll, Bad Carroll

The *Alice* books, noted Alexander Woollcott in 1939, "have known no frontier" (1981, 82). *Alice's Adventures in Wonderland* and *Through the Looking-Glass, and What Alice Found There* have been translated into over 125 languages and have found further translation in the form of imitations, sequels, and satires ranging from traditional print texts to films, cartoons, and videogames. In her introduction to *Alternative Alices: Visions and Revisions of Lewis Carroll's "Alice" Books* (1997), Carolyn Sigler explains that nearly two hundred such alternative *Alice*s were published between 1869 and 1930, after which point they began to shift away from the themes and emphases of Carroll. After around 1930, she observes, alternate *Alice*s began to subside and references to *Alice* became more diffuse and general. Carroll collected some of these and also authorized the merchandising of *Alice*. Like *Peter Pan, Alice* is known by many people, most of whom have not read Carroll. Most people encounter *Alice* through picturebook retellings, or the animated

Disney film, or other variations or revisitations in popular visual culture. The first cinematic *Alice* was a Cecil Hepworth short made in 1903, just five years after Carroll's death, and by 1933 five other films had been made. *Alice* has been embraced by the French surrealists and by the Bloomsbury group, by Walt Disney and Salvador Dalí; the character Alice has found herself starring in advertisements for "Holidayland" (the North-East Railway), "New Wonderland" (Yellowstone National Park), Guinness Beer, and Wonder Bread. Alice or Carroll appear everywhere: in popular music, television, graphic novels, musicals, ballets, operas, plays, and realist theater. *Alice* has at once been preserved intact and transformed dramatically.

Written for a particular child, *Alice* refuses to settle down sensibly in the realm of children's literature. Carroll's *Alice* books are at least partly adult in tone and concern, containing not only fantastical creatures but also mathematical puzzles, educational satires, and not a little narratorial joking at Alice's expense. Carroll was championed by the likes of James Joyce and Virginia Woolf as a forerunner of modernism. His *Alice* books, writes Woolf in a 1939 appreciation, "are not books for children; they are the only books in which we become children. . . . To become a child is to be very literal; to find everything so strange that nothing is surprising; to be heartless, to be ruthless, yet to be so passionate that a snub or a shadow drapes the world in gloom. It is so to be Alice in Wonderland" (1981, 79). This is but one indication in Woolf's work of the influence of *Alice* among the modernists.[6] *Alice* has certainly resonated with psychoanalysts. Writing in 1939, Woollcott muses,

> Everything has befallen Alice, except the last thing—
> psychoanalysis. At least the new psychologists have not
> explored this dream-book nor pawed over the gentle, shrink-
> ing celibate who wrote it. They have not subjected to their
> disconcerting scrutiny the extraordinary contrast between
> the cautious, prissy pace of the man and the mad, gay gait
> of the tale he hold. They have not embarrassingly compared
> the Reverend Charles L. Dodgson with the immortal Lewis
> Carroll, two persons whom he himself never liked to see
> together. (1981, 83)

Actually, psychoanalytic assessments along these lines were already underway. In 1933, A. M. E. Goldschmidt published an essay called

"Alice in Wonderland Psycho-Analysed." Likening Alice's fall down the rabbit hole to the act of coitus, Goldschmidt claims that Lewis Carroll's fantasy is an unconscious distortion of the author's desire for little girls. Despite some evidence that the essay was a parody of Freudian analysis rather than an earnest exercise in such analysis, the notion that *Alice* gave expression to Carroll's repressed pedophilia quickly took root. At the same time, an idealized portrait of Carroll persisted alongside the pop-Freudian one. In his book on Carroll and popular culture, Will Brooker traces the history and consequences of these two strains, the "Saint Lewis" theory (2005, 1) and the pop-Freudian one, which formed two sides of the mythic coin. "In the first discourse," writes Brooker, "Carroll is a sainted innocent, his books are joyous nonsense and Alice is his muse. In the other, Carroll is a pedophile, his books are dark allegories, and Alice is his obsession" (xv). Brooker persuasively shows that "Lewis Carroll" is at once "a national treasure and a vaguely suspect enigma" (64). The interplay of "bad" and "good" Carroll marks and also inspires a staggering number of *Alice* adulterations, among them pornographic films, cross-dressing Web sites, and the gothic video game *American McGee's Alice.*

Psychoanalytic case writing on *Alice* and Carroll continued in earnest after Goldschmidt and found increasing cultural traction. In *Aspects of Alice* (1981), a casebook of *Alice* criticism edited by Robert Phillips, an entire section is devoted to reprints of influential Freudian readings, beginning with Goldschmidt and continuing through essays by Paul Schilder (from 1938), John Skinner (from 1947), Martin Grotjahn (from 1947), Phyllis Greenacre (from 1955), Géza Róheim (from 1955), Kenneth Burke (from 1966), and finally William Empson (from 1935). Empson, writing before any of these authors except Goldschmidt, gets the last word in Phillips's casebook, noting that Carroll's books "are so frankly about growing up that there is no great discovery in translating them into Freudian terms: it seems only the proper exegesis of a classic even where it would be a shock to the author" (1981, 400). "To make the dream-story from which *Wonderland* was elaborated seem Freudian," he remarks further, "one has only to tell it" (414). Empson's purpose, he clarifies, "is not to discover a neurosis peculiar to Dodgson" but rather to see how Dodgson's "shift onto the child . . . of the obscure tradition of pastoral" bespeaks a broader tendency to romanticize the child and thereby deny child sexuality (400).

Empson paves the way for James Kincaid, who argues that by focusing on the "pedophile" we ignore our own child-loving. Kincaid and other contemporary scholars warn against the dangers of psychobiography, shifting the focus from Carroll back to "us" and our collective adoration of/desire for the child. Kincaid points out that Alice does not want to be a child; she "wants so badly to grow up," finds Wonderland to be more an annoying than enchanting place, and all in all "is a great menace to the child" (1992, 288). "Alice remains so distant and desirable," proposes Kincaid, "because she vacates the position of the true child, leaves it for us, and becomes the false child, the child who betrays by growing up" (289). Karen Coats both maintains this focus on "us" and puts the spotlight back on Carroll, asking "where exactly Alice and Peter Pan figure in the structure of desire in their writers and . . . how they figure in the desire of the modernist subject, or us as readers" (2004, 79). The desire of the reader is at stake, not simply the desire of the author, and to examine that, "we must employ a critical discourse of desire that focuses on the symbolic rather than the literal uses of sex" (78). To that end, Coats proposes that Alice is Lewis Carroll's *objet petit a*—in Lacanian terms, a retroactive construction of the Symbolic that promises the illusory wholeness of the Real. Lacan holds that the subject is essentially nostalgic, longing for a sense of wholeness lost with separation from the mother and entry into the Symbolic. Coats suggests that Alice embodies Carroll's deep ambivalence about the mandate to grow up. In her view, Carroll "attempts to preserve in [Alice] the unalienated, undifferentiated self that he is necessarily unable to preserve in himself" (84). I am more intrigued by her suggestion that we understand Carroll's dynamics in light of our own: is Carroll something like an *objet petit a* in the cultural imaginary or interpretive community?[7] In any case, most assessments seem obsessively focused on Carroll's love for little girls rather than on our need to believe in that love.

Unlike some of the other Golden Age texts, *Alice* has not been appropriated for self-help projects. While psychotherapists make references to the *Alice* books in their work, there is no *The Alice Complex*.[8] There is an "Alice in Wonderland syndrome," but it is a medical rather than a psychological diagnosis, for a neurological condition in which subjects, among other things, perceive objects as smaller or larger than they really are. Instead, *Alice* has been used for more psychonovelistic explorations of identity and agency, often in "looking-glass" worlds in which identity is suspect and unstable. Psychoanalytic case writing about Carroll and little girls has surfaced reflecting feminist concerns and has merged with fictional treatments of the subject. Kali Israel takes issue with the celebratory tone of some postmodern *Alice* tales as well as scholarship:

> Celebrations, including scholarly versions, of the endlessly un-
> daunted girl-child who is triumphant despite her vulnerabili-
> ties are deeply appealing. This is especially true when such
> stories are presented as revisionary, when they are marked
> and marketed as alternatives to narratives of feminine pas-
> sivity or helplessness. Despite the fillip of daring that may
> attend them, however, stories of resilient children intersect
> with a cultural truism, a reassuring knowledge that "children
> are resilient," a knowledge that can easily slide into comfort-
> able knowingness. Stories of resilience also risk inadvertent
> collusion with backlash politics in which speaking of victim-
> ization is demonized and liberal autonomy is refetishized.
> (1999, 255–56)

Israel prefers *Alice* revisionings that retain a little bad Carroll or that allow for the possibility of adult use or abuse of children.

One of the more balanced versions of *Alice* admired by Israel is also a favorite of mine, the film *Dreamchild* (Millar 1985), written by Dennis Potter and directed by Gavin Millar. *Dreamchild* merges the *Alice* books with the story of Lewis Carroll's relation to Alice Liddell. The film was shot entirely in the United Kingdom despite its New York setting. Set in 1932, the centenary of Charles Ludwig Dodgson's birth, the film opens with the now eighty-year-old Mrs. Alice Hargreaves sailing to America to receive an honorary degree from Columbia University. She is accompanied by a young woman named Lucy. Upon arrival in New York, they are surrounded by a mob of reporters, one of whom, Jack Dolan, insinuates himself into their company and gradually wins their trust.

The film pits the genteel and refined Mrs. Hargreaves against the vulgar, money-grubbing and celebrity-hounding American public. When she debarks from the boat and is surrounded by journalists eager for a bit of Alice gossip or a picture of "Alice" with a stuffed rabbit, she warns them to respect their elders. It turns out, however, that only vulgar Americanism can save her from the joyful but also traumatic experience of being Alice; help bring back her memories of Carroll, pleasant and not so pleasant; and help her accept both her childhood and her impending death. Put another way, Mrs. Hargreaves is too grown-up and too British; in order to recover her inner Alice, she becomes an American. Earlier in the film, she insists on time to "compose" herself; by the movie's end, she is hanging out in a diner, eating greasy American food, and making small talk with the locals. "Sometimes," Jack Dolan reminds her at one point, "we have to dream a little." Americans may be crass pragmatists, the message goes, but they are also big dreamers, capable of inspiring even the original dreamchild.

While Roger Ebert insists that *Dreamchild* is not "a psychological case study" (1986), the film is arguably a case history of sorts, its visual artistry and creativity part of its psychological dimension. The movie uses fantasy and dream sequences to offset and question the reality of the present moment, suggesting the lingering presence of childhood and fantasy alike. The famous boating expedition down the Thames, for instance, during which Carroll first composed the Wonderland stories for Alice Liddell and her sisters, is presented as an intensely pastoral and dreamy sequence, in which Carroll and Alice compose together and exchange intense glances. This scene recurs throughout, punctuating and confusing the adult Alice's here and now. We meet the characters from the infamous tea party, who turn into rather sinister characters, along with the Gryphon and the Mock Turtle, the Caterpillar (courtesy of Jim Henson's Creature Shop). Memories of her libidinally charged relationship with Carroll are bound up with Alice's anxieties about death. Not only is she old, she is also terminally ill, and in one of several hallucinatory episodes, the adult Mrs. Hargreaves is whisked back to the tea party, where the Hatter menacingly tells her, "You stupid, ugly, old half-wit, you should be dead, dead, DEAD." The film at once hints that Carroll's preoccupation with Alice was sexual or erotic—as when, for example, the adult Mrs. Hargreaves dreams of Carroll in her hotel bedroom—and manages anxiety about that by shifting attention away from Carroll and toward Dolan's romancing of the two women. That is, in opposition to the scenario of a young girl romanced by an older man, the movie furnishes an inverse scenario of an old woman charmed by a young man. The romance between Dolan and Lucy offers relief from the hauntologies of Carroll.

The film's conclusion functions much like the frame conclusion of Carroll's first *Alice* book, which returns Alice safely to pastoral mode and looks sentimentally toward a future of fond childhood memory. The grown-up Alice, having presumably worked through her past and present terrors and gotten in touch with her inner (American) Alice, reads that very passage from Carroll in her speech at Columbia. "At the time," says Mrs. Hargreaves, looking back to childhood and addressing Carroll, "I was too young to see the gift whole, to understand what it was, to acknowledge the love that had given it birth . . . but I see it now, at long, long last. Thank you, Mr. Dodgson, thank you." The film at once indulges in and suppresses the question of an adult's love for a child and frames that story in an American context that is supposed to liberate love but also preserve its innocence. In America, the moral goes, we can give vent to the unconscious but also keep it safely in check. We might read that concluding scene as ironic rather than earnest. Nonetheless, whenever I teach *Dreamchild,* my students usually see something menacing in the Carroll–Alice relationship. The film cues us toward abuse not only through its depiction of Carroll (a stutterer around adults, a magical presence around little girls) but also through its depiction of Mrs. Liddell as disapproving of Carroll, part of bad Carroll mythology.[9]

The feminist revisioning of *Alice* merges and collides with different strains of psychoanalytic-literary discourse, with good and bad Carroll—sometimes *very* bad Carroll. Contemporary writers on both sides of the Atlantic continue to be preoccupied with the sexual politics of Carroll's life and work. A case in point is Richard Peabody's collection of *Alice* stories, *Alice Redux,* published in the United States. In his introduction, Peabody explains how the anthology took shape:

> This anthology was initially intended to revisit Wonderland and its inhabitants, to give contemporary writers a chance to connect with their own childlike fantasies, to mock modern mores even as Lewis Carroll's phantasmagoria parodies the prim morality of Victorian England. But many of the stories

submitted under that rubric, like their nineteenth century for-
bears, seemed forced or tangential compared to the electricity
in the stories that focused on the relationship between Alice
and Lewis. It was that friction—the world of controversy and
speculation; the did he or didn't he?—that sparked so many
imaginations. Once the direction was established, the anthology rapidly took on a life of its own. (2006, xiv)

Many of the contributions center on the alleged sexual activity or attraction between Alice and Carroll, with varying degrees of explicitness
and attitudes. In "Lilith in Wunderland," Bruce Bauman introduces
Alice's older sister Lorina to Freud himself, although she resists the
patriarchal authority of "Siggy," appropriating his cigar and remarking, "Yes, I am free associating. You keep interrupting" (2006, 110).
Lorina recounts in first-person monologue her seduction by Dodgson,
aka "Dodo," who tries to write Lorina out of the Wonderland story, replacing her with Alice, after Lorina tries to assert herself. When Freud
tries to end the session, Lorina retorts, "What do we mean we have to
stop now? I didn't come all the way to Vienna to titillate you and be
thrown out on my own arse. Not again. . . . Nice try Siggy, but I've had
it with doddy old men and their sexual fantasies they claim are my
fantasies. We are done here. For good" (112).

Some of the pieces included in *Alice Redux* are excerpts of novels,
such as Katie Roiphe's *Still She Haunts Me* (2000), a historical reimagin-
ing of the case of Carroll and Alice Liddell that sides with good (if shy)
Carroll. While the section excerpted in *Alice Redux* takes the point
of view of Mrs. Liddell, Roiphe refuses to vilify Carroll, underscoring
Mrs. Liddell's prudery and emphasizing Alice's ability to manipulate
Carroll. Also excerpted in *Alice Redux* is David R. Slavitt's *Alice at 80*
(1984), another retrospective narrative in which an older, wiser Alice
rethinks her childhood rivalry with younger sister Edith over Carroll's
affections and regrets that she let him come between them. Slavitt's
Alice tells us that Edith made false allegations about Carroll's interest in the girls, and she speculates that Carroll made Edith unhappy
not by his inappropriate advances but rather by his restraint. Another
alternate *Alice* that sides with good Carroll is Alison Habens's *Dream-*

house (1994), which offers criticism not of man–girl love but of the institution of marriage.

In contrast, Lisa Dierbeck's *One Pill Makes You Smaller* (2003) and especially A. M. Homes's *The End of Alice* (1996) position Carroll's love for Alice in the context of male sexual abuse of young girls. Set in Manhattan in the 1970s and playing off the countercultural fascination with *Alice,* Dierbeck's novel focuses on the manipulation of eleven-year-old Alice Duncan by the boyfriends of Alice's sister "Aunt Esmé," chief among them J. D. Whereas Carroll is awkward and stuttering, J. D. is suave and self-assured. But what makes the novel the most sinister is that J. D. denies his own agency and indeed the sexual rapaciousness of men, while Alice is all too aware of her own semi-ruin. In *The End of Alice,* Homes tells the story of a pedophile and child-killer who encourages from his prison cell the seduction of another child—this time a boy, and at the hands of a nineteen-year-old woman. The book met with wide disapproval, especially in the United Kingdom. *The End of Alice* is a case study of a sinister and irredeemable pedophile, with little likeness to the historical Carroll.

The specter of bad Carroll lives on in yet another contemporary alternative *Alice,* the lavish, three-volume graphic novel *Lost Girls* (2006), by Alan Moore and Melinda Gebbie, even more of a meta-commentary on *Alice* and its cultural afterlife. As Charles Hatfield (2007) notes in his review, comic-book adulterations of *Alice* are a dime a dozen, but even so, *Lost Girls* offers provocative engagement not just with *Alice* but also with *Peter Pan* and *The Wizard of Oz.* Moore and Gebbie do not so much corrupt these three classics as expose them as always already adult, through what Christopher Eklund aptly calls a "magical realism of the fuck" (2007). *Lost Girls* partakes of what art historian Anne Higonnet (1998) describes as a "Knowing" tradition of childhood and its forms. Moore and Gebbie have great fun with their material. *Lost Girls* succeeds not because it deviates from the originals but because it is perversely faithful to (while obviously playful with) them—to their ambivalent themes and plots, to the peculiarities of their composition, and to their oft-sordid afterlives. And whereas most television and film versions of *Alice* eschew the pedophilia thesis, *Lost Girls* aggressively courts it.

The story opens with the grown-up Alice, aka Lady Fairchild, relocating from Pretoria, South Africa, to a Swiss hotel near the Austrian border. She is soon joined there by the also grown-up but younger Dorothy, straight out of Kansas, and by one Mrs. Potter, formerly Wendy Darling. They get on famously, having sex with one another and trading stories of innocence lost, stories featuring a lively cast of characters, among them Lewis Carroll, Peter Pan, and "Uncle" Henry (really Dad), as well as the Darling brothers, assorted farmhands, even a cyclone. It is the eve of World War I, and for a short while, the women are safe to frolic and dream, to reclaim the girls they once were and the polymorphous sexuality that is rightfully theirs. They find comfort in each other because their stories, so individually strange, have strong resemblances to one another. Like all such idylls, their time together comes to an end by the third volume, as war breaks out and all flee before the German advance.

Lost Girls embraces bad Carroll but leaves behind the discourse of repression, showing Carroll actually molest Alice. With this signal difference, *Lost Girls* continues the perversion thesis, playing off but also against the contemporary hysteria concerning child abuse and child sexuality. Alice is psychologically wounded yet sexually empowered; *Lost Girls* attests to trauma but celebrates erotic power. And it is not just Carroll who is a pervert in *Lost Girls*—it is also Alice. Ever curious, Alice is the ringleader of the group. She initiates their sex and their storytelling. Like her namesake, she turns "evidence" against the absurdity of the real world in a spirit variously childlike and adult, depending upon the moment. "Desire's a strange land one discovers as a child," she notes in the second volume, "where nothing makes the *slightest* sense" (Moore and Gebbie 2006, 2: 3). Wendy and Dorothy likewise stay much in character in *Lost Girls*. Moore and Gebbie also pay homage to the 1939 MGM film *The Wizard of Oz* (Fleming 1939); Dorothy's time in Kansas is drawn in black and white, in sharp contrast to the colorized Oz. Nor is this all a simple matter of fidelity to character and plot. Some of the stranger innovations point all the more insistently to what lies beneath: Tinker Bell, for instance, becomes Annabel, Peter's sister, and Peter and Annabel have an incestuous relationship, which underscores Peter's indifference to female desire in Barrie's work.

Moore and Gebbie pay their respects to Freud explicitly. After Wendy recounts her childhood encounter with Peter in volume 1, she worries that she sounds deranged, to which Alice replies, "Fiddlesticks! Why, there is a notable professor of the mind currently practising not far from here, in Vienna. He would find your image of flight perfectly acceptable and indeed appropriate. I have no doubt you are as sane as I" (1: 8). "Of course," she adds, "I did spend a number of years in a sanatorium" (1: 8).

The Peter Pan Syndrome

Rose reminds us that in Barrie's work, contemporaneous with that of Freud, we see many of Freud's great themes, among them the difficulties of language, the problem(s) of sexuality and origin, and the persistence of childhood. Michael Egan likewise notes resemblances between Barrie's discourse and that of Freud, describing Mrs. Darling—who rummages around in her children's minds while they sleep—as "the maternal superego" (1982, 43) and calling the Neverland "a poetic version of the Freudian id" (44). Barrie "appears to have successfully developed a complex set of metaphors and images which, as we shall see, agrees remarkably with Freud's tripartite theory of the human personality (id, ego, superego)" (40). "Sophocles excepted," he continues, "it would be hard to find a more articulate literary representation of the confusions and gratifications inherent in the Oedipal situation" (50). Egan also attributes the popularity of *Peter Pan* to "its dramatization, in symbolic terms, of the Oedipal Son's victory over the Father. When Peter defeats Hook, every son in the audience crows with glee" (49). For Egan and Rose both, Barrie explores the same territory as did Freud and at around the same time, working in an imaginative rather than a scientific register.

At the same time, as Egan points out, Barrie described himself as a divided personality, as someone not fully aware of or in control of his unconscious. In his preface to the 1928 play script, Barrie finds "suspicious" his inability to remember having composed *Peter Pan*. His right hand having given out during the 1920 composition of a ghost-themed play, Barrie began writing with his left hand, after which he warned that "anything curious or uncomfortable" in his work should be attributed to lefty composition (quoted in Egan 1982, 40). Egan finds "nothing tongue-in-cheek" about these remarks, concluding instead that Barrie "had unusual access to his own unconscious" (40). But Barrie's remarks *do* seem tongue-in-cheek, or at least seem potentially theatrical or performative. Egan also asserts that Barrie cannot have known Freud's work, "given the exigencies of place and time" (40). But it is likely that Barrie would have heard of Freud, whose work had reached England certainly by the time the play version of *Peter Pan* was composed. There is no mention of Freud or Freudian influence in the biographies by Janet Dunbar and Andrew Birkin, although both adopt a Freudian perspective on Barrie as a "flawed genius" (Dunbar 1970, 13). But Barrie might be deliberately playing with Freud's terminology or pandering to the vogue of psychobiography then underway. Barrie was a master of stage and casting and may have presented himself as a "flawed genius." Maybe he did so with a sly wink to Freud, or maybe he fashioned his own language of unconscious motivation independent of Freud's, as he apparently did with the story of Peter Pan.

Either way, *Peter Pan* found quick and enduring popularity in England and the United States because it resonated with an existing fantasy of escape from "civilization," or adulthood, marriage, and polite society. It counts among its fans two other prominent "boy-men" of the age, men preoccupied with boy culture and (by some accounts) still boyish themselves: Mark Twain and Lord Baden-Powell, founder of Boy Scouting.[10] "In innumberable places every week," reports Barrie's biographer J. A. Hammerton, "'Peter Pan' is used to suggest a condition of enduring youth" (1929, 251). That "condition" was understood as joyful but eventually also as dysfunctional. In the camp of affirmation, Paul Hazard winds down his 1933 *Books, Children, and Men* by declaring, "Oh, if men could only fly away like Peter Pan, fly away to gardens that would become their home forever! They would no longer belong entirely to their own wretched species. . . . No longer would wickedness, or self-interest, or jealousy come near them" (1944, 162–63). "Men come to the performance," he writes, "pretending that they have come to bring their children who have been good. They seek a pretext to excuse themselves. . . . They would do better to spare their pretexts, not to blush, but to set out eagerly to those fortunate isles where they will find freshness and youth" (165). But one man's unabashed search

for the freshness of youth is another man's perversion. These two traditions of interpretation or spin persist. *Peter Pan* is still loved as a story
about innocence and the imagination and still serves as a cautionary
tale about immaturity. Retellings for children tend toward the former
tradition, whereas retellings for adults go both ways.

Peter Pan cautionary writing plays off earlier concerns about
boyish men and colludes with Barrie's more recent reputation (fair or
not) as a lover of boys. Questions about Barrie's sexuality do not seem
to have surfaced until the 1970s, although there is a long history of
speculation that Barrie was mother-fixated, as well as haunted by the
death of his older brother. Barrie did not help matters by publishing a
biography of his mother in 1896. Describing this book, Hammerton,
a staunch fan of Barrie (he calls him a genius), writes, "I had almost
called it an epic of mother-love, when I shuddered at the vision of a
Freudian female psycho-analyzing it!" (1929, 200). In the 1970s, Barrie
biographers began to scrutinize Barrie's involvement with the five
Llewellyn Davies boys, whom he eventually adopted after marrying
their mother; that involvement was the focus of Andrew Birkin's 1979
J. M. Barrie and the Lost Boys. Birkin's general thesis is that Barrie
staked his claim on the Llewellyn Davies boys chiefly through *Peter
Pan,* later described by namesake Peter Llewellyn Davies, who threw
himself beneath a train in 1960, as "that terrible masterpiece" (quoted
in Birkin 1979, 1). Birkin decides that Barrie was "platonically in love"
with the boys and hints at desire beyond the platonic (130). In recent
assessments, David P. N. Nunns (2009) and Allison B. Kavey insist
that we respect Barrie's innocence on this matter; Kavey sees a direct
link between speculation about Barrie's sexuality and the case writing
of Rose, which Kavey calls "the most egregious example of the argument that Barrie's desire—for children, to be a child—permeates the
text and inevitably confounds its title character" (2009, 4). Rose's case
writing does indeed resemble the kind of suspicious psychobiography
we see around Barrie and especially Carroll. Even so, most cautionary
Peter Pan narrative points to Peter rather than Barrie as the immature
boy-type to be avoided.[11]

Aside from *Lost Girls,* I do not know of any pornographic retellings
of *Peter Pan* or of any novelizations that pursue a man–boy love theme;
certainly there is nothing comparable to the narratives on Carroll's

alleged girl-love. Recent variants on *Peter Pan,* such as Peter David's *Tigerheart* (2008) and Dave Barry and Ridley Pearson's *Peter and the Starcatchers* (2004) (the first in a series), are marketed to young readers rather than to adults. Given the discussion about Barrie's sexuality and our cultural propensity for scandal, why the lack of popular case writing about Barrie? Rose attributes such silence to the particularity of man–boy desire:

> In the case of *Peter Pan,* the problem is more delicate. Behind *Peter Pan* lies the desire of a man for a little boy (or boys), a fantasy or drama which has only recently caught the public eye. Thus just at the moment when we are accepting the presence of sexuality in children's fiction . . . , we are asked to recognise it in a form which violates not only the innocence of childhood, not just that of children's fiction, but what we like to think of as normal sexuality itself. (1984, 3)

As she shows, the man–boy seduction plot of *The Little White Bird,* in which Peter makes his debut, has been ruthlessly censored and is largely unknown.[12] Another explanation is that Barrie himself directed attention to Peter Pan and to the eternal child for which he stands. Martin Green claims that Barrie inaugurated as much as inherited an English "cult of the male child," turning his "abnormal" sexuality into a national mythology that "implicitly displaced the values of mature manhood" (1982, 159–62). It might be that Barrie's creation of Peter was understood more as an adventure in narcissism or nostalgia than as an expression of pederastic desire, so that Peter seemed a version of Barrie, whereas Alice was not generally perceived as a version of Carroll. For whatever reasons, the Peter Pan "condition" is more generalizable, understood in cultural or national as much as individual terms. Peter takes center stage, with Barrie receding into the shadows.

Kiley's 1983 elaboration of the Peter Pan Syndrome bears traces of older case writing even as it updates the immaturity critique. Highly problematic in its opposition of gayness and manhood, *The Peter Pan Syndrome* is a self-help tome designed for women involved with immature and thus gay-trending heterosexual men. At the end of the book, Kiley advises women not only to avoid Peter Pans but also to avoid becoming Wendy Darlings, or mother-enablers of boyish men. In this he draws inspiration from Colette Dowling's *The Cinderella Complex* (1981), even though Kiley does not cite that book until near the end of his own. Kiley followed up with *The Wendy Dilemma: When Women Stop Mothering Their Men,* in which he advises women to model themselves after Tinker Bell and become a "Tinker," or a "self-possessed person" "who is willing to grow up" and refuses "to indulge [Peter Pannish] ways" (1984, 12–13). In both books, Kiley positions himself as a champion of heterosexual women of the marrying kind. Both books feature questionnaires for its female readers, to see if their significant others have PPS (in the first volume) or if they are themselves suffering from the Wendy Dilemma (in the second). He comes down harder on the men, who suffer from a complex rather than a dilemma. Opening each chapter with a line from Barrie, Kiley claims to have carefully studied Barrie's text. "A careful and thoughtful reading of Barrie's original play opened my eyes to the chilling reality," he reports in *The Peter Pan Syndrome.* "As much as I want to believe the contrary, Peter Pan was a very sad young man. His life was filled with contradictions, conflicts, and confusion. . . . For all his gaiety, he was a deeply troubled boy living in an even more troubling time. He was caught in the abyss between the man he didn't want to become and the boy he could no longer be" (1983, 23).

Kiley's is neither a particularly accurate nor a very nuanced use of *Peter Pan,* but it is certainly a successful one; Kiley's books sold well, and the Peter Pan Syndrome has entered the pop-psychological lexicon. Eschewing the term "oedipal," Kiley talks about the "father hang-up" and the "mother hang-up" (11). The critique of immaturity is derivatively Freudian, committed to a heterosexual model of oedipal development. At the same time, the critique is reminiscent of Marie-Louise von Franz's analysis-critique of the *puer aeternus,* or eternal boy, given in lecture form in 1959–1960 and later published as a book. Kiley offers readers a practical, populist look at male immaturity. "Forget about the ink smudges and hours of psychological diagnostics," he advises in *The Peter Pan Syndrome.* "Just take a quick glance at his daily behavior" (1983, 63). Most telling, there is little mention of Barrie and certainly no mention of Barrie's alleged immaturity or boy-fetish; that would complicate the "wisdom" of Barrie's narrative and of Kiley's in turn. While Kiley claims not "to imply that all gay men are gay because of PPS"

(31), the very structure of PPS presumes exactly that: boyish men are gay, and only straight men can grow up. Perpetual boyhood is conflated with homosexuality.

If not this exact formulation, we see the trace of boy-love and its possible scandal(s) even in more celebratory *Peter Pan* case narratives, including popular film. In Steven Spielberg's *Hook* (Spielberg 1991), for instance, a grown-up Peter "Banning" (echoes of Darling)—having left Neverland and become a real-world pirate, a corporate lawyer— must get in touch with his inner Pan, not merely to redeem himself but to rescue his son Jack, whom Hook has abducted and brought back to Neverland. In this case, the man–boy problematic is displaced not only from Barrie but also from married, presumably heterosexual Peter onto the unmarried and queerish Hook, who seeks to recruit Jack into piratehood. In Barrie's play *Peter Pan,* the boy Peter has no love for the chief pirate; Hook is his foresworn enemy.[13] In *Hook,* however, the chief pirate tries to win Jack over with love. "Aye, Captain," says sidekick Smee gleefully, "You could make them like you!"—the ulti- mate revenge, which would to some degree implicate the children in their own seduction. Hook attempts to educate Jack (and to a lesser extent, Peter's daughter Maggie) as to what parents and children *re- ally* want from each other. Mimicking a grammar school teacher, Hook inscribes on a makeshift chalkboard "Lesson One: Why Parents Hate Their Children." They do so, says Hook, because children are whiny, demanding, and selfish. "He took my toy, she called me names, I want to stay up, me, me, me, no, no, no . . ." he intones. Hook knows that Peter has ignored Jack: "He missed your baseball game, Jack. How could he?" Jack, who has already expressed frustration with his father's ne- glect and career monomania, agrees with Hook that parents "tell you stories in order to shut you up." "Before you were born," the captain tells them, "your parents were happy and free. They could do anything they wanted to." In Barrie's play, storytelling is safely reassigned to Wendy and the nursery, whereas in *Hook* it resurfaces as a man–boy affair, as in the Barrie's *The Little White Bird.* Like the narrator of that book, Hook tries to seduce the boy through stories.

Fortunately for Jack, Peter Pan reemerges from the depths of Peter Banning just as Hook starts to pierce Jack's ear, which Hook warns "is really going to hurt." Hook's queer desire for both Peter and Jack is not opposed to their boyhood but, rather, aligned with it; Hook, too, has boyish tendencies and represents, at least in the film, another possible future for boys who will not grow up: for what are Hook and his pirates, really, beyond adultish versions of Peter and the Lost Boys? *Hook* screens ongoing anxieties about boyishness and sexual or social deviancy, even as it reverses the immaturity critique. We might say that *Hook* offers a *maturity* critique, undercutting what looks like a highly successful manhood in Peter Banning. *Hook* urges the retention rather than erasure of the boy in the man. But the affirmation of boyhood is fraught with anxiety about how such retention might go astray.

In the 1987 vampire film *The Lost Boys* (Shumacher 1987), homosexuality and immaturity are quite clearly linked. Like the figure of Peter, the Lost Boys have come to represent unorthodox sexuality, chiefly homosexuality and pedophilia, both the ostensible consequence of an unresolved oedipal complex. Set in the mythical California boardwalk town of Santa Clara, "murder capital of the world," the film chronicles the encounter of the working-class Emerson family with a gang of teenage vampires. Young Sam watches helplessly as the gang recruits his older brother Michael. Sam then turns to the Frog brothers for help. Together they find and kill the real head vampire, Max, who poses as a local businessman and attempts to seduce Mrs. Emerson (when in fact—like Barrie?—he just wants to get close to the boys). Elaine Showalter holds that "the film brilliantly portrays vampirism as a metaphor for the kind of mythic male bonding that resists growing up, commitment, especially marriage" (1990, 183). The film glamorizes male teen subculture and style but links them to child exploitation and the rejection of family values. However seductive, the Lost Boys are savage and predatory and must be destroyed. Like *Hook, The Lost Boys* echoes contemporary fears about the (homo)sexual corruption of boyhood. Both hinge on a male seduction plot reminiscent of that of *The Little White Bird*, traces of which survive in Barrie's play *Peter Pan*.

And then there is the strange case of the late Michael Jackson. Jackson's breakout 1983 music video *Thriller* was apparently the inspiration for a feature film that Jackson was planning with Spielberg about Peter Pan. Jackson was originally supposed to play Peter Pan, but Spielberg was unable to secure all the movie rights until later, when he finally made *Hook,* casting Robin Williams in the role. Spielberg called Michael "one of the last living innocents," according to biographer Dave Marsh (1985, 210). Though he never became Peter on the silver screen, Jackson long played that role in the public imagination, seeming at once the boy eternal and the boy denied a real childhood. There are of course many rich dimensions to Jackson's life and career, and I do not mean to minimize them. But it is striking how consistently Jackson was portrayed as a Lost Boy or as a pathetic Peter Pan. Jackson courted the comparison, famously naming his California estate Neverland Ranch and remarking, "You know, all over the walls of my room are pictures of Peter Pan. I totally identify with Peter Pan . . . the lost boy of Never-Never Land" (quoted in Taraborrelli 1991, 283). Once at the Encino estate (where Jackson had previously lived), he and his then constant companion Emmanuel Lewis, child star of the TV show *Webster*, read *Peter Pan* together and then pretended to be flying over Neverland. "Believe it and it'll be true," Michael reportedly told the boy (316). Like Peter Pan, Jackson seemed unwilling to leave childhood, even after marrying and having children. "Magic," he claimed, is "easy if you put your mind to it. . . . We can fly, you know. We just don't know how to think the right thoughts and levitate ourselves off the ground" (quoted in Marsh 1985, 119). Playing along, Dave Marsh opens his biography with the following epigraph from Barrie's *Peter and Wendy* (first published in 1911): "He had ecstasies innumerable that other children can never know; but he was looking through the window at the one joy from which he must be for ever barred" (Barrie 2004, 141).[14]

The allegations of child abuse leveled against Jackson return us to the man–boy dynamics of Barrie's work and to the immaturity critique that encapsulates (perhaps overwhelms) it. According to Jackson as well as his biographers, he was denied a normal childhood; his father made him rehearse and perform constantly. He thus remained a boy. "His intelligence," explains his friend Jane Fonda, "is instinctual and emotional, like a child's" (quoted in Marsh 1985, 12). The allegations of child abuse became entangled with Jackson's own story of childhood abuse and resistance to growing up. When Jackson was first accused of molestation in 1993, his defenders held that Jackson could not have abused the boy in question because he was himself still a boy. His former manager Frank Dileo offered what became the formulaic response: "Michael never really had a childhood, and I think he is trying to experience it in later life. I would tell him to keep the knowledge that he is innocent and hold his head up" (quoted in Kennedy 1993, 30). Jackson's lawyer Bert Fields concurs: "Michael never had a childhood. . . . He really lives the life of a 12-year-old" (quoted in Orth 1994, 77). Such claims recall Nicholas Llewelyn Davies's assertion that J. M. Barrie could write *Peter Pan* because he was an innocent (cited in Birkin 1979, 130). The immaturity thesis at once incriminated and cleared Jackson, in classic PPS fashion. Biographer Marsh, who describes himself as a fan, nevertheless admonishes Jackson in an "open letter" that he is *not* Peter Pan, adding, "Your work stays young, but its youth is an anomaly, not a confirmation of anything, but a denial of many things. . . . It's meant to be outgrown" (1985, 79). Jackson never fully escaped from Peter Pan's shadow, even after marrying and having kids of his own. Though never convicted of child abuse, his reputation tanked, and he became even more reclusive, dogged by suspicions of sexual deviancy, racial blurring, and drug use.

Barrie is absent from popular *Peter Pan* case writing save the 2004 *Finding Neverland,* a pseudo-biopic starring Johnny Depp as Barrie (Forster 2004). *Finding Neverland* starts off reveling in Barrie's weirdness, only to safeguard it, linking it to creativity and to heterosexual family life. Like other *Peter Pan* vehicles, which repress *The Little White Bird* as a source text, *Finding Neverland* normalizes Barrie's encounter with the Llewellyn Davies family, making mother Sylvie, rather than her boys, Barrie's primary muse. The general tone is one of inspiration, not obsession, and there is no room for ambivalence or awkwardness, nothing like we see in *Dreamchild.* Barrie is presented as the best sort of Peter Pan figure, the ideal boy-man, imaginative but responsible. Depp has played not a few eccentric, queerish characters, most famously Jack Sparrow in the *Pirates of the Caribbean* series but also Willy Wonka, in a 2005 Tim Burton version of *Charlie and the Chocolate Factory.* Depp's Wonka is reminiscent of Jackson, in fact. *Finding Neverland* goes out of its way to frame Barrie as a family man rather than a problem child. How might it have looked had Depp been allowed queerer license as Barrie?[15] (For that matter, imagine *Hook* with Depp rather than Dustin Hoffman playing Hook, and with Jackson as Peter Pan.)

Psychoanalytic and popular case writing has kept in circulation at least two *Peter Pans*—for children, the magical story about a boy who never grows up, and for adults, that story too, but also the tragic tale of an immature, irresponsible man, who might be representative of men more broadly. Scholars, too, use *Peter Pan* to make their case—about the joys and discontents of the so-called Golden Age, about immaturity or the impossibility of children's fiction, and about the persistence of case writing itself.

Oz Dreaming

In "*The Wizard of Oz:* Professor Marvel's Analysis of an Adolescent Girl," psychiatrist Lee Grossman (2002) offers a parodic yet strangely informative case study of "Dorothy G," ostensibly drawing from the clinical notes of one Professor Marvel, unearthed and annotated by an unnamed "graduate student in the humanities" (who, we learn in a footnote, "has elected to remain anonymous until such time as hell freezes over or he completes his Ph.D., whichever comes first"). As Grossman explains, said graduate student, "exploring alternatives to gainful employment, found himself wondering about certain facts," among them the historical coincidence of *The Wonderful Wizard of Oz* and *The Interpretation of Dreams,* both published in 1900, and the dream motif of the MGM film *The Wizard of Oz,* released in 1939, the year of Freud's death. Asserting that the MGM film was "far too sophisticated and too terrifying to have been made for children," the graduate student asserts that the "notes and the film taken together reveal a successful analytic journey in some detail, depicting the three phases of treatment, the emergence of symptoms, and ultimately the resolution of transference in the termination phase." Grossman is merely the editor of the case, assembled from Marvel's notes as reconstructed by our graduate student.

Grossman's mock case history frames Dorothy as suffering from the usual psychosexual dramas—seeing everyone as a witch (either exclusively good or bad), fantasizing about "being big and powerful in the land of innocent children," and undergoing transference neurosis. In the "termination phase" of the study and treatment, Professor Marvel explains how he (as the analyst) came to be seen by his young patient as a bad wizard but a good man. Grossman remarks that elements of transference and countertransference seem to have eluded Professor Marvel:

When Dorothy began to dismantle her idealized version of
the analyst, Dr. Marvel seemed initially to have deflected
her from her efforts toward resolution of this transference
(the movie has him telling her to pay no attention to that
man behind the curtain), ostensibly to help her see the intra-
psychic nature of her problems. Then, when she began to face
the loneliness and sadness of termination, Dr. Marvel was a
bit quick to conclude that she would be unable to tolerate the
separation. One wonders what went on at that point; it seems
that Professor Marvel lost his perspective and clung to the
fantasy that he alone could rescue his patient, and they would
fly away together. (n.p.)

Grossman's piece appeared in the fall 2002 issue of *fort da,* an online
refereed journal of psychoanalysis that "invites all points of view within
the psychoanalytic community and endeavors to preserve high intellectual standards within the context of a lively, creative exchange."[16]
The humor of Grossman's work depends upon knowledge not only of
the Oz story but also of its importance to popular and especially pop-
psychoanalytic culture—as well as of the specific conceits it employs,
primarily the dreamwork. That Grossman can so humorously ironize
the psychoanalytic project through Oz is telling. Grossman does not so
much resist psychoanalysis as have a good time with it, accentuating its
potential for absurdity without compromising its value.[17]

Grossman's piece is also a rejoinder to more-earnest exercises in
applied analysis, such as David Magder's essay on the various "syn-
dromes" of Oz characters (1980), and Gita Dorothy Morena's *The Wisdom of Oz: Reflections of a Jungian Sandplay Therapist* (1998). The
great-granddaughter of L. Frank Baum, Morena offers Oz as the antidote to today's "fast paced living." Like Grossman's parody, and possibly the inspiration for it, *The Wisdom of Oz* is tripartite in structure,
with "Enchantment of Oz" followed by "The Journey through Oz" and
"Follow Your Own Yellow Brick Road." Morena's clients create healing
sand scenarios using Oz figurines and other objects (dice, teddy bears,
spiders, rainbows, starfish, menorahs, G.I. Joes). Poetry therapist Sherry
Reiter, too, believes in the healing power of Oz, declaring, "It is not accidental that *The Wonderful Wizard of Oz* has become one of the most

popular and beloved stories of all time. Don't we all know the fear of abandonment in Dorothy's experience? Are there not times that we all wish we were smarter or braver or more noble of heart?" (1988, 156).

Like *Alice* and *Peter Pan,* the Oz books have long been associated with psychoanalytic culture. While Baum could not have read Freud by the time the first Oz book appeared, he would have later encountered Freudian ideas as adapted by Americans. Baum shared with Freud a fascination with fairy tales, presenting *The Wonderful Wizard of Oz* as a "modernized fairy tale."[18] Like a number of analysts, Baum was also intrigued by the cinema and its potential for "magic" and transformation. More to the point, the Oz books are rife with inventive, often unsettling explorations of gender, sexuality, embodiment, and animation, inviting Freudian engagement on many levels. Baum wrote fourteen Oz books, the last of which was published in 1920, a year after his death. Twenty-six more were then written by Ruth Plumly Thompson, John R. Neill, Jack Snow, and others. These books have been widely read across generations, even if the 1939 film overshadows them. The books are decidedly stranger than the film, and it is no surprise that they have attracted the attention of psychoanalytic and queer theorists.

The first exploration of Oz from a Freudian standpoint was Osmond Beckwith's 1961 "The Oddness of Oz," intended for the short-lived Beat journal *Neurotica* but appearing instead in *Kulchur.*[19] Baum, Beckwith proposes, "set[s] out, almost like a real artist, to personalize all his anxieties" (1976, 81). Pointing to his many gender-bending child characters, Beckwith underscores Baum's anxieties about gender, sexuality, and reproduction. The attraction of girl readers to the Oz books makes perfect sense, he remarks, because girls "could appreciate his idolization of an immature and impubescent [sic] femininity" (87). As for boys:

> What young boy readers saw in Oz is not so clear. . . . But the boys Oz did strike were struck deep (all or most of the adults who find Oz unforgettable seem to be men). In psychoanalytic language, the boyish girls of Oz are *phallic,* and thus deeply reassuring to boys (or men) with castration anxieties. The reassurance is against their unconscious fear that girlish girls are what they seem to be, castrated boys. (87; emphasis in the original)

That is the closest we get to an answer for the question he raises at the essay's outset: "What made (makes) Oz so popular?" (75). Presumably

Oz is popular because it gives expression to our polymorphous perversity while managing castration anxiety.[20]

Picking up on many of the same issues, Tison Pugh offers a queer theoretical response to the question, reading the Oz tales as both queerly utopian and as exercises in antisocial eroticism.[21] Baum's Oz books especially are suffused with scenes of male–male coupling and generation of life out of inorganic materials—a sawhorse is enlivened and a pumpkinhead man is begotten by a boy (Tip) who turns out to be a girl (Ozma).[22] Moreover, Baum's wonderfully queer land of Oz celebrates both nonreproductive sexuality *and* childhood; "here queers are not blamed for or denigrated as a result of the failure of heterosexual reproduction because reproduction is not a cultural goal of any relevance" (Pugh 2008, 18–19).[23]

But it is the 1939 film, rather than Baum's queerer books or Baum's biography, that drives Oz case writing. Oz restorying or case writing tends to draw upon the storyline of the MGM film. Oz case writing tends away from Baum, who is broadly represented as a colorful character, even something of a trickster figure, but not an adult stuck in childhood. Screened on television every year since 1939 and thus seen by millions across generations, *The Wizard of Oz* is reportedly the most-watched film in history. Adapted primarily from the first Oz book, the film condenses and stands in for Oz narrative at large, centralizing an assortment of storylines, characters, and texts—including Baum's own cinematic efforts. The film is the source text for most Oz case writing, which tends to adapt the dream framework in some way. Whereas the books openly display the oddness of Oz, the film, by employing the dreamwork, suggests a hidden dimension to Oz, an unconscious realm in which fantastical creatures correspond to the more mundane "real" characters of Dorothy's psychic drama. The film not only manages Oz as a dreamscape but also brings Dorothy safely home, whereas in the books Dorothy returns often to Oz and finally settles there, along with Aunt Em and Uncle Henry. The intense gay fandom that surrounds the film, while not always explicitly engaged with Baum's texts, does return some queerness to the story. Another Oz fan and scholar, Dee Michel, is now writing a book about the enduring connection of gay men to Oz, in which he acknowledges the centrality of the film but also the queer fandom around Baum's books.[24] Even so, the dominance of the film in and out of gay culture is not to be doubted; it has become

the story of Oz, an authority not achieved by the cinematic versions of
Alice, Peter Pan, or other Golden Age fantasies.

The film has succeeded even better than Baum's first Oz book
as a modernized fairy tale. It was made during the early heyday of
Hollywood and just two years after Walt Disney's pioneering feature-
length animated film *Snow White and the Seven Dwarfs,* which set
the terms for modernized fairy tales and in fact accomplished more
thoroughly what Baum promised—a tale that "gladly dispenses with
all disagreeable incident" and "in which the wonderment and joy are
retained and the heart-aches and nightmares are left out" (Baum 1996,
iii). Disney's films and *The Wizard of Oz* succeed along these lines, mini-
mizing scary and traumatic moments and positioning them as necessary to the triumph of the protagonist(s).[25] Beverly Lyon Clark (2003)
suggests that Baum could have been Walt Disney had he been born a
little later and under different circumstances. She also notes that the
MGM film has kept Baum's texts alive.

The 1939 MGM film also drew from earlier stage and film versions
of the Oz story that reflected more accurately the plots and scenarios of
Baum's texts. The translation of Oz from book to film began in 1902, as
Mark Evan Swartz reports, just two years after the publication of the
first Oz book, with a stage version directed by Julian Mitchell, a "lavish
musical extravaganza" that "took the country by storm" (2000, 2). In
1908 Baum developed and toured a multimedia show called *Fairylogue
and Radio-Plays,* and 1910 saw the production of a short motion-
picture version of the first Oz book. The first extended movie version,
also entitled *The Wizard of Oz* (Semon 1925) was a silent film made in
1925 starring Larry Semon as the Scarecrow (as well as a young Oliver
Hardy as the Tin Woodman). From the start, Baum was fascinated
with film. He moved to Hollywood in 1910, where he set up his estate,
Ozcot, founded the Oz Film Manufacturing Company in 1914, and then
made three ill-fated Oz films: *The Patchwork Girl of Oz* (1914), *His
Majesty the Scarecrow of Oz* (1914) (which predated the book version),
and *The Magic Cloak of Oz* (1915). These films, notes Swartz, "were a
prime example of a genre of early motion pictures known as the fairy-
tale film, which featured fantastic stories and trick effects" (161). It was
precisely those effects that made the films unsuccessful, as said tricks
were going out of style when Baum used them.[26] In addition, the films
are much like Baum's books, episodic and surreal.

The 1925 Semon vehicle was somewhat more successful, though not as much as Semon himself had hoped; in any case, it was a clear influence on the 1939 film, especially in its use of the dream motif. The 1925 film employs the dream motif alongside a storytelling motif. The film opens with an elderly toymaker (played by Semon) entering his shop and placing on a table dolls of Dorothy, the Scarecrow, and the Tin Man. His young granddaughter then enters the room, carrying a large book by Baum. She sits in her grandfather's lap and opens the book to reveal the film credits, at which point the "story" begins. That story goes back and forth between Oz and Kansas, and the plot comes from a later Oz book as much as from *The Wonderful Wizard of Oz,* confusing viewers who do not know Baum's work. More important, the dream motif is not the only frame for the story; although the little girl wakes up at the end of the film, as the Scarecrow doll tumbles to the floor, the sequence of events both inside and outside the "story" is far from clear. Whereas the 1939 film established clear symbolic and linear correspondences for Dorothy's dream, the granddaughter's dream in this film is more confusing. "Perhaps the most sophisticated aspect of the film," proposes Swartz, "is the idea that its version of *The Wizard of Oz* story is at least in part merely a child's dream. With its loose structure and topsy-turvy logic, the story certainly makes most sense as a dream" (2000, 226). Indeed, the dream-film seems closer to *Alice* than to *The Wonderful Wizard of Oz* in some respects—or at least, than to the MGM film *The Wizard of Oz.* The Semon film raises intriguing questions about time and space, dreaming and plotting, whereas the 1939 version offers a streamlined, linear story. Swartz attributes MGM's use of the dream motif to the example of the 1925 film, while acknowledging that Noel Langley, the screenwriter of the 1939 version responsible for that motif, claimed inspiration from a Mary Pickford movie, *The Poor Little Rich Girl* (Swartz 2000, 247–50). Langley and Semon apparently both felt that fantastic characters were not believable unless introduced as versions of real people. To make Oz seem realistic, it had to be presented via a dream.

That Oz is most believable as a dream suggests how thoroughly the dreamwork became not merely a theme but a mode of narration. The MGM film is not only a cinematic dreamwork of Oz but also a distinctly American one, in which realism is ensured rather than threatened by unconscious psychic life. Put another way: the film does not just perform a certain dreamwork for its viewers, in the manner of the dreamwork as theorized by Freud; rather, the film reflects and sustains a particularly American understanding of the dream—as utilitarian, realistic, psychological. No doubt the film works psychological magic on viewers, but viewers also made the film psychological, and in the wake of theatrical and cinematic dreaming before it.

Both psychoanalytic and literary-critical case writing emphasize the importance of the screen dream for both Dorothy and the film's viewers. Sanford Schreiber (1974), for instance, examines how the film functions generally as a screen memory for one of his psychiatric patients, who associates chronic separation anxiety with particular scenes from the film. Todd Gilman, on the other hand, focuses on Dorothy's psychic life, arguing that the film attributes to Dorothy powerful unconscious desires, giving her the last name of "Gale" and linking her to the tornado. The "film-text implies that the storm represents her buried rage," he writes, her "desire to punish those who have disappointed her, and [her] need to escape" (1995–96, 163). Two stages of dreaming, moreover, mark the film, according to Gilman: first, what Freud calls "introductory dreaming," in the film, the black-and-white sequence during which Dorothy is transported to Oz; and second, the main dream of Oz at large. As persuasive as these readings are, the film performs this psychological work because it was designed and expected to do so. I see the film as an efficient American exercise in dreaming forged out of Baum's materials as well as the broader fascination with cinema, visual culture, and psychic life. The 1939 film made the most of the dreamwork as Americans then understood it—as making fantastic events more believable or realistic. Oz without the dream conceit is now nearly impossible to imagine, and the dream without visual and even musical spectacle nearly as much so. It is no accident that a contemporary, parallel Oz novel, Geoffrey Maguire's *Wicked,* quickly yielded a stage musical with cinematic qualities.

Even other critical interpretations have had to reckon with the dreamwork conceit, which dictates that Oz has latent content. The story of Oz, in other words, suppresses the real story of Oz. Dream interpretation is of course a central method of psychoanalysis, which means that any reading of the film is already positioned within psychoanalytic discourse. Even nonpsychoanalytic interpretations, such as the political reading first put forward by Henry M. Littlefield in 1964 (Oz as an allegory for populism and the 1896 presidential campaign of William Jennings Bryan),[27] endorses the notion of a suppressed or distorted reality behind the screen dream.[28]

While he admired *Alice,* Baum did not like its dream frame and tried to safeguard *The Wonderful Wizard of Oz* from a dream presentation.[29] In Baum's *The Wonderful Wizard of Oz,* Dorothy does fall asleep during the tornado ride to Oz; if she dreams, we do not hear about it; and there is no Miss Gulch or Professor Marvel to transform into the Wicked Witch of the West and the Wizard of Oz; those characters are inventions of the film. Baum's Dorothy gets to Oz quickly and without incident and returns the same way, clicking her heels together and saying "Take me home to Aunt Em!" (Baum 1996, 138) (*not* "There's no place like home"). She does not wake up in bed surrounded by familiar faces, as in the 1939 film, but rather lands on the prairie just outside the family farmhouse. "Baum," asserts biographer Rebecca Loncraine, "wanted to save fairy tales from being collapsed into dreams, where they'd be cordoned off, removing any sense that there were other worlds outside our minds, beyond this one" (2009, 184). Baum, who died in 1919, would have disliked the dream frame of the 1939 film, all the more so because Dorothy's dream is brought about by a knock on the head during the storm, the implication being that she is not only dreaming but quite possibly delusional. And yet, whatever realism the film enjoys is achieved through the dream frame, not in spite of it.

Oz, of course, calls forth and stands in for the American dream. Oz, writes Jack Zipes, "sets apart the utopian imagination from the cynical. It is the measure of a hope, a secular force of humanitarian hope" (1994, 119). Emphasizing Baum's theosophical inclinations, William R. Leach describes *The Wonderful Wizard of Oz* as an exercise in positive thinking, as "an optimistic secular therapeutic text" that helped Americans "appreciate and enjoy, without guilt, the new consumer abundance and way of living produced by that economy" (1991, 174). Jon Savage likewise links Oz with "America's vitalist dream economy" (2007, 55), noting the materialization and commodification of dreams: "Vision became money, given tangible form in theme parks, kinetoscopes, tabloids. . . . You bought your dreams" (54). There is certainly no shortage of optimistic, utopian, dreamy Oz.

But the discontents of Oz dreaming have also found substantial expression. Maguire's *Wicked* series imagines a very different narrative trajectory for Oz, one more sympathetic to witchy women and gay characters and focused on the political landscape of Oz. Geoff Ryman's novel *Was* (1992) is an even darker affair, telling the interwoven stories of Dorothy Gale, Judy Garland, and Jonathan, an Oz fan dying of AIDS who seeks the historical story behind the fantasy. In this version, Dorothy Gael (not Gale), living a bleak existence in 1880s Kansas, is sexually abused by Uncle Henry, turns into a bully herself, and then goes crazy. Tracing Dorothy's steps a century later, Jonathan, like Dorothy, finds himself in the not-so-merry land of Was, a place of spoiled dreams and sad memories. Both *Wicked* and *Was* devise and bring to the surface an unconscious for Oz, one marked especially by sexual and political abuse.

One of the more searching film variants is *The Wiz*, a 1978 Motown vehicle (Lumet 1978) based on the Broadway musical of the same name, which opened in 1975. Set in Harlem, *The Wiz* whisks away schoolteacher Dorothy (played by Diana Ross) to "Oz," which resembles a decaying, almost postapocalyptic New York City. Neither a critical nor a commercial success, the film nonetheless offers an engaging critique of the American dream, featuring scenes of exploitation and neoslavery. African American Dorothy does *not* dream her way into Oz; rather, she is transported by a freak tornado during a snowstorm. Another such cinematic revisitation, one nominated for an Academy Award, is the 1985 *Return to Oz* (Murch 1985), set after the conclusion of *The Wizard of Oz* (and thus a sequel of sorts) and featuring a Dorothy haunted by her adventures. Worried about her niece's insomnia, Aunt Em sends Dorothy to a clinic to undergo electroshock therapy; trying to escape, Dorothy blacks out and dreams herself back into Oz, where her adventures continue. Curiously enough, *Return to Oz* is a Disney film, surprisingly dark and bereft of musical numbers. Like the novels by Maguire and Ryman, these films pursue not a utopian place somewhere over the rainbow but rather a dystopian reality ostensibly suppressed by the screen dream of Oz.

"Home" remains a central theme of Oz stories, thanks again to the 1939 film. In a retrospective piece on the MGM film, Margaret Hamilton, aka the Wicked Witch of the West, asks, "What is it that makes the picture so special, what is it that captures our attention, our imagination, that appeals to us, that makes us want to share with others? . . . The word *home* comes to mind" (1982, 153–54; emphasis in the original). Though she acknowledges the film's uncanniness—remarking that it "gives us a warm and lovely feeling and yet an anxiety" (154)—Hamilton insists upon a happy lesson, that home is where the heart is. That "message" is what accounts for the film's popularity, she decides. Others, however, are not so sure, arguing that despite that overt message the film in fact questions the idea of home, perhaps even makes home impossible. Like Gilman, Salman Rushdie refuses the dream of return in favor of the subtext of displacement and despair, which he links to the wisdom of psychoanalysis. For Rushdie, as perhaps for gay fans, Oz is an allegory of exile and diaspora. The *real* message of the MGM film, he asserts, "is not that 'there no place like home,' but rather that there is no longer any such place *as* home: except, of course, for the home we make, or the homes that are made for us, in Oz: which is anywhere, and everywhere, except the place from which we began" (1992, 57).

Elizabeth Bronfen similarly understands the MGM film as the ur-text for a pervasive American home fantasy, one reinvoked by Hollywood films otherwise as disparate as *Wild at Heart, Good Morning, Vietnam,* and the *Star Wars* trilogy (2004, 91). "Home," she proposes after Freud, is a name for our uncanny experiences of familiarity and estrangement. Bronfen finds Dorothy all too aware that she has rewritten "the script of her own home romance" so that Kansas seems satisfaction enough, so that constraint becomes "a protective fiction declaring that happiness resides in the curtailment of one's desires" (69). Realizing that "home" as an experience or state of plentitude is doomed, we adjust our expectations through the fantasy of, as D. W. Winnicott might say, a good enough place. "Only by having recourse to that dangerous desire for a better home can one learn to live with the home that one feels is inadequate" (Bronfen 2004, 70). If such an interpretation is persuasive, it is in large measure because the screen dream of Oz sets us searching for buried meaning.

Casing Out the Classic

Alice, Peter Pan and the Oz stories mean different things to different people and in different communities and contexts, and it is such overdetermination that keeps them in circulation. At the same time, these texts, ostensibly for children, continue to support adult-oriented (if inner child–themed) discourses of psychic life. They are, as Arac says of *Huck Finn,* hypercanonical, and as with Twain's text, their hypercanonicity derives a great deal from the sorts of case writing being done with, through, and around them. Like fairy tales, they are referenced by analysts and therapists and made to serve clinical and interpretive programs, even as they find endless adaptation in pop-psychological culture—all of which suggests that they might not have become classics were it not for the psychoanalytic turn of the twentieth century. Psychoanalysis both exploits and helps create the cultural capital of classic children's literature. That is not to say that other forces were not at work, too. But at the least, the positioning of these narratives within psychoanalytic discourse and case writing has been a major factor in their cultural success.

4. Maurice Sendak and Picturebook Psychology

I N 1963, HUMORIST LOUISE ARMSTRONG AND illustrator Whitney Darrow Jr. published a picturebook entitled *A Child's Guide to Freud*. Dedicated to "Sigmund F., A Really Mature Person," *A Child's Guide to Freud* is a send-up of Freudian ideas, pitched to adults and specifically to upper-middle-class New Yorkers. Armstrong was a confirmed Manhattanite and Darrow a longtime *New Yorker* cartoonist and children's book illustrator. "This is Mommy," the book begins, showing a woman chasing a naughty little boy.

> When she won't let you play doctor with Susie, call her OVER-PROTECTIVE. This is Daddy. He sleeps in the same room as Mommy. Call this a MEANINGFUL RELATIONSHIP. The feelings you have about Mommy and Daddy closing their door are called OEDIPAL. This means that you want to have a Meaningful Relationship with Mommy. If you think a lot about this, it is called a WISH. If you think about it in your sleep, it is called a DREAM. If you suck your thumb instead of thinking about it, it is called COMPENSATION. (n.p.)

While Freud had a lot to say about children, he did not usually talk to them, and so a picturebook about Freud seems laughable, even absurd.

That year, 1963, saw the publication of another American picture-book inspired by Freud and likewise staged around a naughty if more imaginative boy, Maurice Sendak's *Where the Wild Things Are*. In short order it was hailed as a psychological masterpiece, exploring as it does young Max's anger and adventurous imagination within the safe space of home. While the scenario of teaching Freud to children, especially in the form of a picturebook, remains comic, the idea that the picturebook has something to offer by way of psychological value for children—and psychological insight into childhood for adults—was firmly in place by 1963. With *Where the Wild Things Are,* Sendak affirmed the picture-book genre as deeply concerned with the emotional and imaginative lives of children. Even Bruno Bettelheim, who in 1969 criticized it in his *Ladies' Home Journal* column, changed his mind about Sendak's book; indeed, it may have helped galvanize Bettelheim's exploration of fairy tale enchantments. *Where the Wild Things Are* has never been out of print, and as of February 2008 it had sold over nineteen million copies (Thornton 2008). Winner of the 1964 Caldecott Medal, it is one of the most successful picturebooks of all time.

Where the Wild Things Are emerged in part out of Sendak's ongo-ing fascination with psychoanalysis. Sendak has often talked about its place in his life and work. Sendak's longtime partner, Dr. Eugene Glynn, was a psychoanalyst specializing in adolescence.[1] Sendak under-went analysis in the 1950s during a period of depression. The first picturebook he both wrote and illustrated, *Kenny's Window* (1956), was given shape by a case history that he read on the advice of his analyst. What he calls the "trilogy" of *Where the Wild Things Are, In the Night Kitchen* (1970b), and *Outside Over There* (1981) is concerned with things that go bump in the night, with, in his words, "how children master various feelings—anger, boredom, fear, frustration, jealousy—and manage to come to grips with the realities of their lives" (quoted in Lanes 1980, 227). Sendak's love affair with psychoanalysis cannot be disputed, and there is no shortage of psychoanalytic commentary on his picturebook work.

But Sendak's encounter with discourses of the mind was indirect as well as direct, coming through his apprenticeship with pioneers in the picturebook genre as well as through more personal experiences. This chapter approaches Sendak as a cultural switch point as well as a figurehead for what I am calling *picturebook psychology,* a broader discourse about the psychological value and texture of picturebooks that takes a cue from Freud but has other aspects and influences. Sendak can be linked not only to Freud and to American humanistic psychology but also to fairy-tale discourse (the subject of chapter 1) and to child study and analysis (the subject of chapter 2). In Sendak's picturebook work we see the alignment of fairy tales, the "classical" genre for children, with a creative version of child analysis, one that includes both treatments of the inner child and observations of actual children. Sendak has reworked or illustrated quite a number of fairy tales; those of the Brothers Grimm stand out, but there are also tales by Hans Christian Andersen, Clemens Brentano, Wilhelm Hauff, and E. T. A. Hoffmann (Bodmer 2003, 129). Psychologist Robert Kloss (1989), among others, likens Sendak's picturebooks to fairy tales, which are linked to the dreamwork as theorized by Freud. Sendak's picturebooks work like and resemble fairy tales and the dreamwork. His books also resemble the child–adult playwork practiced by child analysts, which is hardly surprising since Sendak imitates some of their techniques. Sendak, in short, is the consummate picturebook psychologist, bringing together in the picturebook key psychological themes, forms, and practices. It is no coincidence that he is "one of the principal mythologists of childhood," who "has created a kind of map of the emotional and visionary terrain of childhood" (Cech 1995, 7),[2] or that friend and collaborator Tony Kushner can liken his child characters to "the kids described in the best, richest developmental literature, the kids in Piaget and Winnicott, doing the tough work of holding themselves and their world together" (2003a, 10).

There was picturebook psychology before Sendak, and there certainly has been picturebook psychology in his wake. Taking a page from Bettelheim, Ellen Handler Spitz proposes that the "popularity of classic picturebooks derives from their remarkable capacity to tap ongoing issues of deep emotional significance for children" (1999, 8).[3] Spitz acknowledges Sendak's importance, devoting some twelve pages to a reading of *Where the Wild Things Are.*[4] But what Spitz does not provide is a history of the genre, and specifically its pre-Sendakian period. John Cech, Barbara Bader, and Leonard Marcus all suggest that Sendak is both legatee and torchbearer of creatively applied child psychology. Bader especially makes a number of connections between child psychology and picturebooks. While acknowledging that *Where the Wild Things Are* was a watershed, she dates the psychologization of the picturebook to the 1930s. In the first part of this chapter, I explore how child analysis and progressive educational theory helped psychologize the picturebook. Sendak's own practices reach back to this period as much as they reach forward to our current moment of picturebook psychology.

Sendak's book represents picturebook psychology as it stood in the early 1960s but also radically recasts it, paving the way for a groundswell in applied picturebook psychology. The book can be understood as rewriting classical Freudian analysis, retaining some of its rigor and edge while making it more palatably American. *Where the Wild Things Are* has been embraced as a psychological primer, a story about anger and its management through fantasy; it is also a text in which echoes of Freud remain audible. I read it as a bedtime-story version of Freud's Wolf Man case history of 1918, an updated and upbeat dream of the wolf boy. It is to Sendak what the Wolf Man case was to Freud, a career-making feral tale. Standing at the crossroads of Freudian tradition, child analysis, humanistic psychology, and bibliotherapy, the book both clarified and expanded the uses of picturebook enchantment.

Drawing (for) the Child

The picturebook began as a European import, an American tradition not emerging until the 1930s. Early on, notes Bader, picturebooks "came along when someone was inspired, usually by his or her own child" (1976, 25)—much as *Winnie-the-Pooh* and other classics were written for the authors' own children or (as in the case of Lewis Carroll and J. M. Barrie) for children they wished to claim. Even so, as early as the 1920s, interest in the world of the very young or preschool child, bolstered not only by Freudianism but also by the American child study movement and progressive education, led to children's picturebooks that emphasized the experiences of everyday life from the child's perspective. Bader describes Helen Sewell's 1936 picturebook *Ming and Mehitable* as "the first picturebook . . . to turn on the turns of a child's mind" (84), noting the general interest of progressive educators and psychologists in the genre. She also points out that Marie Ets, a contemporary of Sewell, studied child psychology extensively and designed her picturebooks as psychological experiments. We might then think of Sewell and Ets (among others) as the first picturebook psychologists. Some of these author-illustrators observed their own children, even as they also drew from scientific research.

Educator and social reformer Lucy Sprague Mitchell founded the Bureau of Educational Experiments (the Bank Street School) in 1916 in support of progressive education and the new child psychology. In the late 1890s, Mitchell had heard William James argue that children's psychosocial development was dependent upon sensory and motor (what Jean Piaget later called "sensorimotor") experiences. Having also studied under John Dewey, Mitchell hoped "to make a scientific approach to the study of children and on that basis work out experimentally what their schools should be like," as she reports (1953, 222). The bureau was linked with Caroline Pratt's Play School and Harriet Johnson's Nursery School, both in New York City; it was at once a teacher-training institute, a child-observation facility, and a progressive think tank, so well-known, notes Marcus, that "a steady parade of visitors from as far away as the Soviet Union and Australia came to observe the observers observe the children, and to be observed by them in turn" (1992, 61). A central focus of Mitchell and her colleagues was the spontaneous language practices of children. Mitchell was more interested in language use than in the child's visual imagination, which is why she did not herself produce picturebooks. Even so, her focus on child language and storytelling helped legitimate the picturebook form, as well as launch not a few author-artist careers.[5]

Mitchell was convinced of the need for a new literature for children, one that captured their experiences and helped them navigate everyday life. In 1921, she published her *Here and Now Story Book,* an anthology of stories taken from the children with whom she worked and a textbook for teachers and other interested adults. In her introduction, Mitchell positions the book as "experimental," thus aligning it with experimental and applied psychology. "The task," she writes, "is to examine first the things which get the spontaneous attention of a two-year-old, a three-year-old, and so up to the seven-year-old; and then to determine what relationships are natural and intelligible at these ages" (1921, 10).

Mitchell affirms the basic premises of early-twentieth-century child psychology, especially as articulated by Piaget (rather than by Anna Freud or Melanie Klein): in short, that young children are primarily driven by their senses and by motor movements, and only slowly develop spatial understanding and critical reasoning skills.[6] Children "think through their muscles," she writes (59). "Above all [the child's] early stories must be of activities and they must be told in motor terms" (6). "I think none of us would like to hazard a guess as to when the child comes through to a sharp distinction between himself and other things or other persons," she continues. "But we are sure, I think, that this distinction is a matter of growth which extends over many years and that at two, three, and even four, it is imperfectly apprehended" (8). She suggests children have an "embryonic pattern sense," one that delights in both muscle exercise and the repetition of sounds (59). What had been called children's literature, she asserts, really is not for children because it neither reflects nor respects their developmental needs. She claims, "We have never had [a writer for children] of the first order. . . . The world has yet to see a genuinely great creator whose real vision is for children" (41). While she does not claim that role, she begins the work of writing real children's stories. She also recommends against fairy tales and other exercises in the "the strange, the bizarre, the unreal" (15); children should instead hear stories about the real things of the world.[7] Like G. Stanley Hall and other proponents of child study, Mitchell enlists the aid of parents and teachers in the collection of data on childhood, remarking, "Mothers and teachers everywhere should be making these precious records" (70–71).[8]

Many of Mitchell's themes and claims had a direct influence on the creation of picturebooks. For instance, she notes the childhood pleasure "of enumerating objects which are grouped together in some close association, usually physical juxtaposition" (11)—hence *Goodnight Moon* (1947), the most famous and successful picturebook of her protégé Margaret Wise Brown, a recitation of cherished objects within a child's bedroom. Children, Mitchell also asserts, are interested in questions of "Use," citing on this issue an early book on child psychology, Charles Wilkin Waddle's *Introduction to Child Psychology:* "Does [the child] not think of the world largely in terms of active functioning? Has not the typical question of this age become 'What's it for'? Even his early definitions are in terms of use, which has a strong motor implication. 'A table is to eat off of'; 'a spoon is to eat in'; 'a river means where you get drinks out of water, and catch fish, and throw stones'" (Mitchell 1921, 19). "Use" with a strong motor implication is the organizing conceit of another important picturebook, Ruth Krauss's 1952 *A Hole Is to Dig: A First Book of First Definitions,* illustrated by Sendak. "Mashed potatoes are to give everybody enough," the book begins. "A face is so you can make faces. A face is something to have on the front of your head" (Krauss 1989, n.p.). Mitchell's idea that children's books should begin with subjects and settings familiar to the young child and only slowly move toward the unknown is now pretty much the practice of most authors and artists.

Mitchell makes the case for a new and more practical children's literature on the grounds that play is crucial to the child and that words make the best play stuff. Adults have forgotten how to play, she asserts, and especially how to play with words. Mitchell emphasizes the oral aspect of stories, the importance of telling and listening carefully, rather than their visual aspect. She does write about form in children's narrative, but not about visual elements or design. Mitchell seems nearly to suggest that pictures have overshadowed words in children's books and discussions about them. Although it features occasional illustrations, the *Here and Now Story Book* is not by any means a picturebook. In her preface to the book, Caroline Pratt even more clearly expounds the value of the verbal as well as the visual:

> That is, just as children draw and show power to compose
> with crayons and paints, they use language to compose what
> they term stories or occasionally, verse. Often these "stories"
> are a mere rehearsal of experiences, but in so far as they are
> vivid and have some sort of fitting ending they pass as a
> childish art expression just as their compositions in drawing
> do. (1921, xi)

Pratt here alludes to a proliferating professional literature on the drawings of children and child art, a literature spanning psychology, philosophy, art history, and educational theory. The link between childhood and drawing goes back at least to Jean-Jacques Rousseau and was a central aspect of the educational theory of Johann Heinrich Pestalozzi. The idea that children's drawings constitute an art form began in earnest with Rodolphe Töpfer in the early nineteenth century, and the first exhibit of children's drawings took place in London in 1890. Children's drawings became a centerpiece of what is now called developmental psychology through the work of many intellectuals, but especially Herman T. Lukens, Georges Luquet, Georges Rouma, and Jean Piaget. More interested in pedagogy and democracy than in development per se, John Dewey nonetheless characterizes the impulse to draw as a basic instinct of childhood in his *The School and Society* (1899). As early as 1922, Piaget had published his analysis of children's drawings of bicycles, and he returned to the subject of children's drawings as he formulated his account of childhood's developmental stages. Some commentators on children's drawings operated from a pop-evolutionary perspective and argued for developmental equivalences between the child and the savage/primitive. In 1926, nursery school teacher Florence L. Goodenough published her study *Measurement of Intelligence by Drawings,* with representational realism as the central standard (hence the "Draw-a-Man Test"). Piaget and subsequent commentators have concentrated on the issue of "visual realism" vis-à-vis the transition in childhood from egocentrism to an ostensibly more outward-bound subjectivity.[9] The literature on children's drawing was so established by 1921 that Mitchell and Pratt felt the need to temper its influence.

The late 1930s and the 1940s were thus the early heyday of picturebook psychology, with Brown's work being particularly successful. Brown's picturebooks bring together real-world knowledge with the child's imaginative powers. Bader credits Brown above others for ushering in a strong "emotional element" in her picturebooks. Bader also notes the resemblance between Brown's work and Gertrude Stein's 1939 picturebook *The World Is Round,* written at the invitation of William R. Scott, Brown's publisher and an associate of the Bank Street crowd. Brown admired Stein's childlike, incantational prose, and Bader sees Brown as working in the same tradition. Bader finds Brown's *Goodnight Moon* "the closest to Gertrude Stein and to the utterances of children" (1976, 259).[10] Bader notes that a bit later

Ruth Krauss, in her many inventive picturebooks such as *A Hole Is to Dig* and the 1954 *I'll Be You and You Be Me,* likewise captures "the way children play with words and with notions of things" (419). Bader also characterizes as powerfully child-focused the picturebook work of Crockett Johnson, Feodor Rojankovsky, György Kepes, and of course Sendak, who illustrated many of Krauss's books (including those above). Kepes and other author-illustrators, claims Bader, introduced child-centered "new looks" into the picturebooks that "brought back to children, in effect, what children had given to the art that produced them; and the picturebooks, in turn, embodied qualities native to children's art" (332).

Meanwhile, child analysts also studied the drawings and creative play of their young patients, such that the study of drawing became central to child analysis—which, as I suggested in chapter 2, might be understood as a kind of children's literature. While we cannot point to direct influence in the production of children's books, as with Mitchell and Brown, we can speculate that attention to the creative activities of children on the part of analysts helped focus attention on children's texts, sometimes written by children on their own, sometimes collaboratively produced with adults. Melanie Klein's *Narrative of Child Analysis* (1998), composed in 1939 but not published until 1961, might even be described as a psychoanalytic picturebook, featuring as it does reproductions of seventy-one drawings made by the ten-year-old boy who is the subject of her case history. The boy, named Richard, underwent ninety-three sessions with Klein over a four-month period, making drawings from the twelfth session forward. The drawings were the centerpiece of the analysis, and Richard recognized their importance to Klein, understanding them as a "gift" for his therapist (who shared her desire to keep the drawings for further reference).[11] Like both other commentators on children's drawings and more-contemporary picturebook author-illustrators, Klein emphasizes the spontaneity and surprise effect of Richard's drawings, noting, "He did not start out with any deliberate plan and was often surprised to see the finished picture" (17). Although the drawings are richly nuanced and made in the context of World War II, Klein interprets them as straightforward evidence of canonical psychic dramas.[12]

D. W. Winnicott, influenced by Klein, even drew *with* his child subjects. He would draw a "squiggle," have the child draw a squiggle in turn, and keep alternating until a picture emerged, reflecting the collaborative effort of analysis. Psychologist Howard Gardner continues this practice today, pseudonymously reporting on the artistic activities of his own children: "It is as if the young child, hardly out of the crib himself, has begun to create his own offspring—a wholly separate world, a world stocked with marks, forms, objects, scenes, and fledgling artistic works" (1980, 11). For child analysts especially, to watch the child draw or play is to see the unconscious at work. While child analysis and the practice of drawing (and writing) *for* the child are distinct practices, they do overlap, so that the successful picturebook writer or illustrator, who draws for and "with" the child, seems both a perpetual child and a lay child analyst.

This helps explain why pictures of children drawing have become something of a staple in picturebooks. Joan Menefee has identified over seventy-five picturebooks with such illustrations, beginning with Du Bose Heyward's 1939 *The Country Bunny and the Little Gold Shoes* and continuing well into the present day. Crockett Johnson's 1955 *Harold and the Purple Crayon* is perhaps the most famous such text, but another from the same period is *A Very Special House,* written in 1953 by Krauss (who was Johnson's wife) and illustrated by Sendak. In both texts, a child literally draws his world into existence: Harold's adventures are outward-bound; the unnamed protagonist of Krauss and Sendak draws a house of imagination. In both, the drawing spins nearly out of control. As Menefee observes, the incorporation of the artistic child within the picturebook—think Max's self-portrait in *Where the Wild Things Are*—points to the confluence of picturebook practice and child analysis. The author-illustrator often invokes an imago of the creative child to represent both him- or herself and the child reader.

"I have been doodling with ink and watercolor on paper all my life," Sendak notes. "It's my way of stirring up my imagination to see what I find hidden in my head. I call the results dream pictures, fantasy sketches, and even brain-sharpening exercises" (quoted in Cummins 1999, 26). Sendak produced a series of such "fantasy sketches" between 1952 and 1957, some of which were published as *Fantasy Sketches* (1970a) by the Rosenbach Museum and Library, where Sendak's papers are held. Sendak composed the sketches while listening to music, draw-ing freely but following a tempo or pace. Some are captioned after par-ticular musical pieces; some are not. Quite a few have sexual themes or are comically violent. Several are clearly first versions of what would later materialize as picturebooks. "Not necessarily for children," notes George Bodmer, "and not meant for immediate publication, these sketches are more frank, more mysterious, more Freudian" (1986–87, 182). These sketches show Sendak's determination to draw even the more unsettling elements of the unconscious mind. "After 1957," ex-plains Sendak in his preface to *Fantasy Sketches,* "for reasons I'm not quite certain of, I abandoned this particular form altogether. . . . I sus-pect that at some certain time I began consciously to manipulate my unconscious, and it was then that I was compelled to quit" (1970a, n.p.).

When he was broke and living with his parents in the late 1940s, Sendak also sketched Brooklyn street kids playing outside his window. Sendak was not only a theorist-sketcher of the unconscious but also an observer of real children. "I became absorbed in the lives of the children across the street," he reports. "These early, unprecise, wavery sketches are filled with a happy vitality that was nowhere else in my life at the time. They add up to the rough delineation of the child all my future characters would be modeled on. I loved Rosie. She knew how to get through a day" (1988d, 180). The character Rosie made her debut in Sendak's third book, *The Sign on Rosie's Door* (1960). For Sendak, the exuberant Rosie, who casts herself and her friends in street theatricals, becomes a prototype for the creative self, if only to be later eclipsed by Max. Sendak is clear about Rosie's importance. "There is Rosie, the living thread, the connecting link between me in my window and the outside over there. I did, finally, get outside over there. In 1956, after il-lustrating some dozen books by various writers, I did a Rosie and wrote my own. It's called *Kenny's Window* and in it I paid homage to Rosie's street and house" (1988d, 180–81). While Sendak does not draw with the child, he "sketches" the child at play, as does the child analyst. At the same time, he listens for the unconscious in a manner both adultlike and childlike.

Sendak, moreover, was mentored by two women with ties to progres-sive thinking about child psychology and children's literature, namely,

Krauss, an innovative picturebook psychologist in her own right, and Ursula Nordstrom, Harper's legendary children's book editor. Nordstrom worked tirelessly on behalf of writers and artists, serving variously as midwife, muse, and analyst. As Marcus reports in *Dear Genius,* Nordstrom would do "sessions" with mentees that took on "thrilling overtones of an impromptu experiment in self-revelation, a stripping down to one's own raw center as a means toward discovering the core material from which a deeply felt book might emerge" (1998, xxvii). These "sessions" probably mirrored the analytic sessions Sendak underwent.[13]

Finally, Sendak's work took shape amid ongoing debate about the value and function of fairy tales and fantasy (both the narrative form and the psychological process). The value of fairy tales had long been a subject of debate, and in the early twentieth century the so-called fairy tale wars erupted between Mitchell's camp, which attacked fairy tales as distracting nonsense, and children's librarians such as Anne Carroll Moore, who defended them against the encroachments of the modern realist (usually urban) tale. As Jacalyn Eddy reports, many child experts at first inveighed against fantasy, but gradually the tables turned, with the experts championing fantasy along psychological lines (2006, 110–17). By midcentury, fantasy was widely deemed essential to the psychological health of children. The clinical and popular literature on fantasy proliferated in the 1940s and 1950s. By the time *Where the Wild Things Are* appeared, child experts had come to embrace fantasy, whereas some librarians were now among the skeptics. "What had happened was twofold," notes Bader.

> With the insights that psychology afforded, fairy tales, myths, legends had come to be seen as other than simple straight-forward stories (however little agreement there was as to what, exactly, they represented); and children had come to be seen as rather less simple creatures too, and possessed of dark visions of their own. (1976, 514)[14]

Sendak's book, she observes, is at once myth and fairy tale, and as such it "catapulted Sendak to prominence as a prime mover, a vital force. He not only had talent, his work had meaning—interest to adults and

power over children" (514). It is no coincidence that Sendak chose the
fairy tale as a template for his work.

From Kenny's Window *to* Where the Wild Things Are

Sendak styled his first picturebook, *Kenny's Window* (1956), after a
best-selling psychological casebook by Dorothy Baruch about a young
boy named Kenneth. Sendak's text is fascinating but clunky; it features
a dream, but dream logic does not govern it or give it shape. In *Where
the Wild Things Are,* Sendak more successfully brings the dreamwork
to the picturebook. The Wolf Man's dream helped make Freud famous
and came to signify his expertise, and so too with Sendak's dream of the
wolf boy. In the transition from *Kenny's Window* to *Where the Wild
Things Are* we can see Sendak refining his own brand of expertise; the
book is a self-conscious, highly successful experiment in picturebook
psychology.

I am not the first to hear echoes of the Wolf Man in Sendak. In his
chapter on psychoanalytic criticism in *The Nimble Reader,* Roderick
McGillis remarks insightfully on the similarities as well as the differences between these two narratives. McGillis even observes that
several illustrations in *Where the Wild Things Are* are reminiscent of
dream scenes from the Wolf Man case, implying that Freud might be a
source or inspiration for Sendak (1996, 82). McGillis, however, focuses
on the use-value of psychoanalytic interpretation, concluding, "Freud,
then, can provide a model for our understanding of *Where the Wild
Things Are*" (82). McGillis is right to imply that Sendak takes his cue
from Freud, my line of emphasis here.

Although Freud was highly interested in questions of visual–verbal
relation, he was writing before the heyday of picturebooks and thought
of such books only as delivery systems for images and scenes formative to individual experience. Freud noticed that in picturebooks we
encounter powerful scenes that stay with us into adulthood. In *The
Interpretation of Dreams,* published in 1900, he describes a dream as
"a substitute for an infantile scene modified by being transferred on to
a recent experience" (1965, 585)—including experiences with picturebooks. In the case of Little Hans, a picturebook illustration helps Freud

make sense of a horse phobia. In the Wolf Man's case, the patient's dream of the wolves derives in part from a childhood encounter with "the picture of a wolf in a book of fairy tales," in which, as Freud reports, "the wolf was standing upright, striding out with one foot, with its claws stretched out and its ears pricked" (1963e, 187). Freud theorizes that the Wolf Man's recollection of this image gets entangled with his (screen) memory of the fairy tales "The Wolf and the Seven Little Goats" and "Little Red Riding Hood." Freud does not muse explicitly on the picturebook as an imagetext form or genre, despite his sense, in *The Interpretation of Dreams,* of the dreamwork as a "pictographic script," a "picture puzzle" (1965, 312). Others, of course, have pursued this line of inquiry.

Ronald R. Thomas reminds us that Freud's theory of the dreamwork is indebted to scenes of dreaming in Victorian literature as well as to Freud's own dreams. *The Interpretation of Dreams* "may even justifiably be read as Freud's own autobiographical novel," he suggests, "in which he recovers the unconscious material of his own childhood, refashions it into an account of the operations of the mind, and establishes his authority as a scientist of the psyche" (1990, 3). Moreover, the "paradigmatic plot" of both literature and psychoanalysis "as mediated by the dream, revolves around questions of authority. Nineteenth-century literary dreams are *always* dreams of authority" (2; emphasis in the original). While Sendak does not position himself as an authority on the dream, he does self-identify as an authoritative dreamer of childhood and its discontents, drawing from a store of dreamtexts and translating them into picturebooks.

Even as he drew from real life, Sendak styled his work after that of Winsor McCay, creator of the comic strip *Little Nemo in Slumberland.* In a 1973 tribute to McCay, republished in *Caldecott and Co.* (1988e), Sendak remarks, "McCay and I serve the same master, our child selves . . . and neither of us forget our childhood dreams" (78). "McCay re-created dreams that we all had as children," he continues, "but few of us remember—or care to remember. . . . In Slumberland, as in Wonderland, irrational taboos, forbidden places, and terrifying creatures confront our hero at every turn" (81). In every strip, Little Nemo sleeps, dreams, and awakes—often screaming or falling out of bed, as his dreams are usually nightmares. Once Sendak "did a Rosie"—

imagined himself in place of the creative child: he drew kids dreaming as well as drawing. But unlike Little Nemo and the Wolf Man, Sendak's child dreamers do not typically suffer nightmares. In both *Kenny's Window* and *Where the Wild Things Are,* Sendak transforms dreams of Wild Things into fortifying experiences for the child.

The Wolf Man case is the best-known or most canonical of all Freud's case histories. In February 1910, a young, wealthy Russian aristocrat named Sergey Pankejeff came to Freud for help with some serious psychological symptoms. The analysis lasted until 1914 and focused on a neurosis that had occurred between the ages of four and ten, as suggested by the official case title, *From the History of an Infantile Neurosis.* The case revolves around a "specimen dream" occurring just before the Wolf Man's fourth birthday but recollected during the analysis. Here is the Wolf Man's account of the dream, as reproduced by Freud:

> *I dreamt that it was night and that I was lying in my bed. (My bed stood with its foot towards the window; in front of the window there was a row of old walnut trees. I know it was winter when I had the dream, and night-time.) Suddenly the window opened of its own accord, and I was terrified to see that some white wolves were sitting on the big walnut tree in front of the window. There were six or seven of them. The wolves were quite white, and looked more like foxes or sheep-dogs, for they had big tails like foxes and they had their ears pricked like dogs when they are attending to something. In great terror, evidently of being eaten up by the wolves, I screamed* and woke up. (1963e, 186; italics in the original)

To accompany this report the Wolf Man gave Freud a drawing of the dream, the first of many such renderings. In the drawing, against a blank background, five white wolves perch ominously on the craggy branches of a tree. There are five wolves instead of the six or seven in the narrated account. Freud used the dream and the case history to argue for the staying power of infantile experience and to theorize about the origins of obsessional neurosis. While both Freud and the Wolf Man were satisfied with the course of treatment, the Wolf Man's symptoms later returned, and he spent the rest of his life in and out of therapy.[15]

And here is the beginning of *Kenny's Window:*

> In the middle of a dream, Kenny woke up. And he remembered a garden.
>
> "I saw a garden in my dream," thought Kenny, "and a tree."
>
> There was a tree covered white with blossoms. And above the tree shone the sun and the moon side by side. Half the garden was filled with yellow morning and the other with dark green night.
>
> "There was something else in my dream," thought Kenny, and he tried to remember.
>
> "A train," he cried, "and a rooster with four feet and he gave me something."
>
> There was a train puffing its way through the garden and in the caboose sat a rooster with four feet and he gave Kenny a piece of paper.
>
> "Here," said the rooster, "are seven questions and you must find all the answers."
>
> "If I do," asked Kenny, "may I come and live in the garden?"
>
> But before the rooster could answer, the dream ended.

Kenny then sets about answering the seven questions, which are:

1. Can you draw a picture on the blackboard when somebody doesn't want you to?
2. What is an only goat?
3. Can you see a horse on the roof?
4. Can you fix a broken promise?
5. What is a Very Narrow Escape?
6. What looks inside and what looks outside?
7. Do you always want what you think you want? (1956, n.p.)

Instead of six or seven white wolves, we get seven seemingly absurd questions and a tree covered in white blossoms; in place of the eerie moonlight scene depicted by Freud's patient, we have a split scene of day and night. While more philosophical than sexual, at least on the surface, Kenny's questions echo the questions of the Wolf Man and in-

deed the "researches" of small children. Beginning his quest, Kenny
tries to draw a picture on the blackboard, remarking,

> "I'll call it A Dream" (capital letters).
> "NO!" cried an angry voice. "You cannot draw on the
> blackboard today!"
> "Why not?" asked Kenny.
> "Because!" said the voice.

The voice belongs to Bucky, Kenny's stuffed animal, who refuses the
role of collaborator or transitional object. Bucky is upset because Kenny
has neglected him, and after writing a poem for Bucky, Kenny can draw
his dream picture on the blackboard, a picture featuring Bucky astride
the dream rooster, a distorted image of the dream we have been told
about. As he pursues the other questions, Kenny has close encounters
with a white goat, lead soldiers, his dog Baby, and his friend David. At
the book's end, on another dreamy, moonlit night, the rooster returns to
hear Kenny's answers. The hardest of all is the seventh, "Do you always
want what you think you want?" "I thought I wanted to live in the
garden with the moon on one side and the sun on the other, but I really
don't," concludes Kenny. That we don't always want what we think we
want is one of Freud's central lessons.

Sendak has never mentioned any direct influence of the Wolf Man
case on *Kenny's Window* or *Where the Wild Things Are,* although he
has repeatedly acknowledged the general impact of Freudian analysis
on his life and work. Sendak was inspired to write *Kenny's Window*
after reading, in a period of depression and on the advice of his analyst,
Dorothy W. Baruch's 1952 case history *One Little Boy.* Baruch was a
psychoanalytically trained therapist who wrote a number of popular
texts on child-rearing as well as books for children. *One Little Boy* is
an account of a seven-year-old boy named Kenneth brought into treatment because of his failure in school, which turns out to be a symptom for family dysfunction and emotional distress. Baruch adminis-
ters play therapy in the tradition of Klein, working closely with Kenny
and even explaining to him the principles of treatment. The book is
sometimes described as an account of autism; in fact, Kenny's problems
are more generic, the result of family dynamics and childhood anxiety
generalizable to all children. Eschewing Freudian terminology, Baruch

nonetheless takes us through the usual Freudian story of psychosexual development, explaining how she gave Kenny permission to be bad, so that "he would now be a fraction less afraid of two things: of his own inner feelings running wildly out of hand, and of retribution from me" (1964, 39). With her help, Kenny learns to express anger—and his parents learn to put aside their own fears. His imaginative world is "as illogical and full of fantasy as are all children's," writes Baruch. "From the vantage point of adult logic, they looked as strangely distorted as images seen in the mirrors of funhouses" (103).

As Bader notes, while *Kenny's Window* is not a direct translation of *One Little Boy* into picturebook form, "the seven episodes that answer the questions for Kenny deal figuratively with yearnings or fears that Kenneth confronts and comes to terms with in the course of his therapy" (1976, 504–5). By the end of his adventures, Kenny no longer wants to live in isolation in the magic garden, is no longer fearful of himself or others. Sendak aligns himself with Freud and Baruch alike, while taking a cue from an earlier generation of picturebook psychologists. Sendak develops his picturebook as a therapeutic exercise, a working-through of desire, prohibition, and anger undertaken on behalf of the child subject. It is a fascinating picturebook, but not a very successful one. Many readers find it enigmatic or too existential. Bader remarks that the book's shape is "unintelligible because Kenny is indistinct" (505); we do not know enough about his situation to understand his experiences. Another, more significant problem is a hovering adult presence in the text, not the presence of parent figures but rather that of the author, who presides over Kenny's recovery. *Kenny's Window* fails in part because its psychological program is too obvious.

"The picture books that become classics do so," writes Ellen Spitz, "because they dare to tackle important and abiding psychological themes, and because they convey these themes with craftsmanship and subtlety" (1999, 8). By this standard, the "classic" status of *Where the Wild Things Are* should come as no surprise; indeed, the book functions for Spitz (among many others) as the exemplary picturebook. In fact, it helped set the stage for what makes a picturebook a classic; classicism or canonicity is not a naturally occurring phenomenon but rather the result of particular values and practices. Psychological depth alongside "craftsmanship" and "subtlety" are certainly to be found in the book.

Unlike *Kenny's Window, Where the Wild Things Are* gets the dream-work just right. Moreover, there is little sense of authorial presence; the story seems to tell itself.

Sendak made the first dummy for *Where the Wild Things Are* in 1956, calling it "Where the Wild Horses Are." Displeased with it, he put the dummy aside until 1963, after he had written several other books of his own and illustrated many others. At that point, he still struggled with the concept, at first writing several horse-themed versions (including one about "nightmares") before finally deciding he could not draw horses and revising to the generic and far less threatening "things" (see Cech 1995, 126–36). On May 25, 1963, he composed a new dummy featuring eighteen illustrations and only 380 words, far fewer than in the first version. Given the level of revision that went into this book, we might even call it overdetermined, like the dreamwork itself. In one of the best analyses of Sendak's book, Perry Nodelman calls attention to the complexities of its spatial and temporal design, including its alternation of "action" shots with scenes of Max suspended "in a dreamlike stasis" (1988, 162).

Where the Wild Things Are is more clearly about the possibility of self-fulfillment, in keeping with broader cultural trends. Steven Mintz and Susan Kellogg note that while American child-rearing literature had previously been dominated by just a handful of manuals—the foremost being Benjamin Spock's *Baby and Child Care*—the field "rapidly grew more crowded and confused during the 1960s," and by 1981 more than six hundred books on the subject were in print (1988, 220). The new manuals shifted emphasis away from children's thinking and toward their feeling. By the mid-1960s, notes Eugene Schwartz, books on child-care suddenly had "many discussions on 'feelings' (virtually absent from earlier volumes)" (1999, 46). The literature remained focused on the mother–child relationship, and there were strong traces of Freudian thought inherited from the so-called Freudian forties, especially in the extent that "feelings" were thought to be able to signify the unconscious. By the 1960s, the so-called humanistic or third-force psychology of Abraham Maslow, Carl Rogers, and Erich Fromm had come to dominate the popular scene, placing great premium on individual happiness and self-realization. Child-rearing discourse since Spock had already imagined a kinder, gentler parenting, setting the stage for further modification. Accounts of this trend vary; its advocates welcomed it as an alternative to the pessimism of psychoanalysis and behaviorism, whereas skeptics saw it as vacuous and anti-intellectual.

In *Where the Wild Things Are,* published amid this overhaul of child-rearing literature, we see the importance of feelings, both in a residually Freudian sense and in the context of humanistic psychology. Sendak is perfectly attuned to the complexities of his time and represents them as we might well expect: through a dream, one that echoes but tames the Wolf Man's dream and other variants of wolf-boy narrative. Running amok in a wolf suit and making mischief "of one kind / and another," young Max is sent off to bed supperless. His room dreamily becomes a forest—bedposts turning into trees and carpet into grass; the moon escaping the window frame. An ocean tumbles by and Max sails "off through night and day / and in and out of weeks / and almost over a year / to where the wild things are." Five Wild Things welcome Max as their king. The wild rumpus, which runs several pages and constitutes a centerfold of sorts, is wordless, not unlike the Wolf Man's dream of the wolves. Both "dreams" are moonlit, essentially nonverbal episodes. Postrumpus, Max grows bored and homesick and sails back "into the night of his very own room," where he finds his supper waiting for him—"and it was still hot."

There are of course key differences between the Wolf Man's dream of the wolves and Max's dream of the Wild Things. The situation of the protagonist is particularly crucial. The Wolf Man reports in distress: "It seemed as though [the wolves] had riveted their whole attention upon me" (Freud 1963e, 186). Max, too, is the center of attention, but he is firmly and happily in charge, staring into the Wild Things' yellow eyes until they look away and sending them to bed without supper. Max, notes McGillis, is aggressive and destructive and "the book is replete with images of phallic aggressiveness: the strong vertical lines of erect trees, bedposts, Max's scepter, his ship's mast, and the horns of some of the Wild Things" (1996, 80). Because Max's anger is directed partly toward his mother, explains McGillis, the Wild Things are "parodic of adults" rather than scary (81). Even at their most menacing, the Wild Things have a friendly countenance, their arms extended in welcome and their forms suggestively human.[16] "Whereas Freud's patient feared animals," McGillis points out, "Max is one" (82). McGillis notes that in an early version of the story, Max does not wear a wolf suit; rather, he meets a character claiming to be his mother who then turns into a rapacious wolf.[17] This aborted plot resonates with the Wolf Man's dream and with wolf-themed fairy tales, whereas in Sendak's version, the mother is firmly linked with care and feeding (rather than with child-devouring). Whereas the Wolf Man spends the rest of his life in analysis, never successfully overcoming his phobias, Max works through his anger and returns to a hot supper. Max needs no dramatic intervention, only an understanding mother and some time and space of his own.

Avuncular Expertise; or, Sendak's Queer Authority

By midcentury, if not before, picturebook creators were being praised for staying close to childhood—sometimes to such a degree that they had to defend their work as sufficiently adult. The picturebook author-illustrator became something like an expert on childhood, even a lay child analyst, whose knowledge was intuitive, personal, and creative rather than clinical. Expertise came from proximity to childhood alongside skill in the picturebook genre. In keeping with this expectation, some author-illustrators have aligned themselves with adult experts, whereas others identify as fellow travelers of the child.

Even so, the designation of the author as informal or avuncular child expert has occurred on behalf of parents as well as children. Spitz emphasizes the relational role that parents play in reading books with their children and thereby creating a safe holding environment. But just as parents provide safety and guidance for their children, author-illustrators arguably do the same for parents, providing them with imaginative and educational material to use at home. The picturebook provides lessons in visual and cultural literacy for the child even as it ushers the parent into text-centered practices of child-rearing.

Ann Hulbert implies something along these lines when she discusses Dr. Benjamin Spock and Dr. Seuss in relation to American child-rearing:

A child born in the middle of the baby boom might be forgiven for getting Dr. Spock and Dr. Seuss mixed up. It seemed somehow possible that the cat with the striped stovepipe that bossed the kids in the beloved beginner book also inhabited the well-thumbed paperback that told parents what to do. America's lanky, legendary pediatric expert as the Cat in the Hat: the image links two upstart heroes in the postwar generation's pantheon. . . . Dr. Spock joined Dr. Seuss in making room for fantasy—often frightening—in the psyches of the young, and of their parents. . . . Yet they also insisted that everybody come to terms with reality—and more than that, develop a sense of mastery and of social morality. . . . These solicitous doctors, chatty and funny though they could be, were very serious. (2003, 225–27)

Like Spock's baby manual, the picturebook is designed for home use, but unlike the more official child expert, the picturebook creator either fades into the background (as with less well-known author-illustrators) or serves as a fun, friendly, child-knowledgeable personality, as with Dr. Seuss and Sendak after him.

Dr. Seuss is our other hypercanonical picturebook master. By 2001, his work had outsold that of Sendak and indeed every other children's author, including the Harry Potter books of J. K. Rowling (Nel 2006, 12). While Dr. Seuss's earlier books had been reasonably successful, his breakthrough book was *The Cat in the Hat,* published in 1957. Designed as a beginning reader in response to John Hersey's call for an alternative to Dick and Jane primers, *The Cat in the Hat* became so much more; "it is also," writes Maria Tatar, "a vehicle for discovering a world of make-believe . . . a lesson in using imagination" (2009, 171). Unlike Sendak, however, Dr. Seuss routinely disavowed any psychological meaning in his books, despite ongoing attempts to interpret *The Cat in the Hat* along Freudian lines.[18] His picturebooks do function more obviously as moral or cautionary tales, their didacticism softened by zaniness. Dr. Seuss is a master of nonsense and wordplay, heir to Brown, Stein, and Krauss. I would describe him as a daytime psychologist, more interested in daydreams than dreams, which seem to be Sendak's preoccupation. Whereas *The Cat in the Hat* was written to induce children to read, *Where the Wild Things Are* was written to induce them to dream.

But Dr. Seuss and Sendak share an avuncular, creative authority, relishing their role as spokesmen for childhood. They and a few other

picturebook men (Shel Silverstein comes also to mind) are posi
uncles rather than father figures.[19] A humorous acknowledgment of his
father's unfulfilled hope that he would earn a doctorate in literature,
the "Dr." in Theodore Geisel's pen name pokes fun at academic preten-
sion, while also signifying Dr. Seuss's expertise and achievement. He
may not be a doctor of literature or medicine, but he holds something
like an honorary doctorate in childhood thanks to the success of his
books. Neither Geisel nor Sendak had children (nor did Silverstein, to
my knowledge), and not a few other famous children's writers were likewise childless—Philip Nel lists Lewis Carroll, Edward Lear, Beatrix
Potter, Margaret Wise Brown, Crockett Johnson, and Ruth Krauss
(2006, 7). Their childlessness is variously read as dysfunctional or enabling (and sometimes both) in relation to markers such as marital status, gender, and sexuality. Geisel and Sendak at least are assumed to
be close to childhood in part because they do not have children. Their
expertise is bound up with their avuncular singularity or eccentricity,
even their queerness.

Where the Wild Things Are has a curious status, belonging to everyone and celebrated as a universal story, but with an intensely personal
origin. While a queer interpretation of Sendak's work has yet to emerge,
a foundation for such has been established by McGillis, who emphasizes the polymorphous libido of Max. Indeed, a queer reading might
recast many of the observations already made in the scholarship about
Max's hybridity, passion, and performativity. Max may well be (or may
have become) an exemplary subject of humanist child-rearing and child
psychology, but he is also queer to some degree—hard to manage, independent, animal-identified.

Sendak's creative life is integrally connected to his ongoing struggles for personal as well as professional satisfaction. His depression
and adventures in therapy surely had something to do with his life as
a closeted gay man in pre-Stonewall New York. Before that, Sendak
had what might fairly be described as a queer childhood. Talking with
Jonathan Cott, Sendak remarks, "I was miserable as a kid. . . . I couldn't
make friends, I couldn't play stoopball terrific, I couldn't skate great.
I stayed home and drew pictures. You *know* what they all thought of
me: sissy Maurice Sendak" (quoted in Cott 1983, 45). Sendak recalls
that as a teenager he began illustrating his own books, beginning with

Oscar Wilde's *The Happy Prince* and moving on to Bret Harte's *The Luck of Roaring Camp*. "It was my favorite story, and what is it about? A baby that is adopted by a lot of rough men, lumberjacks—an illegitimate child abandoned after the death of its mother" (46). Sendak's creative activity served as a sort of survival or coping strategy. Sendak goes on to discuss the book then in development, *Outside Over There*, also about a baby, albeit with goblins rather than lumberjacks. *Outside Over There* is Sendak's favorite book, not only because it was the hardest to make (as he has often said) but perhaps also because it is a strange and melancholic story, revolving as it does around a baby's abduction by goblins and subsequent rescue by her older sister, Ida. Sendak likens the creative experience to "getting pregnant when you've just gone crazy and you've found out your house has burned down" (60)—an interesting analogy for a male writer to make. It is worth noting that Sendak identifies just as strongly with his girl protagonists (Rosie, Ida) as with his boy ones.

Steven Cheslik-DeMeyer suggests that *Where the Wild Things Are* is a coming-out story in thin disguise, a story about finding community outside civil, straight society (outside, over there). "At the end of the story," he writes, "Max goes home reassured that, no matter how much he may feel at odds with his family, there is another family, his family of wild things like him who dance and howl with joy in a land far away but reachable" (n.d., 7–8). Art historian Whitney Davis offers us another route to the queerness of Max and Sendak by way of a provocative reading of the Wolf Man case, titled (appropriately enough) *Drawing the Dream of the Wolves* (1995). Davis proposes that a major intersubjective dimension of the case has been missed, one vital to Freud's influential construction of homosexuality. The Wolf Man, he points out, draws *for* Freud, both literally and through words, hoping to make Freud interested in and happy with him. Freud in turn "draws" the Wolf Man, giving his patient a mythology linked with the "specimen dream" of the wolves and the various sketches produced in its wake. Identifying the Wolf Man as a "latent" homosexual, Freud fails to acknowledge his homoerotic investment in the Wolf Man, holds Davis, and suppresses his childhood encounters with a suggestive, scary wolf picture.

Even more tellingly, Davis unearths a favorite illustrated book of

Freud's that he sees as key to the case history. The book in question is an 1865 edition of Friedrich von Tschudi's *Animal Life in the Alpine World,* which features an illustration of a wolfish and menacing-looking rescue dog saving a little boy lost in the snow, its ears pricked and its sharp teeth clearly visible (Davis 1995, 200–1). The illustration bears a striking resemblance to the Wolf Man's "memories" of the wolf dream and of the fairy-tale illustrations he apparently encountered in childhood; in fact, notes Davis, the von Tschudi image looks *more* like the latter than does the scene from the Wolf Man's dream. Freud's concept of latent homosexuality emerges out of his intersubjective, unconscious relationship with the Wolf Man, in and around formative if forgotten images.[20]

As Sendak may have taken a cue from Freud in his picturebook work, Freud may have already himself taken a cue from von Tschudi's illustrated book, devising his famous case history out of a children's book, with Sendak translating it back into one. If, as Davis argues, Freud's case history hinges on an unrealized homoerotic dimension, might that have influenced Sendak in some way, and if so, how and to what effects? Was the avuncular Sendak drawn to the case because it deals so extensively with the question of same-sex desire in and around childhood and dreams? Davis emphasizes that for Freud, the theory of latent homosexuality is at root a theory of human intersubjectivity, latency implying the potential for actualization, and not only of sexuality. The Wolf Man was based on a real person, and perhaps Max was, too—perhaps on Sendak himself or on an idealized boy whose dreams he hoped to nurture. In any event, *Where the Wild Things Are* is in part a dreambook and a case history, drawn from Sendak's encounters with real children as well as from his own memories of a queer childhood.

Queerness, of course, extends beyond the sexual, and in Sendak's case might apply to everything about his life and work that is nonconformist or challenging. Sendak, we might say, is queer because he is gay *and* Jewish *and* irascible.[21] "He is not, as children's book writers are often supposed, an everyman's grandpa," notes Patricia Cohen (2008). "His hatreds are fierce and grand, as if produced by Cecil B. DeMille." Even if *Where the Wild Things Are* represents a more easily assimilated Sendak, his larger body of work complicates the story, disassociating the picturebook from happy endings and even the dream of imaginative mastery. We need only point to *Brundibar,* written by Kushner (2003b) and illustrated by Sendak and based on a 1938 opera subsequently performed by children in the Theresienstadt concentration camp; or to *Dear Mili* (Grimm 1988), the grim Brothers Grimm tale that Sendak illustrated; or to Sendak's *We Are All in the Dumps with Jack and Guy* (1993), a response to homelessness and AIDS and dedicated to another gay picturebook artist, the late James Marshall. *Where the Wild Things Are,* while powerful, is but one small part of Sendak's queer achievement.

Wild at Heart

Initially meeting with some disapproval, *Where the Wild Things Are* quickly found status as a psychological as well as aesthetic masterpiece. Psychologist Michael Thompson, for instance, proclaims it "the best book on boy anger" (2000, 165). Whatever its complexities, it has none-theless been received as a psychological primer. Sendak himself au-thorized that view in his 1964 Caldecott acceptance speech: "Through fantasy, Max, the hero of my book, discharges his anger against his mother, and returns to the real world sleepy, hungry, and at peace with himself" (1988a, 151). In that speech, Sendak remarked, "I feel like I am at the end of a long apprenticeship," anticipating work even more attuned to "the child's endless battle with disturbing emotions" (154). *Where the Wild Things Are* has a place in our culture because it made classic the idea of the picturebook as hard psychological work.

Bettelheim seemed to recognize Sendak as a rival authority on childhood. Bettelheim's attention was directed to Sendak's book by a group of mothers with whom he met regularly at the Sonia Shankman Orthogenic School. Bettelheim's "dialogues" with that group were published as a column, "Dialogue with Mothers," in the *Ladies Home Journal.* Sendak's book comes up in the context of one mother's concern, reported in a 1969 column titled "The Care and Feeding of Monsters," about her son's visions of a "bad man" in the home; she worries that Sendak's "beautiful monsters" might have caused the boy's anxieties. Bettelheim then asks, "Why do we give children books with monsters in them?" going on to say,

I don't know the book, but I'm skeptical. You haven't convinced me that the child *really* believes the monsters are his
invention and that he therefore controls them. It's entirely
possible that some children believe this; on the other hand,
like the sorcerer's apprentice, when you've got a monster by
the tail you can't know for sure that it won't turn against you.
(1969, 48)

Bettelheim holds that Sendak's book emerges from "the psychology of
the writer" rather than from "the psychology of the child." "The old-
fashioned fairy-tale, which was gruesome enough, had one redeeming
feature," he writes. "It came out of the fantasy of the adult, not out of
what the adult thought was the fantasy of the child, and in this way
it was more or less authentic." Admitting, "it may be very unfair on
my part," Bettelheim doubts the accuracy of adult claims to knowledge about the child's psychic life. More to the point, he questions the
power of an author to mimic or simulate the therapeutic process. When
it comes to monsters, remarks Bettelheim, a child needs to be shown
"that these persecuting figures are really the creation of his own mind.
Now, if that could be done simply by the reading of a book, people
like me would be out of business." No author, in short, is qualified to
be a *real* psychologist. "It takes me a year or more of very hard work,
of doing a wide variety of things, to get a disturbed child to the point
where he's in control of the persecuting figures he creates in his imagination." The mothers seem resistant to this critique, asking him, "But
why do children *love* this book?" and remarking, "But the book isn't
necessarily harmful to a secure child." Bettelheim struggles to respond.
In this discussion, Bettelheim seems to be thinking through his position
on fairy tales, remarking, "You see, fairy stories were very gruesome,
but most of them held a very clear message: the evil-doer gets punished
and the good are rewarded and live happily ever after. . . . Now, I'm not
pleading here for some of these gruesome fairy stories" (48). He pleads
just so only a little later.

Where the Wild Things Are now stands for a reigning orthodoxy,
its reception perhaps too powerfully determined by a larger psychological plot of adventure and mastery. Sendak himself does not think it is
his best work, but popular opinion and scholarship alike reflect this

orthodoxy. Moreover, there is very little critique of Sendak's book. I have found no class-oriented analysis at all, and feminist commentary is decidedly pro-Sendak.[22] Interpretations from a postcolonial studies perspective likewise tend toward affirmation. Both John Clement Ball (1997) and Jennifer Shaddock (1997–98) acknowledge the book's colonialist echoes but conclude that Sendak's relation to colonialist narrative is ironic. Both situate the book in relation to psychology as well, Ball developing a psychoanalytic reading and Shaddock arguing that Sendak interrogates the opposition of wild and civilized in the idiom of 1960s psychology. Although Shaddock concludes that Sendak's psychological refashioning of wild amounts to a critique, the book's popularity is probably due to the broader cultural success of such refashioning, probably not so ironic. That is, lovers of *Where the Wild Things Are* probably do see it not as a child's version of Joseph Conrad's *Heart of Darkness* but, rather, as a self-help book for children and their parents. It is, in other words, part of the culture of self-help, even if also a deconstruction of such. In different ways, Ball and Shaddock raise the question of how to historicize psychology in a culture largely (in)formed by psychological discourse. We are arguably all colonizers of the psyche, even as we are also all its subaltern subjects, which makes all the trickier the historicist understanding of picturebook psychology.

Offering alternatives to psychological readings of *Where the Wild Things Are,* Nodelman and McGillis nevertheless leave room for the possibility that Sendak's book performs psychological work. McGillis speculates that it "touches on each reader's Oedipal experience," remarking that the "experience of reading this book gives us the pleasure of having our fantasies taken care of. We are complicit with the literary text" (1996, 179–80). Noting that "many good picture books manage to capture a childlike guilelessness—a sort of defenseless and vulnerable fantasizing that comes very close to dream," Nodelman "can only conclude they do so because they speak symbolically to a level of human understanding that is below consciousness" (1988, 109).[23] More recently Nodelman takes a Pierre Bourdieu–inspired position, suggesting that Sendak's "especially intense grasp of the habitus" enabled him to take "a position that was not actually there to be taken in the field of children's literature as it existed at that time"—namely, the position that childhood can itself be monstrous, and usefully so (2008, 121, 120).

Sendak's angle on the monstrosity theme, in and around a broader refashioning of wildness, made for "startling but acceptable innovation" (123) within the field of picturebooks. *Where the Wild Things Are* in turn made possible further domestications of the monstrous (think Muppets). Nodelman anticipates much of what I have suggested in this chapter. While Sendak neither romanticizes the child nor minimizes the child's experiences with trauma, his makeover of monstrosity amounts to a kind of gentling of the child rather than a celebration of childhood's radical alterity.

Sendak's success can be attributed to his alignment with both Freud and revisionist, mainstream psychology. As a point of contrast, consider another picturebook psychologist, author-illustrator William Steig, a former patient and then lifelong devotee of the psychoanalyst Wilhelm Reich, famous for his theories concerning "orgone energy" and for his orgone accumulators (or orgone boxes). "Rarely has a deeper affinity between a psychologist and an artist existed than between Wilhelm Reich and William Steig" (Cott 1983, 90). Prior to his encounter with Reich, Steig was best known for a series of wry pictorial satires on the human condition, but his picturebook work, which began in 1968, is more positive in tone, focused on the potential of children rather than on the neuroses of adults.[24] Steig's picturebooks—among them *Sylvester and the Magic Pebble* (1969), *Dominic* (1972), *The Amazing Bone* (1976), and especially *Gorky Rises* (1980)—seem to illustrate Reich's ideas without amounting to propaganda.[25] Like Sendak, Steig saw himself as an advocate of both childhood and the creative life, in keeping with the general discourse of picturebook psychology.[26] But while Steig's picturebooks are known and loved, the Reichian psychology behind them is not public knowledge; *Where the Wild Things Are,* by contrast, is widely appreciated as applied psychology, even commonsense Freudianism.

Sendak has asserted his independence from Freud by representing himself as having worked-through psychoanalysis or the problems to which psychoanalysis attends. As early as 1964, in his Caldecott acceptance speech, Sendak insisted that Max "is having fun, and not by playing hide-and-see with Sigmund Freud" (1988a, 152). Writing about his response to Jean de Brunhoff's Babar books in the 1950s, Sendak remarks, "I was then a green recruit fresh from the analyst's couch and woe betide any work that failed to loudly signal its Freudian allegiance. With a convert's proverbial fervor, I rushed pell-mell into the very heart of what I considered Babar's unresolved problem: his mother's death, of course" (1988c, 97). Sendak credits de Brunhoff's son Laurent for urging him "out of my frantic Freudian 'dig'" (98) and into more-nuanced modes of understanding and artistic practice. In a 1993 interview with Leonard S. Marcus, Sendak describes *Outside Over There* as "an excavation of my soul, the last archaeological Sendakian dig!" (Marcus 2002, 176). "You could be describing an end to therapy," says Marcus. "In a sense, yes," replies Sendak, "a very rich sense" (176).

Sendak's recent willingness to allow a live-action film version of *Where the Wild Things Are* (Jonze 2009)—and to give its director, Spike Jonze, carte blanche—seems further evidence of Sendak's letting go of the book and what it represents in his own history. Sendak had little to do with the film, in contrast to his intense involvement with a 1973 animated short film and with opera versions of his book. Jonze wrote the screenplay with Dave Eggers, who subsequently wrote a novel based on the screenplay, ostensibly at the urging of Sendak (Eggers 2009, 287). While the film and novel versions of *Where the Wild Things Are* differ significantly from the source text, they retain much of the book's apparent message. Jonze and Eggers give the story a realistic update: Max, played by nine-year-old Max Records, is now a lonely, rebellious child of divorced parents. Whereas Sendak's picturebook does not mention a father, Max's father in the film is explicitly framed as absent. Max longs for attention from his mother and is unhappy about her new boyfriend; he also battles with and craves the company of his older sister. The first part of the film beautifully depicts Max's loneliness, his struggle for visibility, and his rich imagination and is in many ways more compelling than the fantasy encounters that follow. In *Heads On and We Shoot: The Making of "Where the Wild Things Are,"* Jonze and Eggers emphasize the importance of Max's "realism": "We wanted to make sure that Max acts like a real boy—breaking things and throwing tantrums, the kind of kid who would play with swords and slingshots" (2009, xi). Max is modeled on the "real" boyhoods of Eggers, Jonze, and Sendak, as well as ostensibly realistic boy characters in various films (xi).

Max still wears his wolf suit and makes mischief. But rather than transforming Max's bedroom into a forest, as in Sendak's book, Jonze and Eggers send an angry Max running into the woods and then to the edge of a lake, where he discovers the boat that transports him to where the Wild Things are. Sendak objected to this change, as Jonze and Eggers report. "But it seemed like the idea of the movie being real and really dangerous," they explain, "would require Max to actually be in a forest and on a real boat" (x). "If we know everything that follows just takes place in his imagination," they explain, "then there's not as much at stake the next hour of the movie. We really wanted it to seem like a small boy sailed across the ocean, and, when he was on the island, that he was truly in danger of being devoured" (x).

The biggest transformation from book to film, however, is in the Wild Things themselves: in lieu of Sendak's mute beasts, Max encounters seven oversize Wild Things with proper names and distinct, decidedly human personalities—personalities that recall those of Max and his family. There's Carol, leader of the group and generally Max's alter ego, as well as Judith, Douglas, KW (Katherine in Eggers's novel), Alexander, Ira, and the enigmatic, silent Bull. These Wild Things seem at once curious children and knowledgeable, worldly adults. The Wild Things embody and reflect back Max's emotional problems.

While Max loves playing king, his adventures with the Wild Things turn sour and frightening. Sendak's Max quickly masters the Wild Things and then grows bored, but the cinematic Max grows less and less sure of his command over the Wild Things and of his desire to live among them. These Wild Things are not so easily or permanently tamed, and their capriciousness and sheer size—part of their realism[27]—make them quite dangerous. In this respect, Max's feelings hover somewhere between the confidence of Sendak's protagonist and the terror of the Wolf Man. The Wild Things seem to know that they are a menace to Max and help send him on his way home. Max's return, still triumphant, seems also a narrow escape.

While most reviews of the film have been positive, not a few have found it less a film for children than one about them. Whereas the picturebook is designed for very young children, notes A. O. Scott, the film seems "pitched either at 5-year-old graduates of progressive nursery schools or at 25-year-old graduates of progressive liberal arts colleges" (2009). Other reviewers have suggested it might be appropriate for or enjoyed by older children, say in the eight-to-twelve range. (Jonze and Eggers originally imagined their Max to be seven or eight, and Max Records was nine.) Eggers's novelization is explicitly for adults, although some older children might tackle its 288 pages. It seems aimed at those twenty-five-year-old graduates, or at parents who remember the book from their own childhoods. I bought my copy—available in plain or furry binding—at Urban Outfitters, where it was displayed amid other *Wild Things* merchandise. Like the film, the novel expands on the psychology of Max's fractured family. Eggers's Max is more introspective and self-aware than the cinematic Max. Whereas Sendak makes clear that Max's rage springs from the unconscious and lets the shape of the adventure itself speak to/about Max's anger and anger management, Eggers's older Max reflects on his darker impulses and feels guilty about them. "Max wondered why he was the way he was. . . . There were so many things he'd done, so many things he'd broken or torn or said, and always he knew he'd done them, but could only half-understand why" (Eggers 2009, 34). When his mother asks, "What the hell is wrong with you?" we are told, "Max was wondering the same thing about himself" (39). Max seems hostage to his anger, but he is aware of it. At one point, he even wills himself into wildness, as here: "So he had a choice. Would he stay behind the curtain and think about things, marinate in his own confusion, or would he put on his white fur suit and howl and scratch and make it known who was boss of this house and all the world known and unknown?" (73). It is as if Eggers expects his readers to expect Max to own his psychological condition.

If the film and novel retain some of the strangeness of Sendak's tale, they also further humanize it, making it clearly a story about children and parents, about the dynamics of family. This is a family film, whereas Sendak's book is more focused on the young child's emotional life. There is no doubt about the human identities of the Wild Things, since they talk and have names and remind Max of his adult familiars. Moreover, the film and novel openly embrace therapeutic culture. The wolf suit is transformed from a sign of Max's wildness to a therapeutic prop. "He usually felt better when he put on the wolf suit. He felt faster, sleeker, more powerful" (Eggers 2009, 72). Max's other prop is a journal given to him by his father, called a WANT journal. Max finds this journal helpful to a point, but when he is unusually angry, he dons the wolf suit.

Thus, the film and the novel continue the domestication of wildness. That is not to say that they do not have an edge. While humanesque, the Wild Things are also a menace to Max (more so than in Sendak), which suggests that even resourceful children need protection from the destructive power of adults. Max runs away not just because he is mad at Mom but also because home is a complicated place run by oversize creatures that are alternately caring and hurtful. Though the 2009 updates of Sendak's *Where the Wild Things Are* may continue its alignment with the heroic narrative of the child doing imaginative battle with his emotions, they also reflect a more contemporary emphasis on the vulnerability of childhood and of human subjectivity more generally, a vulnerability bordering on the existential.[28] These adaptations or sequels maintain the broader energies of picturebook psychology, even if Sendak has declared for himself an end to therapy.

The Triumph of the Therapeutic

Now in his eighties, Sendak has written or illustrated nearly seventy children's books; he has also illustrated adult classics and designed opera and ballet sets for stage and television. He has been awarded the Hans Christian Andersen Award, a National Medal of the Arts, and the Astrid Lindgren Memorial Award for Literature. Sendak's oeuvre is rich and complex and should not be eclipsed by *Where the Wild Things Are* or by its popularity. Sendak himself has expressed some ambivalence about the book's great esteem. When asked in 2003, "How does it feel to realize that your work—*Wild Things* in particular—is so much a part of public culture?" Sendak responded, "I'm not very impressed with being a catchword every time someone needs something to be 'wild,'" while acknowledging that *Where the Wild Things Are* has enabled him to "do all kinds of books that I probably never would have done" (quoted in R. Sutton 2003, 687). Some of Sendak's picturebook work in fact moves deliberately against the happy message of *Where the Wild Things Are* or against the assumption of that there is such a message, vis-à-vis humanistic psychology.

Even so, *Where the Wild Things Are* marked an important turning point for picturebook psychology, reworking in a contemporary idiom the themes and forms of progressive pedagogy and child analysis as well as those of Freud himself. The book is so much a part of public culture because it captured and expressed the psychological zeitgeist of 1960s America. We are still living with that zeitgeist, more or less. Even more postmodern or more metafictional picturebooks partake in what I have been calling picturebook psychology, inviting the playful engagement of the child and foregrounding the playful inventiveness of their creators. Picturebook psychology still emphasizes the psychosocial utility of the form for both children and their caretakers. In fact, there is a strong trend toward the explicitly bibliotherapeutic from the 1960s forward. Tomie DePaola's 1973 *Nana Upstairs and Nana Downstairs* and John Burningham's 1984 *Granpa,* for instance, were written to help young children cope with death. Often the titles of picturebooks make obvious their applied focus, as with Aliki's 1986 *Feelings,* Mercer Mayer's 1968 *There's a Nightmare in My Closet* and 1988 *There's Something in My Attic,* and of course Stan and Jan Berenstain's popular Berenstain Bears books of the 1980s, such as *The Berenstain Bears in the Dark, The Berenstain Bears Visit the Dentist, The Berenstain Bears and Too Much Junk Food,* and so forth.

If parents are unsure which picturebooks to use with their children, they can turn to resources such as child psychologist Jacqueline Golding's *Healing Stories: Picture Books for the Big and Small Changes in a Child's Life* (2006), an annotated guide to some five hundred picturebooks addressing such problems as sibling rivalry, moving, bullying, death, and war and violence. Dozens of articles in professional psychology and psychiatry journals now deal with the therapeutic value of children's books; Golding merges this professional literature with the literature of annotation provided by librarians. With or without the likes of Golding and such explicit thematizations within the texts, parents routinely turn to picturebooks for help with their children, tacitly acknowledging the author-illustrator as a partner in child-rearing. Some of this, at least, is the legacy of Sendak and of *Where the Wild Things Are.* Sendak has always taken picturebook work very seriously as hard, psychological work. When asked by Walter Lorraine, "Can you define what a picture book is for you?" Sendak replied thus:

> It's my battleground. It's where I express myself. It's where I consolidate my powers and put them together in what I hope

is a legitimate, viable form that is meaningful to somebody else and not just to me. It's where I work. It's where I put down those fantasies that have been with me all my life, and where I give them a *form* that means something. I live inside the picture book; that's where I fight all my battles, and where I hope to win my wars. (Sendak 1988b, 93)

5. "A Case History of Us All"

The Adolescent Novel before and after Salinger

IKE THE ADOLESCENT, THE ADOLESCENT novel has long been understood as a psychological form. This chapter historicizes the psychologization of adolescence and its literature, beginning not with the so-called problem novel for teenagers in the 1960s and 1970s,[1] a familiar starting place, but rather much earlier, with the foundational work of G. Stanley Hall. I identify three major stages in the psychologization of the genre: first, the articulation of adolescence in psychological as well as literary terms, beginning with Hall; second, the literary-psychological-ethnographic framing of a problem interior in and around the notion of "identity" and by way of explorations of gender and sexuality; and third, the transformation of that interior into a "young adulthood" at once confident and highly vulnerable, in such a way that adolescent literature begins to overlap with the literature of trauma.

I am indebted to Leerom Medovoi's *Rebels: Youth and the Cold War Origins of Identity,* which links the midcentury rise of "identity" as an American keyword to the coterminous emergence of two other categories, "teenager" and "rebel." Medovoi argues further that identity became a literary as well as a psychological term, calling this transformation "the protagonization of the American character" (2005, 56) and citing as its exemplary text J. D. Salinger's 1951 novel *The Catcher in the Rye*. The adolescent novel is but one index for Medovoi of the interlocking themes of rebellion and identity; *Rebels* is more a study of youth culture than of adolescent literature. Still, it helps set the stage for my analysis of adolescent literature and psychological discourse.

I also take a cue from Julia Kristeva's essay "The Adolescent Novel." "The adolescent," she proposes, "is a mythical figure of the imaginary that enables us to distance ourselves from some of our failings, splittings of the ego, disavowals, or mere desires, which it reifies into the figure of someone who has not yet grown up" (1995, 135). As a psychoanalyst Kristeva believes in the imaginary, the ego, and so forth, thus tending to universalize adolescence as a psychological experience. But she also gives that mythical figure of the imaginary a cultural history, proposing that adolescence and the novel emerged in relation to one another around the eighteenth century, with the rise of "psychological man" (her term). In her essay we see a productive tension between the historical and the psychological, a tension that Kristeva exploits rather than resolves, allowing for psychology (and adolescence) to be at once historical and ahistorical. Kristeva's formulation of the "'adolescent economy' of writing" (139) helps historicize the psychological aspects of the adolescent and the novel but also instantiates the third stage mentioned above, the construction of a vulnerable subjectivity.

Even if the novel and adolescent writing have eighteenth-century origins, as Kristeva maintains, the adolescent novel is a more modern and rather American phenomenon, one bound up with psychological discourse. With respect to Medovoi, I see the protagonization of the American character as beginning not with the midcentury theorists of identity but rather with Hall and an earlier wave of literary adolescence. In his monumental two-volume 1904 work *Adolescence: Its Psychology and Its Relations to Physiology, Anthropology, Sociology, Sex, Crime, Religion, and Education*, Hall not only takes up these various "relations" but also calls for the creation of a literature specifically for adolescents. Hall's romantic, developmentalist view of adolescence, positioned both alongside and against psychoanalysis, paved the way not only for the rise of teen-affiliated identity and identity politics but also for the prescriptive approach to adolescent literature now called bibliotherapeutic.

In narrating the pre–*Catcher in the Rye* history of adolescent literature, I neglect what Roberta Seelinger Trites calls the "adolescent reform novel," in part because her work on the subject is so illuminating. In *Twain, Alcott, and the Birth of the Adolescent Reform Novel* (2007), Trites proposes that the social reform novel, as pioneered by Mark Twain and Louisa May Alcott, continues to shape writing for adolescents, not only through particular themes and plots but also through their collective promotion of the adolescent as a "metaphor" for reform.[2] Hall's faith in the adolescent as a potential citizen may derive in part from the social reform tradition. While the psychological is not her major focus, Trites reminds us that what looks like psychological writing for adolescents in fact partakes of a broader discourse of social critique. Also, as she notes, adolescent reform literature that is descended from Alcott, including decidedly postmodern texts, often takes the form of the *künstlerroman,* a genre focused on aesthetic and psychological maturation. While I give priority to other material, I am indebted to this study and to her previous book, *Disturbing the Universe* (2000).

Contemporary writing for adolescents tends toward difficult, even traumatic subjects and situations, cycling back to earlier traditions of child rescue but in the contemporary language of vulnerability and endangerment. Some scholars of the genre in fact see adolescence as synonymous with *abjection,* a term introduced by Kristeva, and a more minor argument of this chapter is that abjection needs to be historicized as part of the psychoanalytic-literary repertoire.

Hall, Freud, and Ephebic Literature

As John Neubauer reports in *The Fin-de-Siècle Culture of Adolescence* (1992), the first literary works addressed to adolescents were penned in the late nineteenth century by British, European, and American writers, among them Jules Verne, Karl May, and Louisa May Alcott. Some of this literature appeared in magazines designed to counter the influence of dime novels and penny dreadfuls. Genres such as the bildungsroman and the school story began to portray adolescence as a distinct and crucial time of its own, not just a step toward maturity. By the end of that century, many novelists had turned their attention to the subject, as with Fyodor Dostoyevsky's 1874 work *The Adolescent,* André Gide's 1891 *Les cahiers d'André Walter,* and Henry James's 1897 *What Maisie Knew.* These texts emerged alongside works written for and even by adolescents, the latter in diary form.[3]

This literary groundswell was part of a broader transcontinental concern with adolescence. Adolescence has a rich and massive history, making generalization risky. That said, adolescence has typically been constructed as a problem or challenge. Rapid urbanization, alongside other sociohistorical pressures, gave rise to fears about the ostensible delinquency of youth—often including their mere presence on the streets—which paved the way for institutions such as compulsory schooling, juvenile justice work, and various character-building ventures. Adolescence was at once product and sustaining ideology of a wide array of social discourses as well, especially psychology and the social sciences.

Unlike other problems, however, adolescence is supposed to be a *developmental* problem; the adolescent temporarily looks like troublesome types of humanity but is presumably going to outgrow those patterns or leave them behind. The adolescent is both self and Other, at once a normative subject, formed on the usual model of middle-class WASP identity, and a figure for deviations from that model—deviations hoped to be temporary. In their respective studies, Sarah E. Chinn (2009) and Kent Baxter (2008) emphasize the extent to which adolescence has been entangled with discourses of racial and ethnic otherness, Baxter addressing the articulation of juvenile delinquency in and around the Native American "problem" and Chinn examining the universalization of a generation gap between working-class, U.S.-born youth and their immigrant parents.

While much fin de siècle literature of adolescence is British and European, the idea of adolescence is distinctively American in elaboration.[4] Hall's psychological theorization of adolescence, which deeply influenced its subsequent understandings, drew upon racial and racist developmental logic, even as it offered relief from the easy equation of adolescence with delinquency or even criminality. Hall was the first American to receive a Ph.D. in psychology, under William James at Harvard, and he later became the president of Clark University. Hall pioneered the American form of child study and founded two important journals, the *American Journal of Psychology* and the *Pedagogical Seminary,* in 1887 and 1891, respectively. It was Hall who brought Sigmund Freud to the United States for the first and only time, inviting him to Clark University in 1909. *Adolescence* was the culmination of several decades of research and consolidated popular sentiment as well as scientific thought. *Adolescence* was widely read and admired, and not only by fellow psychologists. Biographer Lorine Pruette nods to "the anxious mothers who hugged its two volumes to their breasts and found within its thousand pages a light to ease their steps and to guide them through the perilous paths of child-rearing" (1970, 120).

In his preface to the first volume, Hall explains that *Adolescence* was published before a planned volume on genetic psychology, "which should logically have been published first" (1907, 1: v) and which is distilled into chapter 10 of that first volume. In fact, it makes sense that *Adolescence* took priority for Hall and remains his best-known work, since the subject of adolescence grounds his approach to psychology rather than the other way around. It is not just that Hall understood adolescence in psychological terms; rather, adolescence is *the* foundation for Hall's psychology. Adolescence, he declares in the preface, is "more worthy of study than any other subject" (1: xviii). For Hall, adolescence constituted a period of chastity and restraint between the onset of puberty and the achievement of maturity and proper adulthood, as sanctified by marriage. Hall pleads for a full cultural accommodation of that period: "We are progressively forgetting that for the complete apprenticeship to life, youth needs repose, leisure, art, legends, romance, idealization, and in a word humanism, if it is to enter the kingdom of man well equipped for man's highest work in the world" (1: xvi–xvii). Hall's life and work reflect the tension between genteel moralism and its modern challenges.

Like many of his contemporaries, Hall drew extensively upon and helped popularize further the evolutionary doctrine of recapitulation, in short, the idea that the individual creature repeats or reenacts the developmental history of the species. The history of the species functioned for Hall as a kind of genetic and collective unconscious (Baxter 2008, 47). In the second volume of *Adolescence,* Hall situates his study in the context of evolutionary science and describes it as "a parallel embryology of the psyche" (1907, 2: 57). Psychic evolution, he remarks, "is even more upsetting than biological evolution, for it lies nearer to all human and practical interests" (2: 55). Hall proclaims the Bible "deeply based on genetic truth" (2: 126) and thus "our great text-book in psychology" (2: 321). Hall's particular understanding or application of recapitulation theory affirmed a traditional and rather racist view of cultural development that made space for adolescence. Whereas the child embodies or recalls a "remoter past," the adolescent, claims Hall, is "neo-atavistic, and in him the later acquisitions of the race slowly become prepotent" (1: xiii). With the help of cultural supports (education, literature, "humanism"), the adolescent in Hall's scheme resists the sexual urges that attend puberty in favor of emotional and cultural maturation.

Hall believed that while evolutionary forces are still at work in adolescence, the individual can acquire new characteristics at that point, even overriding evolutionary programming to some degree. Influenced also by religious psychology, Hall saw adolescence as a rebirth so powerful as to move the adolescent subject into individuality. As Joseph F. Kett (1977) emphasizes, Hall appropriated and semisecularized the notion that adolescence is a time of religious conversion and thus of spiritual rebirth. Hall's adolescent aspires to and achieves ostensibly higher emotional and spiritual states of being. Hall expresses both enthusiasm for and anxiety about the adolescent's upward mobility, at once romanticizing the adolescent as idealistic and heroic while insisting that certain moral codes be followed so as to ensure a proper character. He admired but also worried about the physical and emotional changes of adolescence, which he described as an experience of "Sturm und Drang" (storm and stress), borrowing from Johann Wolfgang von Goethe's 1774 *The Sorrows of Young Werther* and thus blurring the line between literature and psychology.[5]

Although "literature" is not among the many subtitles of *Adolescence,* Hall makes clear his appreciation of adolescence as a literary domain. In the final chapter of the first volume, Hall offers an exhaustive survey of adolescence in literature and then biography, beginning with "Plato's boys" (1: 513), or the Platonic dialogues, in his view "among the best of all literary sources for the study of the pedagogy of adolescence. After many years of teaching them and reading [Benjamin] Jowett in seminary classes," he continues, "it is even clearer to me that some of the best of them owe much of their charm to the noble love of adolescent boys" (1: 513). Plato "presents most of the chief types of ephebic perplexity and the elucidation of each" (1: 519). Hall adopts the Greek term *ephebe* (male youth) throughout the chapter, presumably to emphasize the Greeks as the founding fathers of adolescent literature. After Plato's adolescent boys come those of Aristotle, Jesus, Shakespeare, and biographers and novelists of the eighteenth century forward. Hall concludes with the autobiography of Helen Keller, published in 1903. As is typical of Hall's work, not much analysis accompanies this extensive inventory; it is never clear what these various "types" of adolescence signify. He does make a few generalizations about male versus female adolescence and emphasizes a few tendencies across the sample—the adolescent love for nature, preference for "synthetic" rather than "analytic" life, and propensity for melodrama. The literary record seems important to Hall, but primarily as establishing adolescence as a central and ongoing theme of human history. He makes little attempt to match the literary record to the developmental claims made in rest of the study.

Hall abruptly concludes the chapter with a call for reinvigorated interest in the literature of adolescence:

> It is, I believe, high time the ephebic literature should be recognized as a class by itself, and have a place of its own in the history of letters and criticism. Much of it should be individually prescribed for the reading of the young, for whom it has a singular zest and is a true stimulus and corrective. This stage of life now has what might almost be called a school of its own. Here the young appeal to and listen to each other as they do not to adults, and in a way the latter have failed to appreciate. Again, no biography, and especially no autobiography, should henceforth be complete if it does not describe this period of transformation so all-determining for future life to which it alone can often give the key. To rightly draw the lessons of this age not only saves us from waste ineffable of this rich but crude area of experience, but makes maturity saner and more complete. Lastly, many if not most young people should be encouraged to enough of the confessional private journalism to teach them self-knowledge, for the art

of self-expression usually begins now if ever, when it has a
wealth of subjective material and needs forms of expression
peculiar to itself. (1: 589)

Hall recommends the inclusion of adolescent literature in the canon
and prescribes writing as well as reading for adolescents themselves.
In this last respect especially, his perspective overlaps with that of
Kristeva, who remarks, "We might reasonably ask the following question: must we choose between sending an adolescent to an analyst or
encouraging him to write novels? Or should we perhaps write them
together?" (1995, 152). Kristeva's scenario of the analyst and the adolescent writing together recalls the collaborative practices of child analysts that I discussed in chapter 2. In any case, Hall, like Kristeva,
grounds adolescence as much in literary as in psychological discourse.

Moreover, Hall seems to have identified strongly with adolescents.
Drawing on various materials, Louise Kaplan holds that Hall and
Jean-Jacques Rousseau before him were "characters whose very lives
were dramatic examples of some of the dilemmas and resolutions of
adolescence" (1984, 18). Like Rousseau, Hall struggled to reconcile the
sexual passion of youth with the leading of a moral life; both men drew
from experience when writing about the pursuit of an integrated, al-
truistic personality. Patricia Meyer Spacks proposes that Hall's strong
and personal identification with adolescence set a certain precedent
for literary writers who also took up the subject. If we read his work
for tone as well as content, she proposes, we see "emotional patterns
comparable to those apparent in much twentieth-century fiction" (1981,
229). "His open acknowledgement of the emotional response generated
in adults by adolescents," she writes, not only echoes the emotional patterns of literature but also "represents something new in intellectual
and social history: something new, lasting, and important. We still live
with its consequences" (235–36). "Adolescence," she continues, "*means*
possibility: so writers of all centuries have felt. Not until G. Stanley
Hall's century have novelists sustained a fantasy of preserving its values and its indeterminacy" (250; emphasis in the original).

It is telling that Freud went not to *The Sorrows of Young Werther*
for inspiration but rather to *Faust,* Goethe's darker and arguably more
mature work. We can accuse Freud of many things, but probably not
of holding a romantically adolescent perspective on life. Even so, Freud

contributed to Hall's vision of adolescence and to its subsequent re-finements. While Hall objected to Freud's theories of sexuality, he clearly saw himself as a disciple of Freud, and we might describe adolescence as a discourse with European roots, Freudian inflection, and a strongly American articulation.[6] Adolescence was something of a hot topic in Freud's Vienna. In 1908 Frank Wedekind's tragedy *Spring's Awakening* premiered there, just two years after making its debut in Berlin. The ill-fated protagonists Wendla, Moritz, and Melchoir, all fourteen years old, are victims of both the sudden onset of puberty and the sharp social repression of adolescent sexuality. Melchoir rapes Wendla, leading Moritz, coded as "feminine," to commit suicide. Artists such as Oskar Kokoschka and writers such as Stefan Zweig and Robert Musil also took up the subject of adolescence. What, if any, influence this cultural preoccupation with adolescence had on Freud remains a matter of debate.[7] Certainly Freud never produced anything like *Adolescence,* even if his ideas inspired others interested in the subject. Freud did not think of his eighteen-year-old patient Dora primarily as an adolescent; rather, he saw her as an individual still suffering from infantile dramas. Like Hall, Freud was influenced by the doctrine of recapitulation and adapted it to his own system, but unlike Hall, Freud did not envision adolescence as a new beginning, nor did he seek to protect ideals of chastity and restraint—quite the contrary. In puberty, thought Freud, it is the dramas of early childhood that are reborn, not the individual per se. And while Freud certainly had a soft spot for German Romanticism, he can hardly be described as adolescent himself in sensibility or identification.[8]

In Louise Kaplan's view, Freud became an "unwitting participant in the psychoanalytic neglect of adolescence" (1984, 82), in large measure because of his particular spin on the doctrine of recapitulation. That doctrine, she notes, quickly found its way into theories of the transference relationship, in such a way that adolescent and adult patients alike were assumed to be endlessly working through the experiences of early childhood, bypassing altogether the possibility of an intervening and equally crucial period of life. Kaplan, also a psychoanalyst, faults Ernest Jones more than Freud for this neglect or refusal of the idea of adolescence, as Jones described adolescence in strictly recapitulationist terms in an influential essay.

Yet the lines between psychology and psychoanalysis have always been fuzzy, and this rhetoric of neglect is self-serving to the degree that it enables a fantasy of rescue and redress characteristic of psychology after Freud. Moreover, it is not so clear that Freud neglected adolescence, as Baxter and others have shown. Although the term "adolescence" is "almost entirely absent" from his writings (Baxter 2008, 46), there is strong evidence that Freud was interested in the problem of delinquency and supported efforts to use psychoanalytic theory in clinical work with adolescents, just as he encouraged the development of child analysis without taking a more active role in that emergent field. Freud wrote a foreword to August Aichhorn's *Wayward Youth,* first published in 1925, in which he notes that the child "has become the main object of psychoanalytic research and in this respect has replaced the neurotic with whom the work began" (1983, v). In this book, Aichhorn reports on the results of his clinical work in Vienna with delinquent or "dissocial" adolescents in and out of institutional contexts. That work was only later informed by psychoanalysis, and Aichhorn shows how psychoanalysis confirms his intuitive understanding of asocial behavior and provides a discourse with which he can better frame his findings. In his preface, Freud comments on the relationship between psychoanalysis, education, and "re-education," noting that "the child, even the wayward and delinquent child, should not be compared to the adult neurotic, and re-education is something quite different from the education of the immature" (vii). Here as elsewhere, Freud communicates sensitivity to the problems of adolescents and to the challenges of rehabilitative work with them.

It is almost surprising that Freud so enthusiastically endorses Aichhorn's book, given its practical and upbeat character. Aichhorn does not deny the role of the unconscious or the intensity of sexual longing, but neither does he dramatize them as powerfully as does Freud. Aichhorn's tone is light and conversational. Like Freud, he draws in the reader, but unlike Freud, he sympathizes with the theory-phobic: "I am in the midst of practical work with children," he explains early on, "and theoretical discussions without application seem out of place to me" (1983, 11). Aichhorn's developmental theory is straightforward: children are fundamentally asocial and must learn to endure pain, renounce pleasure, and embrace reality. Delinquency is akin to a neurotic symptom and should not be confused with any underlying psychological problem. The task of the therapist is to use transference to adjust the patient's ego, either by relaxing the superego or by fortifying it, depending on need.

In *The End of Adolescence* (2004), Philip Graham notes that while Hall coined the "Sturm und Drang" theory of adolescence, it was Freud who gave that theory a major boost, not because of his interest in adolescence but rather because of his belief that puberty brought a reactivation of infantile wishes and thus a psychic as well as physical disturbance of self. Peter Blos (1941), a well-known American psychoanalyst who became an expert on adolescence (and who introduced his friend Erik Erikson to the Freuds in Vienna), promoted further the notion that a tumultuous adolescence was the developmental norm. At the same time, Hall's understanding of adolescence as rebirth was also championed, so that traces of both Freud and Hall persist in adolescent literature and in scholarship on it.[9]

In 1959, operating confidently in the collective wake of Hall and Freud, psychologist Norman Kiell published a study called *The Adolescent through Fiction: A Psychological Approach,* devoted to illuminating through a sampling of imaginative writing such adolescent topics as physical development, family relations, vocational choice, and so forth. "Fiction has made us perhaps overfamiliar with the agonies and absurdities of adolescence," notes Kiell (12), hence the need for a more careful analysis. Kiell takes an inclusive view of psychology, borrowing from and citing Freud, Hall, Bruno Bettelheim, Blos, and many less well-known figures in the field (such as Irene M. Josselyn, then a noted authority on adolescent psychology). His appendix on psychology and literature makes clear just how vast that subject had become by 1959. Kiell followed up in 1964 with *The Universal Experience of Adolescence,* which reasserts the universality of adolescence against anthropological critiques of that idea. Kiell returns to and redeems Hall while incorporating more-recent imaginative as well as psychological literature. The book is actually an annotated reader or anthology of primary material, including some literature but mostly autobiographies and other personal documents. Chapter 10, "The Compulsion to Read," proposes that adolescents tend toward obsessive reading because reading allows for a sublimation of the libido, an escape from reality, a testing of philosophical beliefs, and a (largely unconscious) search for identity. Like Hall, and with some hints from Freud, Kiell sees adolescent literature as both part of the larger cultural fabric and as the key to understanding adolescent psychology.[10]

Trouble in the Heartland: The Contribution of Social Science

In the United States, interest in adolescence intensified during the early twentieth century, particularly between the two world wars and again after the close of the second. W. Tasker Witham (1964) argues that before 1920, the American "genteel tradition" held sway in adolescent as well as adult literature. Genteel classics of adolescence from this period—simple, moralizing tales that cherished innocence—include Gene Stratton-Porter's *Freckles,* Harold Bell Wright's *The Winning of Barbara Worth,* and Booth Tarkington's *Seventeen.* Opposed to the genteel tradition were such works of literary naturalism as Stephen Crane's *Maggie: A Girl of the Streets,* Theodore Dreiser's *Sister Carrie,* and Willa Cather's *My Antonia.* After 1920, dramatically changing social conditions helped usher in a new era in adolescent literature, even though many prominent authors did not make a distinction between adolescent and adult literature. Whereas pre-1920s books tended to portray adolescents as somewhat older children, generally untroubled and even innocent, later works give them greater depth and complexity.

Another important context for the literary emergence of adolescence-as-problem is the anthropological and sociological claim to adolescence, made against psychology and psychoanalysis both.[11] In her 1928 work *Coming of Age in Samoa,* Margaret Mead criticizes Hall's assertion of universal adolescent turmoil and theorizes instead that adolescence is merely symptomatic of the (adult) culture to which it belongs. Mead takes issue with what she mocks as the "Yes, stormily" (1961, 3) attitude of psychologists (whom she dismissively calls "theorists") as well as with the notion that advanced civilizations must be fundamentally different from primitive cultures. As Baxter notes, while Hall and Mead seem to represent very different ways of thinking about adolescence, they share a rehabilitative attitude toward the subject, focusing on how to solve its alleged problems. Moreover, while Mead stops just short of debunking psychology and adolescence alike, she seems nearly to appropriate psychological discourse rather than repudiate it. In his preface to *Coming of Age in Samoa,* Mead's mentor, Franz Boas, positions her work as psychological in that it offers a glimpse into the "personal side of the life of the individual" against more standard analyses of cultural systems; he also praises the then young Mead for "having undertaken to identify herself so completely with Samoan youth that she gives us a lucid and clear picture of the joys and difficulties encountered by the young individual in a culture so entirely different from our own" (1961, n.p.). In ethnography, as in literature, psychological and anthropological perspectives on adolescence collude as much as collide.

While Mead leveraged her work on Samoa into an expertise on American life, the Chicago school social scientists observed American life more directly, in and around Chicago especially. With the arrival of Robert E. Park in 1916, the University of Chicago began a prosperous period of urban studies work in the social sciences. The Chicago school sponsored "ecological" studies of local ethnic groups as well as of the nature and distribution of juvenile delinquency, mental illness, and other forms of presumed social pathology.[12] As with anthropology, Chicago school sociology disdained the psychological even as it aped its themes and terminology. Alongside studies of adolescent subcultures, most famously Frederick Thrasher's *The Gang* (1927), there appeared the "sociological life history," essentially an individual case study written to illuminate and dramatize larger problems. The first of these appeared in 1930, *The Jack-Roller: A Delinquent Boy's Own Story,* written by Clifford R. Shaw and his associates at Chicago. The life history, we are told in the preface, is neither "conventional social science 'data'" nor "a conventional autobiography. . . . It is certainly not fiction, although the best life history documents have a sensitivity and pace, a dramatic urgency, that any novelist would be glad to achieve" (1966, v). We follow the alarming misadventures of young Stanley from an impoverished and abusive childhood through a delinquent and even criminal adolescence to, finally, a more promising young adulthood.[13]

Constructed from interviews with the young subject and written on his behalf, *The Jack-Roller* is presented as a sociological study but also expected to communicate something of Stanley's psyche. "There is a much richer psychology concerned with inner mental life, memories, ideations, imageries, etc., with [adolescents'] emotional backgrounds than is dreamed of during an ordinary examination of a delinquent young person," writes Shaw. "Some of this material is so deeply buried that it requires considerable skill on the part of the inquirer to over- come inhibitions and forgetfulnesses so that underlying fundamental truths of the situation may be brought to the surface" (5). The diagnosis of Stanley echoes the language of psychology as well as the "culture and personality" school of anthropology; Stanley is "egocentric," owns "an overorganized personality," and exhibits traits such as "resentment of correction" (Burgess 1966, 192–93). The analysis is framed explicitly as not psychoanalytic, as concerned with the conscious rather than the unconscious mind, and yet, we are told, "The telling or writing one's life-story is itself a part of the treatment. The very act of pouring out one's experiences not only has a cathartic effect . . . but also gives the subject perspective on his life" (195). More convincing is the claim that life histories attend more than do psychological studies to "the powerful factors of group and neighborhood influence" (195). Works such as *The Jack-Roller* set precedent for the problem novel of adolescence.

Across the twentieth century, ethnographic literature cemented as much as challenged the construction of the adolescent as a mysterious, exotic creature. What we might call the "ethnographic imaginary" of ad- olescence persists well into the present, especially in pop-ethnographies of high school life (more journalistic than academic) such as Patricia Hersch's *A Tribe Apart* (1998) or Elinor Burkett's *Another Planet* (2001), which employ the estranging rhetoric of fieldwork and minimize the impact of ethnographer. Whereas Hersch insists on the creation of an autonomous sphere of adolescence, Burkett, much like Mead, turns her focus back to the parent culture, clarifying the adolescent experi- ence as more a "shadow planet" than another planet altogether, one that throws adult society "into bold relief" (2001, 312). These and many other such works operate in the tradition of foundational ethnographies such as August B. Hollingshead's *Elmtown's Youth* (1949), an influen- tial sociological analysis of adolescence in the Midwest, and Edgar Z. Friedenberg's *Coming of Age in America* (1963), a study of high school students across different regions of the country. Hollingshead takes issue with Hall's "liberal sprinkling" of ethnographic facts taken out of cultural context and harnessed in the service of recapitulationist psy- chology; in lieu of "Sturm und Drang" he proposes this sociological definition of adolescence: "the period in the life of a person when the society in which he functions ceases to regard him (male or female) as a child and does not accord to him full adult status, roles and functions" (1949, 6). Friedenberg goes much further in his critique of the professional literature on adolescence, likening adolescents to colonized people and to emigrants who are exploited but refused full social status in capitalist society. This tradition of leftist thinking about adolescence as an exploited group has influenced at least some psychologists, psychoanalysts, and psychiatrists; the contemporary child and adolescent psychiatrist Philip Graham (2004) thus calls for the "end of adolescence" as a concept, proposing that we focus our energies on public policy reform. Louise Kaplan is alarmed enough by such challenges to retort that "the notion that adolescence is a fiction generated by an antiquated breed of psychologists and psychoanalysts has acquired around it a mythology of its own" (1984, 41).[14] Kaplan calls this "invention theory" and asserts that although adolescence is a social artifact, it is also a physical and psychological phenomenon.

The American literature of adolescence that emerged in the early to middle twentieth century reflects the struggle between psychological and anthropological/sociological understandings of adolescence and even seeks to reconcile them. That literature communicates an awareness of adolescence both as a culture or subculture and as a set of experiences. Moreover, it is remarkable how many novels from this period are set in the Midwest, even if not actually in Chicago. In *Making American Boys* (2004), I argued that authors of Bad Boy literature were boy workers of a sort, authorial counterparts to Scoutmasters and YMCA leaders. Likewise, some of the novelists who concerned themselves with adolescence—especially male adolescence—might be seen as also working this new field much as did the Chicago school social scientists, testing out theories of identity and delinquency in the context of urban and rural life, attending to issues of class, race, and gender while plumbing the depths of the psyche. These novelists saw themselves as theorists and practitioners of literature rather than as experts on adolescence, but they wrote with insight and sensitivity about the subject, following Hall in this regard. One famous Bad Boy author, Booth Tarkington, also wrote one of the first novels of adolescence, *Seventeen,* published in 1916. On the one hand, *Seventeen,* set in the

American heartland near an unnamed large city, belongs firmly to the genteel tradition, with its condescending humor, sentimental drama, and blatant racism; on the other hand, the book offers a sensitive if amusing glimpse into the psyche of seventeen-year-old Willie Baxter as he suffers through a summer of infatuation and all its attendant humiliations. When summer comes to close and Willie must renounce his beloved Miss Pratt (who speaks in baby talk and carries around a toy dog named Flopit) the result is comic but a touch poignant:

> To the competent twenties, hundreds of miles suggesting no impossibilities, such departures may be rending, but not tragic. Implacable, the difference to Seventeen! Miss Pratt was going home, and Seventeen could not follow; it could only mourn upon the lonely shore, tracing little angelic footprints left in the sand. To Seventeen such a departure is final; it is a vanishing. (1968, 121)

Four years later, in 1920, Floyd Dell published his autobiographical coming-of-age story *Moon-Calf*. Although written after Dell had moved to New York, *Moon-Calf* is set in western Illinois and emphasizes Dell's adolescence spent in Davenport, Iowa (disguised as "Port Royal"), concluding with its sensitive and artistic young hero, Felix Fay, daydreaming "Chicago! Chicago!" (1957, 346). Dell's work has been variously associated with realism, naturalism, and modernism, and more specifically with what Carl Van Doren (1921) called the "revolt from the village," the critique of mainstream American values and practices largely but not exclusively associated with the Midwest. Despite its central themes of growing up, first love, and intellectual and political awakening—despite Dell's explicit description of adolescence as "that mysterious re-birth of the soul" (1957, 94)—*Moon-Calf* is not usually now considered a novel of adolescence. Neither is F. Scott Fitzgerald's *This Side of Paradise,* published the same year. The novels of Dell and Fitzgerald ushered in a new "frankness," according to Witham, by which he means more-explicit grappling with the social issues of the day as well as with sexuality. Witham sees these and other titles as novels of adolescence rather than as adolescent novels. I do not disagree, but would point out that Dell especially remained fascinated with adolescence, returning to it again and again in novels about boys

(*The Golden Spike,* in 1934) and girls (*This Mad Ideal,* in 1925) striving toward adulthood but thwarted by social expectation as well as by self-doubt. Dell was inspired not only by Hall's vision of adolescence as a rebirth but also by Freud's theories of sexuality and its discontents; reading Freud reinvigorated his novel writing, and *Moon-Calf* and its 1921 sequel *The Briary Bush* were the product of a free-associative process of creative work.[15] Dell even produced nonfiction about childhood and adolescence, first *Were You Ever a Child?* (1919), a treatise on progressive education, and then *Love in the Machine Age: A Psychological Study of the Transition from Patriarchal Society* (1930), an early attempt in psychohistory. Psychiatrist Louis J. Bragman pronounced Dell "a pre-eminent psychologist of adolescence" (1937, 1402), offering a less-than-flattering psychological assessment of the author but concluding thus: "One goes to Floyd Dell as to a vital textbook, for information and advice on the art of 'growing up'" (1411).

In one of the first studies of literary adolescence, Helen White Childers observes that while the novels of the 1920s and 1930s dealing with adolescence tend to cover a long span in the life of the central character and to show him "in broad social context," novels of the 1940s and 1950s focus on a shorter period of time and "are much more concerned with the psychological processes of the protagonist than with flaws in society" (1958, 347–49). Childers notes the emergence in the 1940s and 1950s of a new type of adolescent protagonist, a type that Witham summarized as "a pathetic figure, thrust too early into the world of maturity where even the adults are lonely and insecure" (1964, 21). While adolescence continued to be a serious and legitimate subject, taken up by prominent authors, it also became more and more associated with the psychological domain and with prescriptive writing. Put another way, the novel of adolescence was coidentical with the naturalist novel and the proletarian novel through the first several decades of the century, but gradually split off from those genres, looking more and more like something called the psychological novel, organized around the hypersensitive and anxious character.[16] This, in turn, became the problem novel, hence the general conversion of the novel of adolescence into the adolescent novel. Childers identifies four types of the novel of adolescence: the life history, the sociological study, the psychological study, and the "literary" novel, more concerned with artistry and narrative experimentation.[17] Most histories of the adolescent or young adult novel begin with the 1950s, and usually with *The Catcher in the Rye,* both a psychological and a literary work.

While there is evidence for a shift from the novel of adolescence to the adolescent novel, I should acknowledge that matters are not so simple. Some earlier works are just as preoccupied with psychological as with sociological or socioeconomic issues. Dell, for one, was influenced by Freud and Karl Marx both, as the concerns of *Moon-Calf* make clear. And some later works are likewise attuned as much to social concerns as to psychological ones—hence the advent of the so-called problem novel in the late 1960s, really a return to the earlier novel of adolescence. Evident in the history of literary adolescence is a dialectic of the social and the psychological, a vacillation between realist-naturalist modes of discourse and more psychological modes. The adolescent novel achieves not so much the disappearance of social problems as a streamlined emphasis on their emotional impact, often through first-person narration. Unlike the third-person narrator, more typical in the literature of adolescence, the narrating personality in the adolescent novel is more egocentric, less adult, and less cognizant of the dimensions of sociality. Novels of adolescence tend to be autobiographical first novels, but the adolescent novel goes even further in pursuit of the psyche.

Gender, Sexuality, and the Problem Interior

The adolescent as envisioned by Hall and associates was first and foremost a sexual creature, driven by sexual urges but expected to direct them into properly heterosexual channels. So argues historian Jeffrey P. Moran in *Teaching Sex* (2000), which traces the history of sex education and hygiene programs in the United States back to the foundational ideas and anxieties of Hall, with a nod to the influence of sexology. Boys were the primary subject and target of the new discourse of adolescence, holds Moran, in large measure because boys were expected to make their way in the world, but also because their sexuality was more firmly associated with savage self-indulgence. The (hetero) sexing of the male adolescent accompanied the credentialing of new kinds of experts and the development of new pedagogical or regulatory materials. While certain topics have more openly been addressed in recent years, especially gay sexuality, literature for the adolescent has long been concerned with sexuality and gender.

As the adolescent boy is a troublesome figure for Hall, so is the adolescent girl. The girl represents for Hall not so much the boy's opposite but rather a particular (hopefully temporary) stage in his evolution; for Hall, as for so many other practical theorists of recapitulation, femininity, like savagery and criminality, is not an identity or experience in its own right but rather an evolutionary stage or phase through which boys must pass in order to become men. The girl is key to the successful reproduction of white, middle-class stability (that is, Anglo-Saxon manhood), and yet at the same time, she is the abject of masculinity. Noting Hall's anxieties about the achievement of manhood, Peter Stonely sees him as more concerned with the adolescence of girls than with that of boys (2003, 7–8). Both Stonely and Nancy Lesko stress the destabilizing potential of the girl in Hall's scheme of adolescence. Lesko suggests that girls, seemingly absent in the modern discourse of adolescence, are "in fact, hauntingly present" (2002, 183) in the institutional scene of education and juvenile justice, and Stonely points to their omnipresence in imaginative literature. Stonely claims that the adolescent girl "dominate[d] the American imagination from the nineteenth century into the twentieth" because she represented both rural American character and a more modern consumerist selfhood—she was "the vehicle for both nostalgia and optimism" (2003, 1). Spunky adolescent girls are everywhere in the literature of the period, he points out, from Jo March to Daisy Miller to the heroines of Kate Douglass Wiggin, Jean Webster, Gene Stratton-Porter, and Laura Ingalls Wilder. Many of these characters are tomboys, but that is just part of their appeal, suggests Stonely. The adolescent girl is a fascinating but disturbing figure who must finally be recruited into marriage and motherhood.

Stonely might look to Mead for evidence in a different register of the importance of the girl to the ongoing question of adolescence. In *Coming of Age in Samoa,* Mead notes that she studied girls because they were more accessible to her as a female field worker, and while that may have been the case, her focus on girls forms another part of her rejoinder to Hall. Mead refuses to give priority to the adolescent boy or to see femininity as a developmental stage. Moreover, Mead concludes that Samoan girls and women deferred marriage for many years, in the meanwhile enjoying sexual relations with multiple partners with no negative effects. Hall defined adolescence not only as a sequence of certain developments but also as an ethic of chastity and restraint, and Mead refuses the latter entirely, along with his general supposition that adolescence is necessarily a stressful and even debilitating time. At the same time, Mead offers her own thoughts about social delinquency and adjustment, especially in chapters 10 and 11 of her Samoan study, entitled "The Experience and Individuality of the Average Girl" and "The Girl in Conflict," respectively. Mead insists that homosexuality is of little import in Samoan culture; more significant are cases of "upward" or "downward" deviation. Those deviating upward seek escape from traditional Samoan culture; those tending downward cannot adjust to that culture for reasons of temperament (having "essentially unfortunate" personalities; 1961, 178) or inadequate upbringing. What makes girls queer for Mead is not sexuality but rather resistance to social norms. And queer girls are admired rather than pitied by Mead; Mead hints that while Samoan culture is stress free, *some* girls might need a more complex life. Stonely, too, sees nonconformity both as a positive trait and as a cultural fantasy; the adolescent girl is *expected* to be nonconformist, at least to a point, in the imaginative literature of the period, he remarks.

In writing for adolescents, gender demands and assumptions about sexuality are intimately bound up with the interiorist tendencies of the protagonist. Put another way, the adolescent character's struggle for selfhood, often symbolized by creativity, thought, and other ostensibly psychological and private activities, is often staged around or against expectations about gender and sexuality. This is no less true of pre-1950s literature than of the problem novel. In *Moon-Calf,* for instance, shy and sensitive Felix longs for recognition as a poet even as he insists on working factory jobs to demonstrate his manhood. Dell reports that *Moon-Calf* is a working-through of the author's personal and professional difficulties, and critic Louis Bragman, for one, is quick to diagnose the novel in crudely Freudian terms, taking his cue from Dell's autobiographical writings as well as from the novel. Dell reports that as a young boy he was overly influenced by his mother and became a "sissy," sporting curls and a Little Lord Fauntleroy suit. "'How is he going to become masculine enough in his attitudes to hold a job,'" writes Bragman, "'or accept a responsible relationship to the other sex?' became the all-important question" (1937, 1402). Bragman takes no notice of Dell's social milieu or his lifelong if ambivalent engagement with feminism, offering a brand of mother-fixed, sissy-boy theorizing all too familiar still. Bragman reads Dell as a failed heterosexual. Dell himself turned away in later life from the more radical perspectives of his youth, lamenting in *Critic's Magic* the "mawkish homosexual disguise of life" unveiled by the "franker" literature he helped legitimate (quoted in Bragman 1937, 1410).[18] While the tomboy is encouraged to enjoy a certain outward-bound rebellion, even if she is finally expected to settle down, the sensitive or literary boy must renounce his sissiness and make his way in the world. He must also outgrow adolescence, whereas the girl is expected to stay within its parameters, especially in Hall's scheme, since femininity and adolescence are equivalent. But as Dell's case makes clear, even clear accomplishments in work and love never dispel the specter of perversion or insulate the psyche against negatively queer charges—the boy's psychic life seems perpetually at war with his public persona.

Foundational texts of adolescent literature run the ideological gamut with respect to gender, sexuality, and interiority. As should now be evident, *The Catcher in the Rye* was hardly the first adolescent novel and hardly the first such novel to take up the question of identity in relation to sexuality and gender. Rather, it appropriated and masculinized the genre, returning us to the predicament of the introspective, anxious boy but paying greater attention to sexuality. *The Catcher in the Rye* appeared in the immediate wake of works such as Maureen Daly's 1942 work *Seventeenth Summer* and Carson McCullers's 1946 novel *The Member of the Wedding,* which offer compelling and perhaps more-enabling portraits of the problem interior of the adolescent girl. These works, among others, help fashion an interiority for the adolescent character, stressing her singularity and positioning it as both ordinary and queer.

Seventeenth Summer seems a more legitimate beginning point for adolescent literature than *The Catcher in the Rye,* as some commentators have recognized. In *Books and the Teen-Age Reader* (1967), an influential handbook for teachers and librarians, G. Robert Carlsen emphasizes *Seventeenth Summer's* importance and popularity, recounting that on a visit to a high school library a year or so after the book's publication, Carlsen discovered that the library owned seventy copies, so difficult was it to keep the book on the shelves. Daly was herself barely out of adolescence and in college when she published her autobiographical novel, a first-person story of a summer romance set in the heartland town of Fond du Lac, Wisconsin. *Seventeenth Summer* inspired a rash of imitations, among them Betty Cavanna's 1946 *Going on Sixteen* and Rosamund du Jardin's 1949 *Practically Seventeen,* and it may have also played a role in the 1944 founding of *Seventeen* magazine (Cart 1996, 16–24; Savage 2007, 448). Daly's lack of authorial remove from the events of the novel accounts largely for the book's success, thinks Carlsen. "At the time the book was published it was unique and represented a whole new approach to the junior novel," he notes. "Adolescent problems and reactions were taken seriously, just as seriously as they are taken by the young person experiencing them" (1967, 43). While he sees the book as a direct rather than filtered reflection of Daly's own adolescence, he praises the "subtle understandings Maureen Daly imparts about human relationships" (43). Daly herself saw the book as a mature enterprise, remarking in 1994 that it was written and reviewed as "a full adult novel" (quoted in Berger 1994, 170). But the book quickly became known as a "junior novel," and Daly later wrote a weekly advice column for teens in the *Chicago Tribune,* as well as other adolescent narratives, including one about her daughter's own life at seventeen.

Spacks suggests that while the literature of adolescence has a long and venerable history, the "young person's absorption with his or her own growth, discovery, and pain are reason enough for proclaiming ours the century of the adolescent" (1981, 9). *Seventeenth Summer* is paradigmatic in this regard, reveling as it does in the protagonist Angie Morrow's self-absorption. Like Tarkington's *Seventeen, Seventeenth Summer* is the story of a summer romance, but told from the perspective of an adolescent girl with little if any distance from the narrating subject. At summer's start, middle-class Angie meets Jack, a handsome and easygoing baker's boy, whom she dates until leaving for college in Chicago a few months later. The point of view is first person, intimately so. "I don't know why I'm telling you all this," the novel begins. "Maybe you'll think I'm being silly. But I'm not, really, because this is *important.*" With these opening lines, Angie urges us to take her story seriously. She insists on being respected as a lover, remarking, "It wasn't puppy love or infatuation or love at first sight or anything that people always talk about and laugh." "Maybe you don't know just what I mean. I can't really explain it—it's so hard to put in words but—well, it was just something I'd never felt before. Something I'd never known. People can't tell you about things like that, you have to find them out for yourself. That's why it's so important" (Daly 2002, 3). Divided into three sections for each summer month, the novel vibrates with expectation even as little happens by way of plot: at the end, Jack asks Angie to marry him, she says no, and they go their separate ways.

Angie relishes being in love and the heightened self-consciousness it brings, wanting to share that with the reader, but with the reader only. At times her experiences are positively orgasmic as well as confessional: "Something deep within me stirred and a throbbing warmth surged through my whole body until the very tips of my fingers tingled" (53). Giddy with love or self-love, Angie resists being pulled back into the mundane everyday: "There would be no more of the exquisite uncertainty of last night, no queer, tingling awe at the newness of the feeling, and no strange, filling satisfaction out of just being alive" (23). Angie often freeze-frames scenes to pause, reflect, and savor, to marvel at the moment or at her own powers of anticipation. She exhibits omnipotence of thought, sees coincidence where there probably is none, reads nature as being expressive of her own moods and desires, and suggests that she can predict and control events (not so hard to believe, really, since the novel is retrospective in narration). "You know how it is sometimes," she muses, "when things go along so smoothly that you feel certain something unforeseen must happen" (99). "I could tell beforehand just what it would be like," she remarks earlier (47). Her world is both egocentric and animistic. "It seemed almost as if the darkness beyond was listening, waiting" (272). Even at our most mature, thought Freud, we never quite leave behind animism, which accounts for not only magical thinking but also uncanny effects more generally. While overvaluing her perceptiveness, Angie also delights in *not* knowing exactly who she is or what she is about. "I wonder, I thought, what I am really thinking" (84).

Angie's egocentrism makes difficult any mature recognition of the Other, specifically Jack. The class politics of the novel distinguish it firmly from later explorations of insider–outsider romance, such as S. E. Hinton's *The Outsiders* (1967), likewise written by an adolescent girl. Whatever its shortcomings, *Seventeenth Summer* allows its protagonist a rich and even autoerotic inner life. Angie's capacity for imaginative self-absorption, while annoying at times, is what makes this an exemplary work, if also a potentially queer one. Cart and Carlsen praise the novel for its psychological realism, for capturing what adolescence is really like psychologically, but perhaps what the novel really captures is a certain cultural fantasy about the psychology of adolescence. *Seventeenth Summer* is a love story, but it is not so much a boy–girl romance as a story of self-love, and a rather writerly one at that, one that sets a precedent for ventures in self-discovery. Reading it as a feminist text, Virginia Schaefer Carroll notes that "Angie sees her relationship with Jack as a chance to reveal and develop something within herself. . . . Like the act of writing, the relationship becomes another means of testing, tuning, and strengthening her own voice" (1996, 17).

Consider also Carson McCullers's *The Member of the Wedding,* which has attracted more interest than *Seventeenth Summer* among feminist and queer-studies critics especially. Of particular note is Elizabeth Freeman's reading in *The Wedding Complex,* which attends to the personal and cultural complexities of twelve-year-old Frankie's desire for alternative forms of kinship or belonging (2002, 45–69). Growing fast and feeling freakish, Frankie falls in love with the impending wedding of her brother, or rather with the *idea* of the wedding, which represents not marriage or even couplehood but rather escape from her Georgia home and new forms of social relation. Not much happens by way of plot in this novel, either, but the novel captures the intensity of Frankie's longing to live and love beyond what she already knows. Like Mead's girl in conflict, Frankie aspires upward, or outward. Desire for this or any other wedding is not necessarily a desire for marriage, proposes Freeman, and the novel is neither a straight marriage plot nor a lesbian counterstory. Frankie's search for the "we of me" (McCullers 1986, 39)—she does not know how else to put it—suggests a more complicated politics of relationality. Freeman reads that search as "a figure for queer *para*-representation—representation 'alongside of' the dominant, a self-extension that eschews the choices of self-annihilation or self-reproduction" (2002, 63). The novel features long dialogues between Frankie and her black caretaker Berenice about the weirdness of time and space and the difficulties of giving an account of oneself, especially in the 1940s American South. "Listen," she says to Berenice at one point, "Doesn't it strike you as strange that that I am I, and you are you"? (109). A major difference between this novel and *Seventeenth Summer* is point of view; McCullers uses third person and keeps Frankie at a slight distance, so that the reader feels her pain but is perplexed and helpless before it.

Even so, McCullers brings a certain peace if not closure to Frankie's search for the "we of me." After failing to persuade her brother to take her with him and his bride to their new home—after *not* becoming a member of the wedding—Frankie loses the company of Berenice and her equally queer cousin John Henry (who dies of meningitis) but then makes friends with one Mary Littlejohn. "We're going to travel around the world together," she announces to Berenice (150); Berenice disapproves of the friendship, which cements her break with Frankie, now Frances. But even this friendship cannot be assigned a stable or definitive meaning, lesbian or otherwise; as Freeman emphasizes, the novel ends with Frankie's unfinished declaration "I am simply mad about ——," her words "shattered when, with an instant shock of happiness, she heard the ringing of the bell" (153). Even if we hear wedding bells, we never discover what Frankie is simply mad about. The failure of language is perhaps vital to the success of self. In any event, Frankie's search for the "we of me" seems to have lessened in intensity; she is more confidently herself and the implication is that her psychic turmoil has somehow fortified her. In the end, Frankie is not traumatized by her experiences, any more than is Angie Morrow. In these otherwise very different books the oddness of life takes on a psychological resonance beyond words, or at least beyond easy communication. Daly's book resembles the more upbeat and romantic adolescent psychology envisioned by Hall, albeit without the social idealism he urges, whereas the vision of McCullers seems more creatively Freudian as well as existentialist, concerned with the ambivalences and confusions not just of adolescence but of psychic life at large.

The story of the sensitive, introspective adolescent boy tends by contrast to succumb to homosexual panic as well as to generic existential anxiety. Salinger's Holden Caulfield is obsessed with "flits and Lesbians" (1964, 143) and "damn perverts" (192). At one point in the novel, Holden is stuck in the city with no place to go and spends the night at the home of his former teacher Mr. Antolini, only to find Mr. Antolini patting his head in the middle of the night. Holden bolts but then wonders "if maybe he just liked to pat guys on the head when they're asleep. I mean, how could you tell about that stuff for sure? You can't" (195). Just a few years before, in 1945, William Maxwell had given readers a more queer-affirmative variation on the anxious-boy theme in *The Folded Leaf,* a story of male–male friendship set first in Chicago and then in a small-town college. Whereas Spud is athletic and outward bound, Lymie Peters is slight, intellectual, and effete: a familiar buddy pairing dating back at least to 1857, to Thomas Hughes's *Tom Brown's School Days. The Folded Leaf,* a lyrical and intensely melancholic novel, manages same-sex desire much in the manner described by Judith Butler in *The Psychic Life of Power* (1997), saying "never-never" to same-sex love in and around homosocial friendship. Lymie is almost sacrificed, in keeping with the usual outcome of such stories.[19] Near the end of the novel Lymie attempts suicide but fails, then recovers, and even gets a kiss from Spud, not to be repeated, we are told, but remarkable all the same. And while the narrator or author muses at one point about the universality of the death drive, we are told quite firmly, "Lymie had never wanted to die, never at any time" (1981, 270).[20] Queerness in *The Folded Leaf* is associated not only with an eccentric interior, as with *Seventeenth Summer* and *The Member of the Wedding,* but also with eccentric desire, and Maxwell seems torn between advocating for that desire and capitulating to the expectations of heteronormative masculinity.

Witham notes that "abnormal sexual behavior, such as homosexuality and incest" (1964, 57), gets little mention in 1920s and 1930s novels of adolescence but has become a central theme by the 1950s, for which he cites *The Folded Leaf* as well as, among other titles, Truman Capote's *Other Voices, Other Rooms,* Gore Vidal's *The City and the Pillar,* and Sara Harris's *The Wayward Ones.* Witham does not know what to make of this trend, beyond seeing it as evidence of an increasingly "frank" treatment of sexuality. Homophobic language aside, Witham is not far off the mark. These texts on "abnormal" behavior all give particular attention not merely to sexuality but also, through sexuality, to the psychic lives of their protagonists, variously affirming and transforming the idea of problem interior in relation to social environment. The anxiety about gender and sexuality that marks Hall's work persists but is also reworked in novels such as these, linked to the achievement of a delineated and private self. Put another way, the exploration of same-sex friendships and desire in this literature is integral to the genre's general articulation. In *Disturbing the Universe,* Trites emphasizes the centrality of sexuality to adolescent literature; I would venture further that texts about queer sexualities are especially engaged with the vexing issue of selfhood.

At least to an extent, these novels challenge suppositions about sexuality and gender roles advanced by developmental psychology. In the 1930s and early 1940s, work by Lawrence K. Frank, Caroline Zachry, Daniel Prescott, Caroline Tryon, and Robert J. Havighurst had given rise to the idea of "developmental tasks," subsequently written up in 1948 by Havighurst, a professor of education at the University of Chicago. Havighurst and his colleagues outlined developmental tasks for infancy, early childhood, middle childhood, adolescence, early adulthood, middle age, and later maturity—which would later find integration in Erikson's model of the "life cycle." The first two developmental tasks of adolescence presume the establishment of firm gender roles: "1. Achieving new and more mature relations with age-mates of both sexes," the goal being the conversion of boys into men and girls into women, and "2. Achieving a masculine or feminine social role" (1972, 45–51). Havighurst's scheme was widely adapted, eventually to the point of challenge, "sex role" no longer a self-evident or stable term.[21] Even so, the general pressure of developmental discourse was normative rather than interrogative.

Young Adulthood and the Vulnerable Self

Psychoanalyst Erik Erikson was the chief architect of identity, beginning in 1950 with *Childhood and Society,* an attempt to reconcile psychoanalysis and cultural anthropology. We owe the term "rebel" primarily to another psychoanalyst, Robert Lindner, who in 1944 published a case study entitled *Rebel without a Cause: The Hypnoanalysis of a Criminal Psychopath.* Against the forces of mass culture (and against the figure of the psychopath) Lindner proposed the "positive rebel" (see Medovoi 2005, 31). Only a year later the term "teenager" made its first appearance, in an article by Elliot Cohen in the *New York Times Magazine* (1945, 24). The teenager and the rebel morphed into the rebellious teenager, not the juvenile delinquent of earlier analyses but rather a model American subject—indeed, as Medovoi argues, *the* model American subject. The "'search for identity' that comprises the stage of adolescence for Erikson," writes Medovoi, "reenacts a classical political metanarrative of the enlightened individual entering into full possession of his/her right to self-determination" (2005, 6–7). To this metanarrative, continues Medovoi, Erikson adds "a post-Hegelian psychological requirement. . . . The self must be capable of formulating a satisfactory self-image that is determined by neither blind acceptance nor unthinking rejection of the image offered by the other" (7).

Medovoi also highlights a significantly literary dimension of the discourse of identity organized around the rebellious teenager. Beginning in the 1950s, he argues, the notion of identity became a standard for literary evaluation and even production; "character" was refashioned in literary terms, even as literature was understood as inherently political and cultural. This "protagonization of the American character," suggests Medovoi, "was the process by which the literary value of American texts, old and new alike, became measured for their hermeneutic capacity to be read as allegories of national identity" (56). Put another way, literature became a preferred genre of adolescence. Medovoi's chief evidence is *The Catcher in the Rye,* whose hypercanonicity is perhaps rivaled only by Twain's *Adventures of Huckleberry Finn,* likewise understood as national allegory. *The Catcher in the Rye* offers a gently delinquent vision of the American self, its hero Holden Caulfield pseudo-rebelling against school, family, and all things "phony." Leslie Fiedler, in *Love and Death in the American Novel* (1960) famously observed that the American canon was at heart a literature for boys, and we might say after Salinger and Medovoi that said canon is now more specifically a literature for adolescent boys; as Medovoi notes, Fiedler's "Good Bad Boy" bears a strong resemblance to the rebellious teenager of midcentury forward.

While literary adolescence is not Medovoi's main concern, the argument he makes about the rebel-teenager resonates strongly with what Trites calls "adolescent reform." The American teenager, Medovoi believes, asserts his or her youthful rights and identity against corrupt and repressive paternal powers—sometimes the American government, more typically Communists—*and* against the standardizing forces of American mass culture. The teenager rages against the man, the suburb, and (to use Holden Caulfield's term) "phonies" of every persuasion. In Medovoi's reading, Holden came to represent America's "submerged commitment to a sovereign selfhood, which survives intact beneath pragmatic compromises made with mass society" (72). As Medovoi makes clear, the rebellion of the American teenager is enacted within as much as against American culture; Holden is hardly a radical rebel or social reformer, and *The Catcher in the Rye,* with its ostensible critique of American culture (as shallow, consumerist, and so on) is a highly successful American commodity. While Trites tends toward a more heroic understanding of the adolescent as reform minded, she too recognizes that Holden and other characters function differently than do Jo March and Huck Finn, maintaining that the tradition is not so much broken as reformatted in more contemporary and generally more dystopian literature, with Holden and company serving as victim-reformers (2007, 145).

In time, the idealized rebel-teenager yielded to or metamorphosed into the so-called young adult (YA), or the adolescent tending toward adulthood and ostensible social maturity. The term "young adult" seems to have originated with book publishers and librarians, who sought an alternative to more-negative understandings of the adolescent. The terms "adolescent," "teenager," and "young adult" overlap considerably in usage and inflection, but they emerged more or less sequentially, in particular contexts that continue to shape their meanings. More so than his older cousins, the young adult is associated with education, civic training, and cultural literacy—such that "young adult" has become shorthand for pedagogical programs and materials. The moniker connotes a healthy sort of development into adulthood, one attuned both to the rhythms of development and to the needs of adult society. At the same time, it insists upon a residual immaturity; adulthood is on the horizon but not yet achieved. The term "young adult" works to repudiate the chaos and perils of adolescence—the young adult is what we hope the adolescent or teenager will become. Simultaneously, the young adult embodies and perhaps even restores to the old adult a weird sort of innocence, representing both past and future stability of the self.

Although an overdetermined figure, the young adult is not discontinuous with the adolescent. If the young adult bears a family resemblance to Hall's fin de siècle adolescent, it is thanks to the ongoing project of middle-class uplift and assimilation. The junior high and high school tends to standardize as much as empower or liberate, and so too with the public library, whose genteel origins have long conflicted with its more progressive energies. The first young adult services were aimed at working-class kids between the ages of fourteen and sixteen who dropped out of school in order to earn a living (Hutchinson 1978, 39). Soon, however, YA library work shifted attention to the middle-class kids who could afford to stay in school. In the library and in the school, the focus in YA reading has long been on social adaptation rather than on the development of critical thinking. The kind of prescriptive practice envisioned by Hall in adolescence came to pass. Beginning in the 1930s, high schoolers were surveyed about their reading habits and were then given literary prescriptions. Educators and librarians seem to have been particularly influenced by Havighurst's monographs on adolescence, education, and developmental psychology. In 1943, for instance, Gladys B. Johnson published a booklist for each of the five developmental tasks of adolescence as defined by Havighurst: adjustment to age mates *(Huckleberry Finn)*, independence of family (John Galsworthy's *The Forsyte Saga*), occupational orientation (Paul de Kruif's *Microbe Hunters*), social participation (Ellen Glasgow's *Barren Ground*), and developments of the self (Somerset Maugham's *Of Human Bondage*). This matching of books to tasks fueled the expectation that YA literature should fortify the self. By the end of World War II, notes Margaret Hutchinson, "many people were thinking of books as a means to an end (adjustment) . . . given to youth made intellectually and emotionally mature by the world crisis and by exposure to the media of radio, newspaper, and motion pictures" (47).

Young adult literature is expected to perform psychological and educational work, usually in the utilitarian mode of ego psychology but sometimes in a more classically Freudian vein. While the problem novel is a form of young adult literature, young adult literature has also been asserted against the problem novel. In 1966, for instance, ten years before Bettelheim's fairy-tale study appeared, Carlsen objected to the prescriptiveness of the problem novel on the grounds that it denies the adolescent an opportunity to work-through problems unconsciously and "will not invade his privacy as a counselor would" (1966, 39). While the details vary, the faith in the genre as psychological in form and effect is steady.

Though YA literature tends to be optimistic about the ability of adolescents to solve problems and grow into adulthood, quite a few titles play up their psychological as well as social vulnerability. This more negative or dystopian tradition can also be traced back to *The Catcher in the Rye,* perhaps even to earlier works. Holden Caulfield, after all, became popular not only as a hero but also as an ordinary teenager. In one of its first reviews, psychoanalyst and Freud biographer Ernest Jones calls the novel "a case history of us all," finding it unremarkable as literature but interesting as a record of "what every sensitive sixteen-year-old since Rousseau has felt, and of course what each one of us is certain he has felt" (1990, 24). Calling its insights very "general," Jones says that *The Catcher in the Rye* "depends upon the reader's recollection of merely similar difficulties; the unique crisis and the unique anguish are not re-created." Jones finally finds the novel "predictable and boring" (25). Other readers found the novel and the character of Holden evidence of American immaturity. Citing Dwight Macdonald's remark that "Peter Pan might be a better symbol of America than Uncle Sam" (1957, 66), Medovoi suggests that the immaturity critique was part and parcel of anxiety about the mass-market paperback and the forces of mass culture more generally (2005, 82–83). But the immaturity critique was not fashioned only out of anxiety about the paperbacking of America; critics were responding as much to the character of Holden, to his ostensibly representative fears and anxieties. Those fears and anxieties so artfully conveyed in the first person emerge from a tradition of anxious representation and in turn keep that tradition alive.

We might look to *The Catcher in the Rye* as the beginning point not so much of adolescent literature at large but of adolescent literature as case writing about emotionally troubled youth. From Salinger onward, much adolescent literature has emphasized in both psychological and ethnographic terms the vulnerability as well as the immaturity of adolescents. The introduction of identity made possible the failure of its achievement, a failure that haunts even more cheerful or confident texts. While the book did help sponsor identity and model what Medovoi calls the "identitarian novel," it also points to the precariousness of identity formation. If Holden is a representative male subject, he seems less than confident about his selfhood's sovereignty. Whether his uncertainty bespeaks rebellion, conformity, or both, it is now the overriding mode for the protagonization of the young adult novel.

The problem novel of the 1960s and 1970s had already emphasized the psychological fragility of youth, as Michael Cart observes: "In [problem novels] teens speak their own language, often in the immediacy of present tense. . . . always they create a world apart from adults. . . . Even today many novels echo the familiar angst-filled voice of a sensitive lonely kid near the edge of a nervous breakdown" (1996, 66). Moreover, that voice nearly always belonged to a budding writer or artist, who tells his or her story in order to forestall that breakdown or to recover from trauma. Consider the narrative framework of Salinger. Holden tells his story in retrospect, living in "this crumby place," some kind of treatment facility in California (1964, 1). And at the book's end, he talks about a psychoanalyst who asks dumb questions about Holden's future. "Don't ever tell anybody anything," he says then. "If you do, you start missing everybody" (214). The book, then, is a story that Holden shares with the reader, as he is thinking about his life and at least pretending to get better in a clinical setting. The reader represents both an alternative to and a version of his psychoanalyst.

A similar framework marks S. E. Hinton's *The Outsiders* (1967), another contender for the title of first YA novel. In Hinton's narrative, Ponyboy Curtis also tells his story—*much* more traumatic than Holden's—retrospectively, trying to heal wounds and survive the death of his friend Johnny. This time, the writing is not prompted by (or set against) dumb questions from a psychoanalyst but rather is an assignment in English class—as it happens, the origin of *The Outsiders* itself, written by a sixteen-year-old Hinton. Like *Seventeenth Summer,* *The Outsiders* was written by an adolescent girl, and it shares some of its predecessor's themes and tonalities, among them romantic longing, the joy in being alive, and the pleasure of "family" (here, kinship with fellow greasers). Cart avers that the narrative voice is obviously not that of a Ponyboy but rather a Ponygirl, or that Hinton fails to mask her gender. Perhaps so, but *The Outsiders* blends romance with realism and naturalism, focusing on the class divide between the "greasers" and the "socs" (socials, the economically privileged) and thereby combining psychological with social and ethnographic concerns. Ponyboy does not have the kind of faith in him- or herself that Angie does in Daly's novel; quite the opposite. He feels very vulnerable, as does his friend Johnny, abused by his family and then by the socs.

A decidedly more cynical variant on this bibliotherapeutic tradition of the young adult novel is Robert Cormier's *I Am the Cheese* (1977), about a boy whose life is disrupted by political violence and immersion in an early version of the federal Witness Protection Program (being developed when Cormier wrote the book). Operating in the loose tradition of Oz, Cormier uses three levels of narrative, and we never know which one is most current or privileged. In one, Adam rides his bike toward Vermont in search of his father; in another, he is interrogated by a "doctor" who is probably an enemy; the third is Adam's memory of life before trauma. The book performs the impossibility of witnessing to trauma, or more precisely, the reenactment of trauma that witnessing inevitably brings, even in the form of writing. Through his sessions with the doctor, Adam remembers that he is or was also Paul Delmonte, gradually piecing together the chain of events that destroyed his family, culminating in a car crash that killed his mother. The knowledge is too traumatic, however, and the novel ends with Adam-Paul in a mental institution, riding his bike in circles and having regressed to an infantile personality (clutching a stuffed animal, singing "I Am the Cheese").

I Am the Cheese is deeply suspicious of the institutional discourse of psychoanalysis. The book functions as an anti–case study of sorts, emptying out the self and positioning the doctor as an enemy. In the questioning, Paul challenges the doctor, who responds with the clichés of psychotherapy:

> A: What do you really want to know about me? What's this questioning really about?
> T: Must we discuss motive again? We have agreed that these sessions are journals to discover your past. And I am willing to serve as your guide.
> A: But I sometimes wonder what's more important—what I find out about myself or what you find out about me.

T: You must avoid these needless doubts—they only delay
the process of discovery and you are then left with those
terrifying blanks. (131)

Cormier uses the story of Adam-Paul not to convey a sense of adolescent identity, or even the search for such an identity, but rather to emphasize the sheer vulnerability of selfhood. Identity here has been shattered. All the usual hallmarks of the genre take on dramatic form. The
family romance turns into an actual story of false or invented identity,
and the primal scene is devastating beyond understanding. If Cormier
casts suspicion on the figure of the analyst or therapist, he does so entirely in the contemporary idiom of trauma writing, itself formed from
psychoanalysis. In this respect, Cormier anticipates the turn toward
abjection lately taken by the genre.

A more recent example is Stephen Chbosky's *The Perks of Being a
Wallflower* (1999), about the effects of sexual abuse. Protagonist Charlie
is a more sedate version of Holden, telling his story through an episto-
lary format. He is writing to a mysterious stranger, mailing each chapter as a letter. Charlie, like Adam-Paul, suffers a serious breakdown in
the course of the novel, finally remembering an episode of sexual abuse
by his aunt. Here are the final lines of the book: "So if this ends up being
my last letter, please believe things are good with me, and even when
they're not, they will be soon enough. And I will believe the same about
you" (213). There are many other examples, among them Laurie Halse
Anderson's *Speak* (1999), about a girl recovering from a rape and coming into a more mature selfhood through writing and artistic expression. As Trites notes, the *künstlerroman* lives on in such texts.

The narrative pattern in contemporary YA realistic literature, concludes Frances FitzGerald, "is traumatic/therapeutic" (2004, 64). "How
do kids survive their predicaments? Interestingly, the solutions haven't
changed as much as the problems have. Art is one way: more than half
of these kids are budding writers or painters" (69). Moreover, psychotherapy "is up there with art as a means of survival, and, as is rarely
the case for adult fiction these days, the therapist is a benevolent figure
who, like the High Priest in *The Magic Flute,* appears at the end to put
matters to rights" (69). Adult popular fiction nonetheless shares this
tendency toward the traumatic/therapeutic, with the telling and even

writing of one's story a central conceit.[22] This emphasis on vulnerability alongside and within the achievement of adulthood (or the potential for achieving it) marks the third stage of the genre's psychologization.

The cultural politics of this literary-psychological turn to trauma or recovery writing are hard to assess, especially given the diversity of storylines, contexts of production, and so forth among such works. Stories about rape, murder, and other forms of social violence should not be too easily grouped with stories about vaguely disaffected or alienated youth; the literature of trauma and vulnerability deserves more careful parsing. Another issue is the extent to which the problem novel, whether classic or more contemporary, has been fashioned from stories about minority teens and the racism they encounter. "Books about minority youth with problems," notes Hutchinson, "were the forerunners of books about all sorts of youths with problems" (1978, 57). The dissemination of "problems" to a wider segment of the population—to adolescents in general, including nonminority adolescents—may represent either a positive development or just the opposite, a kind of whitewashing or noncontextual appropriation. There are clearly other factors at work in the rise of the novel of vulnerability and trauma, some of which I have acknowledged, such as delinquency case writing and literary naturalism. Examining particular titles, we might consider whether a character's psychological problems do or do not derive from social problems such as homophobia or xenophobia. Much YA literature, notes Anne Scott MacLeod, reads "less like social criticism than like private psychotherapy sessions" (1997, 126). What are the implications of this turn away from the social or this privileging of adolescent interiority? Such consideration seems especially critical given the tendency of psychological discourse toward ahistoricism or universality.

Abjection and Adolescent Literature

In "The Adolescent Novel," Kristeva holds that the adolescent and the novel share an "open psychic structure" that tends toward maturity but does not necessarily achieve it—and to their credit. "I would tend to see writing," she remarks, "as a semiotic practice that facilitates a renewed organization of psychic space—a process that precedes an idealized maturity" (1995, 138). As a genre, the novel is "quite dependent on the 'adolescent economy' of writing. . . . This view would imply that a novel is the work of a perpetual subject-adolescent. As a permanent witness to our adolescence, the novel would enable us to rediscover the state of incompleteness (which is as depressive as it is joyful) that leads in some respects to what we call aesthetic pleasure" (139). Writing protects the subject from "phobic affects," allowing the reconstruction of psychic space and the evasion of judgment (137). As she puts it, "What, if not an 'open structure,' could motivate someone to write?" (139).[23] In one sense, Kristeva is suggesting that adolescence is never left behind. At the same time, she restores alterity to adolescence, precisely against the normalizing force of identity. She does the same for the novel in relation to adolescence, giving the novel a history of emergence but also declaring it adolescent in energy even if not also in theme.

What Kristeva says about the novel seems particularly true of the contemporary young adult novel. Here, after all, writing about the self often involves writing about writing; in text after text, the teen protagonist is a writer or an artist, proactive in the construction of meaning and trying to manage an unsettling or even traumatic experience. In "The Adolescent Novel," however, Kristeva does not comment on her own theory of abjection. Karen Coats finds it "surprising that Kristeva doesn't link the concepts of adolescence and abjection in her work," and she argues not only that they should be linked but also that "the exploration of abjection has come to dominate the [YA] genre" (1999, 290, 292). Martha Westwater makes a similar case in *Giant Despair Meets Hopeful* (2000), which aligns Kristeva's ideas with the work of six YA novelists.

Kristeva introduced the term "abjection" in *Powers of Horror* to designate "the twisted braid of affects and thoughts . . . [that] does not have, properly speaking, a definable object" (1982, 1). The abject "has only one quality of the object—that of being opposed to *I*" (1). The abject names the human response of horror—sometimes registered or represented physically, linked with feces and bodily fluids and the human corpse—to a real or perceived collapse between subject and object, or self and Other. The abject also names a state of psychological existence prior to identity formation through self–object negotiation, which can be reactivated by trauma or by encounters with the Real.[24] Abjection has proven a very portable and generalizable concept; indeed, it functions more as a metaphor than as anything else, signifying various states and processes of exclusion and alterity.

For Coats, abjection means "the process of expulsion that enables the subject to set up clear boundaries and establish a stable identity" (1999, 291). In adolescence, the theory goes, the unruly, often messy body reasserts itself or can no longer be so easily managed, even as psychic disturbances going back to early childhood are reactivated. Kristeva says as much in "The Adolescent Novel," even if she does not invoke the concept of abjection there. Coats applies the term to the social as well as the individual body, arguing that adolescents not only experience abjection within themselves but also serve as abject figures within the community. Coats identifies a tradition of the "abject hero" (290) in adolescent literature, beginning with Robert Cormier's Jerry Renault in *The Chocolate War* (1974). Such characters are "ordinary people who refuse to reintegrate into society under its terms, but instead haunt and disrupt its borders" (Coats 1999, 296). She identifies *The Outsiders* as a precursor to the tradition, underscoring that Hinton's characters are socially abject (and in fact self-identify as "greasers"). The abject hero of Coats is the hero of the adolescent reform novel as identified by Trites—especially its postmodern variant—more likely a victim than a change agent. While Coats prefers psychological to historical analysis, she does draw an intriguing comparison between Jerry Renault as abject hero of *The Chocolate War* and the returning soldiers of the Vietnam War, at least as abject. Like Kristeva and FitzGerald, Coats proposes that abjection can be combated through writing, art, and spiritual experience.

Both Coats and Westwater see abjection as a worsening social and psychological problem, taking a cue from Kristeva herself, who theorizes abjection in relation to the Holocaust and other mass horrors of the modern age. In *Giant Despair Meets Hopeful,* Westwater underscores the fragility of adolescence, linking it to the decline of religion and the nuclear family and what she more broadly calls "the strange diseases of our time" (2000, 17). There is much to admire in this study; Westwater presents her readings as "meditations" and respects both theory and literature, refusing to give one greater rhetorical authority. But her assertion of cultural decline is less than persuasive. She explains up front her conviction "that we *are* in a state of cultural decay and that writing—whether for children or adults—may preserve for us values that are on the verge of decline" (xvii; emphasis in the original). "Parents and educators," she asserts, and therefore the young people with whom they are involved, are "looking up the devil's nose," unable to differentiate between good and evil. Hence the need for narrative rescue, both literary and psychoanalytic (2). Westwater reads Kristeva as a theorist of hope and renewal, and it is certainly true that Kristeva passionately advocates for writing, art, and psychoanalysis as the cure for the materialism and depersonalization of the modern age. Westwater's alarmist tendencies are inspired by Kristeva, who has her own story to tell about cultural decline and the staying power of symbolic activity.[25]

I am not so sure that we are in cultural decline or, if so, that adolescent literature is really so sturdy a lifeboat. I am suspicious of any scholarship that presumes the breakdown of the family, much less that sees such a breakdown as necessarily bad. In Westwater's study, all the social gains of the 1960s and 1970s are overlooked; rather than seeing young adult literature as gaining maturity with the introduction of difficult topics, she sees young adults as losing it. *Giant Despair Meets Hopeful* plays down the complexity of social history and exhibits a rather utopian faith in the power of literature.

As engaging as are these alignments of abjection and adolescent literature, we should also remember that both terms or discourses have a history that complicates their pairing. The turn toward character vulnerability and trauma is just that, a turn or a stage in the genre's larger evolution. At the same time, the genre has long been preoccupied with both psychological and social difficulty. In short, the literary record does not furnish easy evidence of social reality and is certainly not a straightforward narrative of decline. Moreover, abjection cannot simply be applied to adolescence because abjection is itself a *literary* as well as a psychoanalytic concept. Kristeva's *Pouvoirs de l'horreur* appeared in 1980 (the English translation came in 1982), well after *The Chocolate War* and indeed after many decades of literature reckoning with trauma and social ills. In the first chapter, "Approaching Abjection," Kristeva develops the concept by appealing to the writing of Fyodor Dostoyevsky, Marcel Proust, James Joyce, Jorge Luis Borges, and Antonin Artaud. Like most of Kristeva's concepts, abjection is fashioned out of textual traditions, including literature and psychoanalysis.

Perhaps Kristeva did not want to link abjection with adolescence, whatever her reasons. "The Adolescent Novel," in fact, seems one of the least pessimistic or alarmist chapters of *New Maladies of the Soul*. In that piece, she emphasizes the indeterminacy and liminality of adolescence—its "open psychic structure"—as useful rather than disabling. Furthermore, linking abjection with adolescence, while instructive in some ways, may risk reinscribing the ideology of innocence, exactly when adolescent literature is finally being recognized as a mature enterprise.

The Author as Young Adult

One of the most interesting aspects of Kristeva's essay is its emphasis on the "'adolescent economy' of writing" and her construction of the novelist—not just the young adult novelist—as "a perpetual subject-adolescent" (139). Writing, she thinks, maintains or returns us to an adolescent "state of incompleteness" linked to aesthetic pleasure and personal fulfillment (139). Again leaving aside the provocative claim that all novelists trend adolescent, is the novelist for adolescents also and necessarily an adolescent? Does writing for young adults return one to young adulthood or signal that young adulthood was never relinquished or surpassed? Might the young adult in YA literature be the author as much as the protagonist or the implied reader?

At least two scholars have speculated along these lines. In her analysis of Daniel Handler's Series of Unfortunate Events books (published under the pen name Lemony Snicket), Laurie Langbauer draws upon Kristeva's essay to propose that the Snicket books are representative of the adolescent economy of Gen X literature more broadly. Gen X literature's tendency toward metafiction or self-conscious, ironized authorial exhibition or spectacle "underscore[s] the genre's adolescent elements" (2007, 503), including not only its skepticism but also its strange earnestness (which Langbauer identifies as a kind of ethics). When read through Kristeva, suggests Langbauer, Handler's exhibitionistic tendency (not only in the books but also in op-ed pieces and other writings) "becomes the innocent, even touching fantasy of every adolescent: the fantasy that the zeitgeist culminates in him or her" (509). Langbauer's is not the most flattering of readings, but it is an interesting attempt to apply Kristeva's thesis to the contemporary moment.[26]

Turning her attention to adolescent trauma literature, and also working from a psychoanalytic perspective, Barbara Tannert-Smith theorizes that the process of writing about trauma for adolescents necessarily subjects the author to potentially traumatic experiences and elicits not a little authorial anxiety. Through a persuasive close reading of Anderson's *Speak*, Tannert-Smith holds that "the act of speaking *through* a young adult consciousness is rather analytically complex" and that "the writer of young adult fiction fashioning such a voice may be herself subject to uncanny affects she cannot control" (2010, 398). Tannert-Smith draws not only from the novel but also from Anderson's comments about its composition to show how Anderson reworked various experiences from her own youth. "The young adult author, like the traumatized individual, carries 'an impossible history within them' and in the act of writing through the consciousness of the child they once were may too become 'the symptom of a history that they cannot entirely possess'" (410, quoting Caruth 1995, 5).

At the same time, the adolescent novel, like the picturebook, has been fashioned as a psychological genre and tends to accredit the successful practitioner (the good author) as a lay psychologist very much in control of his or her text. I do not think there is a YA equivalent to Maurice Sendak. The closest match might be Judy Blume. Blume's many books for teens and preteens, organized around the psychological and social challenges of growing up, have made her into a household name. She is frequently appealed to for advice by teenagers and parents alike; her *Letters to Judy* (1986) is a compilation of such appeals and of the advice she gives in return. Another YA author who seems both positioned and self-positioning as an expert on adolescence is Chris Crutcher, who is also a licensed family therapist. As Anne Scott MacLeod observes, Crutcher's novels nearly always feature "a coach or a trainer who functions as a guru" who "applies tough-minded wisdom" and offers therapeutic advice (1997, 127–28). But Crutcher himself functions that way, advocating for the importance of adolescent literature as well as the right to read freely; he is very active in the anticensorship movement. Looking back to authors I discussed earlier, Dell and Maxwell both claim special knowledge about adolescence. To trace out this history, we would need to make distinctions among the various kinds of psychological-therapeutic wisdom claimed or modeled by various authors. Some kind of fieldwork seems to be expected, as well—whether professional (as with Crutcher) or more casual; Anderson reports that she learned the contemporary language of teenagers at "Taco Bell and The Mall" (2000, 25). The larger point is that because adolescent literature has long been understood as a psychological genre, its practitioners are at least tacitly understood as having specialized insight and knowledge.

Moreover, that insight or knowledge must be personal and even autobiographical: writers of adolescent literature must remain in adolescence or young adulthood to some degree, must "identify" with their subjects. I think this is even truer of this genre than of the picturebook. The picturebook author is expected to remain childlike, but no one would expect the picturebook author to actually be a young child (only a child at heart). The young adult author, on the other hand, could conceivably be and is often presented as a young adult—there is not as much of a gap between adult and young adult as between adult and child. Young adult authors increasingly self-present or are presented as teenagers on author Web sites, book tours, and other marketing spaces. Meg Cabot, for example, has worn tiaras when visiting bookstores to promote her Princess Diaries series and apparently does Webcasts dressed up in pajamas as if she is at a slumber party. There is of course tension between the author's identification with young adulthood and assumptions about literary achievement. Sometimes young adult authors can manage to be both sufficiently literary and sufficiently "authentic" in adolescent voice, whereas sometimes literary "failure" affirms the authenticity of the adolescent perspective; Cart's comment that Hinton's narratorial boy voice is obviously that of a girl makes the novel less literary but also more authentic.

In any event, while adolescents are young and must strive for adulthood, authors for adolescents are adults who must retain their youth. Even when sufficiently mature or literary, they are expected to maintain fidelity and proximity to adolescence. Their expertise, in short, comes from their positioning as both young *and* adult. That positioning is cultural as much as individual. Like the abjection of adolescence, the youth of the author is largely an effect of the genre's history and ongoing reputation as psychological. The genre conditions the author as much as it does the subject or reader to be a young adult, with all the complexities of that term. While Kristeva, Langbauer, and Tannert-Smith hold that the adolescent identity of (young adult) novelists comes from the process of writing, which reactivates certain psychological dynamics, we must also acknowledge the legacy of writing, the cultural and institutional pressures shaping the adolescent novel and our expectations of it.

6. *T* Is for Trauma
The Children's Literature of Atrocity

S INCE THE LATE 1980S AND EARLY 1990S, children's texts about trauma, and especially the traumas of the Holocaust, have proliferated. Despite the difficulties of representing the Holocaust, or perhaps because of them, there seems to be consensus now that children's literature is the most rather than the least appropriate forum for trauma work. Thus in "A New Algorithm in Evil: Children's Literature in a Post-Holocaust World," Elizabeth R. Baer emphasizes the urgency of "a children's literature of atrocity," recommending "confrontational" texts and proposing "a set of [four] criteria by which to measure the usefulness and effectiveness of children's texts in confronting the Holocaust sufficiently" (2000, 384). *A* is now for Auschwitz, and *H* for Holocaust (and sometimes Hiroshima).[1] Baer sees as exemplary the picturebook *Rose Blanche* (1985), written by Roberto Innocenti and Christophe Gallaz and illustrated by Innocenti, along with Seymour Rossel's nonfiction history *The Holocaust* (1992) and Jane Yolen's novel *The Devil's Arithmetic* (1988). Such books emphasize their protagonists' direct experiences of the Holocaust, experiences that extend to and presumably interpellate the child reader.

Like the unconscious as theorized by Sigmund Freud, the Holocaust is at once historical event and never-ending story, the primal scene endlessly reconstructed. It must be spoken about but remains inaccessible: this is the necessary paradox of Holocaust writing. Contrary to Theodor Adorno, the sentiment now goes, we must write poetry after Auschwitz, must attempt to reckon with the Holocaust despite the difficulty and potential futility of our efforts.[2] Even so, the Holocaust has only recently become an acceptable narrative project. As Susan Gubar emphasizes in *Poetry after Auschwitz,* silence about the Holocaust, alongside outright denial, held sway through the late 1950s, at which point writers, artists, and critics began finally to engage the Holocaust and its consequences (2003, 3).[3] Lawrence L. Langer's foundational study *The Holocaust and the Literary Imagination,* published in 1975, is one of the earliest long treatments of what he calls the "literature of atrocity." In the United States, the first wave of Holocaust studies coincided with and was in part authorized by the women's and antiwar movements, which established psychological trauma as a pressing sociopolitical problem.[4] The idea of trauma has since gone mainstream, maintaining its medical and psychological meanings while also becoming the stuff of literature and of critical theory. Trauma, writes Kirby Farrell, has become "both a clinical syndrome and a trope" (1998, 2). Trauma writing is an amalgam of literary and psychological discourse, one in which certain kinds of trauma take priority.

We could claim a longer history for children's literature about trauma, one less clearly organized around the Holocaust and less exemplary by Baer's standards. Much depends on how trauma or traumatic experience is constructed and accentuated. There are many children's books about death, for instance, but not all portray death as a destabilizing event. Books for children and adolescents about war date back at least to the nineteenth century, but most do not emphasize the psychological toll of war, death, or genocide.[5] Much "realistic" literature for children and adolescents deals with traumatic experiences—divorce, racism, class struggle, and so forth—even when that literature is not tagged as "trauma" writing per se. What *is* new is the atrocity part, as well as the emphasis on experiences of pain and suffering on the part of principal characters. Older children's literature tends to be about the management of trauma, whereas the children's literature of atrocity makes clear the profound emotional and psychological effects of trauma—even the impossibility of recovery.

A proper history of the children's literature of atrocity would require a thorough psychosocial history of American childhood. Jane
Thrailkill (2003) gestures toward such a history, locating her critique
of recent trauma theory in the larger context of American literary sen-
timentalism, showing how the realist tradition that Mark Twain introduced against "feminine" sentimentality has nonetheless made way for
the reincarnation of the wounded or dead child in that most unlikely of
places, critical theory. As Thrailkill has it, the suffering literary child
made thinkable the wounded child of social reform and psychological
or social discourse around the turn of the century and now survives as
the traumatized child of theory.[6] Writing about the sudden popularity
in the 1990s of adult trauma stories in which childhood looms large,
Patricia Pace, drawing from Viviana Zelizer's work, similarly points
to the historical transformation of the American child from "economically useful" to "emotionally priceless" (1998, 238). The emergence of a
trauma literature for children is part of this complex history of childhood's revaluation, of its merger with the idea of interiority and the
position of vulnerability. As Thrailkill, Pace, and other scholars stress,
childhood is now constructed as a psychic-developmental space at once
sacrosanct and violated.[7]

It is hardly surprising that children's literature has traditionally
been resistant to open acknowledgment of trauma. Psychoanalysis itself, the discipline forged largely from the analysis of trauma and hysteria, tends to deny and suppress traumatic experience, as Judith Lewis
Herman emphasizes in her foundational study *Trauma and Recovery*.
Herman devotes a chapter ("A Forgotten History") to the history of
trauma-discovery-turned-disavowal within psychoanalysis, beginning
with Freud's abandonment of the seduction hypothesis. Herman attributes this pattern of discovery-repudiation to both the difficulty of facing trauma and to male denial of the victimization of women and children, adding, "The systematic study of psychological trauma therefore
depends on the support of a political movement. Indeed, whether such
study can be pursued or discussed in public is itself a political question"
(1997, 9). The acknowledgment of traumatic experience within children's and young adult literature has likewise taken time and remains
a complicated affair, especially given an ongoing conviction that such
literature should be happy and uplifting, or at least not *too* disturbing.

That conviction is not necessarily as retrograde as we might think; contra Baer, it is not so clear that "confrontation" makes for the best approach to trauma. Denial and suppression may be problematic but are not always or necessarily so, and coming to terms with trauma nearly always involves a mix of acknowledgment and denial, remembrance and forgetting.[8]

The genres I have examined so far in this book have all been made into trauma writing within the last few decades. Fairy tales are considered potentially traumatizing because of their sometimes severe scenes and themes (violence, infanticide, child abandonment) even as they are also positioned as therapeutic or cathartic. Picturebooks, including those of Maurice Sendak, are increasingly focused on the child's experience of and responses to loss and trauma. The adolescent novel, as stressed in the previous chapter, trends toward traumatic subjects in more ways than one. Even Golden Age aftertexts move toward as much as away from certain kinds of trauma writing, especially sexual-abuse narratives. The practice of child analysis, as Adam Phillips shows in "Bombs Away" (2001), was forged amid war and genocide, reflecting them in its theming of vulnerability and violence. We might even say that the children's literature of atrocity was first made thinkable in child analysis, especially in the work of Melanie Klein.

The interactive dynamic of children's literature and psychoanalysis I have traced so far thus culminates in the so-called children's literature of atrocity. What seems a more serious or mature children's literature—the children's literature of atrocity—is also a particular moment in the ongoing collaborative project of psychoanalysis and literature, both of which take the Holocaust as, in the words of Shoshana Felman and Dori Laub in their book *Testimony,* "the watershed of our times . . . whose traumatic consequences are still actively *evolving*" (1992, xiv; emphasis in the original). As Petar Ramandanovic (2001) underscores in his introduction to a special issue of *Postmodern Culture,* the term "trauma" first became an important keyword of critical theory with Felman's essay "Education and Crisis; or, The Vicissitudes of Teaching," first published in 1991, just as the new "children's literature of atrocity" was appearing on the scene. Felman's essay is reprinted in *Testimony.* In that volume, Felman and Laub position psychoanalysis and literature both as testimony to the unspeakable, one that recognizes the unconscious witnessing of the subject. In their view, psychoanalysis acknowledged,

> for the first time in the history of culture, that one does not have to *possess* or *own* the truth, in order to effectively *bear witness* to it; that speech as such is unwittingly testimonial; and that the speaking subject constantly bears witness to a truth that nonetheless continues to escape him, a truth that is, essentially, *not available* to its own speaker. (1992, 15; emphasis in the original)

Put another way, the speaker does not possess the truth; the truth possesses the speaker. Psychoanalysis, like literature, is there to witness. So, too, is children's literature, in various ways and with various consequences.

This chapter focuses on trauma writing as the contemporary, largely American mode of interaction between children's literature and psychoanalysis. As such, it also serves as a conclusion to *Freud in Oz*. Trauma writing is not the only dimension of analytic-literary relay or exchange in our time, but it is one of the most significant, especially for children's literature. Whereas the other chapters of this book have been more descriptive than evaluative, this chapter proposes that at least some of the children's literature of atrocity turns away from rather than confronts the difficulties of its subject matter, opting for simplistic narratives of character empowerment adapted from self-help literature. While there are books for young readers that explore the paradox of trauma writing—the need to speak about trauma alongside the difficulty of providing sufficient witness or treatment—the materials I examine take refuge in the very ideology of innocence laid bare by the most powerful trauma writing. I focus first on young adult Holocaust novels that are styled after fairy tales or that are "Americanized," then turn to picturebooks about the 9/11 terrorist attacks. While young adult Holocaust narrative marks trauma as having happened elsewhere in time or space, the 9/11 picturebooks construct Americans as innocent victims or (using Lauren Berlant's term) "infantile citizens" (1997). These are but two subgenres and may not be representative of the broader literary scene.

Fairy-Tale Forms

Although a comprehensive picture of trauma literature for children and young adults is beyond the scope of this chapter, I can at least sketch its more recent American profile. As I have emphasized, trauma work has been authorized by psychoanalysis and by critical theory, as well as by adult literature. Published one year after Langer's *The Holocaust and the Literary Imagination* was Bruno Bettelheim's even more influential study *The Uses of Enchantment* (1976), which codified but also revised the trope of the wounded child. *The Uses of Enchantment* was published to wide acclaim and has had significant influence on how fairy tales signify. Even though Bettelheim knew nothing about children's literature—and in fact posed fairy tales against it—*The Uses of Enchantment* attests to the growing force of that expectation in the 1970s and continues to shore it up.

Not only did Bettelheim show us how to read fairy tales, but the culture also showed Bettelheim. He had no interest in fairy tales originally, but he had long been preoccupied with what I have elsewhere called the "feral tale." Bettelheim was fascinated by accounts of wolf-children and argued as early as 1959 that such accounts were really stories of autistic children. He was also preoccupied with the experiences of Holocaust survivors and the ways in which their behavior resembled that of emotionally disturbed children. The feral tale provides a useful bridge from his studies of particular experiences of trauma, especially in concentration camps, to his more professional focus on everyday trauma and how to manage it. A particular wolf-girl case, about a girl who lived in a bunker in Poland during the war, allowed Bettelheim to move from Holocaust trauma to autism to a more generic sense of trauma and dysfunction—at which point his interest in the fairy tale developed.[9] Put another way, the dead or wounded child of Holocaust experience and of residential clinical work merges in *The Uses of Enchantment* with the traumatized but resilient child of psychoanalysis as theorized by Freud. Freud's detractors have long argued that in emphasizing the power of oedipal fantasy Freud denied or downplayed child abuse. Rather than confront that issue, Bettelheim blurs the distinction between fantasy and reality by way of the fairy tale. It gave pop-intellectual affirmation to the idea that fairy-tale reading amounts to self-help or bibliotherapy.

The wounded-but-resilient (inner) child of pop-psychoanalysis enables a poetics of popular transmission and transference, whose major genre is the fairy tale. The fairy tale at once acknowledges and denies trauma. Through the fairy tale, people tell stories about challenge and survival, hardship and hope. By the 1990s, the fairy tale was ever more entrenched in U.S. pop-literary culture, in the adapted form of picturebooks, novelizations, films, "politically correct" satires, and the like. While it serves other ends as well, the fairy tale has been remodeled as a key genre of the children's literature of atrocity. Building upon some of the work of Jack Zipes, fairy-tale scholar Donald Haase proposes, "Children who have been *displaced* by violence may perceive an affinity between their traumatic experience and utopian projects, on the one hand, and the landscape of the fairy tale, on the other" (2000, 362). Noting that the fairy tale is more typically read in developmental terms, Haase theorizes that it "has the potential to become a template for the actual experience of human displacement and the perception of a defamiliarized geography" (363). Like Maria Tatar in *Off with Their Heads!,* Haase considers the Grimm fairy tale *Dear Mili* and its picturebook rendering by Maurice Sendak, which brings the Holocaust to the forefront.

In "The Hansel and Gretel Syndrome," U. C. Knoepflmacher examines what he calls "survivorship fantasies" in revisions or adaptations of "Hansel and Gretel" by Randall Jarrell, Anne Sexton, and Sendak. The core story, at least that of the Brothers Grimm, revolves around parental desertion and includes the threat of being burned up in the witch's oven. The Grimms do not want to recognize the parental desertion, according to Knoepflmacher. Whereas the Grimms in his reading repress such desertion, post-Freudians like Sexton and Jarrell recognize and emphasize it, insistent on the exposure of parental abandonment and the recovery-survival work of the abandoned. Knoepflmacher faults Bettelheim for defaulting to a Freudian emphasis on infantile sexuality, which downplays the possibility of adult abuse. Both the repression of trauma and its acknowledgment or exposure can be traced back to Freud, he thinks. "Kushner and Sendak's picturebook *Brundibar,*" he proposes, "steers between these camps" (2005, 177) by endorsing the fantasy of survival and triumph over evil central to the opera on which the picturebook is based, while tacitly acknowledging the historical reality that the children of Theresienstadt were murdered.

Fairy-tale structures and motifs are common in young adult novels about trauma. Such structures and motifs allow both the exploration and containment of trauma. Consider, for example, Jane Yolen's 1992 story *Briar Rose,* which adapts the Brothers Grimm tale by the same name (a variant of "Sleeping Beauty"). In this novel, a young woman manages to escape the Chelmno concentration camp alive. This plot, argues Adrienne Kertzer in *My Mother's Voice: Children, Literature, and the Holocaust* (2002), is unthinkable and even irresponsible—a fairy tale, we might say. Following Langer, among others, Kertzer chastises Yolen for pandering to the American desire for a happy ending. In her afterword to her novel, Yolen concedes: "This is a book of fiction. All the characters are made up. Happy-ever-after is a fairy tale notion, not history. I know of no woman who escaped from Chelmno alive" (2002, 241). And yet somehow the fairy-tale form is still appropriate to and as history, the logic seems to run. The fairy tale ostensibly brings us closer to truth (emotional truth, perhaps emotional catharsis for the reader), if not necessarily the truth of historical accuracy. Why else a Holocaust story in fairy-tale dress?

In her introduction to the 2002 edition of *Briar Rose,* Yolen's editor Terri Windling makes clear her own faith in the fairy-tale form as universally useful. "Way back in the 1980s," writes Windling, "I was a young book editor in New York City, and Jane Yolen was one of my heroes. Not only was she, quite simply, one of the finest writers I'd ever read, but also her knowledge of the world's great wealth of fairy tales was second to none. Like Jane, I was crazy about fairy tales, and so I had the notion of publishing a series of novels based on these classic stories. Thus the Fairy Tale series was born" (2002, xiii–xiv). Windling furnishes a nutshell history of the fairy tale, pointing to its juvenilization by the Walt Disney Company and hinting that its legitimacy is now being restored through her series. She implies that Yolen's novel will return to the fairy tale its rightful European seriousness, against Americanizations "stripped of moral ambiguities" and narrative complexities (xiii). There is even an epigraph from Jack Zipes, which sug-

gests how closely our faith in the sociological and historical significance of the fairy tale is entangled with our faith in its psychological
import.[10] Whereas Kertzer sees the novel as a typically American exercise in imaginative denial, Yolen and Windling position *Briar Rose*
as a higher truth. The fairy tale, in short, gives expression to trauma
but in distorted form, offering psychological relief but at the expense of
historical truth.

Young Adult, or Abusing the Holocaust?

In *Using and Abusing the Holocaust,* a sequel of sorts to his 1975 study,
Langer takes issue with what he calls the "abuse" of the Holocaust, in
particular the insistence that Holocaust narrative be hopeful and emphasize survival or resilience. This attitude is more typical in American
culture, he suggests, noting, for instance, that the American publishers of Primo Levi's *If This Is a Man (Se questo è un uomo)* retitled it
Survival in Auschwitz (Langer 2006, xi). But he also criticizes along
these lines the 1997 Italian-language film *La vita è bella* (released in
the United States in 1998 as *Life Is Beautiful*) and the 1952 English-
language translation of Anne Frank's journal, *The Diary of a Young
Girl*; both "are marked by an absence of pain, a muting of anguish, a
neglect of death" (xii). Langer urges recognition of and respect for the
"pursuit of death in Holocaust narrative," the coming to terms with
survival less "as the assertive idea of staying alive" and more as "the
reactive one of fending off death" (1). There is little trace of deathwork
or deathwriting in *The Diary of a Young Girl* or other Holocaust narratives that have been widely embraced. "It appears that when the
Holocaust is the subject," writes Langer, "misdirected popular enthu-
siasms form easily, especially when they deflect us from tackling the
authenticity of unbearable truths" (xiii).

Langer devotes the second chapter of *Using and Abusing the Holocaust* to *The Diary of a Young Girl,* arguing that Anne herself would
have been appalled by the book's transformation into a generic story of
adolescent fears and hopes. He is critical not so much of what the book
is as of what it has become, a hope fetish of sorts. Its readers know
that Anne and her family were rounded up and sent to the concentration camps, where they died, but this tragedy takes place offstage,

after the events of the book, and thus can be more easily repressed or not dwelled upon. Moreover, precisely because they were hidden away, Anne and her family knew little about what was happenings outside their secret annex. Anne, clarifies Langer, "is in no way to blame for not knowing about what she could not have known about. But readers are much to blame for accepting and promoting the idea that her *Diary* is a major Holocaust text and has anything of great consequence to tell us about the atrocities that culminated in the murder of European Jewry" (18–19).[11]

Anne's innocence, emanating from both her youth and her isolation, accounts for the book's alleged universal appeal. Langer even proposes that *The Diary of a Young Girl* is designed to avoid and make manageable the very experience of persecution and hiding that it promises to chronicle. Originally published in 1947, the book was translated into English in 1952 and quickly found an American audience. Langer traces the book's American promotion as embodying "the greater human values" and furnishing "a poignant delight in the infinite human spirit," in the words of reviewer Meyer Levin (quoted in Langer 2006, 23). Langer objects to such descriptions as obscuring the harsh realities of mass murder and crushing despair. Anne's afterstory is not so uplifting.[12] *The Diary of a Young Girl* "is a victim of one of the worst features of American culture," he maintains, "the effort to force us to construe the reality of an event before we have experienced it, to confirm an agenda in advance in order to discourage us from raising disturbing questions that might subvert the tranquility of our response" (21). All too easily, he thinks, we invent the Holocaust we need rather than confronting the things we do not know or do not wish to know.

While Langer does not dwell on the book's reputation as an adolescent or young adult text, it is clear from his discussion that such a reputation is bound up with Americanization or Holocaust "abuse." Its canonization as a (perhaps even *the*) Holocaust masterwork suggests the juvenilization of the reading public as much as its Americanization, its refusal of the ostensibly adult themes of despair and death.[13] Langer argues for its decanonization, praising in its stead texts by Ida Fink and Carl Freidman that are more realistic and informative but still appropriate for younger readers (27–28). Quite a few Holocaust titles have been published in the United States and elsewhere since *The*

Diary of a Young Girl appeared at midcentury. Barbara Harrison reports that, as of 1987, over three hundred children's books had been published in the United States alone on World War II, the Holocaust, and war in general, across a range of genres (1987, 67). The literature has continued to proliferate. But as Harrison notes, despite the acceptance of more-serious topics such as war and genocide within children's literature, "the one characteristic which adults are reluctant to see diminished in any way is hope, traditionally the animating force in children's books. Many adults cannot endure the thought that during the Holocaust, hope, along with the children of Izeiu, was swept into the ovens" (69–70). Harrison has her own favorite Holocaust texts, which reposition hope not as "an idealistic illusion but an existential act" (87). The cultural politics of "hope" are quite messy when it comes to Holocaust narrative and trauma writing more broadly.

The child must now witness trauma, somehow "remember" it without necessarily having been there. The injunction to "remember" the Holocaust without having experienced it firsthand drives not only children's literature but also literature and cultural narrative more generally, especially as the Holocaust becomes more remote as a historical event, with the last actual survivors dying off. One interesting trend in writing for older children and young adults is the preponderance of what we might call strategies of protagonist exposure, whereby the main character is made to experience firsthand the horrors of history. In this way he or she can "remember" those horrors. In not a few Holocaust titles for young readers, such exposure is framed within a narrative that also somehow safeguards the vulnerable protagonist (and by extension the reader) from the full force of the trauma. On the one hand, we continue to believe that children should be protected from trauma, but increasingly we also seem to expect that trauma must be experienced in order to be understood, so that books about trauma can only be effective if they frighten and even endanger the child.[14]

To some degree, the act of reading trauma writing is expected to be traumatizing as well as fortifying. In part this is due to the dual construction of the child in relation to trauma, as Katharine Capshaw Smith explains in her introduction to a special journal forum (in which an earlier version of this chapter appeared). "Because children are imagined as innocent," Smith writes, "they are figured almost iconographically as the ultimate victims of trauma." At the same time, "they are also figured as the survivors of trauma, those who can offer adults spiritual advice in how to triumph over pain through simple, honest, essential values like love, trust, hope and perseverance" (2005, 116). The classic dialectic of innocence and experience intersects with and structures the dialectic of protection and exposure (and also knowledge and denial). The child must be at once young and adult. To the extent that the child still embodies hope, we might say that Holocaust literature for children tends toward the abusive as defined by Langer.

Hamida Bosmajian was the first to note this pattern of exposure and protection in her 2000 article on Doris Orgel's *The Devil in Vienna* (1988) and subsequently in her 2002 study *Sparing the Child*. In some books, such as Orgel's and also Lois Lowry's *Number the Stars* (1989), this strategy of protecting and exposing a protagonist is accomplished through the story of two friends, one more endangered than the other, with the less endangered friend functioning as witness and proxy for the reader.[15] Another strategy is the removal of the protagonist from present-day safety to a danger zone, usually constructed as historical or in the past. Among the confrontational texts recommended by Baer are time travel or "trading-places" novels operating in a magical realist register and emphasizing an experiential, healing relation to Holocaust trauma. These include Jane Yolen's *The Devil's Arithmetic* and Han Nolan's *If I Should Die before I Wake* (1994). These titles represent not a simple banalization of the personal, as with the 9/11 titles I discuss next, but rather the expectation that young readers must find history personally traumatic in order to know it.[16]

The power of time travel and trading-places narratives stems in part from the success of similar texts about African American historical trauma published decades ago, such as Virginia Hamilton's *House of Dies Drear* (1968) and especially Octavia Butler's 1979 *Kindred,* arguably a text cross-written for (or at least cross-read by) adolescents. In the latter, the protagonist Dana is transported to and from 1976 California to 1815 Maryland so that she—and by extension, the reader—can experience firsthand the terrors of slavery. Another if less "historical" example is Hamilton's 1982 *Sweet Whispers, Brother Rush,* in which the female protagonist Teresa (Tree) learns, through a sort of psychological time travel, of her family's traumatic history of porphyria as well as of abuse. Even when time travel or place exchange is not a central element, many, perhaps most, contemporary children's books about African American life are historical and often traumatic in emphasis, so pervasive are the effects of slavery, Reconstruction, and the fight for civil rights. Tellingly, these books have yet to be reclaimed by the emergent field of trauma studies, suggesting again the dominance of Holocaust narrative.[17]

The protagonists of Yolen and Nolan are subjected through their Holocaust exposure to a splitting, even shattering, of their subjectivity, from which they must assemble a more adult self. Here, as in the texts of Hamilton and Butler mentioned above, the psychoanalytic-literary collaboration seems productive and praiseworthy. In Yolen's novel, a bored Jewish girl named Hannah opens the door for Elijah during her family's Passover seder and finds herself in Nazi-occupied Poland in 1942. With the other Polish villagers, Hannah—now Chaya—is rounded up and taken to a concentration camp. Eventually, she sacrifices herself to save her friend Rivka. When she walks into the door leading to the gas chambers, she suddenly returns to her real life in the Bronx, with a new appreciation for history and modern rituals. Nolan's novel likewise whisks a contemporary teen girl back to wartime Poland, but this time that girl, named Hilary, belongs to a white-supremacist group. She becomes Chana, a young Jewish girl, and learns some valuable lessons about racism and genocide. Unlike Hannah, Hilary trades ethnicity as well as place, in keeping with other trading-places texts. I found this aspect of the transformation unbelievable and wonder if ethnicity should be so easily elastic.

These stories are effective precisely to the degree that they capitalize on our conviction that historical trauma should be personal, and in ways that are often surprising or unpredictable. My provisional sense is that historical fiction has become more than ever a metadiscourse of personal suffering that in turn demands pain from readers as proof of their engagement. Whether about the impact of slavery, the Holocaust, or other horrific world events (as in the recent spate of Great Depression stories), the genre seems now to thematize the reader's own exchange with the child protagonist. And such personalization, which seems consonant with post-1960s identity politics and the faith in empathy, can sometimes lead to a denial of history's complexities, which are not always so easily plotted.

While I admire the work of Yolen and Nolan, I find the same conceit of split subjectivity disturbing in another young adult text, Marsha Forchuk Skrypuch's *The Hunger,* in which a fifteen-year-old Canadian girl named Paula simultaneously becomes anorexic and learns about the Turkish massacre of Armenians during the years 1915–1923. Half realistic "problem teen" fiction and half historical fiction, the novel opens as the standard story of a perfectionist girl increasingly preoccupied with her body image but soon takes on another dimension. As she gets sicker, Paula learns more online about the massacres. After a dangerous run, Paula has a heart attack, passes out, and travels through a time tunnel. She finds herself face to face with "a mirror image of herself" (1999, 98), named Marta. "Paula stepped into the mirror image of herself and felt a loving warmth envelop her," writes Skrypuch. "'Paula' no longer existed. She had just stepped inside of Marta" (99). Paula-Marta then wakes up in a Turkish orphanage in 1915, where her hellish history lesson begins. The brutalities she experiences link her specifically to her grandmother Pauline, who emigrated from Armenia in 1923 with her adoptive parents at the age of seven (meaning that she was born within a year of when the novel is set). Paula's grandmother Pauline is the daughter of Mariam, Marta's older biological sister, which makes Paula's grandmother also Paula-Marta's niece in the temporal logic of the story. (To make matters more complicated, Marta was not merely Pauline's aunt but also her adoptive mother.)

The Hunger is commendable for raising consciousness about the massacres, which have long been a taboo subject, especially in Turkey. Even so, I doubt that "real hunger" should serve as a wake-up call for teen girls with eating disorders in contemporary North America. When offered food, Marta seizes it eagerly, thinking, "The Turks may wish us to die . . . but I'm not about to cooperate" (115). Her brutal experiences inspire a new will to live and therefore to eat. She learns how to keep food down: "This is medicine, medicine, medicine, she chanted" (160–61). Eventually she is returned to the present and to Paula, her struggle not over but her fatal aversion to food overcome. The novel enacts a split subjectivity only to portray eating as a matter of will-power and personal experience of history. Clearly eating disorders are cultural, but the will to live and the will to eat are not so transcendent of historical context. Yet Amazon.com reviewers call the book a "skillful blend of the contemporary and the historical" and "an especially suitable gift for a young person struggling to overcome an eating disorder or to deal with personal or family trauma." Skrypuch herself weighs in as a reviewer, describing her research and naturalizing the link between Paula's story and the historical trauma that Paula (re)lives. Asserting that Hitler modeled the Holocaust on the Armenian massacre, Skrypuch claims an even earlier primal scene of genocide, then uses it to authorize an object lesson for contemporary teens. The personal, it seems, is the historical, and both are billed as traumatic.

Why are Yolen and Nolan successful where Skrypuch is less so, at least in my view? Skrypuch is not as masterful a writer as Yolen, to begin with, and *The Hunger* is her first novel. But it is also possible that Skrypuch can take greater license with her story because the Turkish massacre of the Armenians is only now being acknowledged publicly. Even now, perspectives on the event are sharply divided along nationalist and political lines.[18] *The Hunger* at least attempts to grapple with the event and its consequences; it is a consciousness-raising book and was surely published to that end. Another, somewhat contradictory explanation is that whereas the Holocaust is entangled with our ideas about memory, repression, and the unconscious, the Armenian tragedy seems more urgent and also more open to invention, less haunted by mass trauma. I am probably overlooking other possibilities, but in any case, *The Hunger*'s ostensible "historicity" feels almost painfully voluntarist and presentist.

The Hunger is but one example of the ease with which historical trauma is used to authorize personal loss in contemporary young adult literature. In Edward Bloor's novel *Crusader* (1999), to take another, fifteen-year-old Roberta Ritter reconstructs the horrific murder of her mother through the supportive "screening" of Mrs. Weiss, the daughter of Holocaust survivors. Mary Ann Ritter was murdered while working one night in the family arcade, and the case has never been solved. Seven years later, Roberta begins to figure it all out. Just after watching for the first time a news broadcast about her mother's murder (through a video archive), Roberta cries for the first time in those seven years, then stumbles to the home of Mrs. Weiss, who serves as a surrogate mother. Mrs. Weiss just happens to be watching Holocaust footage on television, and a long conversation ensues about human evil and accountability. "I had come here to get away from a horrible video," thinks Roberta, "and I had found another one" (1999, 204). The link is awkward, one of many problems with the book. To make matters worse, Uncle Frank, one of two problematic father figures, hosts parties in the new arcade that revolve around racist or genocidal virtual reality "experiences," among them "White Riot," "Lynch Mob," and "Krystallnacht." Roberta prefers unmediated reality, whatever that might be. *Crusader* is a novel of empowerment, and Roberta's growth depends upon her ambivalence about "enchantment" and her repudiation of her biological family, who are linked to history's worst villains—even as Bloor criticizes anti-Arab sentiment. I suspect that Langer would find *Crusader* to be abusive of the Holocaust.

Picturing 9/11

While the fairy tale and the young adult novel have their Holocaust uses and abuses, the picturebook offers the most dramatic testimony to trauma, precisely because the genre is usually presumed innocent. Because of its association with early childhood and its visual power, a picturebook about the Holocaust has greater power to shock and presumably to educate. Innocenti and Gallaz's picturebook *Rose Blanche* (1985), for instance, tells the story of a young German girl who secretly feeds concentration camp victims and is then mistakenly shot by Americans soldiers who liberate the prisoners. Her death is abrupt and upsetting, but the book affirms the idea that children should be exposed to rather than protected from trauma. Or consider Toshi Maruki's *Hiroshima No Pika,* a devastating account of a seven-year-old Japanese girl's experience of the Hiroshima bombing. Young Mii "saw children with their clothes burned away, lips and eyelids swollen. . . . There were heaps of bodies everywhere" (1980, n.p.). Those heaps evoke the mass graves of the Holocaust, complicating any "adult" argument about the necessary evils of war. In more recent titles, the photograph has become the preferred visual form, in keeping with a faith in the realism of photography (a realism that Kertzer and others question).

The tipping point for the picturebook as a preferred genre for trauma work seems to have come in the 1980s. In his review of nine atrocity-themed picturebooks published in that decade,[19] John Cech responds to concerns voiced by Neil Postman and Ariel Dorfman about the so-called disappearance of childhood. Acknowledging that these books may come as a surprise to the reading public, given their unpleasant subjects and graphic styles, Cech argues against the disappearance thesis, proposing that picturebooks can be more adult in concern and more elastic in form without losing their relevance to childhood. Indeed, Cech holds that picturebooks must engage with the sociopolitical realities of the world, and without condescending to young readers. We should not worry about whether trauma narratives are "really" children's picturebooks. "Rather," he writes, "what we may well ask is whether or not these books matter, or will matter, to our own lives and to our children's. If we cannot protect our children from a violent world, perhaps we can at least equip them with the political insight and the moral courage to recognize and to act to change some of these conditions" (1987, 206).

Like the fairy tale and the young adult novel, the picturebook has long been engaged with war and trauma, although not usually in explicit theme. As I stressed in chapter 4, the picturebook is widely considered a psychological genre and as such has been a site for covert as well as (more recently) overt trauma work, sometimes linked with specific events or atrocities, and sometimes not. Even the seemingly innocuous *Goodnight Moon,* written by Margaret Wise Brown and illustrated by Clement Hurd, is designed to reassure the child who is afraid to fall asleep (perhaps in the dark). Noting that its publication coincided with Brown's entry into analysis, Leonard S. Marcus calls attention to a letter Brown wrote to her female lover Michael Strange just after the book appeared:

> To go in to that hour feeling suddenly alone on the rock itself with no one. Everyone you love is lost. You may blame your own childishness and stupid loving or not. This is an experience of desolation, curses, and prayers, and terrible tears. They

say if you relive this desolation and face it, as you once met it and couldn't face it, then you are free of it. Perhaps, that is what one hopes. You don't even have to know what incidents caused the pain you are facing, as long as you do feel it again and stand it. (Quoted in Marcus 1992, 158).[20]

Mary Galbraith and Judith P. Robertson both offer intriguing takes on Brown's masterpiece. Developing a perspective that informs her understanding of classic picturebooks more generally, Galbraith (1998) sees in *Goodnight Moon* the failure of adult caregivers to respond adequately to the child's situation. Admiring Galbraith's analysis, Robertson (2000–2001) counters that the book's spatial and verbal designs stand in for the good (enough) mother, creating a safe holding environment and thus enabling the child to achieve a sense of self and fall asleep without terror. These readings of *Goodnight Moon* differ not only in their take on Brown's book but on the underlying question of what psychological work the picturebook can be expected to perform. In the letter cited above, Brown leaves the question open, unsure whether analysis will free her from desolation, or (more obliquely) if her creative work will do so. Robertson sees Brown's famous picturebook as a successful working-through of anxiety and depression as well as a template for the child's struggle for selfhood, whereas for Galbraith the book repeats the failure of that process, essentially a parenting failure.

In a series of persuasive articles, Galbraith suggests that not a few classic picturebooks—Wanda Gág's 1928 *Millions of Cats,* for example— emerged from personal or collective trauma. Galbraith holds that beloved picturebooks not only reflect psychological concerns but are essentially unconscious responses of the author-illustrator to experiences of loss and deprivation and to the failure of adult caregivers to provide adequate support. Picturebooks forged in the crucible of trauma, she believes, tend to resonate powerfully with generations of readers, not only because of the ongoing legacy of world war and genocide but also because many of us experienced in childhood "an adult failure in basic protection or attunement" (2000b, 340). For Galbraith, the picturebook operates as a secondary or revised "survival schema" that points to "primary survival schema" developed in childhood. "Paradoxically," she notes, "under the protective cover of a children's storybook, primal scenes that would otherwise stay buried can surface without being consciously recognized" (2000a, 638). This seductive reworking of the primal scene is what transforms a picturebook into a classic, she proposes.[21] Even if trauma has only lately come to the picturebook as a subject, it has been behind the scenes all along.[22]

Without sharing Galbraith's conviction that parental neglect and childhood trauma are the cultural norm, I agree that the picturebook can function as an expression or distortion of trauma for adults as much as (perhaps more than) for children.[23] Adults may create, read, share, or treasure certain picturebooks because they offer protective cover for experiences of loss or terror. If older and "classic" picturebooks tend to screen rather than openly thematize trauma, as she suggests, then what do we make of more contemporary texts that are more open or explicit? Quite a few of these books explore trauma and traumatic situations with nuance and sophistication, including *Rose Blanche* and *Hiroshima No Pika*. In these and other titles, open theming and the kind of readerly confrontation urged by Baer communicate and perhaps transfer the pain of trauma without dumbing down sociohistorical context. We may criticize some texts along the lines suggested by Langer, but by and large such books do not trivialize traumatic experience or amount to American propaganda, as has happened with much of the children's literature about the 9/11 terrorist attacks.

The Holocaust is now understood as the horrific event with which we have slowly and painfully come to terms—as the structuring, residually unconscious trauma of the twentieth century. In contrast, the terrorist attacks of September 11, 2001, in our very American society of the spectacle, constitute the ultimate and ostensibly transparent affront to self and nation. Whereas the Holocaust slowly became an acceptable topic for children's literature, no such lag occurred between 9/11 and the publication of children's and young adult books about that tragedy and the so-called war on terrorism. Only one year later nearly fifty books on the subject had been published for children (Lampert 2010, 18), among them picturebooks as well as diary anthologies, poetry monographs, graphic novels, nonfiction accounts, and comic book issues (single and serialized). These titles are largely disappointing as art and as social commentary. Many claim 9/11 as both a simple story and as a personally traumatic event, figuring the nation as a wounded innocent and ignoring our complicity in the exploitation of the world's people and resources—perhaps even our own terrorism. "In this way," notes Jo Lampert in the first book-length study of 9/11 writing for children, "America suddenly colonized a much bigger issue" (2010, 4).

"One of the most significant trends in the political aftermath of 9/11," Lampert observes, "is the emergence of new discourses about what it means to be a good and responsible citizen and about the nature of national identity" (2). For the most part, however, those discourses are reactive and reactionary, claiming the victimization (hurting) of white American subjects. In *The Queen of America Goes to Washington City*, Lauren Berlant argues that "infantile citizenship" (1997, 21) has displaced any meaningful participation in American public life. With the rise of the Reaganite Right, she holds, "a nation made for adult citizens has been replaced by one for fetuses and children. . . . Portraits and stories of citizens-victims . . . now permeate the political public sphere, putting on display a mass experience of economic insecurity, racial discord, class conflict, and sexual unease" (1). In other words, privileged citizens claim, in the name of children born and unborn, to be traumatized—by progressive social politics, for example, such as feminism and affirmative action, and more recently by the events of 9/11. "Mass national pain threatens to turn into banality," writes Berlant, "a crumbling archive of dead signs and tired plots" (2).[24] Berlant even holds that the "ur-infantile citizen narrative is actually the presidential autobiography" (37), as if anticipating the election of President George W. Bush. The cultural tendencies described by Berlant in 1997 intensified dramatically in the wake of 9/11.

The title of Rosina Schnurr's contribution to the growing body of 9/11 children's books nicely sums up the collective emphasis on the child's perception and traumatization: *Terrorism: The Only Way Is Through. A Child's Story*. Another title, *911: The Book of Help* (Cart 2002), is a collection of essays, poems, short fiction, and drawings created by young adult writers in response to the attacks—sort of a "Chicken Soup for the Traumatized Teen Soul." Then there's Latania Love Wright's *A Day I'll Never Forget: A Keepsake to Help Children Deal with the September 11th, 2001, Attack on America*. I could not find the book in my library (or bring myself to buy it), but according to the product description on Amazon.com, this is a book intended for every child between the ages of 4 to 10 years old who watched the worst attack on America . . . from their television set. This book is a keepsake in which the child's name, date given, and who the book was given by can be recorded. The fact that it is a coloring book involves the child in the reading and is a very educational resource. . . . It is a resource that allows children to express their own individual feelings about that horrible day. Children of all races and ages are captivated by this book.

Not one of these books seems to grapple with the political contexts of the attacks, and certainly not with the bullying practices of the United States or its support for such practices. Instead, young readers are only urged to express their feelings and to appropriate 9/11 as a personal trauma—no matter what their own experiences have been. Choose (and color in) your own 9/11 adventure.

One of the better 9/11 books is *The Day Our World Changed* (Goodman and Fahnestock 2002), an anthology of children's art that confirms our faith not only in the picturebook as testimony but in children as reliable witnesses even if not expert interpreters. The book is a joint project of the New York University Child Study Center and the Museum of the City of New York, which suggests again how psyche and history convene of late. The book features gorgeous artwork by children alongside essays by therapists, journalists, teachers, politicians, and historians (including former mayor Rudy Giuliani, novelist Pete Hamill, and Senator Charles Schumer). The book does represent varied perspectives on the attacks and their import, but once again, it gives no attention to geopolitical context and its language is relentlessly pop-therapeutic. In his foreword, Harold S. Koplewicz, a doctor, explains, "In a single day, the illusion of our nation's invincibility was shattered for [children]. How they handle this new sense of vulnerability and, more importantly, how we as adults help them find their way, will have a tremendous influence on our country's future" (10).

There are a few signs of intelligent life in this anthology. In "Children as Witnesses to History," Sarah Henry traces the history of our national interest in children's voices; she even mentions the importance of *St. Nicholas* (the longest-running and most important children's periodical in the nineteenth and early twentieth centuries), as well as Freud, John Dewey, progressive education, and the infamous 1913 Armory show introducing New Yorkers to contemporary art. Debbie Almontaser's "Growing Up Arab-American" is a welcome contribution about anti-Arab and anti-Muslim backlash after the attacks, even if Almontaser keeps her piece focused on strategies for preventing such bigotry rather than narrating actual incidents. For most of the adult contributors, however, the title of *The Day Our World Changed* is not ironic but a straightforward description of innocence lost that makes possible innocence regained. Pete Hamill titles his piece "Horror through Innocent Eyes." Rhapsody displaces analysis throughout the book. "So much that informs the great works of art of our time," writes Arthur L. Carter in his piece, "comes from the innocence, humor, primal joy, fear, and innate sense of humanity that children typically have. . . . Many adults have tried to respond to the day, but few have done it as eloquently as our children. What a lesson! Their instincts have an emotional incisiveness that few adults can match" (107).[25]

In his spirited interpretation of 9/11, *Welcome to the Desert of the Real!*, Slavoj Žižek proposes that terror has lately been made into "the hidden universal equivalent of all social evils" (2002, 111), in keeping with what he calls "the subjective economy of the realization of the Self's inner potentials" (77). For Žižek, Lacanian psychoanalysis is the cure for traumatic political realities. He puts his faith in the Lacanian Real against the "hegemonic liberal multiculturalist logic" (64), which, he says, makes more feasible notions of Absolute Evil. Counterintuitively he asks, "Is it not that today, in our resigned postideological era which admits no positive Absolutes, the only legitimate candidate for the Absolute are radically evil acts?" (137). He strenuously objects to the elevation of 9/11 to that status, as well as to comparisons of 9/11 to the Shoah. Though he admires some articulations of the Holocaust as the great singularity, he stresses the need to keep historical perspective on the Holocaust, against the kind of personal relativizations that make evil too easily Absolute, as in these children's books.

We do not have to share Žižek's faith in the recuperative power of psychoanalysis, but what better evidence of that "subjective economy" than these 9/11 titles? If the only way to understand terrorism is through a child's story, then we need children's books that actually reckon with the horrific world violence to which our nation handily contributes and that challenge the master plot of childhood innocence that has transformed our very understanding of citizenship. Instead, we have books that promote infantile citizenship, that resort to a thematic of absolute evil and absolute innocence. Among them are books about the bravery of firemen and rescue dogs, alongside *Fireboat: The Heroic Adventures of the John J. Harvey* by Maira Kalman (2002), the vacuous *On That Day* by Andrea Patel (2002), and the twelve-book War on Terrorism series published by ABDO and Daughters.[26] As Lampert observes, "There is now a new demand being made of the American subject in particular: to perform heroically in the face of this hypothetically changed world" (2010, 2). The titles in the War on Terrorism series, perhaps the most reactionary of all the 9/11 books so far, include *Ground Zero, Heroes of the Day, Operation Noble Eagle, United We Stand,* and *Weapons of War* (all published in 2002—a book per month for a full year). This series is dumbly patriotic, with its stars-'n'-stripes covers and its jingoistic support for America's war machine. President Bush comes off as a hero rather than a war zealot or just a politician.[27] These books have wide distribution, as ABDO is a privately held company that publishes children's nonfiction for the school library market. As reported on the ABDO Web site, the War on Terrorism series has garnered praise from the American Library Association's *Booklist* magazine.[28]

In lieu of nuanced history we get the Big Scary Picture Book of Terrorism.[29] The child inside and outside the text is at once the wounded or dead child of trauma theory and the endangered child of our reactionary national imagination. All this picturebook talk of injury and vulnerability is cause for alarm, especially because such talk is supposed to be reassuring. Picturebooks about 9/11 tend to insist on a traumatized reader, but they also redefine trauma as the stuff of pop-psychology, emphasizing—and delimiting—choice, pleasure, and action. We want books to give children hope, to nurture them and aid their development. But a coloring book about 9/11? A personal "keepsake"? Complexity and collectivity are refused in the name of the infantile citizen.

September 11, 2001, was a human tragedy and had all too many victims, starting with those killed in the attacks and their friends and family, as well as the truly heroic official and volunteer responders who lost their lives that day or soon after. The medical fallout is far from over, with many relief workers suffering from serious physical and mental health problems. And many, perhaps most, Americans watching at home *did* feel traumatized or at least unsettled by the attacks, struggling to understand the violence and loss. Trauma writing for children about 9/11 builds on existing discourses of American or child vulnerability, which—for better *and* for worse—helped make trauma thinkable. That said, the quick and easy assimilation of 9/11 to the children's literature of atrocity, alongside the simplicity of its representation, bespeaks the triumph not only of the therapeutic (in the worst possible sense of that phrase) but also of the infantile citizen.[30] "Ultimately," writes Farrell, "trauma is a radical form of terror management" (1998, 7). This is true not only in the sense that Farrell intends here—trauma as a reactive experience—but also in the sense that "trauma" as a category allows us to dodge as much as to process terror. We might also say that "terror" is a form of trauma management. Rather than confronting or acknowledging terror, we declare war on it, drawing dubious distinctions between the good guys and the bad guys and thereby safeguarding American innocence.

Clicking My Heels Together

I have argued throughout this book that children's literature and psychoanalysis have been mutually constitutive across the twentieth century and into our current moment. The narrative forms thereby generated have been powerful, though not always pretty. In the case of the 9/11 materials, a children's genre that is usually rich and dynamic is made to serve rather narrow ideological ends. Whereas Sendak's picturebook work, as I suggested in chapter 4, operates in the wake of and reflects back the rich and complex scene of picturebook psychology, these 9/11 titles represent the worst sort of literary-psychological merger, and in the service of reactionary politics. It may seem counterproductive to give them the last word. Let me emphasize again that many trauma-centered picturebooks are considerably more multidimensional, written to explore difficult questions about loss and memory, trauma and survival. So, too, are many young adult novels, some of which build on fairy-tale discourse. While the specter of "Americanization" and

Holocaust abuse marks some trauma writing, other trauma writing offers substantive and powerful testimony and witnessing.

While I have shared my concerns about some recent trauma writing, my main goal in *Freud in Oz* has been to describe rather than evaluate. I see my primary task as outlining a story about the historical encounter(s) of children's literature and psychoanalysis, and thereby suggesting new directions for research. There are gaps in that history, of course. There is surely more to say about the overall trend toward child vulnerability and bibliotherapeutic treatment, or about the circulation of children's classics in psychological discourse. Genres other than the picturebook and the adolescent novel merit consideration as psychological forms. Conversely, children's literature does not always endorse or collude with psychological discourse and may sometimes resist, critique, or simply ignore it. I hope others will trouble and enrich my account of Freud in Oz, and Oz in Freud.

Acknowledgments

I am grateful to the many people who helped make this book a reality. Top billing goes to my dreamy partner Martin Brooks Smith, whose love is deeply sustaining. Much gratitude also to Carolyn, Allison, Dylan, Austin, Jason, Rosie, and Lou, for welcoming me into the family. My parents, Byron and Doris, gave me ridiculous amounts of support along the way and remain my greatest cheerleaders. Thank you. Love and thanks also to my wonderful sister Kathryn and brother-in-law Lyn. I should also credit Kathryn and her friends Stephanie and Ellyn for showing me the way to the Boathouse (long since renamed but, as Robby reminds us, retaining still the nautical theme).

Freud in Oz was supported by sabbatical and research leaves, and I thank the English Department and the Dean's Office at the University of Florida for crucial support. I have wonderfully generous and smart colleagues from whom I continue to learn. Special gratitude to friends and former chairs John Leavey and Pamela Gilbert, who have guided my development with humor and grace. John Cech, Tace Hedrick, and Anastasia Ulanowicz offered useful feedback on various chapters. Peter Rudnytsky is my mentor in psychoanalysis, and this book reflects some of the lessons I've learned from his work. The book would probably still be languishing were it not for the care and feeding of Barbara Mennel and Jodi Schorb. Marsha Bryant helped me balance work with life by introducing me to such pleasures as Ebony Fashion Fair and the Gainesville Roller Rebels. I've had many a stimulating conversation with Leah Rosenberg over dinner and dog walking. Bob and Grace Thomson are model hosts and collaborators. Susan Hegeman and Phil Wegner welcomed me into the fold from the start; I still think of them as my den parents. Sid Dobrin collaborated with me on the anthology *Wild Things: Children's Culture and Ecocriticism* and inspires me with his unfailing energy. I've learned a lot from Malini Schueller, who has mad Ping-Pong skills. Kim Emery and Kathryn Baker helped me get to Gainesville and still do much to make it a wonderful place. Other colleagues who have supported me include Apollo Amoko, Don Ault, Roger Beebe, Richard Burt, Jill Ciment, Ira Clark, Andy Gordon, Terry Harpold, Sid Homan, Brandy Kershner, David Leavitt, David Leverenz, John Murchek, Scott Nygren, Amy Ongiri, Judith Page, the late Jim Paxson, Raúl Sánchez, Stephanie Smith, Chris Snodgrass, Maureen Turim, and Ed White. Extra gratitude to Tace and Pamela for taking such good care of me. Thanks also to our intrepid office staff: Carla Blount, Melissa Davis, Jan Moore, Jeri White, and Kathy Williams.

Among the many fabulous graduate student colleagues with whom I've had the pleasure of working, I want especially to acknowledge Joel Adams, Poushali Bhadury, Ramona Caponegro, Sophie Croisy, Eric Doise, Lisa Dusenberry, Rebekah Fitzsimmons, Emily Garcia, Marilisa Jimenez Garcia, Cortney Grubbs, Denise Guidry, Cari Keebaugh, Michele Lee, Jaimy Mann, Cathlena Martin, Melissa Mellon, Emily Murphy, Robin Nuzum, Todd Reynolds, Nishant Shahani, Joanna Shearer, Horacio Sierra, Randi Marie Smith, Aaron Talbot, and Andrea Wood. Megan Norcia, Kevin Shortsleeve, Catherine Tosenberger, and Eric L. Tribunella are also University of Florida grads and now inspiring colleagues in children's literature.

Beyond my department, I am grateful to Rita Smith, former curator of the Baldwin Library of Historical Children's Literature, for backstage tours, seminar assistance, picturebook marathons, and of course the Newbery/Caldecott awards banquet. Thanks also to Efraín Barradas, Kendal Broad, Franz Epting, Maria Rogal, and Danaya Wright. Chris McCarty and Alicia Turner have made life in Gainesville extra special with road trips, fancy meals, and *True Blood*. Despite his resistance to Facebook, Chris is my tutor in social networks and all things home improvement. Hats off also to Scott Richards and Gregg and Jean-Marie Ritter. Everyone needs a professor friend in Macon, Georgia, and mine is Patrick Brennan. Hugs to Joseba Gabilondo, theorist, tree assassin, Universal Boyfriend. And to Nancy Reismann, for all the lovely letters. Susan Dauer continues to astound with her flexible sense of fun. Who else would join me at the Holy Land Experience? From Robby Sulcer I have learned the joy of chasing ducks into the wrong ponds. Mary Lenard and Kay Harris remain steadfast friends, as does Laura George, my favorite Romanticist.

Karin Westman and Phil Nel make outstanding interlocutors, and Phil was gracious enough to comment on an early draft of the picture-book chapter. That chapter first appeared in an anthology edited by Julia Mickenberg and Lynne Valone, and I appreciate their wise counsel. Mavis Reimer and Kevin Shortsleeve hosted me at the University of Winnipeg's Centre for Young People's Texts and Cultures, where I gave a short version of what became this book. I thank them and also Perry Nodelman for engagement and hospitality. Joan Menefee's insights into the study of children's drawings were a great help with the picturebook chapter, and Bev Clark put me in touch with Dee Michel, whose research on queers and Oz I cite in chapter 3. I thank also Holly Blackford for her fascinating scholarship on child study and children's literature.

Kate Capshaw Smith and Richard Flynn have been a joy on and off the *Children's Literature Association Quarterly*. Michelle Ann Abate, my coeditor for another project, is a great source of inspiration and fun. Claudia Nelson and Anne Morey remain gracious friends, as does Maude Hines. Thanks to Thomas Crisp for his invaluable friendship and for inviting me to speak in Sarasota. Sarah Park, Gwen Tarbox, and Lance Weldy sustain me with their humor and smarts. Jennie Miskec introduced me to the Pit of Fun, and June Cummins makes it a special place every summer. Grateful nods also to Robin Bernstein, Lori Cohoon, G. B. Cross, Christine Doyle, Eliza Dresang, Leona Fisher, Elizabeth Goodenough, Jerry Griswold, Marah Gubar, Kara Keeling, Adrienne Kertzer, Lois Kuznets, Benjamin Lefebvre, Anne Lundin, Michelle Martin, Chris McGee, Tammy Mielke, Nathalie op de Beeck, Lissa Paul, Anne Phillips, Scott Pollard, Teya Rosenberg, Ellen Ruffin, Joe Sutcliff Sanders, the late Lawrence Sipe, Katie Strode, Jan Susina,

Craig Svonkin, Joseph Thomas, Roberta Seelinger Trites, Annette Wannamaker, Ian Wojcik-Andrews, Naomi Wood, and Jack Zipes for aid and encouragement. I would like especially to thank friends who served as president of the Children's Literature Association: Roberta Seelinger Trites, Martha Hixon, Lisa Rowe Fraustino, Mike Cadden, and Mark West. J. D. Stahl will also be remembered for that service and for other generosities. Kathy Kiessling holds us all together in the Association.

I am fortunate indeed to rehome with the University of Minnesota Press, and I want to thank its staff for its characteristic professionalism. I owe a particular debt to editorial director Richard Morrison for his support and enthusiasm. Editorial assistant Erin Warholm-Wohlenhaus made the publication process a smooth and pleasant experience, as has my wonderful copy editor, Kathy Delfosse. Thanks also to Marah Gubar and an anonymous reader, whose reports for the Press struck that difficult balance of encouragement and useful criticism. The book is much improved by their smart feedback. A deep bow to Erica Nikolaidis for her superb and timely help with manuscript preparation; who knew that Everyday Theory would bring us here?

Notes

Introduction

1. Lewis Carroll's two Alice books, *Alice's Adventures in Wonderland* (1865) and *Through the Looking-Glass, and What Alice Found There* (1871), are often conflated as *Alice in Wonderland*. Hereafter, I use *Alice* to refer to both Carroll texts unless otherwise noted. *Peter Pan* has its own complicated history of publication and condensation, which Rose (1984) reviews; for me, *Peter Pan* refers to the texts of Barrie.

2. In the field, "picturebook" is an accepted alternative to "picture book." The former is sometimes used to underscore the interdependence of image and text. On terminology, see Nikolajeva and Scott 2001, 1–6.

3. Mary Galbraith nicely gives her review of Rollin and West's *Psychoanalytic Responses to Children's Literature* the title "Freud and Toad are Friends." Galbraith alludes to Arnold Lobel's 1979 picturebook *Frog and Toad Are Friends.*

4. In "Analysis Terminable and Interminable," Sigmund Freud calls psychoanalysis one of three "impossible" professions, the other two being government and education. "Impossibility" has since become something of a master trope in psychoanalytic discourse, a way of emphasizing the intractability of a subject but also of self-credentializing (*I* will solve this impossible problem!). Deborah Britzman (2003) has explained how this trope also functions in educational theory and practice.

5. In *Hide and Seek,* Virginia L. Blum reverses Rose's hierarchy, finding

psychoanalysis more suspect than literature or its criticism and arguing that psychoanalytic theories promising insight into childhood in fact mythologize it. The child, she suggests, is an "unknowable subject" and indeed the "ultimate blind spot" of psychoanalysis (1995, 23). The lack of critical attention to the place of the child in psychoanalytic discourse, she asserts, comes "from a general failure on the part of the psychoanalytic enterprise to account for its own unconscious" (23). Rose and Blum agree on the impossibility of the adult–child relationship, but they disagree over which discourse—psychoanalysis or literature—is the problem and which offers a solution to (or at least insight into) the problem. Whereas Rose finds in Freud the antidote to the "fiction[s]" of childhood, Blum sees in "go-between" literary narrative (in which a child functions as a go-between for two or more adults) an exposé of the kind of truth claims about childhood asserted by psychoanalysis. While Peter Pan is Rose's poster boy, Blum concentrates on the "go-between" child figure in Charles Dickens, Henry James, and Vladimir Nabokov. Blum does not disparage children's literature, but she has little to say about it, despite its own preponderance of go-between figures. Neither Rose nor Blum identifies herself as a scholar of children's literature.

6. See Freud 1907. Gay thinks Freud was drawn to *The Jungle Books* because of its theme of savagery and civilization and its emphasis on the superiority of animals who acknowledge their animality over humans who try (unsuccessfully) to repress their animality (1990, 104).

7. See M. Gubar 2009, 29–33; Nodelman 1985; Reynolds 2007, 3–9; Rudd 2010, 2004. The fall 2010 issue of *Children's Literature Association Quarterly,* guest edited by Rudd and Anthony Pavlik, examines the negative as well as the positive legacy of Rose. In *The Hidden Adult,* Nodelman takes on not only Rose but also Karín Lesnik-Oberstein, who in *Children's Literature: Criticism and the Fictional Child* declares the impossibility of children's literature criticism. Lesnik-Oberstein maintains that said criticism relies upon various constructions of the child that are impossible to maintain. Like Rose, Lesnik-Oberstein champions psychoanalysis, arguing in her final chapter that D. W. Winnicott should be our exemplary theorist, since he ostensibly avoids essentializing the child through attention to transference, interpersonal relation, and the analytic space. While children's literature criticism, she claims, is "inextricably tied to a *prescriptive* role," psychoanalysis and psychotherapy function *"non-prescriptively"* (1994, 176). Nodelman counters that "there are certainly as many bad prescriptive therapists with normative assumptions about desirable mental health as there are bad prescriptive critics with normative assumptions about children" (2008, 160).

8. Martha Stoddard Holmes makes much the same point with specific ref-

erence to *Peter Pan:* "*Peter Pan* as a classification problem is a powerful spur for the discipline of children's literature to reformulate its project in broader terms, defining a genre in which adults and children have different engagements throughout their lifetimes, but which they nonetheless share" (2009, 132). The "child/adult binary," she continues, "has always been central to the definition and study of this problematic entity called 'children's literature,' the border of which is habitually patrolled by different authorities and always alive with crossings" (144).

9. Like Nodelman, Hamida Bosmajian finds children's literature to be "a complicated artistic, psychological, and social phenomenon, in some ways more so than adult literature because the author projects memories and libidinal releases through forms pretending innocence" (1985, 36). The screen of simplicity, she thinks, evidences complexity and adult sensibility. Authors "may consciously or unconsciously induce, even seduce, the child to accept and repeat the neurotic discontents of culture and civilization" (36).

10. In recent years *Peter Pan* has been the subject of two very good essay collections that trouble Rose's account and open up new lines of inquiry: *J. M. Barrie's "Peter Pan" In and Out of Time,* edited by Donna R. White and C. Anita Tarr, and *Second Star to the Right: "Peter Pan" in the Popular Imagination,* edited by Allison B. Kavey and Lester D. Friedman.

11. In her editor's preface to the 1974 volume of *Children's Literature,* Francelia Butler asserts, "Important things about children and their literature are to be learned from children at play," and she speculates that the burgeoning interest in children's culture more generally "reflects the theories of Freud and Jung about influences to which children are exposed, including literary influences" (8). The issue features an article by James Hillman, director of the Jung Institute, which is followed by a Jungian reading of *Pinocchio* by James W. Heisig.

12. For critiques, see Hogan 1990; J. Phillips and Wojcik-Andrews 1990; M. Steig 1990; and Zipes 1990.

13. The uncanny remains a key concept for analysis; for recent examples, see Rudd 2008; King 2005.

14. "Reading the Unconscious," Bosmajian's contribution to Peter Hunt's *Understanding Children's Literature,* summarizes key thinkers and theoretical traditions and warns against the tendency within psychoanalytic criticism to universalize. Bosmajian also attends to feminist criticism of and within psychoanalysis.

15. In his famous Rome discourse of 1953 ("The Function and Field of Speech and Language in Psychoanalysis"), Lacan attributes the decline of interest in speech and language—Freud's real concern, he holds—to work on the

imaginary, to object relations theory, and to discussions of countertransference. These three new emphases are "pioneer activities" that have nonetheless led psychoanalysis astray, in his view. The first he attributes directly to "the analysis of children, and . . . the fertile and tempting field offered to the attempts of researchers by access to the formation of structures at the preverbal level" (1977, 35). Lacan's critique of child analysis is interesting for many reasons, not the least of which is that his own essay on the mirror stage returns us to Freud's foundational speculations on infantile helplessness (not just infantile sexuality) and depends upon the existential primal scene of the baby in front of the mirror. Even if he is working to counteract the assumptions of ego psychology and object relations theory, Lacan still reinvents psychoanalysis through childhood; it is no coincidence that he placed the mirror stage essay first in *Écrits*. We could even argue that Lacan develops his theory of subjectivity largely through the case studies of childhood conducted by others. At the least, Lacan owes much to Klein, especially her ideas about symbolic processes. Presumably what differentiates Lacan from child analysis is his attention to language and/as the unconscious, and his remove from the compromised world of mother-analysis. "We would truly like to know more about the effects of symbolization in the child," he remarks, "and psychoanalysts who are also mothers, even those who give our loftiest deliberations a matriarchal air, are not exempt from that confusion of tongues by which Ferenczi designated the law of the relationship between the child and the adult" (36). Lacan holds that mother-analysts do not really or effectively listen for the unconscious.

16. Rose's polemic is patterned after that of Lacan and, as Rudd (2010) explains, also participates in the challenge to literary realism (and the celebration of modernist or "writerly" texts) of then ascendant Continental theory. Lacan's question translates to "Is there a children's literature?"

17. Again from Lacan's Rome discourse: "But we analysts have to deal with slaves who think they are masters, and who find in a language whose mission is universal the support of their servitude, and the bonds of its ambiguity. So much so that, as one might humorously put it, our goal is to restore in them the sovereign freedom displayed by Humpty Dumpty when he reminds Alice that after all he is the master of the signifier, even if he isn't master of the signified in which his being took on its form" (1977, 81). Shuli Barzilai glosses this and other invocations of *Alice* in her chapter "On Chimpanzees and Children" in *Lacan and the Matter of Origins*.

18. Emphasizing the importance of early childhood, Coats devotes chapters 2 and 3 of *Looking Glasses and Neverlands* to picturebooks and early readers, respectively, offering fascinating readings of texts such as *The Story of Babar, Curious George,* and *Stellaluna*. She suggests how entry into the

Symbolic demands the absence or renunciation of mothers. "Children's picture books and beginning readers," she writes, "in their colorful, lively, humorous presentation, can be seen as ads for the Symbolic, attempts to ease the child away from an impossible connection to the mother into a slightly less impossible position as a subject" (2004, 60).

19. See Appleyard 1990 and M. Steig 1989. Steig's project is particularly interesting, derived as it is from reader-response criticism and psychoanalysis. Steig tries to account for his subjective responses to texts, then uses those responses as well as contextual or biographical information about the author to inform his "interpretation" of a book, an interpretation he understands as still subjective and partial. At times he matches experiences from his own childhood to childhood experiences of the authors, while acknowledging that such a match is probably so much nonsense. He remembers the emotional impacts of certain childhood favorites, tries to explain what those moments were all about through remembering and introspective analysis, and then goes from there into biographical data. He points out that such introspective and recollective practice is not the same as a psychoanalysis because he is not forced into any transference and does not otherwise undergo any adjustment to his psyche; he just tries to figure out what had emotional impact, and why. Then he tries to see his own "evasions" of tricky or emotionally laden subjects in first drafts of essays. Through this method, he hopes to bridge the gap between subjective reader-response interpretation and more traditional knowledge-based analysis.

20. The rhymes encapsulate "the curious contrast in the way adults in English-speaking culture handle an infant's body. They alternate between holding it closely, encouraging its growing sense of its own wholeness, and then, in the name of play, threatening it with disintegration by pretending to drop it or to split it into pieces. Such activities accompanied by feeding and by the blandishments of language represent some of the infant's earliest experience with another person, with the external world in which it must define itself" (Rollin 1992, 75).

21. See also Blackford 2008.

22. In *Freudianism and the Literary Mind,* published just a few years after Freud's death, Frederick J. Hoffman warns about the difficulties of charting psychoanalytic "influence" on literature and culture. Hoffman emphasizes, for instance, that "hostility is an extremely important means of spreading any notion" (1945, 86). He also points out that correspondence between literature and psychoanalysis does not necessarily evidence influence; rather, it indicates simultaneous engagements with the same cultural issues.

23. In *Is It Really "Mommie Dearest"?,* Hilary S. Crew uses psychoanalytic

theory to interpret adolescent texts but also approaches the fourth critical proj-ect identified here in her suggestion that adolescent literature imaginatively reworks the cultural plots of psychoanalysis—especially its insistence that growing up requires giving up the mother. Like Coats in *Looking Glasses and Neverlands*, Crew is struck by how frequently mothers are dispensed with in the genre, theorizing that mothers are killed off or made abject so that their daughters can come of age. Crew makes the very important point that psychoanalysis may contribute to as much as help us analyze narrative or cultural plots.

24. See, for instance, Michael Snediker's invocation of Winnicott in *Queer Optimism: Lyric Personhood and Other Felicitous Persuasions.*

25. Among the possible meanings of "psychoanalysis": a clinical method, a critical method, a lay analysis, a theory of culture, a theory of desire, Freud, a science, a religion or cult, a bourgeois Enlightenment project. "Children's literature" might be an oxymoron, or it might mean a literary tradition, a de-velopmental program, things kids read, things adults write, a field of study or profession, or an ideology.

26. On the American reception and adaptation of Freud, see Adelson 1956; Cushman 1995; Demos 1997a, 1997b; Gifford 1991; Hale 1995; F. H. Matthews 1967; Rosenzweig 1992; J. Schwartz 1999; Shakow and Rapaport 1964.

27. Rieff's *The Triumph of the Therapeutic* follows up on his earlier book *Freud: The Mind of the Moralist,* written out of Rieff's experience as the general editor of Freud's papers for Collier-Macmillan and declaring ar-rival of "psychological man." Rieff's Freud is not the unorthodox liberator of the Freudian Marxists but rather an irreligious moralist whose vision of the psychological offered an existential sort of morality. In 1959, when the first book appeared, Rieff approved of the Freudian revolution and even the popu-lar embrace of psychoanalysis. By the time of the latter book, however, Rieff despaired of the humanistic, self-help turn psychoanalysis had taken.

28. Robert C. Fuller (1986) argues against the notion proposed by Rieff, Christopher Lasch, and others that "the therapeutic" emerged as a secular re-placement for religion. In fact, says Fuller, the therapeutic, and psychology more generally, tended to reinforce existing religious commitments. On religion as popular psychology, see Meyer 1965; for a good overview of the American "therapeutic gospel," see Moskowitz 2001.

29. A more materialist variant of this argument comes from Russell Jacoby in *Social Amnesia,* where he maintains that late capitalism requires the repression of Freud's program and a compensatory "pseudo-selfhood."

30. Van Wyck Brooks's psychobiography *The Ordeal of Mark Twain* (1920) is probably the most famous, since it set off a storm of controversy about Twain (Samuel L. Clemens) and his place in American letters.

1. Kids, Fairy Tales, and the Uses of Enchantment

1. My chapter glosses over important distinctions between the folk tale (often called the wonder folk tale or the magic tale) and the literary fairy tale; for information, see Zipes 2009.

2. On Freud and recapitulation theory, see especially Kern 1970; Morss 1990; Ritvo 1990; and Sulloway 1979. John R. Morss argues that developmental psychology, ostensibly based on Darwinian science, in fact is pre-Darwinian and radically outdated, maintaining themes and correspondences no longer credible.

3. Dundes observes that in pre-Freudian psychiatric literature there is already an association of fairy tales with mental illness.

4. Dundes contends that neither neo-Freudians nor ego psychologists have contributed much to the psychoanalytic study of the fairy tale. Erich Fromm's *The Forgotten Language: An Introduction to the Understanding of Dreams, Fairy Tales and Myths,* as Dundes notes, offers only one narrow reading of a fairy tale (1987, 33).

5. In the second of two chapters on the Little Hans case of 1909, Peter L. Rudnytsky (2002) offers a reading complementary to that of Sarah Winter (1999), proposing that Freud invoked the Greek figure of Oedipus as part of a disavowal of his own Jewishness and the Jewishness of psychoanalytic culture.

6. Rachel Bowlby notes that Freud's use of tragedy to buttress his theory "was not in itself unusual: quite the contrary: Since Hegel's extensive use of Sophocles' *Antigone,* it had been almost standard practice for German philosophers to do this: Greek tragedy came naturally to hand as historical-literary matter for thinking with" (2007, 5). See also Alford 1992; R. Armstrong 2005.

7. On psychoanalytic approaches to myth from Freud to ego psychology, see Segal 2003. Segal points out that ego psychologists tend to make more distinctions between myth and fairy tale than do Freudians, seeing the former as a useful part of ego fortification.

8. Jung and his collaborator C. Kerényi emphasize especially the "archetype of the 'child-god'" (Jung 1949, 106) among other aspects of the Child archetype. The archetype is "extremely protean and assumes all manner of shapes" (107).

9. See Jung 2008. The four seminars were given from 1936 to 1940 to a small group of Jung's students. The second seminar, printed first in the published volume, serves as a theoretical overview and distinguishes Jung's approach from that of Freud. The rest of the seminars focus on specimen dreams and clarify Jung's approach to dream interpretation.

10. Eugene Taylor argues that in American culture at least, Jung came before Freud, literally as well as figuratively, and should be understood not

as a fallen Freudian but as "the twentieth century exponent of the symbolic hypothesis in the tradition of the late nineteenth century psychologies of transcendence" (1998, 97). On Jung's early relations with the United States and the United Kingdom, see also McGuire 1995.

11. On Jung's esotericism, see Noll 1994; Main 1997.

12. Von Franz authored *Puer Aeternus: A Psychological Study of the Adult Struggle with the Paradise of Childhood,* outlining what Dan Kiley later called "the Peter Pan Syndrome," or the mother-complex of a young man who "remains too long in adolescent psychology" (von Franz 1981, 1), unable to commit to heterosexual relationships and achieve sufficient maturity— hence "the strange attitude and feeling that the woman is *not yet* what is really wanted" (2; emphasis in the original).

13. For persuasive Jungian treatments of children's texts, see Hamida Bosmajian's (1989) reading of *Johnny Tremain,* Sally Rigsbee's (1983) analysis of *The Lion, the Witch, and the Wardrobe* and *The Princess and the Goblin,* John Cech's (1995) study of Sendak, and Susan Hancock's (2009) discussion of symbols and images. Focusing on imagoes of "the child" in fairy tale and miniature literature, Hancock suggests that the central insight of poststructuralist work on children's literature—that childhood is a confusing, perhaps unknowable mishmash of adult fantasies and projections—is compatible with Jung's emphasis on childhood as a symbol or archetype with infinite and unpredictable iterations.

14. Robin J. G. Nicks (2006) proposes that the psychological thrillers of Edgar Allan Poe, for instance, share much with the European fairy-tale canon, most disturbingly, a fascination with the bodies of dead woman—a necrophilic desire. In any case, nineteenth-century authors and readers readily drew connections between the European fairy tale and the American sensational story.

15. In 1954 Wolfenstein published *Children's Humor: A Psychological Analysis,* applying the insights of Freud's *Jokes and Their Relation to the Unconscious* to theorize about "the joke façade" and to account for such joke traditions as "the legend of the moron." "Children are not so remote from us," she concludes. "If we cannot always laugh with them, we can at times laugh like them" (Wolfenstein 1978, 214).

16. Wolfenstein goes on to say that "many Americans find it difficult to 'let themselves go' by voluntary relaxation of ego restraint. They oscillate between severe ego-dominance and a knocking out of the ego by means of drinking" (1946, 51).

17. The term "mental hygiene" seems to have been introduced in the 1870s. It gained widespread currency in the early twentieth century, with the publication of Clifford Beers's *The Mind That Found Itself* (1908). The book's success

prompted the founding of several American mental hygiene societies within the next few years. Originally the movement was focused on reforming the treatment of the insane and the mentally ill, especially the conditions of their institutionalization, but by the 1920s mental hygiene had expanded to include many other aims and emphases. The movement joined forces with child study and child guidance work, focusing especially on the rehabilitation of juvenile delinquents.

18. "Psychiatry suggests, too, that in fairy tales, as well as in the great literature of myths and legends, children may find expression for feelings and wishes for which modern civilization allows them no outlet" (J. Frank 1937, 38).

19. For critiques, see especially Darnton 1984; Dundes 1991; Zipes 1984.

20. See Kidd 2005.

21. In *Freud and Man's Soul,* Bettelheim argues for a better understanding of the myths to which Freud appeals, especially the myth of Oedipus but also the story of Cupid and Psyche. He attempts to reeducate his (American) readers about the classic myths that inform and give texture to psychoanalysis, even as he also underscores the beauty and subtlety of Freud's language, which he feels is lost in the translations of James Strachey. The real Freud was more intimate and informal—more "spiritual" even—than the Freud of Strachey and company, Bettelheim holds. Freud, according to Bettelheim, concerned himself with the "soul" rather than the "mind." And if Freud got soul, then so too does Bettelheim, likewise committed to the cause of psychoanalytic humanism.

22. Rose sees Bettelheim as seriously distorting the agenda of Freud, pointing especially to his fantasy of the integrated personality (Rose 1984, 10).

23. Pollak's biography, *The Creation of Dr. B,* is the latest and most devastating in a series of harsh reassessments of Bettelheim's legacy. Echoing some of the criticism leveled by earlier biographer Nina Sutton, Pollak exposes not only the plagiarism but also Bettelheim's forged credentials, his pretended acquaintance with Freud, his exaggerated claims of clinical success, and even alleged sexual abuse of young girl patients at the Shankman facility. For Sutton (1996), Bettelheim's lies or distortions are merely unfortunate, evidence of the man's complexity; she insists that whatever his faults, Bettelheim was a gifted therapist. The debate goes on, with Bettelheim's friend and literary agent Theron Raines (2002) defending him as a humane practitioner of tough love, and David James Fisher (2008) acknowledging Bettelheim's dark side but objecting to "Bettelheim bashing" and insisting on Bettelheim's brilliance as well as humanity. Fisher also attributes Bettelheim's late-life suicide not to shame about his behaviors (as Pollak does) but rather to physical decline, loss of loved ones, and ongoing depression stemming from "the unbearable legacy of shame

and guilt after surviving in two concentration camps" (11). It would seem that Bettelheim's emphasis on childhood's vulnerability and on the devastations of abuse has come back to haunt him. In the fairy tale/family romance of psychoanalysis, he is not only Hansel scrambling for nuts and berries but also the child-devouring witch or Big Bad Wolf.

24. Heuscher sums up how the fairy tale benefits the child: "In the first place, the fairy tale awakens in the child the feeling of participating with other human beings, with people not only of his immediate environment, but of all nations. He begins to sense that he is not alone with his, at times horrid and violent, fantasies, and that the latter are meaningful and valuable sources for strength for useful sublimations, as long as they never become confused with the outward reality. He also feels understood in his most tender longings, in his highest wishes. In the second place, the fairy tale communicates to the child a dim, intuitive understanding of his own nature and of his future positive potentialities. And he starts to sense that he became a human being primarily because in this world of ours he is meant to meet challenging and wondrous adventures. And so the fairy tale nourishes the child's courage to widen his horizons and to tackle all the challenges successfully. Then only, like some of the fairy tale heroes, he can hope to become a 'king' within whose maturity spiritual wisdom will harmonize with his power over earthly things" (1963, 185–86).

25. Smith worked for the Toronto Public Library from 1912 to 1952 and in 1949 was designated curator of its important Osborne Collection of children's books.

26. Hence such self-help titles as *The Wisdom of Oz* (Morena 1998), *The Peter Pan Syndrome* (Kiley 1983), and *Counselling for Toads: A Psychological Adventure* (de Board 1998). The overlap of fairy tales and children's classics is not surprising given that some of the latter—*The Wonderful Wizard of Oz* and *Peter Pan* most notably—were forged out of the fairy tale as much as against it. With his first Oz book, L. Frank Baum famously set out to write a modernized, American fairy tale. As for *Peter Pan*, Zipes finds it an "imaginative radicalization of the fairy tale" (2009, 32–33).

27. Fairy-tale experts now tend to be based in two disciplines, usually at the same time: children's literature, and comparative language and literature studies. Fairy-tale experts such as Zipes and Tatar thus also know a great deal about language, linguistics, and translation.

28. For a succinct account of the debate in relation to Bottigheimer's "new history," see Howard 2009.

29. See also Bottigheimer 2002. Leslie Fiedler, not a fairy-tale scholar, observed in 1973 that fairy tales "do not come to us orally and anonymously, but in

print and associated with the names of writers" (xi). In the 1950s, Richard M. Dorson invented the term "fakelore" to designate material falsely claiming origins in folk tradition; Alan Dundes applied the term to the Grimm tale collections in "Nationalistic Inferiority Complexes and the Fabrication of Fakelore." Dundes encouraged folklorists not to dismiss fakelore but rather to study it.

30. See also Dan Ben-Amos's foreword to Lüthi's *The European Folktale.* Lüthi makes a similar observation in *The Fairy Tale as Art Form and Portrait of Man,* noting that the "inner form" of the fairy tale "corresponds to that of man" (1984, 166).

31. Stephen Benson points out that the rise of fairy-tale studies in America from about 1979 onward closely parallels the rise of postmodern fairy-tale narrative, especially by women; he identifies Jack Zipes and Angela Carter as figureheads for such narrative (2008, 5). Feminism was central to both enterprises; while Zipes's work is Marxist, focusing on the sociohistorical transformations of the fairy tale and its role in the "civilizing process," Zipes pays great attention to the ideological tendencies of fairy-tale discourse, including its sexism. The "synchronicity of critical and creative work" (Benson 2008, 6) is indeed remarkable and underscores the ongoing relays between interpretation and storytelling.

32. Bottigheimer suggests something similar: "Perhaps fairy tales are better understood not as direct and unmediated expressions of human beings' emotional need, but as people's conscious or unconscious incorporation of tales that suit their needs which canny suppliers recognize and respond to" (2009, 107).

2. Child Analysis, Play, and the Golden Age of Pooh

1. Milne published the Pooh stories in two volumes, *Winnie-the-Pooh* (1926) and *The House at Pooh Corner* (1928). Hereafter, I use *Pooh* to refer to all these stories unless otherwise noted.

2. The Chicago Exhibition of 1893, as Stephen Kern (1970) points out, energized the founding of such organizations, beginning in the American Midwest: in Illinois and Iowa in 1894, in Nebraska in 1895, and in Kansas and Minnesota in 1896.

3. Freud's only direct clinical experience with children came in the clinic of Adolph Baginski, where he studied the organic diseases of children.

4. As Steedman points out, Freud's vision of childhood was also inspired by cell theory, the seeming radicalism of which was its "denial of extinction: nothing goes away. It was this understanding that Freud used to delineate the unconscious: the place where childhood (an individual history) is put, and thus released from time" (1995, 93).

5. A picturebook furnishes a vital link between Little Hans's horse phobia and the story that babies are delivered by storks. In this picturebook, reports Hans's father, is "a picture of a stork's nest with storks, on a red chimney. . . . Curiously enough, on the same page there was also a picture of a horse being shod" (S. Freud 1963a, 113). Freud does not suspect that the picturebook might have helped shape Hans's neurosis.

6. "If we examine the presentation of sexual difference in the case of Little Hans," remarks Rudnytsky, "we find confusion perpetrated at every turn by adults—by Little Hans's parents and above all by Freud—and the child doing his best to sort things out for himself" (2002, 25).

7. Burlingham and Anna Freud founded the Hampstead War Nurseries during World War II, and their joint work there resulted in the volume *Infants without Families* (1943). The nurseries later became the Hampstead Clinic.

8. Women analysts are routinely figured as mothers, not only because they often have been mothers, but also because mothering furnishes a lingua franca for professional practice. The teaching and study of children's literature was likewise long presumed to be a feminine and maternal project, only more recently recuperated as a suitable vocation for men.

9. "The Child's Concept of Death" (first published in 1912). Other key works include "The Nature of the Child's Soul (or Psyche)" (from 1913), "On Early Loving and Hating" (from 1917), and "New Ways to the Understanding of Youth" (from 1924). She was an interesting thinker and a graceful stylist.

10. On October 8, 1913, Hug-Hellmuth delivered a favorable report to the Vienna Psychoanalytic Society on a paper by G. Stanley Hall and C. Ellis on doll play. The men of Freud's circle "did not notice that before their eyes Hug-Hellmuth was giving birth to analytic play therapy!" (Balsam 2003, 338).

11. The "Controversial Discussions" were a series of "scientific meetings" of the British Psychoanalytic Society between October 1942 and February 1944 focusing on the conflict between the Viennese School and supporters of Klein. A core issue was the onset of oedipality. Shuli Barzilai notes that Klein's understanding of the young child as deeply conflicted is not so much a refusal of Freud's oedipal complex as a kind of "backshifting": "On a sliding scale, if Klein pushes the Oedipus complex back from ages 3–4 to 0, Freud and his followers would hold it at around 3–5" (1999, 34).

12. "Winnie" was the name of a bear that Christopher often saw in the London Zoo (relocated from the city of Winnipeg, in Manitoba, Canada); "Pooh" was originally the name of a swan that Christopher saw on holiday.

13. More recently scholars have emphasized "how much of the child within Alan Arthur, the father, rather than Christopher the son, can be discerned in the books" (Kuznets 1994, 47). Writes Christopher Milne: "It was

precisely because he was not able to play with his small son that his longings sought and found satisfaction in another direction. He wrote about him instead" (quoted in Carpenter 1987, 201). Milne himself acknowledged the role of both observation and recollection in the making of *Pooh*.

14. See Victoria Hamilton 1993.

15. On play in American culture, see Dulles 1952; Nasaw 1993; Grover 1992; G. Brown 2003; and Gleason 1999. On child play in relation to national anxieties and class formation, see Sánchez-Eppler 2003 and G. Brown 2003.

16. Winnicott was not the only one who broadened the category of play. Johan Huizinga prefaces his *Homo Ludens: A Study of the Play-Element in Culture,* written in 1938, with the observation that "It is ancient wisdom, but it is also a little cheap, to call all human activity 'play'" (1955, n.p.). But Huizinga goes on to prove it exactly so, linking play to virtually every aspect of human society and proposing that play "is older and more original than civilization" (75).

17. In 2005, in its animated project *My Friends Tigger and Pooh,* the Walt Disney Company tried gender reassignment on the character Christopher Robin, transforming him into a tomboy named Darby. Adult fans mounted a "Save Christopher Robin" campaign and the project was scrapped.

18. Milne later tried to distance himself from his children's stories, hoping to achieve more adult literary fame. A pity, notes Carpenter, as Milne's works are "more successful as works written for children than anything else produced during children's literature's Golden Age" (1987, 205).

19. For Elliott Gose, each Pooh adventure "functions as a testing of physical and psychological realities from which the listening child can learn" (1988, 29). Basic childhood appetites drive Pooh, he notes; moreover, the gently pastoral setting of the 100 Aker Wood is "a recognizable environment, one in which children can easily imagine themselves" (31). Gose finds in *Pooh* a happy shoring up of self and other.

20. In *Postmodern Pooh,* Crews takes aim at more-contemporary modes of criticism, such as deconstruction, postcolonial studies, and feminist studies, showing very little affection or amusement this time around. He ends with the line I use as this chapter's epigraph, playing on the final line of *The House at Pooh Corner:* "So they went off together. But wherever they go, and whatever happens to them on the way, in that enchanted place on the top of the Forest, a little boy and his Bear will always be playing" (Milne 1957, 313–14).

21. Pooh satire has migrated from literary studies to psychology/psychiatry; see Shea et al. 2000.

22. Crews continues the assault in *Follies of the Wise,* calling psychoanalysis "the queen of modern pseudosciences [which] has pioneered the methods and directly supplied some of the ideas informing other shortcuts to 'depth'"

(2006, 12); psychoanalysis functions as "a kind of metaphysical morale booster for the science-impaired" (58).

23. Faced with this kind of criticism, in 2006 Hoff published a defensive online essay entitled "Farewell to Authorship and Why We're Losing Literature."

3. Three Case Histories

1. Stone reworks these ideas in *Gradiva* and *Freud after Freud,* elaborating in the latter the Pinocchio Complex "to provide a nomenclature for elements of the Oedipus complex that Freud had trouble classifying right until the end of his writing career, namely his theories between 1919 and 1938 of the uncanny, disavowal and fetishism, and the splitting of the ego in the process of defence" (2006a, n.p).

2. For more on Brooks and his immaturity critique, see Kidd 2004, 81–85.

3. In addition to the texts I discuss in this chapter, see also Robert de Board's *Counselling for Toads: A Psychological Adventure,* which uses another Golden Age text, Kenneth Grahame's 1908 *The Wind in the Willows,* to introduce transactional analysis. The back cover reads, "Appropriate for anyone approaching counselling, whether as student, client, or counsellor, *Counselling for Toads* will appeal to both children and adults of all ages."

4. A case in point would be Robert Coover's novel *Pinocchio in Venice,* which is perversely faithful to plots and themes of Collodi's original tale.

5. Peter Brooks defines the case history as "the story of an individual presented to the public for didactic purposes: it is a form of exemplary biography" (1985, 284). The term "case" has much broader purchase, as Lauren Berlant observes: "The case represents a problem-event that has animated some kind of judgment. Any enigma will do—a symptom, a crime, a casual variable, a situation, a stranger, or any irritating obstacle to clarity. What matters is the idiom of the judgement" (2007, 663). She notes that the "case study" "took aesthetic form in documentary and ficto-narrative genres (the detective story, the fictional autobiography, the medical mystery, the still life) and then in interpretive scholarship" (663–64).

6. Juliet Dusinberre (1987) holds that the "radical experiments" of Lewis Carroll and other nineteenth-century children's writers helped inspire modernist interest in stream of consciousness, rhythm, sensory experience, and non-sequentiality. See also Westman 2007.

7. Coats does not rehearse the long history of Freudian readings that support her theoretical direction in equating Alice with the phallus, after Otto Fenichel's 1936 formula "girl = phallus." This perspective on *Alice* begins with

Paul Schilder's 1938 remarks: "Fenichel has lately pointed to the possibility that little girls might become symbols for the phallus. Alice changes her form continually; she is continually threatened and continually in danger. There may have been in Carroll the wish for feminine passivity and a protest against it. He plays the part of the mother to little girls but the little girl is for him also the completion of his own body. The little girl is his love object, substituting for the mother and substituting for the sister. These are complicated discussions and are not fully justified, since we do not know enough about the fantasy life of Carroll and probably shall never know about it. But on the basis of other experiences we are reasonably sure that the little girls substitute for incestuous love objects. Besides this object relation, there must have existed a strong tendency to identification, especially with female members of the family. As in all forms of primitive sexuality, the promiscuity in Carroll's relation to children is interesting" (1981, 341).

8. Concordia University's Centre for the Arts in Human Development has sponsored a musical adaptation of *Alice* called "The Alice Project (Creative Arts Therapy in Action)" (2008) in which performers "face the challenges of emoting, physical expression, line memorization, and confronting Carroll's themes of exclusion and alienation."

9. *Dreamchild* screenwriter Dennis Potter was a victim of childhood sexual abuse, but he has acknowledged, as Israel reports, "that such deeply damaging experiences can generate many kinds of stories, many kinds of containments, and [that those stories'] representations should not be reduced to their traumatic origins" (cited in Israel 1999, 263).

10. Tim Jeal titled his biography of Baden-Powell *The Boy-Man.*

11. The sexual dynamics of Barrie's fable become even more complicated when we consider its theatrical history. Traditionally the highly coveted part of Peter has been played by a woman, including such famous actresses as Nina Boucicault, Maude Adams, Pauline Chase, Mary Martin, Sandy Duncan, and Cathy Rigby. Originally, Barrie's play was conceived as a pantomime, a Christmas entertainment in which an actress played the part of the hero or Principal Boy. Marjorie Garber theorizes that this tradition continued in Britain after the waning of the pantomime (and consistently in the United States, which has no "analogous mainstream transvestite theater") because the play's "split vision" of transvestitism fascinates Anglo-American viewers. Peter Pan and Hook she respectively dubs "a dream and a nightmare of transvestitism" (1992, 176); "transgression without guilt, pain, penalty, conflict, or cost: this is what Peter Pan—and *Peter Pan*—is all about" (184). Peter must played by a woman and not a boy, suggests Garber, because a woman cannot grow up to be a man.

12. *The Little White Bird* is narrated by a bachelor clubman who describes his involvement with Mary A—— and her son David. The narrator first sees Mary from the windows of the "Junior Old Fogies Club"; he watches, and even facilitates, her courtship with a "selfish young zany of a man" whom she eventually marries. Anonymously he befriends them, sending them money, buying the house in which they live, and finally taking an interest in David. He "has never had [a child] to play with," and his fascination with David intensifies to the point that he decides to "burrow under Mary's influence with the boy, expose her to him in all her vagaries, take him utterly from her and make him mine" (1902, 128). He carries out his "sinister design" (130) in part by telling David stories, echoing Barrie's own practice of telling stories to the Llewelyn Davies boys. These include the story of their own evolving relationship (beginning before David's birth), and the famous tale, elaborated in chapters 14–18, of Peter Pan.

13. Many critics read the Hook–Peter relationship as an (unresolved) oedipal conflict in which Hook doubles for Mr. Darling.

14. Writing about Jackson as a cultural figure, Garber dubs him the "quintessential incarnation of Peter Pan" because of his ability to blur "the boundaries between male and female, youth and age . . . and black and white" (1992, 184–85).

15. Allison Kavey (2009) and David Nunns (2009) see as positive these very aspects of the film; in their view, the film refuses to pathologize Barrie.

16. On Freud's *fort/da* game, see chapter 2.

17. Grossman is hardly the first to offer such comic fare. In 1984, Glenn C. Ellenbogen launched the now-defunct *Journal of Polymorphous Perversity,* with the lead article "Psychotherapy of the Dead." Several book anthologies followed, all edited by Ellenbogen: *Oral Sadism and the Vegetarian Personality* (1986), *The Primal Whimper* (1989), and *Freudulent Encounters (for the Jung at Heart)* (1992).

18. Baum promises a fairy tale in which "the stereotyped genie, dwarf and fairie are eliminated, together with all the horrible and bloodcurdling incidents devised by their authors to point a fearsome moral to each tale" (1996, iii).

19. A revised version, my source, was published in *Children's Literature* in 1976.

20. While Alan C. Elms (1994) develops a psychobiographical approach to Baum, most subsequent readings center on Dorothy, treating her as if she were a real person. See Dervin 1978; Greenberg 1975.

21. Joel D. Chaston (2001) likewise explores the subversive utopianism of Baum's life and work but with a Bakhtinian emphasis on the carnivalesque.

22. For Tison Pugh, *The Tin Woodman of Oz* is the queerest of all of Baum's Oz titles—indeed, he told me in an e-mail, it "should be required reading for any queer theory class" as "THE GAYEST BOOK EVER WRITTEN!" For a more critical view of Baum's politics of gender and sexuality, focused especially on representations of women and girls, see Culver 1992.

23. Thanks to its tendency toward dreaming, fantasy, eccentric characterization, and multilevel narrative, as well as its preoccupation with the child–adult relationship, Golden Age children's literature is starting to catch the attention of queer theorists just as it caught the attention of psychoanalysts, and for much the same reasons. See especially Steven Bruhm and Natasha Hurley's "Curiouser: On the Queerness of Children." In her chapter "Up the Ante, Oedipus! Deleuze in Oz," from her *Is Oedipus Online?*, Jerry Aline Flieger mounts a pro-Freudian and queerish rejoinder to Gilles Deleuze and Félix Guattari's *Anti-Oedipus* by way of Oz, replacing the Tin Man with the desiring machine/cyborg "Kettlepus" and casting Deleuze as the Wizard of Theory.

24. In 2005 Michel curated an exhibit at the University of Massachusetts at Amherst called *Oz Books, the Movie, Gay Men, Oh My!* in which were displayed books, cards, ads, musical recordings, collectibles, and Web sites related to the Oz books and films.

25. In fact, many of the scenes with the Wicked Witch of the West were cut out of the film because they were deemed too terrifying.

26. Looking at Baum's Oz films, Anne Morey (1995–96) argues that Baum tried to appeal to both children and adults, thereby undermining his own popularity. What later worked for Disney did not work for Baum. Baum's use of the "trick" visual style—editing footage to produce special effects—backfired, as that style was passé by 1914.

27. The Yellow Brick Road, in Littlefield's view, represents the gold standard; Dorothy's slippers (changed from silver to ruby in the film), the mobility of silver; and so forth. The Cowardly Lion is purportedly Bryan, and the Wizard, William McKinley. The Scarecrow and the Tin Man represent the demoralized farmer and the dehumanized industrial worker, respectively. Littlefield later recanted the reading.

28. Another major reading of Oz, put forward by Paul Nathanson, concentrates on the film and attempts to decode the latent content behind the manifest screen dream. Drawing from semiotic as well as cultural analysis, Nathanson argues that the film functions as a "secular myth" of America, or more precisely, "functions as a myth in the context of an ostensibly secular culture" (1991, xvii), by referencing and reformulating religious as well as narrative traditions linked with an idealized national past. While the film's popularity is

obviously bound up with its ongoing life on television, Nathanson holds that there is more to its staying power. Acknowledging other sorts of engagements with Oz—as well as the wide range of Oziana in American culture (the subject of his appendix 2)—Nathanson focuses on how the film illustrates the "flexible boundary between religion and secularity" in American culture (18) even as it "is in many ways a religious or quasi-religious phenomenon" (241). *The Wizard of Oz,* he thinks, has characteristics of both a folktale (or a "fallen" myth) and a "risen tale" (a story beginning to take on the function and status of myth).

29. Alice's dream is often interpreted to be a daydream, which might make her adventures seem both less frightening and less consequential. But it might also explain the story's appeal. Lili Peller notes that daydreams structure many children's books and adds that the most successful such books refuse the more nightmarish complexities that trouble children (sexual difference, parent–child difference) and therefore build "on the defense mechanisms of denial" (1959, 430).

4. Maurice Sendak and Picturebook Psychology

1. Dr. Glynn died in 2007. A year later, Sendak acknowledged the relationship and his sexuality in the *New York Times.* Noting that he has given hundreds of interviews over the years, Patricia Cohen asks Sendak if there is any question that was never asked in all that time. "He paused for a few moments and answered, 'Well, that I'm gay. . . . All I wanted was to be straight so my parents could be happy. They never, never, never knew'" (2008, n.p.).

2. John Cech's *Angels and Wild Things* adopts a Jungian perspective on Sendak.

3. Giving priority to "the formative power of early cultural experience and its role in determining the attitudes and behavior of adults" (1999, 5), as well as to the relation between child readers and their adult caregivers, Spitz identifies those issues and their handling in picturebooks while eschewing standard psychoanalytic terminology, writing instead about "inner possibilities" (10) and "children's mental museums" (14).

4. "This picturebook has been so successful over so many years," writes Spitz, "because of the skill with which Sendak demonstrates two major developmental agendas of early childhood: first, the push toward language and socialization, toward the acceptance of limits, losses, and diachronic time; and second, the pull toward impulse, wish, and desire" (1999, 134).

5. Julia Mickenberg acknowledges Mitchell's importance while identifying two major strains of thinking about the psychological and cultural work of children's books in early-twentieth-century America, both heavily influ-

enced by the Lyrical Left movement as well as by the popularization of Freud and by the rise of progressive education. These two strains or philosophies—what she calls "Liberation through Imagination" and "Liberation through Knowledge"—overlapped especially when it came to children's books (2006, 33–46).

6. On Piagetian psychology, see Morss 1990.

7. "Obviously," Mitchell clarifies, "fairy tales cannot be lumped and rejected en masse. I am merely pleading not to have them accepted en masse on the ground that they 'have survived the ages' and 'cultivate the imagination'" (1921, 23).

8. While Mitchell's book got mixed reviews from critics and librarians, it was hailed as "revolutionary" by the *Journal of Educational Psychology* and was praised by such child experts as Arnold Gesell. See Marcus 1992, 58.

9. Piaget initially thinks the movement toward visual realism takes place as part and parcel of the rise of socialized thought and the demise of egocentrism around the age of seven or eight. Intellectual realism arrives earlier, he thinks, but does not result in pictorial accuracy. Piaget's subsequent study of infancy disrupts this picture, because it turns out that very young children, not just older kids, can achieve spatial realism or understanding (see Morss 1990, 135). Piaget fixes this problem by arguing that young children's construction of reality is still egocentric even if they have "optical realism." Piaget reformulates egocentrism in spatial or geometric terms, rather than in the social-cognitive terms of the 1920s, notes Morss (138). We could conclude the opposite, that the developmental narrative, which posits egocentrism as the first stage, is just wrong or overstated. Piaget makes it all work and in so doing affirms sensationism (or the primacy of unmediated sensory experience) and recapitulation.

10. Brown, then, would continue the experimentation of modernist writers like Gertrude Stein and Virginia Woolf, experimentation that Juliet Dusinberre (1987) traces back to Lewis Carroll especially.

11. Here, as with so much of the professional literature on drawings, the child draws "for" the adult. The Wolf Man likewise drew for Freud, later giving him his first sketch of the wolf dream and turning out dozens of such pictures as gifts for subsequent analysts.

12. The drawings are generally of starfish and various naval or ocean scenes; in some, a line actually separates above from below. Klein interprets all concerns with Adolf Hitler and the war as being really about the bad father, the bad penis, and various persecutory and sadistic anxieties and fantasies.

13. Indeed, in a 1954 letter to Krauss, Nordstrom relays this comment from one of Harper's vice presidents, Raymond C. Harwood: "All the psychiatrists will be out of business by the time the children who now read her books

are grown up. This last one *[A Very Special House]* surely takes care of many repressions" (quoted in Marcus 1998, 69). Nordstrom herself championed the children's book against "messy adult maladjustments," as she puts it in another 1954 letter concerning Krauss (73).

14. Bader holds in her chapter "Feelings Extended" that the picturebooks of midcentury America reflect this new emphasis on fantasy and emotional-imaginative exploration. She discusses a number of important texts that seem nearly to emanate from childish joys and longings, identifying a "new literature for the kindergarten, or, in educational parlance, k–2, kindergarten to second grade.... The 'area of direct communication to children's feelings'—[publisher William] Scott's characterization—expanded to embrace the transmission, in fictional form, *of* children's feelings" (1976, 478). She sees in picturebooks from this period a shift toward the individual and to "the particular" and notes the ways the observations of children by individual author-artists helped inspire some of our most beloved texts. Bader acknowledges that there is more to picturebooks than meets the eye and that the best specimens—whatever their use of line or color—do not necessarily stick to the familiar or to realism.

15. Pankejeff sought Freud's help with his nervous compulsions and inability to have bowel movements without an enema. Freud thought that his patient was resisting full analysis and gave the analysis a one-year deadline; at the end of that time, analysis had ostensibly led to a successful outcome. Freud came up with two explanations for the Wolf Man's symptoms: first, he concluded that the Wolf Man had witnessed his parents having coitus *a tergo* ("from behind") while still very young; later, he suggested that his patient had perhaps witnessed animal sex and had projected anxieties about it onto his parents, in keeping with classic oedipal formation. Freud emphasized the Wolf Man's identification with his mother as well as his father, underscoring the foundational presence of same-sex identification and desire. The case is still used in the training of analysts.

16. The Wild Things were in fact modeled on Sendak's uncles and aunts.

17. By having Max replace his mother as the wolf, suggests McGillis, Sendak acknowledges the boy's overriding narcissism as well as the dynamics of aggression and sublimation (1996, 82). And by making this particular change, he revises the fairy-tale formula behind the Wolf Man's dream, emphasizing the adaptive power as well as the psychic wildness of the child.

18. While the picturebooks of Dr. Seuss have generally been interpreted as political rather than psychological texts, some psychological readings have appeared. For details, see the introduction and annotated bibliography of Philip Nel's *Dr. Seuss: American Icon.* In their biography *Dr. Seuss and Mr. Geisel,* Judith and Neil Morgan interpret *The Sneetches and Other Stories* (especially

"What Was I Scared Of?") as self-therapy on the part of Geisel. The 1937 book *And to Think That I Saw It on Mulberry Street* is arguably one of the first picturebook explorations of the child imagination, even if its character opts for realism at the end. "Sendak's work develops from the primal fears and joys of childhood," suggests Nel, "but Seuss's comes from the subversiveness of adolescence" (2004, 98). Responding to my query about Dr. Seuss and picturebook psychology more generally, Nel notes that Dr. Seuss's *Oh, the Places You'll Go* "would get my vote for book-as-psychology manual" (e-mail correspondence, May 7, 2007).

19. "Forget the Name of the Father," Eve Kosofsky Sedgwick urges us. "Think about your uncles and aunts" (1993, 59). The "avunculate," or the social formation of aunt and uncle—which may or may not involve blood relation—can, she says, provide relief from and alternative wisdom to the nuclear family.

20. The tree motif also shows up in the Wolf Man's dream, in *Where the Wild Things Are*, and in Freud's vision of the psyche as "a system or network of branching interconnections." Freud "depended on this image throughout his mature psychoanalytic writings" (Davis 1995, 97).

21. Observes Kushner: "Maurice is a child of the Great Depression and of Jewish Depression, if I may generalize. Jewish Depression is that inherited awareness of the arduousness of knowing God, the arduousness of knowing *anything,* an acute awareness of the struggle *to know,* the struggle against not knowing; and it is that enduring sense of displacement, yearning for and not securely possessing a home. It is the conviction, passed through hundreds of generations, that true home is elsewhere, promised but not attained, perhaps not even attainable. Maurice's is a *Yiddische kopf,* a large, brooding, circumspect, and contemplative mind, darkened by both fatalism and faith" (2003a, 190).

22. Deborah Thacker, for example, argues that Sendak "claims the feminine domain as the rightful place of the child" (2001, 12). Max's return to Mom represents a triumph of maternal love and feminine domesticity, in her view. For a similar conclusion, see Gross 2002.

23. William Moebius (1986), using *Where the Wild Things Are* as a case study, notes how frequently picturebook characters learn to appreciate the intangible (here, mother love). He links that story pattern to the cognitive development of children as traced by Piaget and also notes the picturebook leitmotif of the threshold (doors, gates, windows, stairs, roads, and so forth). As with Nodelman in *Words about Pictures,* Moebius's careful attention to the genre's codes leads him to theorize about its psychological function(s).

24. Steig was a respected *New Yorker* cartoonist before he underwent analysis with Reich and turned to picturebook work. They met in 1946, when Steig sought help for depression, and remained friends until Reich's untimely

death in prison (he was prosecuted by the U.S. Food and Drug Administration for use of the accumulators). Reich apparently already owned a copy of Steig's 1942 cartoon volume *The Lonely Ones,* and soon after they met he asked Steig to illustrate the 1948 work *Listen, Little Man!*

25. On Reich and Steig, see Cott 1983 and Ihas 2005.

26. In his interview with Marcus, Steig talks about Reich's influence on his work but also more generally emphasizes the otherness of childhood, remarking, "All kids feel misunderstood. . . . How can you understand a kid unless you are one?" (Marcus 2002, 190). Steig sticks up for kids, while his wife likens Steig's compositional method to the spontaneous drawing of children.

27. Jonze insisted that his Wild Things be giant puppets rather than computer-generated imagery productions to maintain a certain authenticity. The puppets were made by the Henson Creature Shop and shipped to Australia for filming.

28. Existential anxiety and the fear of death mark the 2009 film and novel. In a scene lifted from Woody Allen's film *Annie Hall,* Max learns in school that someday the sun will explode and everything will go dark and the earth will die. In the novel, Max gets "a sick feeling in his stomach. There was something about the words 'go dark permanently' that didn't sit well with him" (Eggers 2009, 57). Max shares with the Wild Thing Ira a fear of "the void."

5. "A Case History of Us All"

1. Kenneth L. Donelson and Alleen Pace Nilsen define the young adult (YA) "problem novel" as having unidealized settings and characters; realistic, often idiomatic language; plots that emphasize realistic problems; and conclusions that are not necessarily or improbably happy (2001, 113–14).

2. "If Twain is cited for vernacular, first-person narrators, the picaresque, irony, and male bonding," explains Trites, "Alcott is the author credited with creating both the quintessential sister novel about female community and the prototypical *künstlerroman* of the female writer" (2007, 146).

3. On literature by adolescents, see Neubauer 1992, 84–86; and Savage 2007, chap. 1.

4. Like Neubauer and most other historians, John and Virginia Demos view adolescence as "on the whole an American discovery" (1969, 632). The most comprehensive history of adolescence in America remains Joseph F. Kett's *Rites of Passage: Adolescence in America, 1790 to the Present.*

5. Hall's work found a quick and warm reception among parents, teachers, and vocational workers. Those working with adolescents in high school

and other institutional settings applauded Hall's attitudes toward adolescence, even if they were more resistant to the idea of rebirth. Rather than rebirth, they preferred more continuous models of adolescent development and psychology, turning instead to Freudian theory and to experts such as E. L. Thorndike and Irving King, who emphasize continuity rather than rupture with the past (Kett 1977, 237).

6. Hall biographers Lorine Pruette (1970) and Dorothy Ross (1972) emphasize his lifelong fascination with psychoanalysis.

7. "What a gold mine for Freud, one might think, but such would not be the case," writes Alessandra Comini. Freud "was far more interested in the insights his growing collection of Egyptian and classical antiquities might render him than in the goings-on of local artists" (2002, 172).

8. Hall, Neubauer points out, seems torn between seeing adolescence as a stage to be championed in our evolution toward the "superanthropoid" and fearing adolescence as a time of dangerous precocity and thus a threat to civilization itself. As for Freud, Neubauer pronounces him an antagonist of adolescence. Reading Freud's 1901 case history of Dora, Neubauer echoes contemporary feminist critics in exposing Freud's manipulations of his eighteen-year-old patient. "Instead of strengthening her ego by accepting her story," writes Neubauer, "Freud proceeded to construct his own complicated account of her life and forced her into a position of mere negation" (1992, 131). Against Dora's case Neubauer poses the adolescent diaries of revisionist psychoanalyst Karen Horney, which he sees more sympathetically. "Like Dora," he concludes in the last line, "Karen was the victim of the adolescence of psychoanalysis" (140).

9. In the applied psychological literature of the period Kett also sees a shift away from Hall's faith in the singular adolescent and toward the promotion of conformity. By 1920, adolescence was virtually equated with the high school experience, and "adolescent psychology became as much a method for controlling the behavior of young people as a tool of description and explanation" (Kett 1977, 238).

10. W. Tasker Witham's *The Adolescent in the American Novel, 1920–1960*, also published in 1964, likewise presumes great continuity among adolescence, literature, and psychology. Witham sounds most of the same themes as Kiell and imagines an audience just as broad, composed of literature students, parents, teachers, psychologists, and sociologists. Like Hall and Kiell before him, Witham treats adolescence as part of literature and psychology alike.

11. On Mead's relation to Freud and psychoanalysis, see Baxter 2008, 59–60.

12. In 1899, the state of Illinois passed the Juvenile Court Act, which set up the nation's first juvenile court and established parameters for the identification and handling of delinquency.

13. "Jack-rolling" means mugging, especially the mugging of drunks or otherwise easy prey.

14. Psychiatrist Aaron H. Esman offers a similar deconstruction of adolescence in *Adolescence and Culture,* taking on the conceit of "youth culture" and arguing that adolescent behavior is symptomatic of and indistinguishable from cultural behavior at large. This line of thought can also be traced to F. Musgrove's *Youth and the Social Order.*

15. In 1920 Dell published an essay called "Psycho-analytic Confession," a dialogue between his political consciousness and his hedonistic unconscious.

16. Surveying early scholarship on literary adolescence, Witham remarks, "All of the critics here mentioned see the adolescent in fiction as a symbol of modern man in a period of doubt and confusion" (1964, 26). The adolescent shared much with the antihero of modernist, naturalist, and existentialist literature, becoming a representative subject but also disturbing the terms through which subjectivity is typically normalized, made into maturity, adulthood, and "identity."

17. Witham traces the transition from genteel and sentimental treatments of adolescence to what he calls "modern realism." He characterizes each decade thus: in the 1920s greater "frankness" in subject(s) appeared; in the 1930s social disenchantment and proletarian novels arose; and in the 1940s, depth psychology and symbolism took priority "in novels of careful and conscious artistry" (1964, 16).

18. In *Love and the Machine Age,* Dell proposes that modern civilization is just beginning to break decisively with "patriarchal society," which suppresses "true" or "full" heterosexuality in favor of "permanently infantile attitudes" and cultural formations (1930, 9). He quotes child expert Dr. Frankwood E. Williams: "If hetero-sexuality is not accomplished in these four or five years [of later adolescence] it never will be accomplished in a normal way. . . . Hetero-sexuality cannot be attained in a vacuum. It cannot be attained by itself. It does not just happen; it is a development and growth that is nourished and continued by what it feeds upon" (quoted in Dell 1930, 310).

19. See Eric Tribunella's "Refusing the Queer Potential."

20. Rather than tell the story in first-person voice, Maxwell often plays psychoanalyst to the characters and their situations.

21. For a critique, see Carlsen 1967.

22. Not a few ostensibly adult works are concerned with traumas of or

during adolescence, ranging from Sylvia Plath's *The Bell Jar* to Susanna Kaysen's memoir *Girl, Interrupted,* which shares the emphasis on writing as recovery work.

23. Patricia Meyer Spacks concurs that "something in the notion of youth, clearly, supports the fantasies that make fiction" (1981, 15). Like Kristeva, Spacks explores the connections between "the adolescent idea" and the novel.

24. Kristeva understands the maternal as ground zero for the abjection-formation of the subject. In her view, the mother, struggling for recognition in and from the symbolic, has little incentive to advance the child. The child thus pursues "a reluctant struggle against what, having been the mother, will turn into an abject" (1982, 13). This formulation has rightly troubled feminists, even though it attempts to compensate for the glaring sexism of some versions of psychoanalysis.

25. Coats also thinks that "we have lost the social and cultural supports for those processes needed to keep abjection at bay" (1999, 294). "The failure of absolutes or even agreement among church, family, and state," she writes, "has precipitated a diffusion of superegoic injunctions: conflicting demands and prohibitions come from everywhere all the time rather than being focalized through a paternal presence functioning within and bolstered by a master discourse" (293).

26. Langbauer also stresses the tendency of adolescent literature to reveal "adolescence as a category through which (as parents of teenagers sometimes feel) simple notions of the human come to grief" (2007, 505).

6. T *Is for Trauma*

1. In the *New England Primer, A* stands for Adam and original sin: "In Adam's fall / We sinned all." Early children's books on both sides of the Atlantic were exercises in shame and abjection, written to subdue children and curb their sinful natures. Rather than argue for the newness of evil or trauma in children's literature, Baer introduces into her analysis a mathematical conceit; what the twentieth century bears witness to during and after the Holocaust, she holds, is a new "algorithm" of evil, a new configuration or formula.

2. Adorno later revised his original claim, remarking in *Negative Dialectics,* "It may have been wrong to say that after Auschwitz you could no longer write poems. But it is not wrong to raise the less cultural question whether after Auschwitz you can go on living" (1973, 362–63).

3. Susan Gubar argues that poetry is the most ideal genre for engaging the Holocaust, since it "provides spurts of vision, moments of truth, baffling

but nevertheless powerful pictures of scenes unassimilated into an explanatory plot and thus seizes the past 'as an image which flashes up at the instant when it can be recognized and is never seen again'" (2003, 7).

4. See Herman 1997, chap. 1.

5. Margaret R. Higonnet (2005) positions historical fiction about war as a form of trauma writing. She also points out, after Jerry Griswold, that many classic American children's books are essentially orphan stories, like one of the war texts she examines, Esther Forbes's *Johnny Tremain*. For a wide-ranging collection of essays on childhood "in the shadow of war," see Goodenough and Immel 2008. In a particularly important essay on the "storying of war," Mitzi Myers notes that war-themed writing for the young "coincides with accelerating late twentieth-century violence and reflects adult preoccupations with human evil: all forms of moral, psychological, and material destruction; past and present genocides, from the Holocaust to more recent 'ethnic cleansings'; the ever-present possibility of nuclear disaster" (2000, 328). "Adult social history," she continues, "cultural studies, and postmodern/postcolonial literary theory—all much concerned with redefining what counts as 'war' and with exploring how conflicts escalate and how war is represented in history, memory, and words—filter into the expanding and impressive volume of war stories for the young" (328).

6. Long a literary staple—think of Harriet Beecher Stowe's little Eva, for instance, or any of Charles Dickens's angelic and all-too-mortal children— the trope of the dead or wounded child entered the psychoanalytic domain in 1900 in Freud's dream of the burning child in *The Interpretation of Dreams.*

7. Kirby Farrell gives this construction of childhood an even broader history: "It seems safe to say that sensitivity toward the condition of children, women, and the poor has taken on a new moral force in the two centuries since the great democratic revolutions and campaigns against slavery. This suggests that in the current fascination with abuse, imaginations may be acting on a rising standard of justice and empathy, even as they blindly wrestle with shadowy cultural changes of a magnitude greater than we like to think" (1998, 214).

8. One of the countertropes of Holocaust narrative and theory is that confrontation with the Holocaust is impossible or always already insufficient.

9. See Bettelheim 1959, 1943, and 1956.

10. The epigraph also suggests that Zipes has displaced Bettelheim as the fairy-tale critic of choice in this particular series.

11. "Instead of asking what we can learn about the Holocaust from *The Diary of a Young Girl,*" suggests Langer, "perhaps it would be useful to begin by inquiring what we cannot" (2006, 20).

12. Anne and her sister Margot died from typhus and exposure while in

the concentration camp Bergen-Belsen. "The journey from 'Anne-in-her-own-right' to an undifferentiated corpse in a mass grave at Bergen-Belsen marked a defeat for everything Anne Frank had hoped for and believed in," writes Langer, and the celebration of her diary glosses over that sad reality (2006, 26).

13. *The Diary of a Young Girl* has long been positioned as an adolescent narrative, appropriate for other adolescents in part because an adolescent wrote it. Berteke Waaldijk tells us that beginning in the 1950s, "many Dutch, and probably also British and American, girls were given the diary to relieve their parents (mothers) from the obligation of telling them about menstruation. Anne's words were considered a beautiful and pure description of what a growing girl went through" (2000, 113). Other critics have emphasized Anne's usefulness as a role model entirely outside the context of the Holocaust. Such decontextualization and universalization of Anne's character and her diary lead to some rather disturbing conclusions: "Like Anne," assert Linda Irwin-DeVitis and Beth Benjamin, "[modern adolescent girls] are in danger of having their real selves shrivel up and disappear" (1998, 38).

14. Books about the Holocaust without such confrontation are generally met with disapproval. For an analysis, see Ulanowicz 2008b.

15. Lowry's *Number the Stars,* so far the only Holocaust narrative for young readers to be awarded the prestigious Newbery Medal, tells the story of a Danish family and their friends who help smuggle Jewish neighbors out of Nazi-occupied Denmark into Sweden. Ten-year-old Annemarie Johansen becomes involved with the Resistance when her family hides Annemarie's best friend, Ellen Rosen, from the Nazis. Lowry alternately safeguards her protagonist Annemarie and puts her in harm's way, through changes in place and an emphasis on the defensive power of ignorance rather than innocence. Midway through the book, Annemarie discovers that her Uncle Henrik has been lying to her about their mysterious family business near the sea, and she confronts him. "How brave are you, little Annemarie?" he asks, saying that the larger truth of their situation is too much for anyone, much less a child, to bear. Annemarie accepts this explanation, thinking, "They protect[ed] one another by not telling" (1989, 91)—by not knowing or claiming too much individually, they avoid giving others away under German torture. In the book's climactic event, Annemarie is instructed to take a basket of food to her uncle on a docked boat. She knows her task is dangerous, but not why. Hidden in the basket is a handkerchief soaked with a concoction designed to throw off the German dogs brought aboard the boats to sniff out stowaways headed across the sea to Sweden. On her way she encounters German soldiers, who confiscate the lunch but let her take the basket to her uncle. The handkerchief arrives in the nick of time and prevents the dogs from sniffing out the Rosen family members hiding

in a secret compartment. While on the path, Annemarie realizes that she must seem as ignorant as possible. She thinks of herself as Little Red Riding Hood, and even tells herself that story as she walks along. Remembering the child-ishness of her younger sister, Annemarie feigns anger and confusion when the soldiers confiscate the lunch: "'*Don't!*' she said angrily. 'That's Uncle Henrik's lunch!'" (114–15). Innocence, she knows, is a defense. Some critics even hold that *Number the Stars* is not a story of lost innocence at all but rather a medita-tion on the uses and abuses of innocence.

Lowry hopes details will suggest the larger picture. In her Newbery ac-ceptance speech for *Number the Stars,* Lowry remarks: "As a writer I find that I can cover only the small and the ordinary—the mittens on a shivering child—and hope that they evoke the larger events. The huge and the terrible are beyond my powers" (1990, 416).

16. In "The Anxiety of Trauma in Children's War Fiction," Kertzer sug-gests that most trauma narratives strive to protect young readers from the effects of trauma rather than to expose them to such effects. Like Langer, she notes that much historical information is missing from such texts and that authors tend to self-censor when it comes to disturbing subjects. "In children's war fiction," she writes, "sustained exploration of psychological trauma re-mains the exception rather than the rule" (2008, 208). I do not disagree, but I would underscore the dialectic between strategies of protagonist protection and exposure, especially in recent years.

17. "A trauma history of the United States," writes Ann Cvetkovich, "would address the multigenerational legacies of the colonization and genocide of indigenous peoples as well as of the African diaspora and slave trade—a project, it should be noted, that is necessarily transnational in scope" (2003, 119). Cvetkovich's work demonstrates the value of an integrative approach to trauma, one in which psychoanalysis does not dominate the interpretive scene but rather is understood as one heuristic among many.

18. Another recent and higher-profile return to this tragedy is the docu-mentary film *Ararat,* directed by the Armenian-Canadian director Atom Egoyan (2002). In January 2004, the Turkish minister of culture and tourism, Erkan Mumcu, gave official and controversial permission to Turks wanting to see the film, emphasizing that Turkey is now a democracy. By and large, Turks and Armenians have told different stories about the events that began in 1915. Armenians avow that they were chased out of their ancestral homeland and executed brutally, whereas the official Turkish line is that the Armenians, en-couraged by Russia, were rebelling against the Ottoman Empire and were thus suppressed. Belonging to the skeptical genre of political documentary, the film raises consciousness not only about this traumatic episode but also about the difficulties of coming to terms with history and/as trauma.

19. The nine titles include the aforementioned *Rose Blanche* and *Hiro-shima No Pika,* as well as *The Butter Battle Book* by Dr. Seuss, and my favorite, *The Tin-Pot Foreign General and the Old Iron Woman* by Raymond Briggs, both published in 1984.

20. Marcus also calls Brown's 1950 book *The Dark Wood of the Golden Birds* "a haunting, albeit vexingly elliptical allegory of the artist's heroic struggle against the dark forces that constitute the wellsprings of creativity" (1992, 244–45).

21. "I hypothesize that a necessary ingredient to make a picturebook a classic—that is, a book of great and enduring literary value and appeal that meets the conventional criteria of a picturebook for a manifestly light tone and happy ending—is that the book be motivated throughout by a creator's restaging of early trauma (primarily through allegorical narrative and line drawing)" (Galbraith 2000a, 638).

22. See also Margaret R. Higonnet's "Picturing Trauma in the Great War," which examines French visual culture during World War I, including drawings by French children alongside picturebooks.

23. Galbraith calls for a mode of children's studies informed by and attuned to "radical attachment theory" or "emancipatory theories of childhood" that demand adults change their behavior. She writes, "I subscribe to a psychodynamic model that, *contra* Freud, Klein, and Lacan, sees the meeting of children's needs for 'continuous live support' (Winnicott's phrase) as an achievable goal that needs never to be renounced in favor of so-called 'transitional objects' so long as adults adhere to two basic principles of human intimate care: prevent all attachment breaks you can, and recognize and repair all attachment breaks you can't prevent. . . . Since normative European-American parenting practices still mandate attachment breaks and forbid the processes required for repair, it is not surprising that this model has been slow to emerge" (2001b, 192).

24. Berlant notes that "the pregnant woman becomes the child to the fetus, becoming more minor and less politically represented than the fetus, which is in turn made more *national,* more central to securing the privileges of law, paternity, and other less institutional family strategies of contemporary American culture" (1997, 85; emphasis in the original).

25. Another such collection of children's testimony is *Messages to Ground Zero: Children Respond to September 11, 2001,* featuring writings by children collected by Shelley Harwayne in cooperation with the New York City Board of Education.

26. In a more generous analysis of 9/11 picturebooks, Paula T. Connolly argues that *Fireboat* and other titles manage to contextualize the attacks "outside an insulated narrative position to include wider contexts of people,

geography, and time" (2008, 299–300). "Whether framing the event through stories of recovery, heroism, individual accomplishment, or community resolve, these books also reveal a range not only of responses but of ideological paradigms about 9/11" (289).

27. Picturebooks with 9/11 themes conspire with other primers in infantile citizenship, such as neocon Lynne Cheney's *America: A Patriotic Primer* (2002). See Ulanowicz 2008a.

28. Here is the magazine's review of *Weapons of War,* as quoted on the ABDO Web site: "Clear and well focused, this highly accessible text delivers the basic facts and the advantages of various craft. Excellent color photos show a dozen different planes, as well as five helicopters, and four support planes in flight, and the others *[sic]* major weapons in use" (http://www.abdopub.com/c/@tBd4Eoatol4KA/Pages/pressmay.html).

29. ABDO and Daughters is not the only children's publisher to hop on the bandwagon; there is also Scholastic, often championed as socially progressive. In his very engaging paper "Marketing 9/11: Children as Victims, Agents, and Consuming Subjects," Richard Flynn turns his attention to "the good corporate citizen" Scholastic, which "mobilizes" its resources on behalf of the wounded nation and the vulnerable child (2002, 2–3). As Flynn remarks, Scholastic.com constructs the child as not only vulnerable but already traumatized, in need of expert help, shopping incentives, and patriotic pedagogy. Speaking more broadly about corporate children's culture, Flynn holds that such materials "reinforce an image of children as infantile, vulnerable, voracious consumers" (10).

30. There are exceptions to this trend, of course. As Emily Murphy argues in "Life on the Wire," Mordicai Gerstein's 2003 book *The Man Who Walked between the Towers* develops the story of Philippe Petit's infamous tightrope walk between the twin towers of the World Trade Center as an allegory for the shock of 9/11 and for trauma more generally. But the trend persists.

Bibliography

Adelson, Joseph. 1956. "Freud in America: Some Observations." *The American Psychologist 2*, no. 9 (September): 467–70.

Adorno, Theodor W. 1973. *Negative Dialectics*. New York: Continuum.

Aichhorn, August. 1983. *Wayward Youth*. Foreword by Sigmund Freud. Evanston, Ill.: Northwestern University Press. First published in 1925.

Alford, C. Fred. 1992. *The Psychoanalytic Theory of Greek Tragedy*. New Haven: Yale University Press.

Allen, Roger E. 1994. *Winnie-the-Pooh on Management: In Which a Very Important Bear and His Friends Are Introduced to a Very Important Subject*. New York: E. P. Dutton

Allen, Roger E., and Stephen D. Allen. 1995. *Winnie-the-Pooh on Problem Solving: In Which Pooh, Piglet, and Friends Explore How to Solve Problems so You Can Too*. New York: E. P. Dutton.

———. 1997. *Winnie-the-Pooh on Success: In Which You, Pooh, and Friends Learn about the Most Important Subject of All*. New York: E. P. Dutton.

Almontaser, Debbie. 2002. "Growing Up Arab-American." In *The Day Our World Changed: Children's Art of 9/11*, edited by Robin F. Goodman and Andrea Henderson Fahnestock, 68–71. New York: Harry N. Abrams.

Anderson, Laurie Halse. 1999. *Speak*. New York: Puffin.

———. 2000. "Speaking Out." *Alan Review* 27, no. 3: 25–26.

Appignanesi, Richard. 1979. *Freud for Beginners*. Illustrated by Oscar Zarate. New York: Pantheon.

Applebee, Arthur N. 1978. *The Child's Concept of Story: Ages Two to Seventeen.* Chicago: University of Chicago Press.

Appleyard, J. A. 1990. *Becoming a Reader: The Experience of Fiction from Childhood to Adulthood.* Cambridge: Cambridge University Press.

Armstrong, Louise. 1963. *A Child's Guide to Freud.* Illustrated by Whitney Darrow Jr. New York: Simon and Schuster.

Armstrong, Richard H. 2005. *A Compulsion for Antiquity: Freud and the Ancient World.* Ithaca, N.Y.: Cornell University Press.

Bader, Barbara. 1976. *American Picture Books from Noah's Ark to the Beast Within.* New York: Macmillan.

Baer, Elizabeth R. 2000. "A New Algorithm in Evil: Children's Literature in a Post-Holocaustal World." *Lion and the Unicorn* 24, no. 3 (September): 378–401.

Ball, John Clement. 1997. "Max's Colonial Fantasy: Rereading Sendak's *Where the Wild Things Are.*" *ARIEL* 28, no. 1: 167–79.

Balsam, Rosemary H. 2003. "Women of the Wednesday Society: The Presentations of Drs. Hilferding, Spielrein, and Hug-Hellmuth." *American Imago* 60, no. 3 (Fall): 303–42.

Barrie, J. M. 1902. *The Little White Bird.* London: Hodder and Stoughton.

———. 2004. *Peter Pan: Peter and Wendy and Peter Pan in Kensington Gardens.* Introduction by Jack Zipes. New York: Penguin.

Barry, Dave, and Ridley Pearson. 2004. *Peter and the Starcatchers.* Illustrated by Greg Call. New York: Disney Editions / Hyperion Books.

Baruch, Dorothy W. 1964. *One Little Boy.* New York: Dell. First published in 1952.

Barzilai, Shuli. 1999. *Lacan and the Matter of Origins.* Stanford: Stanford University Press.

Baum, L. Frank. 1996. *The Wonderful Wizard of Oz.* Illustrated by W. W. Denslow. New York: Dover. First published in 1900.

Bauman, Bruce. 2006. "Lilith in Wunderland." In *Alice Redux: New Stories of Alice, Lewis, and Wonderland,* edited by Richard Peabody, 109–12. Arlington, Va.: Paycock Press.

Baxter, Kent. 2008. *The Modern Age: Turn-of-the-Century American Culture and the Invention of Adolescence.* Tuscaloosa: University of Alabama Press.

Beckwith, Osmond. 1976. "The Oddness of Oz." *Children's Literature* 5: 74–91.

Beers, Clifford Whittingham. 1908. *The Mind That Found Itself: An Autobiography.* New York: Longmans, Green.

Ben-Amos, Dan. 1982. Foreword to *The European Folktale: Form and Nature,* by Max Lüthi, vii–xiii. Translated by John D. Niles. Philadelphia: Institute for the Study of Human Issues.

Benson, Stephen. 2008. "Introduction: Fiction and the Contemporaneity of the Fairy Tale." In *Contemporary Fiction and the Fairy Tale,* edited by Stephen Benson, 1–19. Detroit: Wayne State University Press.

Berger, Laura Stanley, ed. 1994. *Twentieth-Century Young Adult Writers.* Detroit: St. James.

Berlant, Lauren. 1997. *The Queen of America Goes to Washington City: Essays on Sex and Citizenship.* Durham, N.C.: Duke University Press.

———. 2007. "On the Case." *Critical Inquiry* 33 (Summer): 663–72.

Bettelheim, Bruno. 1943. "Individual and Mass Behavior in Extreme Situations." *Journal of Abnormal and Social Psychology* 38 (October): 417–52.

———. 1950. *Love Is Not Enough: The Treatment of Emotionally Disturbed Children.* Glencoe, Ill.: Free Press.

———. 1956. "Schizophrenia as a Reaction to Extreme Situations." *American Journal of Orthopsychiatry* 26 (July): 507–18.

———. 1959. "Feral Children and Autistic Children." *American Journal of Sociology* 64, no. 5 (March): 455–67.

———. 1969. "The Care and Feeding of Monsters." *Ladies' Home Journal,* March, 48.

———. 1972. *The Empty Fortress: Infantile Autism and the Birth of the Self.* New York: Free Press. First published in 1967.

———. 1976. *The Uses of Enchantment: The Meaning and Importance of Fairy Tales.* New York: Alfred A. Knopf.

———. 1983. *Freud and Man's Soul.* New York: Alfred A. Knopf.

Birkin, Andrew. 1979. *J. M. Barrie and the Lost Boys.* London: Constable.

Blackford, Holly. 2007. "Apertures in the House of Fiction: Novel Methods and Child Study, 1870–1910." *Children's Literature Association Quarterly* 32, no. 4 (Winter): 368–89.

———. 2008. "Child Consciousness in the American Novel: *Adventures of Huckleberry Finn* (1885), *What Maisie Knew* (1897), and the Birth of Child Psychology." In *Enterprising Youth: Social Values and the Project of Acculturation in Nineteenth-Century American Children's Literature,* edited by Monika Elbert, 245–58. New York: Routledge.

Bloor, Edward. 1999. *Crusader.* New York: Scholastic.

Blos, Joan. 1978. "Of Children's Literature and Child Psychology: Some Heuristic Considerations." *Children's Literature in Education* 9, no. 2: 101–5.

Blos, Peter. 1941. *The Adolescent Personality.* New York: D. Appleton-Century.

Blum, Virginia. 1995. *Hide and Seek: The Child between Psychoanalysis and Fiction.* Urbana: University of Illinois Press.

Blume, Judy. 1986. *Letters to Judy: What Your Kids Wish They Could Tell You.* New York: Putnam.

Boas, Franz. 1961. Foreword to *Coming of Age in Samoa: A Psychological Study of Primitive Youth for Western Civilization,* by Margaret Mead. First published in 1928. New York: William Morrow.

Boas, George. 1966. *The Cult of Childhood.* London: Warburg Institute.

Bodmer, George R. 1986–87. "Ruth Krauss and Maurice Sendak's Early Illustration." *Children's Literature Association Quarterly* 11, no. 4 (Winter): 180–83.

———. 2003. "Arthur Hughes, Walter Crane, and Maurice Sendak: The Picture as Literary Fairy Tale." *Marvels and Tales* 17, no. 1: 120–37.

Bosmajian, Hamida. 1985. "*Charlie and the Chocolate Factory* and Other Excremental Visions." *Lion and the Unicorn* 9: 36–49.

———. 1989. "The Cracked Crucible of *Johnny Tremain.*" *Lion and the Unicorn* 13, no. 1 (June): 53–66.

———. 1999. "Reading the Unconscious: Psychoanalytical Criticism." In *Understanding Children's Literature,* edited by Peter Hunt, 100–12. London: Routledge.

———. 2000. "Doris Orgel's *The Devil in Vienna:* From Trope into History." *Children's Literature* 28: 112–31.

———. 2002. *Sparing the Child: Grief and the Unspeakable in Youth Literature about Nazism and the Holocaust.* New York: Routledge.

Bottigheimer, Ruth B. 2002. *Fairy Godfather: Straparola, Venice, and the Fairy Tale Tradition.* Philadelphia: University of Pennsylvania Press.

———. 2009. *Fairy Tales: A New History.* Albany: State University of New York Press.

Bourdieu, Pierre. 1998. *Distinction: A Social Critique of the Judgment of Taste.* Translated by Richard Nice. Cambridge, Mass.: Harvard University Press.

Bowlby, Rachel. 2007. *Freudian Mythologies: Greek Tragedy and Modern Identities.* New York: Oxford University Press.

Bragman, Louis J. 1937. "The Case of Floyd Dell: A Study in the Psychology of Adolescence." *American Journal of Psychiatry* 93, no. 6 (May): 1410–11.

Britzman, Deborah P. 2003. *After-Education: Anna Freud, Melanie Klein, and Psychoanalytic Histories of Learning.* Albany: State University of New York Press.

Bronfen, Elizabeth. 2004. *Home in Hollywood: The Imaginary Geography of Cinema.* New York: Columbia University Press.

Brooker, Will. 2005. *Alice's Adventures: Lewis Carroll in Popular Culture.* New York: Continuum.

Brooks, Peter. 1985. *Reading for the Plot: Design and Intention in Narrative.* New York: Vintage Books.

Brooks, Van Wyck. 1920. *The Ordeal of Mark Twain*. New York: E. P. Dutton.

Brown, Gillian. 2003. "Child's Play." In *The American Child: A Cultural Studies Reader,* edited by Caroline F. Levander and Carol J. Singley, 13–39. New Brunswick, N.J.: Rutgers University Press.

Brown, Margaret Wise. 1947. *Goodnight Moon*. Illustrated by Clement Hurd. New York: Harper.

Bruhm, Steven, and Natasha Hurley. 2004. "Curiouser: On the Queerness of Children." Introduction to *Curiouser: On the Queerness of Children,* edited by Steven Bruhm and Natasha Hurley, ix–xxxviii. Minneapolis: University of Minnesota Press.

Bühler, Charlotte. 1918. *Das Märchen und die Phantasie des Kindes*. Leipzig: J. A. Barth.

Burgess, Ernest W. 1966. "Discussion." Afterword to *The Jack-Roller: A Delinquent Boy's Own Story,* by Clifford R. Shaw, 184–205. Introduction by Howard S. Becker. Chicago: University of Chicago Press. First published in 1930.

Burkett, Elinor. 2001. *Another Planet: A Year in the Life of a Suburban High School*. New York: HarperCollins.

Burlingham, Dorothy, and Anna Freud. 1944. *Infants without Families*. New York: International University Press.

Butler, Francelia. 1974. "Preface: The Editor's High Chair." *Children's Literature* 3: 8.

Butler, Judith. 1997. *The Psychic Life of Power*. Stanford: Stanford University Press.

Butler, Octavia E. 2003. *Kindred*. 25th anniversary ed. Boston: Beacon Press.

Carlsen, G. Robert. 1966. "Patterns in Reading." *Publishers' Weekly,* August 8, 29–39.

———. 1967. *Books and the Teen-Age Reader*. New York: Bantam.

Carpenter, Humphrey S. 1987. *Secret Gardens: The Golden Age of Children's Literature*. London: Unwin Hyman.

Carroll, Lewis. 1993. *Alice's Adventures in Wonderland*. Illustrated by John Tenniel. New York: Dover. First published in 1865.

Carroll, Virginia Schaefer. 1996. "Re-reading the Romance of *Seventeenth Summer*." *Children's Literature Association Quarterly* 21, no. 1 (Spring): 12–19.

Cart, Michael. 1996. *From Romance to Realism: Fifty Years of Growth and Change in Young Adult Literature*. New York: HarperCollins.

———. 2002. *911: The Book of Help*. With Marc Aronson and Marianne Carus. Chicago: Cricket Books.

Carter, Arthur L. "Memories Will Shape the Future. In *The Day Our World*

Changed: Children's Art of 9/11, edited by Robin F. Goodman and Andrea Henderson Fahnestock, 107–15. New York: Harry N. Abrams.

Caruth, Cathy. 1995. "Introduction." In *Trauma: Explorations in Memory,* edited by Cathy Caruth, 3–12. Baltimore: The Johns Hopkins University Press.

Cashdan, Sheldon. 1999. *The Witch Must Die: The Hidden Meaning of Fairy Tales.* New York: Basic Books.

Cech, John. 1987. "Some Leading, Blurred, and Violent Edges of the Contemporary Picture Book." *Children's Literature* 15: 197–206.

———. 1995. *Angels and Wild Things: The Archetypal Poetics of Maurice Sendak.* University Park: Pennsylvania State University Press.

Chaston, Joel D. 2001. "Baum, Bakhtin, and Broadway: A Centennial Look at the Carnival of Oz." *Lion and the Unicorn* 25 (January): 128–49.

Chbosky, Stephen. 1999. *The Perks of Being a Wallflower.* New York: MTV.

Cheney, Lynne. 2002. *America: A Patriotic Primer.* New York: Simon and Schuster.

Cheslik-DeMeyer, Steven. N.d. "Where the Wild Things Are Gay." Unpublished essay cited with permission.

Childers, Helen White. 1958. "American Novels about Adolescents, 1917–1953." Ph.D. diss., George Peabody College for Teachers.

Chinn, Sarah E. 2009. *Inventing Modern Adolescence: The Children of Immigrants in Turn-of-the-Century America.* New Brunswick, N.J.: Rutgers University Press.

Clark, Bevery Lyon. 2003. *Kiddie Lit: The Cultural Construction of Children's Literature in America.* Baltimore: The Johns Hopkins University Press.

Coats, Karen. 1999. "Abjection and Adolescent Fiction." *Journal for the Psychoanalysis of Culture and Society* 5, no. 2 (Fall): 290–300.

———. 2004. *Looking Glasses and Neverlands: Lacan, Desire, and Subjectivity in Children's Literature.* Iowa City: University of Iowa Press.

Cockett, Lynn S. 1996. "Writing for Parents about Children's Literature in Mass Market Publications, 1900–1950." *Library Trends* 44, no. 4 (Spring): 794–812.

Cohen, Elliott E. 1945. "A 'Teen-Age Bill of Rights.'" *New York Times Magazine,* January 7: 16–18.

Cohen, Patricia. 2008. "Concerns beyond Just Where the Wild Things Are." *New York Times,* September 11. http://www.nytimes.com/2008/09/10/arts/design/10sendak.html.

Comini, Alessandra. 2002. "Toys in Freud's Attic: Torment and Taboo in the Child and Adolescent Themes of Vienna's Image-Makers." In *Picturing*

Children: Constructions of Childhood between Rousseau and Freud, edited by Marilyn R. Brown, 167–88. Burlington, Vt.: Ashgate.

Concordia University, Centre for the Arts in Human Development. 2008. "The Alice Project." February 3. http://shopware.films.com/id/13314/The_ Alice_Project_Creative_Arts.

Connolly, Paula T. 2008. "Retelling 9/11: How Picture Books Re-envision National Crises." *Lion and the Unicorn* 32, no. 3 (September): 288–303.

Coover, Robert. 1991. *Pinocchio in Venice.* New York: Linden Press / Simon and Schuster.

Cormier, Robert. 1974. *The Chocolate War.* New York: Dell Laurel-Leaf.

———. 1977. *I Am the Cheese.* New York: Pantheon Books.

Cott, Jonathan. 1983. *Pipers at the Gates of Dawn: The Wisdom of Children's Literature.* New York: Random House.

Crew, Hilary S. 2000. *Is It Really "Mommie Dearest"? Daughter-Mother Narratives in Young Adult Fiction.* Lanham, Md.: Scarecrow Press.

Crews, Frederick C. 1963. *The Pooh Perplex.* New York: E. P. Dutton.

———. 1966. *The Sins of the Fathers: Hawthorne's Psychological Themes.* Berkeley: University of California Press.

———. 1975. *Out of My System: Psychoanalysis, Ideology, and Critical Method.* New York: Oxford University Press.

———. 1986. *Skeptical Engagements.* New York: Oxford University Press.

———. 2001. *Postmodern Pooh.* New York: North Point Press.

———. 2006. *Follies of the Wise: Dissenting Essays.* Emeryville, Calif.: Shoemaker and Hoard.

Culver, Stuart. 1992. "Growing Up in Oz." *American Literary History* 4, no. 4 (Winter): 607–28.

Cummins, Julie, ed. 1999. *Wings of an Artist: Children's Book Illustrators Talk about Their Art.* New York: Harry N. Abrams.

Cushman, Philip. 1995. *Constructing the Self, Constructing America: A Cultural History of Psychotherapy.* Reading, Mass.: Addison-Wesley.

Cvetkovich, Ann. 2003. *An Archive of Feelings: Trauma, Sexuality, and Lesbian Public Cultures.* Durham, N.C.: Duke University Press.

Daly, Maureen. 2002. *Seventeenth Summer.* New York: Simon Pulse. First published in 1942.

Daniels, Steven V. 1990. "*The Velveteen Rabbit:* A Kleinian Perspective." *Children's Literature* 18: 17–30.

Danto, Elizabeth Ann. 2005. *Freud's Free Clinics: Psychoanalysis and Social Justice, 1918–1938.* New York: Columbia University Press.

Darling, Richard L. 1968. *The Rise of Children's Book Reviewing in America, 1865–1881.* New York: R. R. Bowker.

Darnton, Robert. 1984. *The Great Cat Massacre and Other Episodes in French Cultural History.* New York: Basic Books.

David, Peter. 2008. *Tigerheart.* New York: Del Ray.

Davis, Whitney. 1995. *Drawing the Dream of the Wolves: Homosexuality, Interpretation, and Freud's "Wolf Man."* Bloomington: Indiana University Press.

de Board, Robert. 1998. *Counselling for Toads: A Psychological Adventure.* New York: Routledge.

Deleuze, Gilles, and Félix Guattari. 1983. *Anti-Oedipus: Capitalism and Schizophrenia.* Translated by Robert Hurley, Mark Seem, and Helen R. Lane. Minneapolis: University of Minnesota Press.

Dell, Floyd. 1919. *Were You Ever a Child?* New York: Alfred A. Knopf.

———. 1920. "Psycho-analytic Confession." *Liberator* 3 (April 1920): 15–19.

———. 1930. *Love in the Machine Age: A Psychological Study of the Transition from Patriarchal Society.* New York: Farrar and Rinehart.

———. 1957. *Moon-Calf.* New York: Sagamore Press. First published in 1920.

Demos, John. 1997a. "History and the Psychosocial: Reflections on 'Oedipus and America.'" In *Inventing the Psychological: Toward a Cultural History of Emotional Life in America,* edited by Joel Pfister and Nancy Schnog, 79–83. New Haven: Yale University Press.

———.1997b. "Oedipus and America: Historical Perspectives on the Reception of Psychoanalysis in the United States." First published in 1978. In *Inventing the Psychological: Toward a Cultural History of Emotional Life in America,* edited by Joel Pfister and Nancy Schnog, 63–78. New Haven: Yale University Press.

Demos, John, and Virigina Demos. 1969. "Adolescence in Historical Perspective." *Journal of Marriage and the Family* 31, no. 4 (November): 632–38.

Dervin, Daniel. 1978. "Over the Rainbow and under the Twister: A Drama of the Girl's Passage through the Phallic Phase." *Bulletin of the Menninger Clinic* 42: 51–57.

Dewey, John. 1899. *The School and Society.* Chicago: University of Chicago Press.

Dierbeck, Lisa. 2003. *One Pill Makes You Smaller.* New York: Picador.

Donelson, Kenneth L., and Alleen Pace Nilsen. 2001. *Literature for Today's Young Adults.* 6th ed. Glenview, Ill.: Scott-Foresman.

Dorson, Richard M. 1959. *American Folklore.* Chicago: University of Chicago Press.

Dowling, Colette. 1981. *The Cinderella Complex: Women's Hidden Fear of Independence.* New York: Summit Books.

Dulles, Foster Rhea. 1952. *America Learns to Play: A History of Popular Recreation, 1607–1940.* New York: Peter Smith.

Dunbar, Janet. 1970. *J. M. Barrie: The Man behind the Image.* Boston: Houghton Mifflin.

Dundes, Alan. 1985. "Nationalist Inferiority Complexes and the Fabrication of Fakelore: A Reconsideration of Ossian, the *Kinder- und Hausmärchen,* the *Kalevala,* and Paul Bunyan." *Journal of Folklore Research* 22, no. 1 (April): 5–18.

———. 1987. "The Psychoanalytic Study of Folklore." In *Parsing through Customs: Essays by a Freudian Folklorist,* 3–46. Madison: University of Wisconsin Press.

———. 1991. "Bruno Bettelheim's Uses of Enchantment and Abuses of Scholarship." *Journal of American Folklore* 104, no. 411 (Winter): 74–83.

Dusinberre, Juliet. 1987. *Alice to the Lighthouse: Children's Books and Radical Experiments in Art.* New York: St. Martin's Press.

Ebert, Roger. 1986. Review of *Dreamchild* (film), directed by Gavin Millar. *Chicago Sun-Times,* January 10. http://rogerebert.suntimes.com/apps/pbcs.dll/article?AID=/19860110/REVIEWS/601100301/1023.

Eddy, Jacalyn. 2006. *Bookwomen: Creating an Empire in Children's Book Publishing, 1919–1939.* Madison: University of Wisconsin Press.

Egan, Michael. 1982. "The Neverland of Id: Barrie, *Peter Pan,* and Freud." *Children's Literature* 10: 37–55.

Eggers, Dave. 2009. *The Wild Things.* San Francisco: McSweeney's Books.

Egoyan, Atom, director. 2002. *Ararat.* Simon Abkarian, Charles Aznavour, Christopher Plummer, Arsinée Khanjian, David Alpay, Marie-Josée Croze, Elias Koteas, Brent Carver, Max Morrow. Alliance Atlantis Communications.

Eklund, Chris. 2007. "A Magical Realism of the Fuck." *ImageTexT: Interdisciplinary Comics Studies* (Department of English, University of Florida) 3, no. 3. http://www.english.ufl.edu/imagetext/archives/v3_3/lost_girls/eklund.shtml.

Elms, Alan C. 1994. "The Mother of Oz: L. Frank Baum." In *Uncovering Lives: The Uneasy Alliance of Biography and Psychology,* 142–61. New York: Oxford University Press.

Empson, William. 1981. "*Alice in Wonderland:* The Child as Swain." First published in 1935. In *Aspects of Alice: Lewis Carroll's Dreamchild as seen through the Critics' Looking-Glasses, 1865–1971,* edited by Robert Phillips, 400–433. New York: Penguin.

Erikson, Erik. 1950. *Childhood and Society.* New York: W. W. Norton.

Esman, Aaron H. 1990. *Adolescence and Culture*. New York: Columbia University Press.

Farrell, Kirby. 1998. *Post-traumatic Culture: Injury and Interpretation in the Nineties*. Baltimore: The Johns Hopkins University Press.

Felman, Shoshana. 1977. "To Open the Question." *Yale French Studies* 55–56: 206–28.

———. 1992. "Education and Crisis; or, The Vicissitudes of Teaching." First published in 1991. In *Testimony: Crises of Witnessing in Literature, Psychoanalysis, and History*, by Shoshana Felman and Dori Laub, 1–56. New York: Routledge.

Felman, Shoshana, and Dori Laub. 1992. *Testimony: Crises of Witnessing in Literature, Psychoanalysis, and History*. New York: Routledge.

Fenichel, Otto. 1936. "Die Symbolische Gleichung: Mädchen = Phallus." *International Zeitschrift für Psychoanalyse* 22: 299–315.

Fiedler, Leslie. 1960. *Love and Death in the American Novel*. New York: Dell.

———. 1973. Introduction to *Beyond the Looking Glass*, edited by Jonathan Cott, xi–xx. New York: Stonehill Publishing.

Fisher, David James. 2008. *Bettelheim: Living and Dying*. New York: Rodopi.

Fiske, John. 1881. "Koschei the Deathless; or, the Diffusion of Fairy Tales." *Atlantic Monthly*, September, 310–21.

FitzGerald, Frances. 2004. "The Influence of Anxiety: What's the Problem with Young Adult Novels?" *Harper's*, September, 62–70.

Fleming, Victor, director. 1939. *The Wizard of Oz*. Judy Garland, Margaret Hamilton, Frank Morgan, Ray Boldger, Bert Lahr, Jack Haley, Billie Burke, Charley Grapewin, Clara Bandwick. MGM.

Flieger, Jerry Aline. 2005. *Is Oedipus Online? Siting Freud after Freud*. Cambridge: MIT Press.

Flynn, Richard. 2002. "Marketing 9/11: Children as Victims, Agents, and Consuming Subjects." Unpublished essay.

Forster, Marc, director. 2004. *Finding Neverland*. Johnny Depp, Kate Winslet, Julie Christie, Radha Mitchell, Dustin Hoffman, Freddie Highmore. Miramax.

Fraiberg, Selma H. 1959. *The Magic Years: Understanding and Handling the Problems of Early Childhood*. New York: Charles Scribner's Sons.

Frank, Anne. 1995. *The Diary of a Young Girl*. Edited by Otto H. Frank and Mirjam Pressler. Translated by Susan Massotty. New York: Doubleday.

Frank, Josette. 1937. *What Books for Children? Guideposts for Parents*. Introduction by Sidonia Matsner Gruenberg. New York: Doubleday.

———. 1948–49. "Books and Children's Emotions." *Child Study* 26, no. 1 (Winter): 5–7, 24–26.

Freeman, Elizabeth. 2002. *The Wedding Complex: Forms of Belonging in Modern American Culture.* Durham, N.C.: Duke University Press.

Freud, Anna. 1946. *Introduction to the Technique of the Analysis of Children.* In *The Psycho-analytical Treatment of Children: Technical Lectures and Essays,* 3–52. Translated by Nancy Procter-Gregg. London: Imago. First published in 1926.

Freud, Sigmund. 1907. "Contribution to a Questionnaire on Reading." *SE* 9: 245–47.

———. 1955. "The Uncanny." In *The Standard Edition of the Complete Works of Sigmund Freud,* vol. 17, pt. 1, 219–56. Edited and translated by James Strachey. London: Hogarth Press.

———. 1960. *The Psychopathology of Everyday Life.* Edited and translated by James Strachey. New York: W. W. Norton.

———. 1961. *Beyond the Pleasure Principle.* Translated and edited by James Strachey. Introduced by Peter Gay. New York: W. W. Norton. First published in 1920.

———. 1963a. "Analysis of a Phobia in a Five-Year-Old Boy (1909)." In *The Sexual Enlightenment of Children,* edited and introduced by Philip Rieff, 47–183. New York: Collier-Macmillan.

———. 1963b. "Family Romances." First published in 1908. In *The Sexual Enlightenment of Children,* edited and introduced by Philip Rieff, 41–45. New York: Collier-Macmillan.

———. 1963c. "The Occurrence in Dreams of Material from Fairy-Tales." First published in 1913. In *Character and Culture,* edited and introduced by Philip Rieff, 59–66. New York: Collier-Macmillan.

———. 1963d. "On the Sexual Theories of Children." First published in 1908. In *The Sexual Enlightenment of Children,* edited and introduced by Philip Rieff, 25–40. New York: Collier-Macmillan.

———. 1963e. *Three Case Histories: The "Wolf Man," the "Rat Man," and the Psychotic Doctor Schreber.* Edited and introduced by Philip Rieff. New York: Collier-Macmillan.

———. 1965. *The Interpretation of Dreams.* Translated and edited by James Strachey. New York: Avon Books. First published in 1900.

———. 1983. Foreword to *Wayward Youth,* by August Aichhorn, v–vi. Evanston, Ill.: Northwestern University Press. First published in 1925.

———. 2002. "Analysis Terminable and Interminable." In *Wild Analysis,* 171–208. Translated by Alan Bance. New York: Penguin.

Friedenberg, Edgar Z. 1963. *Coming of Age in America: Growth and Acquiescence.* New York: Random House.

Friedlaender, Kate. 1942. "Children's Books and Their Function in Latency and Prepuberty." *American Imago* 3, nos. 1–2 (April): 129–50.

Fuller, Robert C. 1986. *Americans and the Unconscious.* New York: Oxford University Press.

Galbraith, Mary. 1998. "'Goodnight Nobody' Revisited: Using an Attachment Perspective to Study Picture Books about Bedtime." *Children's Literature Association Quarterly* 23, no. 4 (Winter): 172–80.

———. 2000a. "Primal Postcards: *Madeline* as a Secret Space of Ludwig Bemelmann's Childhood." *Michigan Quarterly Review* 39, no. 3: 638–46.

———. 2000b. "What Must I Give Up in Order to Grow Up? The Great War and Childhood Survival Strategies in Transatlantic Picture Books." *Lion and the Unicorn* 24, no. 3 (September): 337–59.

———. 2001a. "Freud and Toad Are Friends." Review of *Psychoanalytic Responses to Children's Literature,* by Lucy Rollin and Mark I. West. *Children's Literature* 29: 267–74.

———. 2001b. "Hear My Cry: A Manifesto for an Emancipatory Childhood Studies Approach to Children's Literature." *Lion and the Unicorn* 25, no. 2 (April): 187–205.

Garber, Marjorie. 1992. *Vested Interests: Cross-Dressing and Cultural Anxiety.* New York: Routledge.

Gardner, Howard. 1980. *Artful Scribbles: The Significance of Children's Drawings.* New York: Basic Books.

Gay, Peter. 1990. *Reading Freud: Explorations and Entertainments.* New Haven: Yale University Press.

Gifford, Sanford. 1991. "The American Reception of Psychoanalysis." In *1915, the Cultural Moment: The New Politics, the New Woman, the New Psychology, the New Art, and the New Theatre in America,* edited by Adele Heller and Lois Rudnick, 128–45. New Brunswick, N.J.: Rutgers University Press.

Gilman, Todd S. 1995–96. "'Aunt Em: Hate You! Hate Kansas! Taking the Dog. Dorothy': Conscious and Unconscious Desire in *The Wizard of Oz.*" *Children's Literature Association Quarterly* 20, no. 4 (Winter): 161–67.

Gleason, William A. 1999. *The Leisure Ethic: Work and Play in American Literature, 1840–1940.* Stanford: Stanford University Press.

Golding, Jacqueline. 2006. *Healing Stories: Picture Books for the Big and Small Changes in a Child's Life.* New York: M. Evans.

Goldschmidt, A. M. E. 1981. "*Alice in Wonderland* Psychoanalysed." First published in 1933. In *Aspects of Alice: Lewis Carroll's Dreamchild as Seen through the Critics' Looking-Glasses, 1865–1971,* edited by Robert Phillips, 329–32. New York: Penguin.

Goodenough, Elizabeth, and Andrea Immel, eds. 2008. *Under Fire: Childhood in the Shadow of War.* Detroit: Wayne State University Press.

Goodenough, Florence L. 1926. *Measurement of Intelligence by Drawings.* New York: World Book.

Goodman, Robin F., and Andrea Henderson Fahnestock, eds. 2002. *The Day Our World Changed: Children's Art of 9/11.* New York: Harry N. Abrams.

Gose, Elliott. 1988. *Mere Creatures: A Study of Modern Fantasy Tales for Children.* Toronto, Ontario: University of Toronto Press.

Graham, Philip. 2004. *The End of Adolescence.* Oxford: Oxford University Press.

Green, Martin. 1982. "J. M. Barrie: Peter Pan and the Idealization of Boyhood." Review of *J. M. Barrie and the Lost Boys,* by Andrew Birkin. *Children's Literature* 10: 159–62.

Green, Roger Lancelyn. 1980. "The Golden Age of Children's Books." First published in 1962. In *Only Connect: Readings on Children's Literature,* edited by Sheila Egoff, G. T. Stubbs, and L. F. Ashley, 2nd ed., 1–16. New York: Oxford University Press.

Greenberg, Harvey R. 1975. "*The Wizard of Oz:* Little Girl Lost—and Found." In *The Movies on Your Mind,* 13–32. New York: Saturday Review Press.

Grimm, Wilhelm. 1988. *Dear Mili.* New translation by Ralph Manheim. Illustrated by Maurice Sendak. New York: Farrar, Straus and Giroux.

Griswold, Jerry. 1992. *Audacious Kids: Coming of Age in America's Classic Children's Books.* New York: Oxford University Press.

Grolnick, Simon A. 1986. "Fairy Tales and Psychotherapy." In *Fairy Tales and Society: Illusion, Allusion, and Paradigm,* edited by Ruth B. Bottigheimer, 203–15. Philadelphia: University of Pennsylvania Press.

Gross, Melissa. 2002. "Why Children Come Back: *The Tale of Peter Rabbit* and *Where the Wild Things Are.*" In *Beatrix Potter's Peter Rabbit: A Children's Classic at 100,* edited by Margaret Mackey, 145–58. Children's Literature Association Centennial Studies 1. Lanham, Md.: Scarecrow Press.

Grossman, Lee. 2002. "*The Wizard of Oz:* Professor Marvel's Analysis of an Adolescent Girl." *fort da,* 8 (November 17). http: www.fortda.org/fall_02/pages5htm.

Grotjahn, Martin. 1981. "About the Symbolization of *Alice's Adventures in Wonderland.*" First published in 1947. In *Aspects of Alice: Lewis Carroll's Dreamchild as Seen through the Critics' Looking-Glasses, 1865–1971,* edited by Robert Phillips, 360–68. New York: Penguin.

Grover, Kathryn. 1992. *Hard at Play: Leisure in America, 1840–1940.* Amherst: University of Massachusetts Press.

Gubar, Marah. 2009. *Artful Dodgers: Reconceiving the Golden Age of Children's Literature.* London: Oxford University Press.

Gubar, Susan. 2003. *Poetry after Auschwitz: Remembering What One Never Knew.* Bloomington: Indiana University Press.

Haase, Donald. 2000. "Children, War, and the Imaginative Space of Fairy Tales." *Lion and the Unicorn* 24, no. 3 (September): 360–77.

Habens, Alison. 1994. *Dreamhouse.* New York: Picador.

Hale, Nathan G. Jr. 1995. *Freud and the Americans: The Beginnings of Psychoanalysis in the United States, 1876–1917.* New York: Oxford University Press.

Hall, Granville Stanley. 1907. *Adolescence: Its Psychology and Its Relations to Physiology, Anthropology, Sociology, Sex, Crime, Religion, and Education.* 2 vols. New York: D. Appleton. First published in 1904.

Hamill, Pete. 2002. "Horror through Innocent Eyes." In *The Day Our World Changed: Children's Art of 9/11,* edited by Robin F. Goodman and Andrea Henderson Fahnestock, 28–30. New York: Harry N. Abrams.

Hamilton, Margaret. 1982. "There's No Place Like Oz." *Children's Literature* 10: 153–55.

Hamilton, Victoria. 1993. *Narcissus and Oedipus: The Children of Psychoanalysis.* London: Karmac Books.

Hamilton, Virginia. 1968. *The House of Dies Drear.* New York: Simon and Schuster.

———. 2001. *Sweet Whispers, Brother Rush.* New York: HarperCollins. First published in 1982.

Hammerton, J. A. 1929. *Barrie: The Story of a Genius.* London: Sampson Low, Marston.

Hancock, Susan. 2009. *The Child That Haunts Us: Symbols and Images in Fairytale and Miniature Literature.* New York: Routledge.

Harries, Elizabeth Wanning. 2001. *Twice upon a Time: Women Writers and the History of the Fairy Tale.* Princeton: Princeton University Press.

Harrison, Barbara. 1987. "Howl Like the Wolves." *Children's Literature* 15: 67–90.

Harwayne, Shelley, and the New York City Board of Education, eds. 2002. *Messages to Ground Zero: Children Respond to September 11, 2001.* Portsmouth, N.H.: Heinemann.

Hatfield, Charles. 2007. "A Review and a Response." *ImageTexT: Interdisciplinary Comics Studies* (Department of English, University of Florida) 3, no. 3. http://www.english.ufl.edu/imagetext/archives/v3_3/lost_girls/hatfield .shtml.

Havighurst, Robert J. 1972. *Developmental Tasks and Education.* 3rd ed. New York: Longman.

Hazard, Paul. 1944. *Books, Children, and Men.* Translated by Marguerite Mitchell. Boston: Horn Book. First published in 1933.

Heisig, James W. 1974. "Pinocchio: Archetype of the Motherless Child." *Children's Literature* 3: 23–35.

Henry, Sarah M. 2002. "Children as Witnesses to History." In *The Day Our World Changed: Children's Art of 9/11,* edited by Robin F. Goodman and Andrea Henderson Fahnestock, 18–22. New York: Harry N. Abrams.

Herman, Judith Lewis. 1997. *Trauma and Recovery.* New York: Basic Books.

Hersch, Patricia. 1998. *A Tribe Apart: A Journey into the Heart of American Adolescence.* New York: Ballantine.

Heuscher, Julius E. 1963. *A Psychiatric Study of Fairy Tales: Their Origin, Meaning, and Usefulness.* Springfield, Ill.: Charles C. Thomas.

Higginson, Thomas Wentworth. 1879. "Address." *Library School Journal* 4 (September–October): 357–59.

Higonnet, Anne. 1998. *Pictures of Innocence: The History and Crisis of Ideal Childhood.* London: Thames and Hudson.

Higonnet, Margaret R. 2005. "Time Out: Trauma and Play in *Johnny Tremain* and *Alan and Naomi.*" *Children's Literature* 33: 150–70.

———. 2008. "Picturing Trauma in the Great War." In *Under Fire: Childhood and the Shadow of War,* edited by Elizabeth Goodenough and Andrea Immel, 115–28. Detroit: Wayne State University Press.

Hillman, James. 1974. "A Note on Story." *Children's Literature* 3: 9–11.

Hinton, S. E. 1967. *The Outsiders.* New York: Dell.

Hoff, Benjamin. 1983. *The Tao of Pooh.* New York: Penguin. First published in 1982.

———. 1993. *The Te of Piglet.* New York: Penguin. First published in 1992.

———. 2006. "Farewell to Authorship and Why We're Losing Literature." http://web.archive.org/web/20071215041107/http://www.benjaminhoffauthor.com/essay.htm.

Hoffman, Frederick J. 1945. *Freudianism and the Literary Mind.* Baton Rouge: Louisiana State University Press.

Hogan, Patrick. 1990. "What's Wrong with the Psychoanalysis of Literature?" *Children's Literature* 18: 135–40.

Hollingshead, August B. 1949. *Elmtown's Youth: The Impact of Social Classes on Adolescents.* New York: John Wiley and Sons.

Holmes, Martha Stoddard. 2009. "Peter Pan and the Possibilities of Child Literature." In *Second Star to the Right: "Peter Pan" in the Popular Imagination,* edited by Allison B. Kavey and Lester D. Friedman, 132–50. New Brunswick, N.J.: Rutgers University Press.

Homes, A. M. 1996. *The End of Alice.* New York: Scribner.

Howard, Jennifer. 2009. "From 'Once upon a Time' to 'Happily Ever After':

Fairy Tale Scholars Explore the Nuanced History of the Genre." *Chronicle Review,* May 22, B6–8.

Hug-Hellmuth, Hermine. 1991a. "The Child's Concept of Death." First published in 1912. In *Hermine Hug-Hellmuth: Her Life and Work,* edited by George MacLean and Ulrich Rappen, 63–75. New York: Routledge.

———. 1991b. "The Nature of the Child's Soul (or Psyche)." First published in 1913. In *Hermine Hug-Hellmuth: Her Life and Work,* edited by George MacLean and Ulrich Rappen, 87–93. New York: Routledge.

———. 1991c. "New Ways to the Understanding of Youth." First published in 1924. In *Hermine Hug-Hellmuth: Her Life and Work,* edited by George MacLean and Ulrich Rappen, 154–213. New York: Routledge.

———. 1991d. "On Early Loving and Hating." First published in 1917. In *Hermine Hug-Hellmuth: Her Life and Work,* edited by George MacLean and Ulrich Rappen, 135–37. New York: Routledge.

———. 1991e. "On the Technique of Child Analysis." First published in 1920. In *Hermine Hug-Hellmuth: Her Life and Work,* edited by George MacLean and Ulrich Rappen, 138–53. New York: Routledge.

Huizinga, Johan. 1955. *Homo Ludens: A Study of the Play-Element in Culture.* Boston: Beacon Press. First written in 1938.

Hulbert, Ann. 2003. *Raising America: Experts, Parents, and a Century of Advice about Children.* New York: Random House.

Hunt, Peter, ed. 1999. *Understanding Children's Literature.* London: Routledge.

Hutchinson, Margaret. 1978. "Fifty Years of Young Adult Reading, 1921–1971." In *Young Adult Literature in the Seventies: A Selection of Readings,* edited by Jana Varlejs, 36–69. Metuchen, N.J.: Scarecrow Press.

Ihas, Joann. 2005. "Recurrent Themes in William Steig's Picturebooks." M.A. thesis, University of Florida.

Innocenti, Roberto, and Christophe Gallaz. 1985. *Rose Blanche.* Mankato, Minn.: Creative Education.

Irwin-DeVitis, Linda, and Beth Benjamin. 1998. "Anne as a Role Model for Other Adolescents." In *Readings on the "The Diary of a Young Girl,"* edited by Myra H. Immel, 30–39. San Diego: Greenhaven Press.

Israel, Kali. 1999. "Asking Alice: Victorian and Other Alices in Contemporary Culture." In *Victorian Afterlife: Postmodern Culture Rewrites the Nineteenth Century,* edited by John Kucich and Dianne F. Sadoff, 252–87. Minneapolis: University of Minnesota Press.

Jacobson, Lisa. 2004. *Raising Consumers: Children and the American Mass Market in the Early Twentieth Century.* New York: Columbia University Press.

Jacobus, Mary. 2005. *The Poetics of Psychoanalysis: In the Wake of Klein.* Oxford: Oxford University Press.

Jacoby, Russell. 1975. *Social Amnesia: A Critique of Conformist Psychology from Adler to Laing.* Boston: Beacon Press.

Jeal, Tim. 1990. *The Boy-Man: The Life of Lord Baden-Powell.* New York: William Morrow.

Johnson, Gladys B. 1943. "Books and the Five Adolescent Tasks." *Library Journal* 68 (May): 350–52.

Jones, Ernest. 1990. "Case History of Us All." First published in *Nation,* September 1, 1951, 176. Reprinted in *Critical Essays on Salinger's "The Catcher in the Rye,"* edited by Joel Salzberg, 24–25. Boston: G. K. Hall.

Jonze, Spike, director. 2009. *Where the Wild Things Are.* Max Records, Ryan Corr, Catherine Keener, James Gandolfini, Paul Dano, Catherine O'Hara. Warner Bros.

Jonze, Spike, and Dave Eggers. 2009. Introduction to *Heads On and We Shoot: The Making of "Where the Wild Things Are,"* ix–xi. New York: It Books.

Jung, Carl G. 1949. "The Psychology of the Child-Archetype." In *Essays on a Science of Mythology: The Myth of the Divine Child and the Mysteries of Eleusis,* by C. G. Jung and C. Kerényi, 95–119. Translated by R. F. C. Hull. New York: Pantheon Books.

———. 1954. "On the Psychology of the Trickster-Figure." In *The Collected Works of C. G. Jung,* vol. 9, ed. Herbert Read, Michael Fordham, and Gerhard Adler, trans. R. F. C. Hull, 255–72. New York: Pantheon Books.

———. 1954. "The Phenomenology of the Spirit in Fairytales." In *The Collected Works of C. G. Jung,* vol. 9, edited by Herbert Read, Michael Fordham, and Gerhard Adler, trans. R. F. C. Hull, 207–54. New York: Pantheon Books.

———. 2008. *Children's Dreams: Notes from the Seminar Given in 1936–1940.* Edited by Lorenz Jung and Maria Meyer-Grass. Translated by Ernest Falzeder, with Tony Woolfson. Princeton: Princeton University Press. First published in 1987.

Kalman, Maira. 2002. *Fireboat: The Heroic Adventures of the John J. Harvey.* New York: Putnam.

Kaplan, Louise J. 1984. *Adolescence: The Farewell to Childhood.* New York: Simon and Schuster.

Kavey, Allison B. 2009. "Introduction: From Peanut Butter Jars to the Silver Screen." In *Second Star to the Right: "Peter Pan" in the Popular Imagination,* edited by Allison B. Kavey and Lester D. Friedman, 1–12. New Brunswick, N.J.: Rutgers University Press.

Kavey, Allison B., and Lester D. Friedman, eds. 2009. *Second Star to the Right: "Peter Pan" in the Popular Imagination.* New Brunswick, N.J.: Rutgers University Press.

Kaysen, Susanna. 1993. *Girl, Interrupted.* New York: Turtle Bay Books / Random House.

Kennedy, Dana. 1993. "Michael Jackson: Time to Face the Music." *Entertainment Weekly,* December 17, 30.

Kern, Stephen Roger. 1970. "Freud and the Emergence of Child Psychology: 1880–1910." Ph.D. diss., University of Michigan.

Kerrigan, William. 1985. Introduction to *Opening Texts: Psychoanalysis and the Culture of the Child,* edited by Joseph H. Smith and William Kerrigan, ix–xix. Baltimore: The Johns Hopkins University Press.

Kertzer, Adrienne. 2002. *My Mother's Voice: Children, Literature, and the Holocaust.* Peterborough, Ontario: Broadview Press.

———. 2008. "The Anxiety of Trauma in Children's War Fiction." In *Under Fire: Childhood in the Shadow of War,* edited by Elizabeth Goodenough and Andrea Immel, 207–20. Detroit: Wayne State University Press.

Kett, Joseph F. 1977. *Rites of Passage: Adolescence in America, 1790 to the Present.* New York: Basic Books.

Kidd, Kenneth. 2004. *Making American Boys: Boyology and the Feral Tale.* Minneapolis: University of Minnesota Press.

———. 2005. "Bruno Bettelheim and the Psychoanalytic Feral Tale." *American Imago* 62, no. 1 (Spring): 75–99.

Kiell, Norman. 1959. *The Adolescent through Fiction: A Psychological Approach.* New York: International Universities Press.

———. 1964. *The Universal Experience of Adolescence.* New York: International Universities Press.

Kiley, Dan. 1983. *The Peter Pan Syndrome: Men Who Have Never Grown Up.* New York: Dodd, Mead.

———. 1984. *The Wendy Dilemma: When Women Stop Mothering Their Men.* New York: Arbor House.

Kincaid, James R. 1992. *Child-Loving: The Erotic Child and Victorian Culture.* New York: Routledge.

King, Shelley. 2005. "'All Wound Up': Pullman's Marvelous/Uncanny Clockwork." *Children's Literature* 33: 66–93.

Kipling, Rudyard. 1992. *The Jungle Books.* Edited by W. W. Robson. New York: Oxford University Press. First published in 1894–95.

Kirkland, Russell. 1988. "Teaching Taoism in the 1990s." *Teaching Theology and Religion* 1, no. 2 (1998): 111–19.

———. 2009. "The Taoism of the Western Imagination and the Taoism of China: De-colonizing the Exotic Teachings of the East." Paper presented at the University of Tennessee, October 20, 1997. http://kirkland.myweb.uga.edu/rk/pdf/pubs/pres/TENN97.pdf.

Klein, Melanie. 1988a. "The Development of a Child." First published in 1921. In *Melanie Klein: "Love, Guilt, and Reparation" and Other Works, 1921–1945*, edited by R. E. Money-Kyrle, 1–53. London: Vintage Books.

———. 1988b. "The Importance of Symbol-Formation in the Development of the Ego." First published in 1930. In *Melanie Klein: "Love, Guilt, and Reparation" and Other Works, 1921–1945*, edited by R. E. Money-Kyrle, 219–32. London: Vintage Books.

———. 1988c. "The Role of the School in the Libidinal Development of the Child." First published in 1923. In *Melanie Klein: "Love, Guilt, and Reparation" and Other Works, 1921–1945*, edited by R. E. Money-Kyrle, 59–76. London: Vintage Books.

———. 1998. *Narrative of Child Analysis.* London: Vintage Press. First published in 1961.

Kloss, Robert J. 1989. "Fantasy and Fear in the Work of Maurice Sendak." *Psychoanalytic Review* 76, no. 4 (Winter): 567–79.

Knoepflmacher, U. C. 1990. "The Doubtful Marriage: A Critical Fantasy." *Children's Literature* 18: 131–34.

———. 1998. *Ventures into Childland: Victorians, Fairy Tales, and Femininity.* Chicago: University of Chicago Press.

———. 2005. "The Hansel and Gretel Syndrome: Survivorship Fantasies and Parental Desertion." *Children's Literature* 33: 171–84.

Koplewicz, Harold S. 2002. Foreword to *The Day Our World Changed: Children's Art of 9/11*, edited by Robin F. Goodman and Andrea Henderson Fahnestock, 10–11. New York: Harry N. Abrams.

Krauss, Ruth. 1989. *A Hole Is to Dig: A First Book of First Definitions.* Illustrated by Maurice Sendak. New York: HarperCollins. First published in 1952.

Kristeva, Julia. 1982. *Powers of Horror: An Essay on Abjection.* Translated by Leon S. Roudiez. New York: Columbia University Press.

———. 1995. "The Adolescent Novel." In *New Maladies of the Soul* (First published as *Les Nouvelles maladies de l'âme*, 1993), 135–53. Translated by Ross Guberman. New York: Columbia University Press.

———. 2001. *Melanie Klein.* Translated by Ross Guberman. New York: Columbia University Press.

Kushner, Tony. 2003a. *The Art of Maurice Sendak: 1980 to the Present.* New York: Harry N. Abrams.

———. 2003b. *Brundibar.* Illustrated by Maurice Sendak. New York: Hyperion.

Kuznets, Lois R. 1994. *When Toys Come Alive: Narratives of Animation, Metamorphosis, and Development.* New Haven: Yale University Press.

Lacan, Jacques. 1977. *Écrits*. Translated by Alan Sheridan. New York: W. W. Norton.

Lampert, Jo. 2010. *Children's Fiction about 9/11: Ethnic, Heroic, and National Identities*. New York: Routledge.

Lanes, Selma G. 1980. *The Art of Maurice Sendak*. New York: Harry N. Abrams. First published in 1971.

Langbauer, Laurie. 2007. "The Ethics and Practice of Lemony Snicket: Adolescence and Generation X." *PMLA* 122, no. 2 (March): 502–21.

Langer, Lawrence L. 1975. *The Holocaust and the Literary Imagination*. New Haven: Yale University Press.

———. 2006. *Using and Abusing the Holocaust*. Bloomington: Indiana University Press.

Lasch, Christopher. 1979. *The Culture of Narcissism: American Life in an Age of Diminishing Expectations*. New York: W. W. Norton.

Leach, William R. 1991. "A Trickster's Tale: L. Frank Baum's *The Wonderful Wizard of Oz*." In *The Wonderful Wizard of Oz*, by L. Frank Baum, edited by William R. Leach, 157–88. Belmont, Calif.: Wadsworth.

Lenard, Alexander. 1958. *Winnie ille Pu*. Translation into Latin of A. A. Milne's *Winnie-the-Pooh*. New York: Penguin.

Lesko, Nancy. 2002. "Making Adolescence at the Turn of the Century: Discourse and the Exclusion of Girls." *Current Issues in Comparative Education* 2, no. 2 (April): 182–91.

Lesnik-Oberstein, Karín. 1994. *Children's Literature: Criticism and the Fictional Child*. Oxford: Clarendon Press.

Lindner, Robert. 1944. *Rebel without a Cause: The Hypnoanalysis of a Criminal Psychopath*. New York: Grune and Stratton.

Littlefield, Henry M. 1964. "*The Wizard of Oz*: Parable on Populism." *American Quarterly* 16, no. 1 (Spring): 47–58.

Loncraine, Rebecca. 2009. *The Real Wizard of Oz: The Life and Times of L. Frank Baum*. New York: Gotham Books.

Lowry, Lois. 1989. *Number the Stars*. New York: Dell.

———. 1990. "Newbery Medal Acceptance." Published speech. *Horn Book*, July–August, 412–21.

Lumet, Sidney, director. 1978. *The Wiz*. Diana Ross, Michael Jackson, Nipsey Russell, Ted Ross, Mabel King, Lena Horne, Richard Pryor, Theresa Merritt. Universal Pictures.

Lurie, Alison. 1973. "Back to Pooh Corner." In *Children's Literature: The Great Excluded*, edited by Francelia Butler, 2: 11–17. Storrs, Conn.: Children's Literature Association.

Lüthi, Max. 1982. *The European Folktale: Form and Nature.* Translated by John D. Niles. Philadelphia: Institute for the Study of Human Issues.

———. 1984. *The Fairytale as Art Form and Portrait of Man.* Translated by Jon Erickson. Bloomington: Indiana University Press.

Macdonald, Dwight. 1957. "A Theory of Mass Culture." First published in 1953. In *Mass Culture: The Popular Arts in America,* edited by Bernard Rosenberg and David Manning White, 59–73. New York: Free Press.

MacLean, George, and Ulrich Rappen, eds. 1991. *Hermine Hug-Hellmuth: Her Life and Work.* Routledge: New York.

MacLeod, Anne Scott. 1997. "The Journey Inward: Adolescent Literature in America, 1945–1995." In *Reflections of Change: Children's Literature since 1945,* edited by Sandra L. Beckett, 125–29. Westport, Conn.: Greenwood Press.

Magder, David. 1980. "*The Wizard of Oz:* A Parable of Brief Psychotherapy." *Canadian Journal of Psychiatry* 25, no. 7 (November): 565.

Maguire, Gregory. 1995. *Wicked: The Life and Times of the Wicked Witch of the West.* New York: Regan Books.

Main, Roderick, ed. 1997. *Jung on Synchronicity and the Paranormal.* Introduction by Roderick Main. Princeton: Princeton University Press.

Marcus, Leonard S. 1992. *Margaret Wise Brown: Awakened by the Moon.* New York: HarperCollins.

———, ed. 1998. *Dear Genius: The Letters of Ursula Nordstrom.* New York: HarperCollins.

———. 2002. *Ways of Telling: Conversations on the Art of the Picture Book.* New York: E. P. Dutton.

Marsh, Dave. 1985. *Trapped: Michael Jackson and the Crossover Dream.* New York: Bantam.

Maruki, Toshi. 1980. *Hiroshima no pika.* New York: Lothrop, Lee and Shepard.

Massé, Michelle A. 2003. "Constructing the Psychoanalytic Child: Freud's 'From the History of an Infantile Neurosis.'" In *The American Child: A Cultural Studies Reader,* edited by Caroline F. Levander and Carol J. Singley, 149–66. New Brunswick, N.J.: Rutgers University Press.

Matthews. F. H. 1967. "The Americanization of Sigmund Freud: Adaptations of Psychoanalysis before 1917." *Journal of American Studies* 1, no. 1 (April): 39–62.

Matthews, Gareth B. 1980. *Philosophy and the Young Child.* Cambridge, Mass.: Harvard University Press.

Maxwell, William. 1981. *The Folded Leaf.* Boston: Nonpareil Books. First published in 1945.

McCullers, Carson. 1986. *The Member of the Wedding.* New York: Bantam. First published in 1946.

McGillis, Roderick. 1996. *The Nimble Reader: Literary Theory and Children's Literature.* New York: Twayne.

McGuire, William. 1995. "Firm Affinities: Jung's Relations with Britain and the United States." *Journal of Analytical Psychology* 40, no. 3 (July): 301–26.

Mead, Margaret. 1961. *Coming of Age in Samoa: A Psychological Study of Primitive Youth for Western Civilization.* Foreword Franz Boas. New York: William Morrow. First published in 1928.

Medovoi, Leerom. 2005. *Rebels: Youth and the Cold War Origins of Identity.* Durham, N.C.: Duke University Press.

Meltzer, Françoise. 1987. "Introduction: Partitive Plays, Pipe Dreams." In *The Trial(s) of Psychoanalysis,* edited by Françoise Meltzer, 1–7. Chicago: University of Chicago Press.

Menefee, Joan. 2007. "The Shape of a Hand: Children's Drawings in 20th-Century Psychology." Paper presented at the Children's Literature Association Conference, Newport News, Virginia, June 16. Unpublished paper cited with permission.

Meyer, Donald. 1965. *The Positive Thinkers: A Study of the American Quest for Health, Wealth, and Personal Power from Mary Baker Eddy to Norman Vincent Peale.* New York: Doubleday.

Mickenberg, Julia L. 2006. *Learning from the Left: Children's Literature, the Cold War, and Radical Politics in the United States.* New York: Oxford University Press.

Michel, Dee. n.d. "Friends of Dorothy: Why Gay Men and Gay Boys Love *The Wizard of Oz.*" Unpublished book manuscript.

Millar, Gavin, director. 1985. *Dreamchild.* Jane Asher, Alan Bennett, Coral Browne, Peter Gallagher, Ian Holm, Rupert Wainwright, Julie Walters. PfH Ltd.

Milne, A. A. 1944. *Autobiography.* New York: E. P. Dutton. First published as *It's Too Late Now: The Autobiography of a Writer* (London: Methuen, 1938).

———. 1957. *The World of Pooh: The Complete "Winnie-the-Pooh" and "The House at Pooh Corner."* Illustrated by E. H. Shepard. New York: E. P. Dutton.

Mintz, Steven, and Susan Kellogg. 1988. *Domestic Revolutions: A Social History of American Family Life.* New York: Free Press.

Mitchell, Lucy Sprague. 1921. *Here and Now Story Book: Two- to Seven-Year-Olds.* Illustrated by Hendrik Willem van Loon. New York: E. P. Dutton.

———. 1953. *Two Lives.* New York: Simon and Schuster.

Moebius, William. 1986. "Introduction to Picturebook Codes." *Word and Image* 2, no. 2: 141–58.

Moore, Alan, and Melinda Gebbie. 2006. *Lost Girls.* 3 vols. Atlanta: Top Shelf.

Moran, Jeffrey P. 2000. *Teaching Sex: The Shaping of Adolescence in the 20th Century.* Cambridge, Mass.: Harvard University Press.

Morena, Gita Dorothy. 1998. *The Wisdom of Oz: Reflections of a Jungian Sandplay Therapist.* Berkeley, Calif.: Frog.

Morey, Anne. 1995–96. "'A Whole Book for a Nickel'? L. Frank Baum as Filmmaker." *Children's Literature Association Quarterly* 20, no. 4 (Winter): 155–60.

Morgan, Judith, and Neil Morgan. 1995. *Dr. Seuss and Mr. Geisel.* New York: Random House.

Morss, John R. 1990. *The Biologising of Childhood: Developmental Psychology and the Darwinian Myth.* Hove, U.K.: Lawrence Erlbaum Associates.

Moskowitz, Eva S. 2001. *In Therapy We Trust: America's Obsession with Self-Fulfillment.* Baltimore: The Johns Hopkins University Press.

Murch, Walter, director. 1985. *Return to Oz.* Fairuza Balk, Nicol Williamson, Jean Marsh, Piper Laurie, Matt Clark, Michael Sundin, Tim Rose, Sean Barrett, Brian Henson. BMI.

Murphy, Emily. 2010. "Life on the Wire: Post-9/11 Mourning and the Figure of the Tightrope Walker." Unpublished essay, cited with permission.

Musgrove, F. 1964. *Youth and the Social Order.* Bloomington: Indiana University Press.

Myers, Mitzi. 2000. "Storying War: A Capsule Overview." *Lion and the Unicorn* 24, no. 3 (September): 327–36.

Nasaw, David. 1993. *Going Out: The Rise and Fall of Public Amusements.* New York: Basic Books.

Nathanson, Paul. 1991. *Over the Rainbow: The Wizard of Oz as a Secular Myth of America.* Albany: State University of New York Press.

Nel, Philip. 2004. *Dr. Seuss: American Icon.* New York: Continuum.

———. 2006. *The Annotated Cat: Under the Hats of Seuss and His Cats.* Introduced and annotated by Philip Nel. New York: Random House.

Neubauer, John. 1992. *The Fin-de-Siècle Culture of Adolescence.* New Haven: Yale University Press.

Nicks, Robin J. G. 2006. "Fairy Tales and Necrophilia: A New Cultural Context for Antebellum America." Ph.D. diss., University of Florida.

Nikolajeva, Maria, and Carole Scott. 2001. *How Picturebooks Work.* New York: Garland.

Nodelman, Perry. 1985. "The Case of Children's Fiction; or, The Impossibility of Jacqueline Rose." *Children's Literature Association Quarterly* 10, no. 3 (Fall): 98–100.

———. 1988. *Words about Pictures: The Narrative Art of Children's Picture Books.* Athens: University of Georgia Press.

———. 2008. *The Hidden Adult: Defining Children's Literature.* Baltimore: The Johns Hopkins University Press.

Nolan, Han. 1994. *If I Should Die before I Wake.* New York: Harcourt Brace.

Noll, Richard. 1994. *The Jung Cult: Origins of a Charismatic Movement.* Princeton: Princeton University Press.

Nunns, David P. D. 2009. "'Gay, Innocent, and Heartless': *Peter Pan* and the Queering of Popular Culture." In *Second Star to the Right: "Peter Pan" in the Popular Imagination,* edited by Allison B. Kavey and Lester D. Friedman, 219–42. New Brunswick, N.J.: Rutgers University Press.

Orenstein, Catherine. 2002. *Little Red Riding Hood Uncloaked: Sex, Morality, and the Evolution of a Fairy Tale.* New York: Basic Books.

Orgel, Doris. 1988. *The Devil in Vienna.* New York: Puffin.

Orth, Maureen. 1994. "Nightmare in Neverland." *Vanity Fair,* January, 69–77, 131–38.

Osgood, Samuel. 1865. "Books for Our Children." *Atlantic Monthly,* December, 724–35.

Pace, Patricia. 1998. "All Our Lost Children: Trauma and Testimony in the Performance of Childhood." *Text and Performance Quarterly* 18, no. 3 (July): 233–47.

Patel, Andrea. 2002. *On That Day: A Book of Hope for Children.* Berkeley, Calif.: Tricycle Press.

Payne, Michael. 2005. "What Difference Has Theory Made? From Freud to Adam Phillips." *College Literature* 32, no. 2 (Spring): 1–15.

Peabody, Richard. 2006. Introduction to *Alice Redux: New Stories of Alice, Lewis, and Wonderland,* edited by Richard Peabody, xi–xvi. Arlington, Va.: Paycock Press.

Peller, Lili. 1959. "Daydreams and Children's Favorite Books." *Psychoanalytic Study of the Child* 14: 414–33.

Pfister, Joel. 1997. "Glamorizing the Psychological: The Politics of the Performances of Modern Psychological Identities." In *Inventing the Psychological: Toward a Cultural History of Emotional Life in America,* edited by Joel Pfister and Nancy Schnog, 167–213. New Haven: Yale University Press.

Phillips, Adam. 2001. "Bombs Away." In *Promises, Promises: Essays on Literature and Psychoanalysis,* 35–58. New York: Basic Books.

Phillips, Jerry, and Ian Wojcik-Andrews. 1990. "Notes toward a Marxist Critical Practice." *Children's Literature* 18: 127–30.

Phillips, Robert, ed. 1981. *Aspects of Alice: Lewis Carroll's Dreamchild as Seen through the Critics' Looking-Glasses, 1865–1971.* New York: Penguin.

Piaget, Jean. 1962. *Play, Dreams, and Imitation in Childhood.* Translated by G. Gattegno and F. M. Hodgson. New York: W. W. Norton.

Plath, Sylvia. 1971. *The Bell Jar.* New York: Harper and Row. First published in 1967.

Pollak, Richard. 1988. *The Creation of Dr. B: A Biography of Bruno Bettelheim.* New York: Touchstone Books.

Pratt, Caroline. 1921. Preface to *Here and Now Story Book: Two- to Seven-Year-Olds,* by Lucy Sprague Mitchell. Illustrated by Hendrik Willem van Loon. New York: E. P. Dutton.

Pruette, Lorine. 1970. *G. Stanley Hall: A Biography of a Mind.* Introduction by Carl Van Doren. Freeport, N.Y.: Books for Libraries Press. First published in 1926.

Pugh, Tison. 2008. "'There Lived in the Land of Oz Two Queerly Made Men': Queer Utopianism and Antisocial Eroticism in L. Frank Baum's Oz Series." *Marvels and Tales* 22, no. 2: 217–39.

Raines, Theron. 2002. *Rising to the Light: A Portrait of Bruno Bettelheim.* New York: Alfred A. Knopf.

Ramandanovic, Petar. 2001. "Introduction: Trauma and Crisis." In "Trauma: Essays on the Limit of Knowledge and Experience: A Special Issue," edited by Petar Ramadanovic. Special issue, *Postmodern Culture: An Electronic Journal of Interdisciplinary Criticism* 11, no. 2 (January): 1–12. http://www.iath.virginia.edu/pmc/text-only/issue.101/11.2introduction.txt.

Reiter, Sherry. 1988. "The Wizard of Oz in the Land of Id: A Bibliotherapy Approach." *Journal of Poetry Therapy* 1, no. 3 (Spring): 149–56.

Reynolds, Kimberly. 2007. *Radical Children's Literature: Future Visions and Aesthetic Transformations in Juvenile Fiction.* New York: Palgrave.

Ricklin, Franz. 1915. *Wishfulfillment and Symbolism in Fairy Tales.* Translated by William A. White. Nervous and Mental Disease Monograph Series 21. New York: Nervous and Mental Disease Publishing Company. First published in German in 1908.

Rieff, Philip. 1959. *Freud: The Mind of the Moralist.* New York: Viking Press.

———. 1966. *The Triumph of the Therapeutic: Uses of Faith after Freud.* New York: Harper and Row.

Rigsbee, Sally. 1983. "Fantasy Places and Imaginative Belief: *The Lion, the Witch, and the Wardrobe* and *The Princess and the Goblin.*" *Children's Literature Association Quarterly* 8, no. 1 (Spring): 10–12.

Ritvo, Lucille B. 1990. *Darwin's Influence on Freud: A Tale of Two Sciences.* New Haven: Yale University Press.

Robertson, Judith P. 2000–2001. "Sleeplessness in the Great Green Room: Getting Way under the Covers with *Goodnight Moon.*" *Children's Literature Association Quarterly* 25, no. 4 (Winter): 203–13.

Roiphe, Katie. 2000. *Still She Haunts Me.* New York: Dial Press.

Rollin, Lucy. 1990. "The Reproduction of Mothering in *Charlotte's Web.*" *Children's Literature* 18: 42–52.

———. 1992. *Cradle and All: A Cultural and Psychoanalytic Study of Nursery Rhymes.* Jackson: University Press of Mississippi.

Rollin, Lucy, and Mark I. West, eds. 1999. *Psychoanalytic Responses to Children's Literature.* Jefferson, N.C.: McFarland.

Ronda, Bruce A. 1995. "'The Theater of Feelings': Psychodrama and Historical Context in American Children's Fiction." Review of *Audacious Kids: Coming of Age in America's Classic Children's Books,* by Jerry Griswold. *Children's Literature Association Quarterly* 20, no. 4 (Winter): 191–93.

Rose, Jacqueline. 1984. *The Case of Peter Pan; or, The Impossibility of Children's Fiction.* Philadelphia: University of Pennsylvania Press.

Rosen, Richard D. 1975. *Psychobabble: Fast Talk and Quick Cure in the Era of Feeling.* New York: Avon Books.

Rosenzweig, Saul. 1992. *Freud, Jung, and Hall the King-Maker: The Historic Expedition to America (1909).* Seattle: Hogrefe and Huber.

Ross, Dorothy. 1972. *G. Stanley Hall: The Psychologist as Prophet.* Chicago: University of Chicago Press.

Rossel, Seymour. 1992. *The Holocaust: The World and the Jews, 1933–1945.* Springfield, N.J.: Berhman House.

Rudd, David. 2001. Review of *Psychoanalytic Responses to Children's Literature,* by Lucy Rollin and Mark I. West. *Lion and the Unicorn* 25, no. 1 (January): 174–79.

———. 2004. "Theories and Theorising: The Conditions of Possibility of Children's Literature." In *International Companion Encyclopedia of Children's Literature,* edited by Peter Hunt, 2nd ed., 1: 29–43. London: Routledge.

———. 2008. "An Eye for an I: Neil Gaiman's *Coraline* and Questions of Identity." *Children's Literature in Education* 39, no. 3 (September): 159–68.

———. 2010. "Children's Literature and the Return to Rose." *Children's Literature Association Quarterly* 35, no. 3 (Fall): 290–310.

Rudd, David, and Anthony Pavlik. 2010. "The (Im)Possibility of Children's Fiction: Rose Twenty-Five Years On." *Children's Literature Association Quarterly* 35, no. 3 (Fall): 223–29.

Rudnytsky, Peter L. 2002. *Reading Psychoanalysis: Freud, Rank, Ferenczi, Groddeck.* Ithaca, N.Y.: Cornell University Press.

Rushdie, Salman. 1992. *The Wizard of Oz*. London: British Film Institute.

Rustin, Margaret, and Michael Rustin. 1987. *Narratives of Love and Loss: Studies in Modern Children's Fiction*. London: Verso.

Ryman, Geoff. 1992. *Was*. New York: Alfred A. Knopf.

Salinger, J. D. 1964. *The Catcher in the Rye*. New York: Bantam. First published in 1951.

Sammond, Nicholas. 2005. *Babes in Tomorrowland: Walt Disney and the Making of the American Child, 1930–1960*. Durham, N.C.: Duke University Press.

Sánchez-Eppler, Karen. 2003. "Playing at Class." In *The American Child: A Cultural Studies Reader*, edited by Caroline F. Levander and Carol J. Singley, 40–62. New Brunswick, N.J.: Rutgers University Press.

Savage, Jon. 2007. *Teenage: The Creation of Youth Culture*. New York: Viking Press.

Schilder, Paul. 1981. "Psychoanalytic Remarks on *Alice in Wonderland* and Lewis Carroll." First published in 1938. In *Aspects of Alice: Lewis Carroll's Dreamchild as seen through the Critics' Looking-Glasses, 1865–1971*, ed. Robert Phillips, 333–43. New York: Penguin.

Schnurr, Rosina. 2002. *Terrorism: The Only Way Is Through. A Child's Story*. Gloucester, Ontario: Anisor.

Schreiber, Sanford. 1974. "A Filmed Fairy Tale as Screen Memory." *Psychoanalytic Study of the Child* 29: 389–410.

Schwartz, Eugene. 1999. *Millennial Child: Transforming Education in the Twenty-First Century*. Hudson, N.Y.: Anthroposophic Press.

Schwartz, Joseph. 1999. *Cassandra's Daughter: A History of Psychoanalysis in Europe and America*. New York: Allen Lane / Penguin.

Scott, A. O. 2009. "Unleashing Life's Wild Things." *New York Times*, November 5. http://www.nytimes.com/2009/11/08/movies/08scot.html.

Sedgwick, Eve Kosofsky. 1993. "Tales of the Avunculate: *The Importance of Being Earnest*." In *Tendencies*, 52–72. Durham, N.C.: Duke University Press.

Segal, Robert A. 2003. "Psychoanalyzing Myth: From Freud to Winnicott." In *Teaching Freud*, edited by Diane Jonte-Pace, 137–62. New York: Oxford University Press.

Semon, Larry, director. 1925. *The Wizard of Oz*. Larry Semon, Oliver Hardy, Mary Carr, Dorothy Dwan, Virginia Pearson, Bryant Washburn, Josef Swickard, Charles Murray. Chadwick Pictures.

Sendak, Maurice. 1956. *Kenny's Window*. New York: Harper.

———. 1960. *The Sign on Rosie's Door*. New York: Harper and Row.

———. 1963. *Where the Wild Things Are.* New York: Harper.

———. 1970a. *Fantasy Sketches.* Philadelphia: Rosenbach Museum and Library.

———. 1970b. *In the Night Kitchen.* New York: Harper and Row.

———. 1981. *Outside Over There.* New York: Harper and Row.

———. 1988a. "Caldecott Medal Acceptance." Speech given in 1964. In *Caldecott and Co.: Notes on Books and Pictures,* 145–56. New York: Farrar, Straus and Giroux.

———. 1988b. "A Conversation with Walter Lorraine." In *Caldecott and Co.: Notes on Books and Pictures,* 185–93. New York: Farrar, Straus and Giroux.

———. 1988c. "Jean de Brunhoff." First published in 1981. In *Caldecott and Co: Notes on Books and Pictures,* 95–105. New York: Farrar, Straus and Giroux.

———. 1988d. "Really Rosie." In *Caldecott and Co: Notes on Books and Pictures,* 179–84. New York: Farrar, Straus and Giroux.

———. 1988e. "Winsor McCay." First published in 1973. In *Caldecott and Co: Notes on Books and Pictures,* 77–86. New York: Farrar, Straus and Giroux.

———. 1993. *We Are All in the Dumps with Jack and Guy: Two Nursery Rhymes with Pictures.* New York: HarperCollins.

Shaddock, Jennifer. 1997–98. "*Where the Wild Things Are:* Sendak's Journey into the Heart of Darkness." *Children's Literature Association Quarterly* 22, no. 4 (Winter): 155–59.

Shakow, David, and David Rapaport. 1964. *The Influence of Freud on American Psychology.* New York: International Universities Press.

Shaw, Clifford R. 1966. *The Jack-Roller: A Delinquent Boy's Own Story.* Introduction by Howard S. Becker. Chicago: University of Chicago Press. First published in 1930.

Shea, Sarah E., Kevin Gordon, Ann Hawkins, Janet Kawchuk, and Donna Smith. 2000. "Pathology in the Hundred Acre Wood: A Neurodevelopmental Perspective on A. A. Milne." *CMAJ* 163, no. 12 (December): 1557–59.

Showalter, Elaine. 1990. *Sexual Anarchy: Gender and Culture at the Fin de Siècle.* New York: Viking Press.

Shumacher, Joel, director. 1987. *The Lost Boys.* Jason Patric, Dianne Wiest, Corey Haim, Barnard Hughes, Edward Hermann, Kiefer Sutherland, Jami Gertz, Corey Feldman. Warner Bros.

Sibley, Brian. 2001. *Three Cheers for Pooh: The Best Bear in All the World.* New York: E. P. Dutton.

Sigler, Carolyn. 1997. Introduction to *Alternative Alices: Visions and Revi-*

sions of Lewis Carroll's "Alice" Books, edited by Carolyn Sigler, xi–xxiii. Lexington: University Press of Kentucky.

———. 1998. "Authorizing Alice: Professional Authority, the Literary Marketplace, and Victorian Women's Re-visions of the *Alice* Books." *Lion and the Unicorn* 22, no. 3 (September): 351–63.

Singer, Dorothy G., and Tracey A. Revenson. 1977. *A Piaget Primer: How a Child Thinks.* Madison, Conn.: International Universities Press.

Skrypuch, Marsha Forchuk. 1999. *The Hunger.* Toronto, Ontario: Boardwalk Books.

Slavitt, David R. 1984. *Alice at 80.* New York: Doubleday.

Smith, Katharine Capshaw. 2005. Introduction to "Trauma and Children's Literature." Special forum, *Children's Literature* 33: 115–19.

Smith, Lillian H. 1991. *The Unreluctant Years: A Critical Approach to Children's Literature.* Introduction by Kay E. Vandergift. Chicago: American Library Association. First published in 1953.

Snediker, Michael D. 2009. *Queer Optimism: Lyric Personhood and Other Felicitous Persuasions.* Minneapolis: University of Minnesota Press.

Spacks, Patricia Meyer. 1981. *The Adolescent Idea: Myths of Youth and the Adult Imagination.* New York: Basic Books.

Spielberg, Steven, director. 1991. *Hook.* Dustin Hoffman, Robin Williams, Julia Roberts, Bob Hoskins, Maggie Smith, Carolyn Goodall, Charlie Korsmo. Columbia-Tristar.

Spitz, Ellen Handler. 1999. *Inside Picture Books.* New Haven: Yale University Press.

Spufford, Francis. 2002. *The Child That Books Built.* New York: Picador.

Stanger, Carol A. 1987. "*Winnie the Pooh* through a Feminist Lens." *Lion and the Unicorn* 11, no. 2 (December): 34–50.

Steedman, Carolyn. 1995. *Strange Dislocations: Childhood and the Idea of Human Interiority, 1780–1930.* Cambridge, Mass.: Harvard University Press.

Steig, Michael. 1989. *Stories of Reading: Subjectivity and Literary Understanding.* Baltimore: The Johns Hopkins University Press.

———. 1990. "Why Bettelheim? A Comment on the Use of Psychological Theories in Criticism." *Children's Literature* 18: 125–26.

Steig, William. 1969. *Sylvester and the Magic Pebble.* New York: Windmill.

———. 1972. *Dominic.* New York: Farrar, Straus and Giroux.

———. 1976. *The Amazing Bone.* New York: Farrar, Straus and Giroux.

———. 1980. *Gorky Rises.* New York: Farrar, Straus and Giroux.

Stevenson, Robert Louis. 1878. "Child's Play." http://www.readbookonline .net/readOnLine/8387/.

Stone, Jennifer Arlene. 1994. "Pinocchio and Pinocchiology." *American Imago* 51, no. 3 (Fall): 329–42.

———. 2006a. *Freud after Freud: Little Hans Encore.* JavariBooks (print-on-demand). http://javari.com/books.html.

———. 2006b. *Gradiva: Freud in Italy.* JavariBooks (print-on-demand). http://javari.com/books.html.

Stonely, Peter. 2003. *Consumerism and American Girls' Literature, 1860–1940.* Cambridge: Cambridge University Press.

Sulloway, Frank J. 1979. *Freud, Biologist of the Mind: Beyond the Psychoanalytic Legend.* New York: Basic Books.

Sully, James. 2000. *Studies of Childhood.* Introduction by Susan Sugarman. London: Free Association Books. First published in 1895.

Susina, Jan. 2002. Review of *Postmodern Pooh,* by Frederick Crews. *Lion and the Unicorn* 26, no. 2 (April): 274–78.

Sutton, Nina. 1996. *Bettelheim: A Life and a Legacy.* Translated by David Sharp. New York: Westview.

Sutton, Roger. 2003. "An Interview with Maurice Sendak." *Horn Book,* November–December: 687–99.

Swartz, Mark Evan. 2000. *Oz before the Rainbow: L. Frank Baum's "The Wonderful Wizard of Oz" on Stage and Screen to 1939.* Baltimore: The Johns Hopkins University Press.

Tannert-Smith, Barbara. 2010. "'Like Falling Up into a Storybook': Trauma and Intertextual Repetition in Laurie Halse Anderson's *Speak.*" *Children's Literature Association Quarterly* 35, no. 4 (Winter): 395–414.

Taraborrelli, J. Randy. 1991. *Michael Jackson: The Magic and the Madness.* New York: Birch Lane Press.

Tarkington, Booth. 1968. *Seventeen.* New York: Harper and Row. First published in 1916.

Tatar, Maria. 1987. *The Hard Facts of the Grimms' Fairy Tales.* Princeton: Princeton University Press.

———. 1992. *Off with Their Heads! Fairy Tales and the Culture of Childhood.* Princeton: Princeton University Press.

———. 2009. *Enchanted Hunters: The Power of Stories in Childhood.* New York: W. W. Norton.

Taylor, Eugene. 1998. "Jung before Freud, Not Freud before Jung: The Reception of Jung's Work in American Psychoanalytic Circles between 1904 and 1909." *Journal of Analytical Psychology* 43, no. 1 (January): 97–114.

Thacker, Deborah. 2001. "Feminine Language and the Politics of Children's Literature." *Lion and the Unicorn* 25, no. 1 (January): 3–16.

Thomas, Ronald R. 1990. *Dreams of Authority: Freud and the Fictions of the Unconscious.* Ithaca, N.Y.: Cornell University Press.

Thompson, Michael. 2000. *Speaking of Boys: Answers to the Most Often Asked Questions about Raising Sons.* New York: Random House.

Thornton, Matthew. 2008. "Wild Things All Over." *Publisher's Weekly,* February 4. http://www.publishersweekly.com/pw/by-topic/childrens/childrens-book-news/article/12192-wild-things-all-over-.html.

Thrailkill, Jane F. 2003. "Traumatic Realism and the Wounded Child." In *The American Child: A Cultural Studies Reader,* edited by Caroline F. Levander and Carol J. Singley, 128–48. New Brunswick, N.J.: Rutgers University Press.

Thrasher, Frederick. 1927. *The Gang: A Study of 1,313 Gangs in Chicago.* Chicago: University of Chicago Press.

Tribunella, Eric L. 2002. "Refusing the Queer Potential: John Knowles's *A Separate Peace. Children's Literature* 30: 81–95.

———. 2010. *Melancholia and Maturation: The Trauma of Loss in American Children's Literature.* Knoxville: University of Tennessee Press.

Trites, Roberta Seelinger, 2000. *Disturbing the Universe: Power and Repression in Adolescent Literature.* Iowa City: University of Iowa Press.

———. 2007. *Twain, Alcott, and the Birth of the Adolescent Reform Novel.* Iowa City: University of Iowa Press.

Tucker, Nicholas. 1981. *The Child and the Book: A Psychological and Literary Exploration.* Cambridge: Cambridge University Press.

———. 1992. "Good Friends, or Just Acquaintances? The Relationship between Child Psychology and Children's Literature." In *Literature for Children: Contemporary Criticism,* edited by Peter Hunt, 156–73. London: Routledge.

Ulanowicz, Anastasia. 2008a. "Preemptive Education: Lynne Cheney's *America: A Patriotic Primer* and the Ends of History." *Children's Literature Association Quarterly* 33, no. 4 (Winter): 341–70.

———. 2008b. "Sitting Shivah: Holocaust Mourning in Judy Blume's *Starring Sally J. Freedman as Herself." Children's Literature* 36: 88–114.

Van Doren, Carl. 1921. "Contemporary American Novelists—X. The Revolt from the Village: 1920." *Nation,* October 12, 408–9, 410, 412.

von Franz, Marie-Louise. 1981. *Puer Aeternus: A Psychological Study of the Adult Struggle with the Paradise of Childhood.* Sigo Press. First published in 1970.

———. 1996. *The Interpretation of Fairy Tales.* Rev. ed. Boston: Shambhala.

Waaldijk, Berteke. 2000. "Reading Anne Frank as a Woman." In *Anne Frank:*

Reflections on Her Life and Legacy, edited by Hyman Aaron Enzer and Sandra Solotaroff-Enzer, 110–20. Urbana: University of Illinois Press.

Wald, Priscilla. 1995. *Constituting Americans: Cultural Anxiety and Narrative Form.* Durham, N.C.: Duke University Press.

Warner, Marina. 1994. *From the Beast to the Blonde: On Fairy Tales and Their Tellers.* London: Chatto and Windus.

———. 2009. "Out of an Old Toy Chest." *Journal of Aesthetic Education* 43, no. 2 (Summer): 3–18.

Westman, Karin, ed. 2007. "Children's Literature and Modernism: The Space Between." Special issue, *Children's Literature Association Quarterly* 32, no. 3 (Winter).

Westwater, Martha. 2000. *Giant Despair Meets Hopeful: Kristevan Readings in Adolescent Fiction.* Edmonton: University of Alberta Press.

White, Donna R., and C. Anita Tarr, eds. 2006. *J. M. Barrie's "Peter Pan" In and Out of Time: A Children's Classic at 100.* Children's Literature Association Centennial Studies 4. Lanham, Md.: Scarecrow Press.

Williams, John Tyerman. 1996. *Pooh and the Philosophers: In Which It Is Shown That All of Western Philosophy Is Merely a Preamble to "Winnie the Pooh."* New York: E. P. Dutton.

———. 1999. *Pooh and the Millennium: In Which the Bear of Very Little Brain Explores the Ancient Mysteries at the Turn of the Century.* New York: E. P. Dutton.

———. 2001. *Pooh and the Psychologists: In Which It Is Proven That Pooh Bear Is a Brilliant Psychotherapist.* New York: E. P. Dutton. First published in 2000.

Wilner, Arlene. 1990. "'Unlocked by Love': William Steig's Tales of Transformation and Magic." *Children's Literature* 18: 31–41.

Windling, Terri. 2002. Introduction to *Briar Rose,* by Jane Yolen, xi–xiv. New York: Tor Books.

Winnicott, D. W. 1989. *Playing and Reality.* New York: Routledge. First published in 1971.

Winter, Sarah. 1999. *Freud and the Institution of Psychoanalytic Knowledge.* Stanford: Stanford University Press.

Witham, W. Tasker. 1964. *The Adolescent in the American Novel, 1920–1960.* New York: Frederick Ungar.

Wolfenstein, Martha. 1946. "The Impact of a Children's Story on Mothers and Children." *Monographs of the Society for Research in Child Development* 11, no. 1: i–iii, 1–54.

———. 1978. *Children's Humor: A Psychological Analysis.* Foreword Alan Dundes. Bloomington: Indiana University Press. First published in 1954.

Woolf, Virginia. 1981. "Lewis Carroll." First published in 1939. In *Aspects of Alice: Lewis Carroll's Dreamchild as Seen through the Critics' Looking-Glasses, 1865–1971*, edited by Robert Phillips, 78–80. New York: Penguin.

Woollcott, Alexander. 1981. "Lewis Carroll's Gay Tapestry." First published in 1939. In *Aspects of Alice: Lewis Carroll's Dreamchild as Seen through the Critics' Looking-Glasses, 1865–1971*, edited by Robert Phillips, 81–88. New York: Penguin.

Wullschläger, Jackie. 1995. *Inventing Wonderland: The Lives and Fantasies of Lewis Carroll, Edward Lear, J. M. Barrie, Kenneth Grahame, and A. A. Milne*. New York: Free Press.

Yolen, Jane. 1988. *The Devil's Arithmetic*. New York: Puffin.

———. 2002. *Briar Rose*. New York: Tor Books. First published in 1992.

Zipes, Jack. 1983. *Fairy Tales and the Art of Subversion: The Classical Genre for Children and the Process of Civilization*. London: Heinemann.

———. 1984. *Breaking the Magic Spell: Radical Theories of Folk and Fairy Tales*. New York: Methuen.

———. 1990. "Negating History and Male Fantasies through Psychoanalytic Criticism." *Children's Literature* 18: 141–43.

———. 1994. *Fairy Tale as Myth, Myth as Fairy Tale*. Lexington: University Press of Kentucky.

———. 2006. *Why Fairy Tales Stick: The Evolution and Relevance of a Genre*. New York: Routledge.

———. 2009. "Origins: Fairy Tales and Folk Tales." In *Children's Literature: Approaches and Territories*, edited by Janet Maybin and Nicola J. Watson, 26–39. New York: Palgrave Macmillan.

Žižek, Slavoj. 2002. *Welcome to the Desert of the Real!* London: Verso.

Index

ABDO and Daughters, 203, 240n28–29

abjection and adolescence, xxvi, 141, 172, 173–77, 179, 235n24–25

Abraham, Karl, 5

Absolute Evil: concept of, 202

abuse of children. *See* child abuse

"abuse" of Holocaust, 189–90, 196, 205

Adams, William Taylor (Oliver Optic), 12

Adolescence (Hall, 1904), 140, 143–46

adolescence and adolescent novels, xxvi, 139–80; abjection and adolescence, xxvi, 141, 172, 173–77, 179, 235n24–25; in American culture and psychology, 139, 140, 142–43, 150, 153–54, 157, 166–67, 232n4; articulation of concept of adolescence, 141–50; author as adolescent, 159–60, 161, 177–80; authority of authors, 178–79;

bibliotherapeutic, 169–73; delinquency, 148–49, 151–52, 158, 234n12; "end of adolescence," calls for, 153; gender and sexuality issues, 145, 146, 147, 156–65, 172; Holocaust stories, xxvi–xxvii, 181–82, 184, 189–96; identity, rebellion, and teenagerdom, codependent rise of concepts of, 139–80, 165–70, 172; mythical figure, adolescent as, 140; problem novels, 139, 152, 155, 156, 158, 168–69, 170, 173, 232n1; reform novels, 141; Salinger's *Catcher in the Rye*, 140, 156, 159, 163, 166–67, 169–70; social science and anthropology on, 150–56; "Sturm und Drang," adolescence as time of, 144, 149, 152–53; as trauma writing, 169–73, 184; "young adult," concept of, 167–69

Adolescent, The (Dostoyevsky, 1874), 142

Kenneth B. Kidd is associate professor of English at the University of Florida. He is author of *Making American Boys: Boyology and the Feral Tale* (Minnesota, 2004) and coeditor (with Sidney I. Dobrin) of *Wild Things: Children's Culture and Ecocriticism* and (with Michelle Ann Abate) of *Over the Rainbow: Queer Children's and Young Adult Literature.*